Notorious

Also by Maureen Dowd

BUSHWORLD

ARE MEN NECESSARY?

THE YEAR OF VOTING DANGEROUSLY

PORTRAITS OF STARS
FROM HOLLYWOOD, FASHION,
CULTURE, *and* TECH

Notorious

MAUREEN DOWD

HARPER

An Imprint of HarperCollins*Publishers*

HarperCollins books may be purchased for educational, business, or sales promotional use. For information, please email the Special Markets Department at SPsales@harpercollins.com.

FIRST EDITION

Library of Congress Cataloging-in-Publication Data has been applied for.

ISBN 978-0-06-339222-9

25 26 27 28 29 LBC 5 4 3 2 1

For Peggy, the best sister ever.

CONTENTS

Part 3: Funny People

Part 4: Creative Class

Part 5: Fashion Savants

Part 6: Writers, Moguls, Visionaries

INTRODUCTION

It's an astonishing thing to have a column at *The New York Times*. When I first got it, sometimes I would sit bolt upright in the middle of the night, wondering who on earth would entrust *me* with such a weighty responsibility.

But it is not always easy to express yourself in 800 words. Sometimes, it feels like you're struggling to wriggle into a dress two sizes too small.

When I first got the prestigious gig in 1995, Anna Quindlen and Tom Friedman, my friends who had already mastered the art of columnizing, advised me not to quote too many other people, to mainly use my own voice, because there just wasn't room.

They were right. The genre is more suitable for a let-it-rip polemic than interviews or features.

After a couple of decades, I longed to write longer. I wanted to hear other voices, not just my own. My late friend Janet Elder, a deputy managing editor at the *Times*, arranged for me to split my job so that I still wrote my Sunday column but was also able to do more scopious pieces for the feature sections.

I was so excited that the first few stories I handed in were verging on *War and Peace* length. After so many years of triage, I was sautéing in words and more words, letting them run amok on the page.

Dean Baquet, the executive editor at the time, suggested that I do profiles, akin to the wonderful lunchtime interviews featured in the weekend *Financial Times*. Instead of describing the food and how much it cost, as the *FT* does, I decided to add a bonus at the end called

"Confirm and Deny," named after an old Don Ameche movie. It was a dada Q-and-A that encouraged spontaneity.

I had written some profiles for Arts & Leisure when I first started at the *Times*, and I had done a bunch of celebrity cover stories for magazines such as *Vanity Fair*, *Rolling Stone*, and *GQ*, so I was happy to get back to a format I loved—letting someone else talk. And, as much as I savor writing about Washington and politics, it's fun sometimes to change the subject to Hollywood and Silicon Valley. It's interesting to see how the rulers of other universes—entertainment gods and the tech lords of the cloud—see the world. All three kingdoms traffic in illusion, and obsess on winning and losing, but in different ways.

I've always been fascinated with how powerful people wield power, how charismatic people create charisma, how talented people nurture or squander their talent. As a Shakespeare fan, I am endlessly intrigued by the high and mighty self-destructing, and by those who topple from great heights and somehow soar back, phoenixlike.

They say life is just a series of snapshots. This book certainly is. It's pioneering, talented, brilliant people at a certain moment in their lives—and these moments can be illuminating.

There's a snapshot of Elon Musk in 2017 when he was more the quirky visionary, before he commandeered Twitter and transformed into a right-wing crank that embraced racist conspiracies, flirted with antisemites, endorsed and endowed Donald Trump, and devolved into more frequent manifestations of "demon mode," as Grimes, his former partner and mother of three of his (at least) 12 children, put it.

There's Eddie Murphy in 1992, at the peak of his Hollywood power, truculent about reports of his big entourage and star demands.

There's Al Pacino in that same year, talking about how his life changed post-*Godfather*. He was suddenly inundated with booze, tranquilizers, women, deals, money and sycophants. "When you become visible and notorious, you start accepting people into your world that you wouldn't normally be associated with," he told me. The shy star did not handle it well. "It was anarchy," he recalled.

There's Bob Iger in 2019, at the height of his Cary Grant reign as the king of Disney, before he stepped away and then came back to rescue a turbulent Mouse House.

There's Jann Wenner in 2022, relaxing at his gorgeous Montauk home on the ocean, the year before he gave the *Times*'s David Marchese an interview explaining why his book *The Masters* featured seven top musicians who were all white guys. When Wenner said there were no women musicians who were "articulate enough on this intellectual level" to be included in his book, he ended up losing his spot on the board of the Rock and Roll Hall of Fame, the organization he had helped found.

My older brother instilled a love of old movies in me when I was young; he took me to the American Film Institute at Kennedy Center to see *Shane*, with Alan Ladd, and *Singin' in the Rain*, with its fantastic dance sequence with Gene Kelly and Cyd Charisse. I love the way those movie stars burned through the screen. These days, twinklies, as the late superagent Sue Mengers called stars, are in short supply. As are great movies that aren't based on comic books.

I've always thought of the real-deal Hollywood celebrities as creatures from another planet. I don't expect to become friends with them, any more than I want to become friends with politicians.

I think that we fall in love with stars on-screen because they're playing very appealing versions of the people we see in our own lives, the reporters and police detectives and lawyers. It's the fusion of their magnetism with our ordinary existence that creates the magic.

Oftentimes, famous people are just giving you a well-rehearsed riff that they've given thousands of times before. But sometimes, you can lead them to some weird subject that gets them off script. And occasionally, they'll simply surprise you.

The very cool Daniel Craig told me that he and Rachel Weisz had a ban on technological devices in the bedroom and recommended that for everyone. "If the iPad goes to bed, I mean, unless you're both watching porn on the Internet, it's a killer," he said.

Some celebrities are the opposite of what you are expecting. Paul Newman, my crush growing up and one of the biggest sex symbols in

Hollywood history, was not sexy in person; he was so besieged wherever he went, pestered by hordes of women, irritated by his sex-symbol reputation, that he just stopped transmitting any vibes and retreated into a shell.

Barry Diller, who seems so fierce in the business world, was sweetly nervous during our interview at his Beverly Hills mansion and began smoking to calm down.

I always dare to be trivial, because I love hearing the colorful bits, which can be remarkably revealing: what Jane Fonda considers her biggest amorous mistake (not sleeping with Marvin Gaye) or what Larry David carries in his pocket (brush picks) or that Bob Iger would get mad when his wife would leave the kitchen cabinets open.

The most unpleasant Hollywood encounter I had, sadly, was with another big crush, Kevin Costner. I interviewed him in New Orleans back in 1991, when he was 36 and Hollywood's head hunk. He was promoting his movie *Robin Hood: Prince of Thieves*, in which he had an unfortunate now-you-hear-it-now-you-don't English accent.

Things got off to a bad start as we were walking through the French Quarter to his hotel for the interview. A group of sweet seniors shyly asked Costner to pose for a picture with them as he waited at a red light, tapping his cowboy boot in irritation.

"O.K.," he snapped at the women, "but can't you see I'm being interviewed?" It was like watching someone kick kittens.

As we talked, he asked me with cocky assurance if I was going to play the tape of the interview for my girlfriends.

I told him starchily, "I interviewed Paul Newman and didn't play that tape for my girlfriends. So I think I can refrain from playing yours." As we walked out of the interview room, he reached over and squeezed the back of my neck.

"Don't worry," he said condescendingly, as he sauntered away. "Everybody has an off day now and then."

The most daunting moments came during my interview with Uma Thurman about her harrowing experiences with Harvey Weinstein and Quentin Tarantino. Even though Weinstein was supposed to be in some sort of rehab in Arizona playing Scrabble and repenting for his disgusting crimes, he still was able to reach out from the ashes of his career to try to sabotage the story. Dealing with him even when his power was so drained was chilling.

Some of my favorite interviews, funnily enough, since I don't speak high fashion fluently, were with fashion savants: my late friend, the inimitable, operatic André Leon Talley at the Duke Diet and Fitness Center in Durham, N.C., where he was once more trying to cure his addiction to biscuits, a food he associated with his beloved grandmother, who raised him; the ever-sultry cat woman of the catwalk, Diane von Furstenberg, purring in her Venice palazzo; and the soigné Tom Ford at the San Vicente bungalows in Hollywood.

Ford came to the interview early to rearrange the furniture in the hotel room to his liking. (He started rearranging the furniture in his house when he was six.) I realized then that, despite the glamour of his life, being Tom Ford could be exhausting. His aesthetic sensibility is so finely, painfully tuned. He can see 20 different shades of black. He objects to brunch because it occurs in daylight and he doesn't like shorts because they're, well, short. Life can always be more sensual and beautiful, and he's always thinking about how it can be. His flawless flaw detector is always on. But the man is a sweetheart.

These are stardust sketches of ensorcelling, electric, arrogant, narcissistic, whimsical, notorious people. Some have grace, others don't. Some fly higher, others have wax wings.

I loved writing these pieces — even during Covid, when they had to be done on Zoom — and strived to make them like small impressionist oil portraits. I commend them with the T. S. Eliot line that Robert Redford told me is his favorite: "There is only the trying. The rest is not our business."

PART 1

Leading Ladies

THIS IS WHY UMA THURMAN IS ANGRY

—FEBRUARY 3, 2018

Yes, Uma Thurman is mad.

She has been raped. She has been sexually assaulted. She has been mangled in hot steel. She has been betrayed and gaslighted by those she trusted.

And we're not talking about her role as the blood-spattered bride in "Kill Bill." We're talking about a world that is just as cutthroat, amoral, vindictive and misogynistic as any Quentin Tarantino hellscape.

We're talking about Hollywood, where even an avenging angel has a hard time getting respect, much less bloody satisfaction.

Playing foxy Mia Wallace in 1994's "Pulp Fiction" and ferocious Beatrix Kiddo in "Kill Bill," Volumes 1 (2003) and 2 (2004), Thurman was the lissome goddess in the creation myth of Harvey Weinstein and Quentin Tarantino. The Miramax troika was the ultimate in indie cool. A spellbound Tarantino often described his auteur-muse relationship with Thurman—who helped him conceive the idea of the bloody bride—as an Alfred Hitchcock–Ingrid Bergman legend. (With a foot fetish thrown in.) But beneath the glistening Oscar gold, there was a dark undercurrent that twisted the triangle.

"Pulp Fiction" made Weinstein rich and respected, and Thurman says he introduced her to President Barack Obama at a fund-raiser as the reason he had his house.

"The complicated feeling I have about Harvey is how bad I feel about all the women that were attacked after I was," she told me one recent night, looking anguished in her elegant apartment in River House on Manhattan's East Side, as she vaped tobacco, sipped white wine and fed empty pizza boxes into the fireplace.

"I am one of the reasons that a young girl would walk into his room alone, the way I did. Quentin used Harvey as the executive producer of 'Kill Bill,' a movie that symbolizes female empowerment. And all these lambs walked into slaughter because they were convinced nobody rises to such a position who would do something illegal to you, but they do."

Thurman stresses that Creative Artists Agency, her former agency, was connected to Weinstein's predatory behavior. It has since issued a public apology. "I stand as both a person who was subjected to it and a person who was then also part of the cloud cover, so that's a super weird split to have," she says.

She talks mordantly about "the power from 'Pulp,'" and reminds me that it's in the Library of Congress, part of the American narrative.

When asked about the scandal on the red carpet at the October premiere for her Broadway play, "The Parisian Woman," an intrigue about a glamorous woman in President Trump's Washington written by "House of Cards" creator Beau Willimon, she looked steely and said she was waiting to feel less angry before she talked about it.

"I used the word 'anger' but I was more worried about crying, to tell you the truth," she says now. "I was not a groundbreaker on a story I knew to be true. So what you really saw was a person buying time."

By Thanksgiving, Thurman had begun to unsheathe her Hattori Hanzo, Instagramming a screen shot of her "roaring rampage of re-venge" monologue and wishing everyone a happy holiday, "(Except you Harvey, and all your wicked conspirators—I'm glad it's going slowly— you don't deserve a bullet)—stay tuned."

Stretching out her lanky frame on a brown velvet couch in front of the fire, Thurman tells her story, with occasional interruptions from her 5-year-old daughter with her ex, financier Arpad Busson. Luna is in her pj's, munching on a raw cucumber. Her two older kids with Ethan Hawke, Maya, an actress, and Levon, a high school student, also drop by.

In interviews over the years, Thurman has offered a Zen outlook—

even when talking about her painful breakup from Hawke. (She had a brief first marriage to Gary Oldman.) Her hall features a large golden Buddha from her parents in Woodstock; her father, Robert Thurman, is a Buddhist professor of Indo-Tibetan studies at Columbia who thinks Uma is a reincarnated goddess.

But beneath that reserve and golden aura, she has learned to be a street fighter.

She says when she was 16, living in a studio apartment in Manhattan and starting her movie career, she went to a club one winter night and met an actor, nearly 20 years older, who coerced her afterward when they went to his Greenwich Village brownstone for a nightcap.

"I was ultimately compliant," she remembers. "I tried to say no, I cried, I did everything I could do. He told me the door was locked but I never ran over and tried the knob. When I got home, I remember I stood in front of the mirror and I looked at my hands and I was so mad at them for not being bloody or bruised. Something like that tunes the dial one way or another, right? You become more compliant or less compliant, and I think I became less compliant."

Thurman got to know Weinstein and his first wife, Eve, in the afterglow of "Pulp Fiction." "I knew him pretty well before he attacked me," she said. "He used to spend hours talking to me about material and complimenting my mind and validating me. It possibly made me overlook warning signs. This was my champion. I was never any kind of studio darling. He had a chokehold on the type of films and directors that were right for me."

Things soon went off-kilter in a meeting in his Paris hotel room. "It went right over my head," she says. They were arguing about a script when the bathrobe came out.

"I didn't feel threatened," she recalls. "I thought he was being super idiosyncratic, like this was your kooky, eccentric uncle."

He told her to follow him down a hall—there were always, she says, "vestibules within corridors within chambers"—so they could keep talking. "Then I followed him through a door and it was a steam room. And I was standing there in my full black leather outfit—boots, pants, jacket. And it was so hot and I said, 'This is ridiculous, what are you doing?' And he was getting very flustered and mad and he jumped up and ran out."

The first "attack," she says, came not long after in Weinstein's suite at the Savoy Hotel in London. "It was such a bat to the head. He pushed me down. He tried to shove himself on me. He tried to expose himself. He did all kinds of unpleasant things. But he didn't actually put his back into it and force me. You're like an animal wriggling away, like a lizard. I was doing anything I could to get the train back on the track. My track. Not his track."

She was staying in Fulham with her friend, Ilona Herman, Robert De Niro's longtime makeup artist, who later worked with Thurman on "Kill Bill."

"The next day to her house arrived a 26-inch-wide vulgar bunch of roses," Thurman says. "They were yellow. And I opened the note like it was a soiled diaper and it just said, 'You have great instincts.'" Then, she says, Weinstein's assistants started calling again to talk about projects.

She thought she could confront him and clear it up, but she took Herman with her and asked Weinstein to meet her in the Savoy bar. The assistants had their own special choreography to lure actresses into the spider's web and they pressured Thurman, putting Weinstein on the phone to again say it was a misunderstanding and "we have so many projects together." Finally she agreed to go upstairs, while Herman waited on a settee outside the elevators.

Once the assistants vanished, Thurman says, she warned Weinstein, "If you do what you did to me to other people you will lose your career, your reputation and your family, I promise you." Her memory of the incident abruptly stops there.

Through a representative, Weinstein, who is in therapy in Arizona, agreed that "she very well could have said this."

Downstairs, Herman was getting nervous. "It seemed to take forever," the friend told me. Finally, the elevator doors opened and Thurman walked out. "She was very disheveled and so upset and had this blank look," Herman recalled. "Her eyes were crazy and she was totally out of control. I shoveled her into the taxi and we went home to my house. She was really shaking." Herman said that when the actress was able to talk again, she revealed that Weinstein had threatened to derail her career.

Through a spokesperson, Weinstein denied ever threatening her prospects and said that he thought she was "a brilliant actress." He acknowledged her account of the episodes but said that up until the Paris steam room, they had had "a flirtatious and fun working relationship."

"Mr. Weinstein acknowledges making a pass at Ms. Thurman in England after misreading her signals in Paris," the statement said. "He immediately apologized."

Thurman says that, even though she was in the middle of a run of Miramax projects, she privately regarded Weinstein as an enemy after that. One top Hollywood executive who knew them both said the work relationship continued but that basically, "she didn't give him the time of day."

Thurman says that she could tolerate the mogul in supervised environments and that she assumed she had "aged out of the window of his assault range."

She attended the party he had in SoHo in September for Tarantino's engagement to Daniella Pick, an Israeli singer. In response to queries about Thurman's revelations, Weinstein sent along six pictures of chummy photos of the two of them at premieres and parties over the years.

And that brings us to "the Quentin of it all," as Thurman calls it. The animosity between Weinstein and Thurman infected her creative partnership with Tarantino.

Married to Hawke and with a baby daughter and a son on the way, Thurman went to the Cannes Film Festival in 2001. She says Tarantino noticed after a dinner that she was skittish around Weinstein, which was a problem, since they were all about to make "Kill Bill." She says she reminded Tarantino that she had already told him about the Savoy incident, but "he probably dismissed it like 'Oh, poor Harvey, trying to get girls he can't have,' whatever he told himself, who knows?" But she reminded him again and "the penny dropped for him. He confronted Harvey."

Later, by the pool under the cypress trees at the luxurious Hotel du Cap, Thurman recalls, Weinstein said he was hurt and surprised by her accusations. She then firmly reiterated what happened in London. "At some point, his eyes changed and he went from aggressive to ashamed," she says, and he offered her an apology with many of the sentiments he would trot out about 16 years later when the walls caved in.

"I just walked away stunned, like 'O.K., well there's my half-assed apology,'" Thurman says.

Weinstein confirmed Friday that he apologized, an unusual admission from him, which spurred Thurman to wryly note, "His therapy must be working."

Since the revelations about Weinstein became public last fall, Thurman has been reliving her encounters with him—and a gruesome episode on location for "Kill Bill" in Mexico made her feel as blindsided as the bride and as determined to get her due, no matter how long it took.

With four days left, after nine months of shooting the sadistic saga, Thurman was asked to do something that made her draw the line.

In the famous scene where she's driving the blue convertible to kill Bill—the same one she put on Instagram on Thanksgiving—she was asked to do the driving herself.

But she had been led to believe by a teamster, she says, that the car, which had been reconfigured from a stick shift to an automatic, might not be working that well.

She says she insisted that she didn't feel comfortable operating the car and would prefer a stunt person to do it. Producers say they do not recall her objecting.

"Quentin came in my trailer and didn't like to hear no, like any director," she says. "He was furious because I'd cost them a lot of time. But I was scared. He said: 'I promise you the car is fine. It's a straight piece of road.'" He persuaded her to do it, and instructed: "'Hit 40 miles per hour or your hair won't blow the right way and I'll make you do it again.' But that was a deathbox that I was in. The seat wasn't screwed down properly. It was a sand road and it was not a straight road." (Tarantino did not respond to requests for comment.)

Thurman then shows me the footage that she says has taken her 15 years to get. "Solving my own Nancy Drew mystery," she says. (Note: There is no audio.)

It's from the point of view of a camera mounted to the back of the

Karmann Ghia. It's frightening to watch Thurman wrestle with the car, as it drifts off the road and smashes into a palm tree, her contorted torso heaving helplessly until crew members appear in the frame to pull her out of the wreckage. Tarantino leans in and Thurman flashes a relieved smile when she realizes that she can briefly stand.

Uma Thurman said she didn't want to drive this car. She said she had been warned that there were issues with it. She felt she had to do it anyway.

"The steering wheel was at my belly and my legs were jammed under me," she says. "I felt this searing pain and thought, 'Oh my God, I'm never going to walk again,'" she says. "When I came back from the hospital in a neck brace with my knees damaged and a large massive egg on my head and a concussion, I wanted to see the car and I was very upset. Quentin and I had an enormous fight, and I accused him of trying to kill me. And he was very angry at that, I guess understandably, because he didn't feel he had tried to kill me."

Even though their marriage was spiraling apart, Hawke immediately left the Abbey of Gethsemani in Kentucky to fly to his wife's side.

"I approached Quentin in very serious terms and told him that he had let Uma down as a director and as a friend," he told me. He said he told Tarantino, "Hey, man, she is a great actress, not a stunt driver, and you know that." Hawke added that the director "was very upset with himself and asked for my forgiveness."

Two weeks after the crash, after trying to see the car and footage of the incident, she had her lawyer send a letter to Miramax, summarizing the event and reserving the right to sue.

Miramax offered to show her the footage if she signed a document "releasing them of any consequences of my future pain and suffering," she says. She didn't.

Thurman says her mind meld with Tarantino was rattled. "We were in a terrible fight for years," she explains. "We had to then go through promoting the movies. It was all very thin ice. We had a fateful fight at Soho House in New York in 2004 and we were shouting at each other because he wouldn't let me see the footage and he told me that was what they had all decided."

Now, so many years after the accident, inspired by the reckoning on violence against women, reliving her own "dehumanization to the point of death" in Mexico, and furious that there have not been more legal repercussions against Weinstein, Thurman says she handed over the result of her own excavations to the police and ramped up the pressure to cajole the crash footage out of Tarantino.

"Quentin finally atoned by giving it to me after 15 years, right?" she says. "Not that it matters now, with my permanently damaged neck and my screwed-up knees."

(Tarantino aficionados spy an echo of Thurman's crash in his 2007 movie, "Death Proof," produced by Weinstein and starring Thurman's stunt double, Zoë Bell. Young women, including a blond Rose Mc-Gowan, die in myriad ways, including by slamming into a windshield.)

As she sits by the fire on a second night when we talk until 3 a.m., tears begin to fall down her cheeks. She brushes them away.

"When they turned on me after the accident," she says, "I went from being a creative contributor and performer to being like a broken tool."

Thurman says that in "Kill Bill," Tarantino had done the honors with some of the sadistic flourishes himself, spitting in her face in the scene where Michael Madsen is seen on screen doing it and choking her with a chain in the scene where a teenager named Gogo is on screen doing it.

"Harvey assaulted me but that didn't kill me," she says. "What really got me about the crash was that it was a cheap shot. I had been through so many rings of fire by that point. I had really always felt a connection to the greater good in my work with Quentin and most of what I allowed to happen to me and what I participated in was kind of like a horrible mud wrestle with a very angry brother. But at least I had some say, you know?" She says she didn't feel disempowered by any of it. Until the crash.

"Personally, it has taken me 47 years to stop calling people who are mean to you 'in love' with you. It took a long time because I think that as little girls we are conditioned to believe that cruelty and love somehow have a connection and that is like the sort of era that we need to evolve out of."

JANE FONDA, INTERGALACTIC ECO-WARRIOR IN A RED COAT

I wanted to be schooled by Jane Fonda.

There was a decent chance that we would get into a Megyn Kelly–type dust-up, where I waded into some topic she didn't want to discuss. But I was ready to take the risk.

I wanted Ms. Fonda, a glam Forrest Gump who has popped up on the front lines of culture, fitness, politics and Hollywood for more than half a century, to give me the lowdown on everything:

From Black Panthers to the Green New Deal, from a legendary sex life to no sex life, from plastic surgery to plastic prison handcuffs, from "Barbarella" to Quentin Tarantino, from Richard Nixon to Donald Trump, from Marilyn Monroe to TikTok, from bad vibes over Hanoi Jane to good vibrators.

And there she was on Zoom, looking fetching with her new gray pixie cut, speaking from her chic townhouse in Los Angeles.

"I went gray at just the right moment," she said. "I didn't know Covid was coming along. I got tired of the chemicals and the time and the money to keep myself this particular color of blond, you know—enough already! And so I talked to the producers of 'Grace and Frankie' and I said, 'I want to go gray, but that would mean that Grace is going to have to go gray,' and they were all for it."

At 82, she still has the same intensity that made her a two-time Oscar winner, an antiwar activist and an intergalactic sexpot. And a repeater.

"Do you know what a repeater is?" she said, her Pacific blue eyes trained on me. "Repeaters are the antennae that you see on top of mountains."

She continued: "They don't originate the signals, but the bottom-of-the-valley signals get picked up and then the repeaters take them from the valley and spread them to a much wider audience. That's what celebrities are."

PAGING IVANKA

Ms. Fonda considered herself an environmentalist before this year "but I hadn't really put my body on the line for it," she said. She had "fished the high seas with every important man in my life, starting with my father."

She knew about sea turtles strangling and polar bears starving. She used windmills and solar, bought an electric BMW, recycled, cut back on red meat and plastic. (But she still sneaks in the occasional order of spareribs.) She had co-produced and starred in "The China Syndrome" in 1979, about the dangers of nuclear power.

But then, last Labor Day weekend, driving up to Big Sur to hike with her pals Rosanna Arquette and Catherine Keener, she began keening about doing more.

"I was quivering all over," she writes in her new book, "What Can I Do?"

Inspired by Greta Thunberg and by Naomi Klein's book about the Green New Deal, she decided to dig out her sleeping bag, move to Washington for a year and camp out in front of the White House to protest climate change. (Her father, Henry Fonda, made "The Grapes of Wrath" about the Depression-era drought and the Dust Bowl.)

"Where will I poop and pee?" she wondered. "I'm way older now and have to get up during the night more often."

She didn't want to be dismissed as "an aging star bopping in from Hollywood." But then, as she says, she "got off my duff," bought a chic red coat from Neiman's and moved to D.C.

She felt that she understood Donald Trump because she recognized what she thought could be a similar dynamic in the upbringing of her third husband, Ted Turner.

"I thought, he's been traumatized as a child, kind of like Ted as a child, so there are certain things that I understand about this kind of man," she said. "So I thought, OK, I will find four of the most beautiful, sexy, smart, climate-interested women I can, and we'll go in, and we'll kneel and we'll plead and beg."

For the "Charlie's Angels"–style eco-mission, she called Pamela Anderson, "and she was up for it," she said. Ms. Fonda was still thinking about who else—"Maybe Sharon Stone."

"We'll tell him what needs to be done and what a serious crisis this is and we'll tell him that he will be the world's greatest hero, that kind of thing," she said. "I actually called Jared, or whatever his name is, and I told him my idea and he said, 'Well, Ivanka is the environmentalist in the family.' Yeah, sure. So she called me and I told her my idea and she laughed and I never heard from her again."

Ms. Fonda got backup from Annie Leonard, the executive director of Greenpeace USA, who said that camping out was a bad idea—"'There are going to be rats,'" Ms. Leonard told her—but that there were other ways to practice civil disobedience.

Ms. Fonda had a famous mug shot from a 1970 arrest in Cleveland on charges trumped up by the Nixon White House. President Richard Nixon was angry about the actress's protests against the Vietnam War and growled on tape, "What in the world is the matter with Jane Fonda?" And: "She looks pretty but, boy, she's often on the wrong track."

As Troy Garity, her son with Tom Hayden, joked at Ms. Fonda's American Film Institute tribute in 2014, "My mother never hired a nanny to watch after me. That's what the F.B.I. was for."

For four months, she played her role as a repeater, becoming the star of Fire Drill Fridays, a climate protest in front of the Capitol. She got arrested five times, and checked to see whether the black plastic handcuffs used by police were recyclable.

'THIS IS WHERE CIVIL DISOBEDIENCE COMES IN'

Back in Los Angeles, Ms. Fonda moved the action online, where she has been pleasantly surprised by the reaction. "We keep growing," she said of the number of viewers of the Fire Drill Fridays video series with

Greenpeace. "It was 100,000, it was 300,000, 400,000, now 600,000." She has guests, including Mary Trump, who offered insights into the president's climate denialism. And she has the new book, offering lots of helpful tips to the ecologically challenged. "Eat less fish!" (And if you have to eat fish, do it lower on the food chain, like sardines.)

Her time in the slammer caught the attention of President Trump, who told a rally in Louisiana: "They arrested Jane Fonda, nothing changes," he said.

"She's always got the handcuffs on, oh, man. She's waving to everybody with the handcuffs. I can't believe it." He added: "Every 25 years they arrest her."

She laughed when I brought it up.

"I am of the belief that evil deeds, which Trump is committing, is the language of the traumatized," she said. "And you can hate the deeds. Don't hate the person because he wins if we hate him. Don't even give him that much energy.

"So, actually, I have empathy for him. I look at this person and I see a frightened child who is very, very dangerous because he's got his hands on all the buttons."

How does Trump compare to Nixon?

"Oh, it's far more dangerous," she said. "I can't even believe I'm saying this. In the '70s, I didn't even think about the positive things about Nixon. But there was the Clean Air Act, and he did great things for the tribal nations. I mean, he actually did some pretty good stuff and he was kind of smart and he knew foreign policy. So it wasn't so dangerous as somebody who has absolutely no limits to what he is prepared to do to take the country down."

While she declared herself "an Elizabeth Warren girl," she's happy with Kamala Harris and had a virtual fund-raiser with Lily Tomlin for Joe Biden.

"My attitude is, Look, I'd rather push a moderate than fight a fascist," she said. "You can push him," she said, referring to Mr. Biden. "He's already moved very far on climate."

She continued: "We have to cut fossil-fuel emissions in half by 2030 and that's going to be hard for him and we have to make them do it but we can. This is where civil disobedience comes in. And I will be one of the people in the streets as soon as 'Grace and Frankie' is over."

When she was living with her father and hanging out with the Black Panthers, Henry Fonda told her, "If I ever find out you're a Communist, I'll be the first to turn you in." In the early '80s, she unofficially adopted Mary Williams, the daughter of two Black Panthers who could no longer take care of her.

She notes that there is "a feeling of love" about Black Lives Matter protests "that was missing with the Panthers back in the '70s. I think one reason is because women are in the leadership." She said that around the time of the unrest in Ferguson, Mo., "one day I got in the mail some fliers about self-care from Black Lives Matter. And it was like, this is a movement that's talking to activists about self-care? That's new."

In this moment when we're having a cultural re-examination of some classic works of art, I was curious to hear what she made about the conversation around "Gone With the Wind," the movie so cherished by her ex, Mr. Turner.

"Ted bought MGM so he could own 'Gone With the Wind,'" Ms. Fonda said. "I mean, 'Gone With the Wind,' he lives by that. 'The land is the only thing that matters, Scarlett. The land is the only thing that lasts!' That's why he owns two million acres, because of Scarlett O'Hara.

"He recited lines from 'Gone With the Wind' a lot. He was obsessed with Scarlett O'Hara. You know the painting from the movie, the great big painting with Scarlett? He owned it."

Was it the actual one or a replica?

"Well, Rhett threw a drink at one and shattered it," she said. "So it was the one that wasn't shattered. It was pre-shattered."

She says the movie should not be canceled, but "the context has to be given."

Also up for debate is the reputation of John Wayne, a good friend of her father's, because of a horrifying history of remarks on race.

"I personally don't think we should cancel John Wayne," she said. "But way more important is, what are we going to do about the banking system, the redlining, the mortgages, the policing, all of those things that make it impossible for Black people to lift themselves up?"

In her book, she is surprised when she meets a young woman from Hanoi who has never heard of her incarnation as "Hanoi Jane."

"Oh, I've been there a few times," she told the young woman dryly.

No matter how many times she has apologized for an ill-advised photo op on a North Vietnamese antiaircraft gun, explaining that being antiwar did not mean she was against American soldiers, she knows that some on the right will never let her live it down.

"I think, just as there are some people who actually believe that Trump is doing a good job and has fulfilled all his promises, there are people who think that I was against the troops and that what I did was treasonous, and that probably will not change," she said. "I never did let it stop me. I apologize. I try to explain the context. And then I move on."

JANE FONDA IS ON TIKTOK. YES.

I wonder what she thinks about #MeToo and Hollywood. What was her experience?

"I was raped once by an actor," she said, "and I had one director, who is a French director, who said, 'Your character has to have an orgasm, so I have to see what your orgasms are like.' And I just pretended I couldn't understand him. He was talking in French."

Would "Barbarella," directed by her first husband, Roger Vadim, even be made now?

"Oh, 'Barbarella' could be made, but I would be one of the producers, and it would be a feminist movie," she said. "It was almost a feminist movie. She flew the spacecraft herself, right? She was the one that the president assigned to go to the planet to save the scientist. She was already pretty good, OK?"

If she returned to that planet with its molten lake made out of hatred and fear, she said she could come back as the matriarch bringing an army of women to rescue her child, who hatched from an egg she laid after an encounter with a blind angel.

Even though Ms. Fonda has a fascinating past, and even though she has done a lot of excavating of her past, she emphatically does not live in the past.

The woman who revolutionized the market for home videos with her fitness tape and leg warmers in the '80s is lately playing around on TikTok, doing one video that is a homage to her iconic workout for people stuck at home in fattening quarantine.

She has done ads for Uncle Bud's CBD. "My doctor told me to give up all sleeping pills and to just use CBD," she said.

She will politely ask a new acquaintance which pronouns she should use. "I've been working with really young people," she said. "When you meet them, they give the pronouns that they go by. I'm going on 83. Do I really have to say what pronouns I go by, you know? The answer is yes and there's a learning curve."

Although a battalion of gray-haired women showed up to the Fire Drill Fridays, saying they had been "summoned by Jane," as though they knew her, the actress has friends of all ages. Unlike most, she is not down on millennials. "I think they are absolutely great and they are making a huge difference, and I feel absolutely hopeful," she said.

She drolly notes that "one of the good things about being an activist is that you come in contact with woke men."

Does Ms. Fonda, who used to hang around with Marlon Brando and Warren Beatty, think that Netflix has eclipsed the glamour of old Hollywood?

She told me to snap out of it.

"Oh, I don't share that feeling about that time," she said briskly. "I don't watch old movies, almost never. I was always outside. I didn't care about movies." She continued: "I don't romanticize that time at all, and I find that the actors today are just brilliant."

In particular, she says, she's really digging Saoirse Ronan; Michaela Coel and her show on HBO, "I May Destroy You"; Issa Rae and her HBO show, "Insecure"; and Ramy Youssef's show on Hulu called "Ramy." She said she loved Charlize Theron's Netflix superhero movie, "The Old Guard."

She grew up around John Ford, a friend of her father's, and started her career with Joshua Logan, but the two directors she fantasizes about working with now are Quentin Tarantino and Wes Anderson.

"What I want is for Wes Anderson to come along and cast me in something that I never, ever would have thought of for myself," she said.

And what would she envision doing for Mr. Tarantino?

"Whatever he wanted," she said.

THE COAT TO END ALL COATS

In her Netflix series, Ms. Fonda's character, Grace, is an uptight WASP, who falls into an odd-couple relationship with the free-spirited Frankie, played by her real-life friend Lily Tomlin, after their husbands declare they are in love with each other.

Ms. Tomlin said that Ms. Fonda's mantra, from the time she was a child, has been: "I can make it better."

"She's so clearly outspoken and it's always well intentioned," Ms. Tomlin said, "but she'll still say out loud on the set, 'You need a haircut,' and then she'll go around until she finds someone to cut the person's hair. And then the person will come back and say, 'Actually, it does look better.'"

"I didn't have much parenting, so it's really been my women friends that have taught me how to be," said Ms. Fonda, whose mother died by suicide while in a psychiatric facility.

Like Ms. Fonda, Grace allows herself to be molded by the men in her life, until she suddenly declares to one boyfriend that she doesn't really like golf or hoagies and she's not going to pretend anymore. Frankie teases Grace about her sparse eating habits, saying she could fit in a glove compartment, and about her plastic surgery.

I asked Ms. Fonda why she says she is renouncing plastic surgery. "I'm almost 83 years old," she said. "I mean, enough already."

She talks poignantly in the Susan Lacy documentary "Jane Fonda in Five Acts" about her bulimia, saying she started purging at boarding school. She would sometimes try to survive, feeling famished, on a soft-boiled egg and a bit of spinach for the whole day.

She writes in her memoir that her father's criticisms of her weight when she was a teenager messed her up. I ask her why her father would complain, when she was already so thin.

"He had issues," she said, summing up a world of pain and psychoanalysis in three words.

Yet even when she pulled away from bulimia, she kept a lithe figure.

"There was a time when I was anorexic, but I never got below 112," she said. "I don't let it get too far out of hand. I'm not at my fighting weight right now. I'm 127. My fighting weight is about 119. So, you know, when we get three weeks out from shooting 'Grace and Frankie,' I'll lose 10 pounds."

She said that she eats healthy and works out with a trainer, wearing masks and gloves. "And I have fillers," she said. "And I'm an activist, so I feel good, and I think that's the most important part of it. If I felt grumpy and depressed, I wouldn't look so good.

"And the other thing is, I have good posture. And, believe it or not, that is critical. I've worked hard to have a very strong back."

In keeping with her focus on the environment, she has sworn off shopping and said that her renowned red coat from Fire Drill Fridays would be the last thing she ever buys.

Really?

"Really," she replied. "Never again. I have two closets full of clothes. I have clothes that I wore 30 years ago. I can still wear them. That's one thing about not putting on too much weight. And when I can't wear anything anymore, I just sell it now."

She said she sold 40 of her 50 pairs of bluejeans two weeks ago.

"Well, let me just explain," she said. "When I met Ted, he had six properties. When I left, he had 23. And we kept clothes at each place. And so I would have to buy in bulk. I remember very often at Saks Fifth Avenue, the sales girl would say, 'Are these gifts?' And I'd say, 'No, they're all for me.'"

Although she dates up a storm in "Grace and Frankie," and gets involved in selling yam lube cooked up by Ms. Tomlin's character, as well as vibrators for older women, with large-print instructions and a grip that won't aggravate arthritis, Ms. Fonda said two years ago that she had "closed up shop down there."

After a lifetime of being a chameleon, changing to please her father and three very different husbands, Ms. Fonda breezily says now, "I have no interest."

"I don't have time," she said. "I am fully complete with me and my children and my grandchildren and my friends. I don't want any more romance. I don't have time for it."

She recalled that when she was with Mr. Turner, in order to find time to write, she would have to abscond with her laptop in the middle of their fishing trips.

"You know, just about every day," she said, "I'll be in the middle of something and think, I would never have had time to do this or read this if I was trying to keep a relationship good."

But she must get hit on. I told her that my researcher, Shawn Mc-Creesh, has just watched "Barbarella" for the first time. Also, he saw her in the elevator at The Times when she visited our office during Fire Drill Fridays and thinks she's a stone-cold fox.

"Is that good or bad?" she wondered.

She said no one propositions her anymore.

"Zero," she said. "No, and I'm not lonely. I've never been lonely. I've never been bored or lonely in my life."

So if she had a free Saturday night, what would she do?

"Read," she said. "And between the fact that I'm alone plus the Covid, I'm discovering so much TV."

After the "Grace and Frankie" plotline about her company selling sex toys was introduced, and after she talked on "Ellen" about one vibrator, which hangs from a silver necklace and looks like jewelry, fans began sending her vibrators.

"I have a drawer full of vibrators," she said. "It's amazing."

I asked if she would be scared to use one that came in the mail from a fan.

"I don't know," she said, grinning. "Maybe I'd ask someone else to try it first."

Confirm or Deny

MAUREEN DOWD: *Your greatest regret is that you never had sex with Che Guevara.*

JANE FONDA: No, I don't think about him. Who I do think about, and what is a great regret is Marvin Gaye. He wanted to and I didn't. I was married to Tom. I was meeting a lot of performers to try to do concerts for Tom and the woman who was helping me do that introduced me to Marvin Gaye.

Please tell me his pickup line included the words "sexual healing."

I needed some but he didn't say that, no. But then I read, apparently he had my picture on his refrigerator. I didn't find that out until later, after he was dead.

You went to birthday parties at Christina Crawford's and hung up your coat on wire hangers.

I was too young to know from a wire hanger. In fact, I don't think I had ever seen a wire hanger in my life. We were very young. We all had governesses in uniforms. And there was a Ferris wheel and an elephant.

Joan Crawford terrified you.

I didn't know who she was, except that she had these dark eyebrows and she seemed to be very tall and imposing and she was responsible for this whole mishegoss, and I had to curtsy.

Simone Signoret is the sexiest woman you ever met.

Ava Gardner was the sexiest woman I ever met. Without question. She was a mensch, a true mensch, and she was a babe.

You and Tom Hayden walked out of "Last Tango in Paris."

Yes. But it was because North Vietnam was being bombed. Kissinger started bombing the north again, and we were so upset.

You love the song "Jane Fonda" by Mickey Avalon.

I've heard it. I don't know if I love it.

Ted Turner used to dress up like Rhett Butler, play the music from "Gone With the Wind" and sweep you up the stairs.

(Laughs.) No. However, one day when we were driving to one of his ranches in his Jeep over the bumpy roads and my brother and his wife were with us, he suddenly stopped the car and got out and pulled me out and grabbed me in his arms and sang "Don't Fence Me In."

Your leg warmers are more famous than Jennifer Beals's "Flashdance" leg warmers.

Probably. Because my leg warmers came into people's living rooms day after day after day after day. And so they became friends of people.

You bought a white stallion from Mike Nichols.
I bought a mare, a bay mare, Evita, from Mike Nichols.

You are related to Jane Seymour, one of the wives of Henry VIII.
That's what my mother always told me and it's why my name until the fourth grade was Lady.

Your character in "Monster-in-Law" brags at a dinner party about sitting next to me, the Sultan of Brunei, Carrie Fisher and Snoop Dogg.
I don't remember.

You regret not taking the Mia Farrow role in "Rosemary's Baby."
I don't think about it.

Katharine Hepburn gave you some good advice when you were filming "On Golden Pond."
She watched me fumble my way into learning how to do a back flip and she knew that I had been very scared to do it. And she said, "Don't get soggy," meaning always confront your fears.

Marlon Brando was . . .
Disappointing. But a great actor.

You were in Lee Strasberg's acting class with Marilyn Monroe.
Yes. She liked me. I think she liked me because she sensed my insecurities and she was drawn to vulnerable things. I'll never forget a party that Lee Strasberg gave and she came late, and she walked in and men there started to shake. I mean, they were physically excited and agitated by the fact that she was there. And she walked straight to me and wanted to talk.

Marilyn was not as striking in person.
She glowed! There was a glow coming out of her that was unbelievable! It came from her skin and her hair and her being. I've never seen anything like it.

KATE WINSLET HAS NO FILTER

—MAY 31, 2021

Philly's a tough town.

If there's a quintessential story about the City of Brotherly Love, it's this one: In 2015, when Canadian researchers developed a child-sized hitchhiking robot with a big smile and yellow wellies, the hitchbot made it across Europe and halfway down the East Coast, offering friendly small talk to anyone it encountered. Then it got to Philadelphia, where it was promptly torn limb from limb and left in an alley.

Residents have pelted Santa with snowballs and hurled batteries and beer at their own quarterback. They flip cars and set things on fire even when they *win* the Super Bowl and World Series.

The unloved cousin of Boston and New York is often overlooked by Hollywood. The accent is so tricky to replicate, most actors won't go near it. (Even Rocky didn't even have a proper Philly twang.)

So it's funny, then, that it took a Brit with an elegant voice, creamy complexion and sunny outlook to parachute into the Philly burbs and totally nail the look, feel, sound and salty attitude of the denizens of Delaware County, or Delco, as it's known.

Kate Winslet gets emotional talking about the end of her HBO limited series, "Mare of Easttown," which scored its own "Saturday Night Live" skit and found a fan in the self-described Philly girl in the White House, Jill Biden. ("You don't screw around with a Philly girl," Joe Biden said of his wife last year, after she blocked an anti-dairy activist who bum-rushed him at a campaign stop.)

Ms. Winslet has said, in the past, that it's hard for an actor to tell what will wow audiences while you're shooting, that sometimes you think you're doing great work and then it turns out to be "a limp biscuit."

Mare Sheehan is anything but a limp biscuit. The police detective exists in a cloud of vape smoke, trysts, flannel, Rolling Rock and Jameson shots—"A very hot grandma," as Guy Pearce's character calls her, sparring with a mother (Jean Smart) who loves drinking Manhattans.

Ms. Winslet said that she has been bowled over by how audiences have fallen "in love with this wildly flawed, messy, broken, fragmented, difficult woman. I loved her marks and her scars and her faults and her flaws and the fact that she has no off switch, no stop button. She just knows 'Go.'"

"Not only did I have to hide myself in the character completely, but I had to hide this story, carry the secret," she said. "I kept it hidden since 2018 when I first read the scripts. My job was to take them on this horrendous journey and hope to God that they'd be prepared to come into the attic with me at the end. It has been agony, agony, agony. You can see I'm still like . . ." She sounds as if she might cry—something she would never let Mare do—then pulls herself together and lets fly one of her frequent, merry F-bombs. "I can't deal with it. It's ridiculous."

'BAD JEANS' AND CHEESESTEAK

The show is a murder mystery with many motifs: grief, the opioid crisis, small-town life. Ms. Winslet, a mother of three, sees it from this perspective: "It's about mothers protecting their children at all costs, and the lengths that a parent will go to in order to protect their children," she said. About the finale's twist ending, she adds, "Oh God, it's just unbelievable, it's heartbreaking."

Underneath Mare's facade, she said, "is a woman who is so entrenched in grief for her son that she has not processed, and as she shares it, as she talks about it with a therapist, she will crack. She doesn't want affection. She doesn't want to be loved. And she doesn't want to be cared for because if she has to experience those things, it makes her feel vulnerable, and if she feels vulnerable, then she can't be strong anymore, and she can't carry on."

Ms. Winslet is known for what one producer called her "insane work ethic." She prepares elaborate back stories for her characters, and she said she prepped more for Mare than any other role in her life. (But she is not Daniel Day-Winslet; she is said to be fun once the shooting wraps for the day.)

She was Zooming in from her house on the south coast of England, curled up with bare feet, her blond mane looking much glossier than Mare's. She's wearing an old white Calypso T-shirt, a couple of gold necklaces and some black Sweaty Betty pants.

The actress often saves something from her sets, and she shifted her camera to show off the sign from the Easttown police station she has hung on a wall. She kept Mare's jacket and badge, too.

She has been harking back to her breakout role as another strong, but more upper crust, Philly girl: Rose DeWitt Bukater. "It's like 'Titanic' again," she said, chuckling. "I'm on the side of buses again! It's like going back in time 24 years where I'm walking down the street and people are nudging and pointing and whispering again." When the actress was on a bike ride in England recently, a woman ran up to stroke her arm and offer all her theories about whodunit.

Ms. Winslet said she knows people are saying, "Oh my God, how can she let herself look so unglamorous?" When Craig Zobel, the director, assured her he would cut "a bulgy bit of belly" in her sex scene with Guy Pearce, she told him, "Don't you dare!" She also sent the show's promo poster back twice because it was too retouched. "They were like 'Kate, really, you can't,' and I'm like 'Guys, I know how many lines I have by the side of my eye, please put them all back.'"

She said she balked when she saw an early cut in which her ordinarily luminous skin looked too good. "We tried to light it to make it look not nice," she said.

She continued: "Listen, I hope that in playing Mare as a middle-aged woman—I will be 46 in October—I guess that's why people have connected with this character in the way that they have done because there are clearly no filters. She's a fully functioning, flawed woman with a body and a face that moves in a way that is synonymous with her age and her life and where she comes from. I think we're starved of that a bit.

"In episode one, she's having sex on a couch. I said to my husband, 'Am I OK with that? Is it all right that I'm playing a middle-aged woman who is a grandmother who does really make a habit of having one-night stands?' He's like, 'Kate, it's great. Let her do it.'"

In moments of doubt, she tortured herself and her assistant director, wondering about other actresses—"Three real people were haunting my mind, I will not name them"—who might have done a better job.

The show's costume designer did recon in Wawa, finding inspiration for Mare's flannel, inexpensive T-shirts, Ocean City sweatshirts and "bad jeans," as Ms. Winslet said.

"Whenever we'd find something unflattering," Ms. Winslet recalled, "we'd be jumping up and down like, 'Yes! We're wearing this.'"

She would leave her clothes in a crumpled pile on the floor of her trailer after filming "and they would stay in a rumpled up ball overnight. We were not washing and drying and hanging those clothes. Never."

They filled in her shapely eyebrows to give her face a heavier look, and left the sunspots and imperfections. "We're so used to seeing this stuff airbrushed away," she said.

She wanted Mare to reflect the burdens she carried, a physical and emotional "heftiness." She borrowed a Peloton to work out at night to make her thighs more muscular. "There's a sloppiness to her, and there's a looseness to how she sits and how she walks and just how she holds herself," she said. "Her body posture is totally different to mine. I actually stand quite upright."

In one peak-Mare scene, she comes home and scarfs down a cheesesteak that her mother has gotten her, without taking off her jacket, still clutching her police files. "This is so clearly a woman who does not cook, doesn't care about what she puts into her mouth, also probably forgets to eat, so that when she does eat, she's so starving, she doesn't even care what it is that she's shoveling in," she said.

Her father, Roger, also an actor, helped inform this bit. "My dad actually reminds me quite a lot of Mare, to be honest. He was slightly the inspiration," she said. "He basically moves like Mare and eats like Mare. Well, he does eat with his mouth full. We do tell him all the time, 'Dad!' He's going to be so mad I just said that."

VISITING THE BADLANDS

And yet, Ms. Winslet, a vegetarian, could only get into character so much. She sheepishly confessed to a Philly sacrilege: The show's hoagies contained no meat and, most shockingly, no onions. "I felt really, really bad because I know onions are a very important part of a hoagie," she said, "but because we had so many hours of filming scenes with all of this food, it basically wasn't fair on the crew to have all this stinky onion food on our tiny set all day long." (She said she was aware of the existence of scrapple but did not try it.)

Even with the counterfeit hoagies, locals are thrilled with Ms. Winslet's metamorphosis. They even named a hoagie after Mare.

Shawn McCreesh, who works with me at The Times and grew up, like the first lady, in a nearby town very similar to Easttown, spotted someone he recognized from back home on the show. Patsy Meck, who plays the woman working the desk at the police station, said that Ms. Winslet was "genuinely who you would want her to be—she was so real." Ms. Meck, whose three grandchildren were extras on the show, said that it was "amazing" to see Ms. Winslet "walk off set, sit down and talk to me in a deep British accent, then pop right back on set and start talking like the rest of us."

Ms. Winslet said she had to change the way the muscles in her face moved—often in freezing weather—in order to emulate Philly's mid-Atlantic dialect, with its selectively elongated vowels and smushed consonants. "Look, when you've done Polish-Armenian and German," she said, referring to her accents in "Steve Jobs" and her Oscar-winning turn as a Nazi in "The Reader," "frankly, I thought, 'Delaware County, oh, it'll be fine. The vowel sounds a little bit different, but it'll be fine.' Honestly, it was just so hard."

Still, mastering the sound wasn't the hardest part. Stepping into the shoes of a mother raising a child with severe mental health issues, as

Mare did, was. (Mare's son, Kevin, had struggled with depression and addiction before taking his own life.) Ms. Winslet met with parents who had been through it all, and worked with a grief counselor.

"There's that moment," she recalled, "when the therapist says to Mare, 'Did he frighten you?' and she just says, 'Sometimes.' A huge admission for Mare to even say out loud, 'My son scared me.' Of course, you see it in that flashback when Carrie and Kevin take Mare's money for drugs in the bathroom." She said the detective strives to fix everything else because she could not fix Kevin.

In order to truly understand the opioid epidemic, how its many tendrils can wrap around a place like Easttown, she went to what Philadelphians call "the badlands"—the North Philly neighborhood of Kensington and its open-air drug markets. "We would go in an undercovery type of car and just drive around a lot," she said.

"I remember seeing—and actually it broke my heart—a man with the most beautiful face and a beard. You could see there was a soul right there. He had been amputated from the knee down on his right leg, and he was injecting into the toes of the other foot.

"People are fighting for their sliver of life there. I would see people in these teeny-tiny houses, and they would be not just sweeping their front stoop but sweeping the pavement and the guttering in front of their home. Sometimes, for some people, that's as much as they can do to keep their pride, to keep a feeling of something that is theirs and that is intact."

What did the dark heart of America's opioid crisis look like to a Brit? "I have to be honest," she said, "I was really staggered that there aren't more of those support networks in place to help with people. In this country, we do definitely have better support networks for people in crises like that, we absolutely do."

'FACES ARE BEAUTIFUL'

Ms. Winslet has been known to warn young actors on a set not to confuse social media fame with the hard work of acting.

"I have certainly heard, twice, of certain actors being cast in roles because they have more followers," she said. "I've actually heard people say, 'She's not who we wanted to cast, but she has more followers.' I almost don't know what to say. It's so sad and so extraordinarily wrong. I think the danger is not just for young actors but younger people in general now. I think it makes you less present in your real life. Everyone is constantly taking photographs of their food and photographing themselves with filters."

She leans her face close to the camera, and noted her lack of filters, with an expletive.

"What worries me is that faces are beautiful. Faces that change, that move, are beautiful faces, but we've stopped learning how to love those faces because we keep covering them up with filters now because of social media and anyone can photoshop themselves, and airbrush themselves, and so they do. In general, I would say I feel for this generation because I don't see it stopping, I don't see or feel it changing, and that just makes me sad because I hope that they aren't missing out on being present in real life and not reaching for unattainable ideals."

The actress is so famous for disrobing in movies that her IMDb profile says her trademark is her "voluptuous figure." But she says nude scenes may be in her past.

"I think my days are getting a little bit numbered of doing nudity," she said. "I'm just not that comfortable doing it anymore. It's not even really an age thing, actually. There comes a point where people are going to go, 'Oh, here she goes again.'" She jokes that it's not fair to camera operators to have to work to get the best angles as her body changes.

Ms. Winslet has a daughter, Mia, 20, with her first husband, Jim Threapleton, a director whom she met on the set of "Hideous Kinky." She has a son, Joe, 17, with Sam Mendes, her second husband. And she also has a son, Bear, 7, with her current husband, who has gone back to his original name, Edward Abel Smith, from his playful pseudonym, Ned Rocknroll.

"He added 'Winslet' as one of his middle names, just simply because the children have Winslet," the actress said. "When we're all traveling together, to all have that name on the passport makes life easier."

(Bear's middle name is Blaze, after the fire that Kate and Ned escaped that burned down the British Virgin Islands home of Richard Branson, her husband's uncle.)

"He's the superhot, superhuman, stay-at-home dad," she said of her husband, as she smiled happily. "He looks after us, especially me. I said to him earlier, like, 'Neddy, could you do something for me?' He just went, 'Anything.'" She swoons, noting that his long hair now gives him the look of "an ocean warrior."

She breaks into song, crooning that they go together like "shama lama ding dong." "He is an absolutely extraordinary life partner," she said. "I'm so, so, so lucky. For a man who is severely dyslexic, as he is, he's great at testing me on lines. It's so hard for him to read out loud, but he still does it."

She added that "He didn't particularly plan on meeting and marrying a woman who is in the public eye and therefore having been so judged." She finds it amusing that, instead of being rock 'n' roll, he's very Zen. "He's vegan, does yoga, breath work and cold water swims."

Ms. Winslet grew up in Reading, west of London, in a modest house and worked slicing ham in a deli when she was young. "I came from a small community not dissimilar to Easttown in the sense that there were paper-thin walls," she said. "You could hear the neighbors rowing through the wall. You could hear the verbal grenades that were being hurled at one another."

She said her father had called to tell her he loved an episode of "Mare," then added his usual caution: "But you know, babes, don't rest on your laurels. You're only as good as your last gig."

Confirm or Deny

MAUREEN DOWD: *Bob Iger approached you about making "Titanic II" for Disney Plus.*

KATE WINSLET: No, never did, and I never would.

You pocketed a few things before you jumped ship from the set of "Titanic."

People stole the White Star Line cups and saucers. I was good. I did take a pair of Rose's earrings, but somewhere I lost one.

Like Mare, you have a gloriously filthy mouth in real life.
(Laughs.) True, yes.

You can't stop reading about Ben Affleck and Jennifer Lopez.
What? No! I've never read about Jennifer in my life. What are these questions?

"Hideous Kinky" was neither hideous nor kinky.
I don't even know how to answer these questions.

You keep your Oscar on the back of your toilet.
I don't actually know where the Oscar is at the moment. I think it's possibly in my son's bedroom. But it was on the back of the toilet for a long time, yes.

You lived in New York for 10 years and never once went to Philly.
That's true.

You've incorporated the Philly slang word "<u>jawn</u>" into your vocabulary.
John, as in a man's name?

You went to Rita's for wooder ice.
No, I didn't go to Rita's.

This role is the first time you held a gun, and you didn't like it.
True.

In John Turturro's "Romance & Cigarettes," you simulated sex with James Gandolfini bouncing on an exercise ball.
I had ripped all the ligaments on the left side of my foot. I'm nursing my son. As I'm bouncing on that ball, I'm actually bouncing using one foot with my leg in the cast improvising at three o'clock in the morning. We were in hysterics. Oh, God, I loved Jimmy Gandolfini so much. He was just so wonderful, so insecure and just so honest.

Guy Pearce washes cans in the dishwasher before he puts them in the recycling can.
That is true.

MUSING ON MARILYN MONROE

Mike Nichols told me this story once: He called Marilyn Monroe to work on a scene.

"Are you sure you weren't hitting on her?" I asked.

"I wouldn't have dared dream of it," he replied.

It was the mid-1950s, and they were both taking an acting class in New York with Lee Strasberg. Nichols recounted his conversation with the woman with the familiar breathy voice: "The phone rang and somebody said, 'Hello,' and I said, 'Hi, is Marilyn there?' and she said, 'No, she's not,' and I said, 'Well, this is Mike. I'm in class with her. Could you take a message?' And she said, 'Well, it's a holiday,' because it was the Fourth of July weekend, and that, to her, was an excuse for not taking a message for herself."

No one ever said Marilyn wasn't complicated.

Nichols directed the Tony Award–winning revival of her third husband's play, "Death of a Salesman." During one of our interviews, the charming director surprised me when he said he was present at what he dryly calls the "historic moment" in May 1962 when Marilyn sang "Happy Birthday" to Jack Kennedy, who was turning 45. Marilyn was wearing that shrink-wrap, sheer Jean Louis gown ablaze with rhinestones—"Skin and beads," she called it. Nichols and Elaine May were also performing that night in Madison Square Garden, not that anyone remembers.

"I was standing right behind Marilyn, completely invisible, when she sang 'Happy birthday, Mr. President,'" Nichols said. "And indeed, the corny thing happened: Her dress split for my benefit, and there was Marilyn, and yes, indeed, she didn't wear any underwear."

At a party afterward, "Elaine and I were dancing, and Bobby Kennedy and Marilyn danced by us, and I swear to God the conversation was as follows: [Here Nichols put on, first, a feathery voice and then a nasal one] "'I like you, Bobby.' 'I like you too, Marilyn.'"

The famous director has worked with many famous beauties. So I asked him, as we mark the 50th anniversary of Marilyn's death, if he could explain her astonishing staying power.

"I think that the easy answer might be that she had the greatest need," he said. "She wasn't particularly a great beauty, that is to say, Hedy Lamarr or Ava Gardner would knock the hell out of her in a contest, but she was almost superhumanly sexual."

Feminism has come and gone, and women now routinely puff their lips, inflate their chests, dye their hair and dress with sultry abandon. But Nichols said Marilyn's heat went deeper, with a walk, a look and movements that were an "out-and-out open seduction right in front of everyone."

Arthur Gelb, the former Times managing editor, likes to tell how he won a $10 bet as a slightly inebriated rewrite man in the '50s when he reached out and, much to her annoyance, touched Marilyn's flawless porcelain back as she dined with friends at Sardi's.

"When she walked, it was as though she had a hundred body parts that moved separately in different directions," Gelb told me on the BBC show. "I mean, you didn't know what body part to follow."

Wherever I travel in the world, I run across the luminous image of the heartbreaking and breathtaking sex symbol who was smart enough to become the most famous "dumb blonde" of the 20th century. Marilyn, her white pleated halter dress flying up over the New York subway grate, is as deeply etched in the global imagination as Audrey Hepburn in a black Givenchy dress at Tiffany's.

Starting as the 1948 Castroville, Calif., Artichoke Queen, Marilyn was a genius at self-creation, high gloss over deep wounds. "Marilyn's like a veil I wear over Norma Jean," she said.

Lois Banner, a professor of history and gender studies at the University of Southern California, hails the star in her new book, "Marilyn: The Passion and the Paradox," as a proto-feminist who had to swim upstream past a mentally ill mother, 12 foster homes, a stutter, sexual abuse as a child, sexism as a star, manic-depressive cycles, addiction, Joe DiMaggio's abuse and Arthur Miller's condescension. "She is the child in all of us," Banner writes, "the child we want to forget but can't dismiss."

Half a century after Marilyn was found on Aug. 5, 1962, in her Brentwood bedroom, nude, holding her phone, soaked in drugs, she continues to bewitch: her death at 36 and the sketchy cover-up; her tempestuous marriages to a famous baseball player and famous playwright; her role, with Jack and Bobby Kennedy, in the most intriguing film noir triangle of all time.

She gazes wistfully from the latest People, beside Robert Pattinson and Kristen Stewart, with the headline, "Was Marilyn Murdered?"

"Could the iconic bombshell," USA Today asked, "be any more alive?"

Her estate made $27 million in 2011, gobs more than she ever earned in life. She was the poster girl at Cannes, a festival she never attended. And her time in England making "The Prince and the Showgirl" was the subject of a movie that got two Oscar nominations, even though the golden girl never won a gold statuette herself.

There's a cascade of books, photos, Twitter messages, Blu-ray box sets, Marilyn Monroe Cafes, Marilyn nail salons, and a MAC makeup collection. You can buy Marilyn Monroe underwear at T.J. Maxx. Nicki Minaj, the rapper, had a song called "Marilyn Monroe."

While making her last movie, "Something's Got to Give," Marilyn posed nude for a young photographer, Larry Schiller, hoping to ratchet up her $100,000 salary to Elizabeth Taylor's million-dollar territory for "Cleopatra."

Schiller wrote in Vanity Fair that he saw the confidence that spurred Marilyn to become one of the first stars to create her own production company. "There isn't anybody that looks like me without clothes on," she laughed.

He also saw her dark companion, insecurity. "Is that all I'm good for?" she keened about nudity.

Yet Schiller told The Associated Press that "it's women that have kept Marilyn alive, not men." He says teenage girls flock to see gallery shows, and that the photos selling now accentuate her humanity, not her anatomy.

"I think," he said, "people want to see her now as a real person."

Casanova's rule for seduction was to tell a beautiful woman she was intelligent and an intelligent woman she was beautiful. The false choice between intellectualism and sexuality in women has persisted through the ages. There was no more poignant victim of it than Marilyn.

Photographers loved to get her to pose in tight shorts, a silk robe or a swimsuit with a come-hither look and a weighty book, a history of Goya or James Joyce's "Ulysses" or Heinrich Heine's poems. A high-brow bunny picture, a variation on the sexy librarian trope. Men who were nervous about her erotic intensity could feel superior by making fun of her intellectually.

Marilyn was not completely in on the joke. Scarred by her schizo-phrenic mother and dislocated upbringing, she was happy to have the classics put in her hand. What's more, she read some of them, from Proust to Dostoyevsky to Freud to Carl Sandburg's six-volume biogra-phy of Lincoln (given to her by husband Arthur Miller), collecting a library of 400 books.

Miller once called Marilyn "a poet on a street corner trying to recite to a crowd pulling at her clothes."

"Fragments," a new book of her poems, letters and musings, some written in her childlike hand with misspellings in leather books and others on stationery from the Waldorf-Astoria and the Beverly Hills Hotel, is affecting. The world's most coveted woman, a picture of lumi-nescence, was lonely and dark. Thinking herself happily married, she was crushed to discover an open journal in which Miller had written that she disappointed him and embarrassed him in front of his intel-lectual peers.

"I guess I have always been deeply terrified to really be someone's wife since I know from life one cannot love another, ever, really."

Her friend Saul Bellow wrote in a letter that Marilyn "conducts herself like a philosopher." He observed: "She was connected with a very powerful current but she couldn't disconnect herself from it," adding: "She had a kind of curious incandescence under the skin."

The sad sex symbol is still a candle in the wind. There's a hit novel in Britain narrated by the Maltese terrier Frank Sinatra gave her, which she named "Maf," for Mafia, and three movies in the works about her. Naomi Watts is planning to star in a biopic based on the novel, "Blonde," by Joyce Carol Oates; Michelle Williams is shooting "My Week With Marilyn," and another movie is planned based on an account by Lionel Grandison, a former deputy Los Angeles coroner who claims he was forced to change the star's death certificate to read suicide instead of murder.

At least, unlike Paris Hilton and her ilk, the Dumb Blonde of '50s cinema had a firm grasp on one thing: It was cool to be smart. She aspired to read good books and be friends with intellectuals, even going so far as to marry one.

The celebrity-drenched culture that dawned in the dazzling aura of Marilyn, J.F.K. and Jackie reached nauseating new depths in a world obsessed with celebrity lifestyle and deathstyle.

Back in 1999, I covered the display for the Christie's auction of Marilyn's personal property. It was invasive and inviting at the same time. The Christie's galleries were chock-a-block with Ferragamo stilettos, Maximilian furs, Pucci silks, Norell beaded gowns, lace bustiers, see-through nighties and marabou capelets and mules.

Some of the Marilyn stuff, bequeathed by the star to her acting teacher, Lee Strasberg, and sold by his widow, Anna, was glamorous: the gilt lighters from Frank Sinatra's Cal-Neva Lodge, the gold sandals she wore to entertain the troops in Korea, and the dog license of the small white pooch the singer gave her. Here are her scripts with penciled notes to herself, like the scene in "Some Like It Hot" when she tells herself to act "delighted" when she gets on the yacht with Tony Curtis.

Her ambitious library got its own room—Thomas Mann, D. H. Lawrence, Tennessee Williams, Colette, a first edition of "On the Road," a book on mixing cocktails signed by Dean Martin, who wrote the introduction, the works of Freud. Stuck inside her copy of "The Joy of Cooking" was a typed diet starting at 8 A.M. with stewed prunes and ending at 11 P.M. with eggnog.

The "nudest dress," as the designer Jean Louis called that skin-tight, flesh-tone, rhinestone-dotted gown that Marilyn wore to Madison Square Garden—was reverently displayed in a room by itself, lit from above as though it were the Pieta or the David.

Curators told me they had to send for a petite mannequin from Paris. (More than two decades later, it was irreverently displayed when Kim Kardashian procured it from the museum of Ripley's Believe It or Not! to wear to the Met Gala, causing alarm among clothes historians who worried that, even with Kim's crash diet, the dress would be stretched and damaged.)

But other Marilyn items on display at Christie's were forlorn: her Mexican sombreros, her certificate of conversion to Judaism when she married Miller, her platinum-and-diamond "eternity band" from DiMaggio, her heart-shaped cookie cutters, her poem entitled "A Sorry Song."

"It's great to be alive, they say I'm lucky to be alive," she wrote in pencil in one melancholy notation. "It's hard to figure out when everything I feel—hurts!"

But it was, after all, Marilyn's troubles that kept her so compelling. As the actress said in "Some Like It Hot," she always got stuck with the fuzzy end of the lollipop.

CANDICE BERGEN, WOMAN WHO'S HAD IT ALL

There may be some things more fun than hanging out with Candice Bergen and talking about Michael Caine, Sean Connery, Steve McQueen, Jack Nicholson, Princess Diana, Princess Grace, John Belushi, Donald Trump, Charles Manson, getting fat, getting old, getting wrinkled and not giving a damn.

But I don't know of anything.

The woman who once specialized in playing icy Nordic beauties has a great throaty, spontaneous laugh. She's an adventuress who has traveled to the most exotic spots, often solo with her camera. And she's a Scheherazade who can tell witty stories about a Tiffany's window of glitterati.

I mean, she was at Truman Capote's legendary Black and White Ball in 1966 at the Plaza, wearing Halston's white mink mask with the long bunny ears and pink satin nose, chatting up newlyweds Mia Farrow and Frank Sinatra. Need I say more?

"There was a guy who wore an executioner's hood," Ms. Bergen recalled of the party. "It got a little creepy." She doesn't wear fur and hasn't eaten meat in 40 years, but still has the bunny mask on display in her living room in New York.

The Bergen family traces the history of show business in America, from the rise of her father, Edgar, in vaudeville, radio and fledgling TV as a ventriloquist—with a smart-aleck dummy named Charlie McCarthy—to Candice's own half-century career in movies and TV, capped by her five Emmys for "Murphy Brown."

When she was young, her parents had Christmas smorgasbords at their Beverly Hills house with the cream of Old Hollywood: the Reagans schmoozing; Fred Astaire twirling her mother, Frances; and Rex Harrison singing songs from "My Fair Lady" accompanied by Henry Mancini on the piano.

Then, in the 1970s, Ms. Bergen became the first woman to host "Saturday Night Live." She chummed around with Mr. Nicholson, Mike Nichols and the hip crowd of moviemakers who ushered in what was then known as New Hollywood.

Now, at 74, Ms. Bergen is in the swim with streaming, starring with Meryl Streep and Dianne Wiest in "Let Them All Talk," an extemporaneous movie for HBO Max, directed and filmed by Steven Soderbergh with a hand-held camera on board the Queen Mary 2, as actual passengers wandered about.

"The passengers were really overweight," Ms. Bergen recalled with a mischievous smile. "They were good little eaters on this incredibly elegant ship."

As we started our nearly three-hour Zoom interview, she walked with her iPad to the window to show me the view from her "tiny" house in Pacific Palisades, high above the ocean.

"The neighborhood is very comforting because it's just lovely little houses," she said. "A couple of big ones have come crashing in." She had come to Los Angeles for Thanksgiving with her younger brother, Kris. Usually, she can be found at the posh Fifth Avenue apartment she shares with Marshall Rose, a widowed real estate developer and philanthropist she married in 2000. He "has been facing health challenges with grace and elegance for the past few years," she said. Ms. Bergen had difficult caretaking duties with her first husband, Louis Malle, the French director. Their marriage lasted 15 years, until Mr. Malle died in 1995 after an agonizing battle with lymphoma.

When she was single, Ms. Bergen lived in another little house in Los Angeles that was once occupied by Katharine Hepburn and, before that, by John Barrymore's birds.

"I found fantastic paintings of men with plumes in their turbans and fantastic birds with elaborate plumage," she said of the Barrymore aviary-turned-guesthouse. "It was like a little tiny chapel. There were stained-glass windows in the cupola. One showed he and Dolores Costello in a scene from 'The Sea Beast.' Nobody wanted the house. There was no garage. It was just useless. But it was heaven."

Bruce, half–Saint Bernard and half-poodle, was by Ms. Bergen's side. She was wearing a striped T-shirt and shoes made out of African indigo cotton by Ibu, an online group of women's cooperatives from around the world, which features designs by her old friend, Ali MacGraw. (Ms. Bergen also sells bags and other merch online featuring her whimsical artwork, all for charity.)

I asked how she felt about the election.

"When I found out that Biden had won, I was going out of my building and I heard honking and people screaming and I said to the doorman, 'What's happening? Is there a parade?' He said, 'He won.' And I just burst into tears. It was just such a relief. We just needed a sense of decency, a sense of kindness." She added, for the president-elect: "May the wind be at his back because he's going to need it."

I noted that she will have to put away her "Free Melania" sweater.

"Yes," she said, smiling. "That'll have to be repurposed somehow."

"My life is a very tiny life now," she said, referring to coronavirus restrictions and tending Mr. Rose. "I don't mind it, frankly. For someone in their 70s, it's not a tragedy." The couple have quiet dinners and watch "The West Wing" in a dark red room covered with dog paintings. "I'm an old person," Ms. Bergen said, and then, later, stretching out her neck for me to see: "I have a wattle."

"I would like to embrace being 74," she said. "I mean, my hair is white up here. My Covid color, turns out, is white. I probably will leave my wattle."

Ms. Bergen, who had her eyes done during "Murphy Brown"—"Because they were very hooded and people were talking"—continued, "I know I should have injections. I have deep lines along my lip." But "I can't take the pain.

"When I go to get my makeup done, the woman who does it says, when she is finished, 'Now you look like Candice Bergen again.' Because when I start, it's like, 'Uh, what a wreck.' Stuff goes."

'THE ELEPHANT IN THE ROOM'

Ms. Bergen has always been blunt about not starving herself or doing extreme procedures to preserve her looks. She declared in her second memoir, "A Fine Romance," published in 2015: "I am a champion eater. No carb is safe—no fat either."

She told me, "I was never a good dieter," adding brightly: "I ate an entire pumpkin pie at Thanksgiving, all by myself in my kitchen. Without the crust, but the entire filling of the pie."

Her daughter, Chloe Malle, a writer and contributing editor at Vogue, said that Ms. Bergen's lack of vanity is an extension of her I-don't-give-a-damn attitude, which can be both stressful and refreshing.

"She really doesn't care and would rather eat the cookie," Ms. Malle said. "She has eaten mocha ice cream and Cheetos for her entire dinner. Most of quarantine, she has been strolling through Central Park with Bruce in her pajamas and the coat she got on Amazon, her hair sticking up, going into a Big Edie and Little Edie vibe."

Ms. Malle continued: "I grew up with my friends' dads saying 'Oh, my God, I remember when your mom was young. She was a knockout.' I think she had great insecurity around the fact that people have always focused on that. It can be quite a burden. There's something freeing about her beauty not being the only thing people are focused on."

Ms. Bergen writes perceptively in her two memoirs about the phenomenon of beauty creating its own rules of conduct. "It's often the elephant in the room and you're the elephant handler," as she put it.

After her 1967 Vogue cover in her modeling days and her movie debut in "The Group" in 1966, where she played the risky role of Lakey, a lesbian—"People saw posters of me in gay bars after that," she said, pleased—Ms. Bergen's perfect nose spurred a flood of plastic surgeries.

"Doctors used to come up to me and say could they take a cast of my nose," she said. "I said, 'Go away.' My nose was very important to people. I never even thought about it. It's strange."

When she gave birth to her daughter, she mused about whether it would be better if Chloe were not beautiful.

"Obviously, I don't deal with it anymore," the actress told me. When she thinks back, Ms. Bergen said, the problem is "that's all you are to people is what you look like. No one tries to find out if there's anyone home. It works against your own self-development, because it's hard to find out what you think about things and what your opinions are because nobody cares. You don't have to engage your brain for any reason. I think that's why I went off and photographed and wrote pieces, just to get out of the line of fire."

Ms. Bergen has seen this happen to the opposite sex as well. "You're semi-glorified but you're also negated. You really have to make an effort to become someone more than what your presentation is."

She speaks highly of her famous leading men: Caine, McQueen, Connery and especially Nicholson. Early in her career, she got scathing reviews. After "The Group" came out, Pauline Kael wrote about Ms. Bergen in Life magazine that "As an actress, her only flair is in her nostrils." Reviewing "The Adventurers," The New York Times said that Ms. Bergen "performs as though clubbed over the head."

But on "S.N.L." and in the 1979 film "Starting Over," in which she belted out songs like a cat in pain, and then in "Murphy Brown," Ms. Bergen discovered she had comedic timing, perhaps honed as a child in her father's holiday skits with Charlie McCarthy. Younger fans laughed at Ms. Bergen as a rabid former beauty queen in "Miss Congeniality" and as a Vogue editor in "Sex and the City."

She recalled her first "S.N.L." hosting gig, in 1975, as "pure, distilled terror." (Lorne Michaels, a friend, said the expression in her eyes that night was "like Patty Hearst when the Symbionese Liberation Army rang her doorbell." She eventually joined the show's Five-Timers Club.)

Ms. Bergen recalled: "Belushi and Danny Aykroyd, who were best friends, were being very cute, and sort of flirtatious, kind of like young guys with an older woman. They were very dear, actually. Belushi had not yet started going to California to do drugs. They were all jealous of Lorne and resentful of his authority. I always got that from cast members. Lorne was a miracle. It was just staggering, the things they could pull off."

Is it harder for beautiful women to be funny?

"I think men don't like beautiful women to make fun of themselves," the actress said. "They don't like you to wear funny hats. They don't like you to look less than a dignified, beautiful woman. I've noticed that. For me, being funny is my joy. Doing 'Murphy' was just such a gift for me." She was very disappointed that the reboot did not catch on.

Her new movie is about three women who go to college together, fall out of touch and reunite when Alice, a Pulitzer Prize–winning novelist played by Ms. Streep, invites the other two on a crossing to London. It turns out that Alice learned about an affair that Ms. Bergen's character, Roberta, had, which caused her rich husband to divorce her, stranding her to a life selling lingerie at a high-end department store—and then appropriated this plotline for a book.

Unlike Ms. Bergen, Roberta is pinched and bruised by grievances. At one point, Roberta wonders if men will want her given that she's "old rotten meat." It's startling, more so knowing Ms. Bergen improvised the line.

In her big confrontation scene with Ms. Streep's character on the boat, Ms. Bergen was jittery. As they sat down to shoot a scene, they received an outline from Deborah Eisenberg, the short story writer and Columbia professor (and Wallace Shawn's longtime companion).

"They tell you what the nub of the scene is, and then you just have to flail around," Ms. Bergen said.

She did do research. "Candy told us she actually flew to Houston to see oil rigs as preparation for her role," Ms. Wiest said, adding that Ms. Bergen conjured a character who "was so poor as a child, her only pet was a snake and her single mother worked as a housekeeper. I thought, 'Wow, Hollywood royalty does deep research!' She dressed herself like a real Texas babe. I sat across the table from her in the film and thought, she's doing nothing obvious and yet I'd swear she sprang from Texas dirt."

SHE PODS

Ms. Streep said she was surprised when Ms. Bergen, whom she did not know previously, was standoffish. "I thought, 'She hates me.'" Then she realized that Ms. Bergen was using a "method-y" approach.

Now, she notes, "Candy is sort of like a sister I never had," with traits that are shy and sly, kind and sharp, all at the same time. And then, she said, there's that surprising, throwing-her-head-back laugh, which Ms. Bergen used to great effect in the 1971 film "Carnal Knowledge."

Ms. Bergen had never done improv. "At her age, she doesn't have to do any of this," said her friend Diane English, the creator of "Murphy Brown." "She has such respect for the script and the written word and she works so hard to get it exactly right. This is a huge challenge for her. But she wants another challenge. It's daunting but she totally embraced it."

Mr. Soderbergh agreed, noting that he has seen many older actors "move bag and baggage into the third person, as though their names are in quotation marks, sort of disconnected from themselves."

He said that with Ms. Bergen, on the other hand, "You can't throw one past her. You better know what you're talking about and what you're doing."

I told Ms. Bergen that in her climactic confrontation with Ms. Streep's character on the boat, she could have channeled the moment in 1980 when she had her only Oscar nomination, for "Starting Over," and lost to Ms. Streep, who won for "Kramer vs. Kramer."

"One of the first of her 18 nominations," Ms. Bergen said dryly. (It's 21.)

I wondered about the movie's theme about strained female friendship. Ms. Bergen wrote in her first memoir, "Knock Wood," that she did not have many women friends when she was younger, and that women were often "wary" of her.

"Certainly, going into parties, my task for myself was to disarm myself, to go, 'I've got no weapons. I'm here. I come in friendship,'" she said. "Because the women would back way up."

She added: "Of course, as you get older, women's relationships become primary relationships because we know so many women are widows, so many women are single, and they become their own pod and form these groups."

Her friends gush about her. Ali MacGraw loves the fact that Ms. Bergen—"A real American beauty with enormous class"—never wears anything that's trying too hard and that she entertains and decorates with a sense of whimsy.

"When she lived in the fabulous former artist's studio on Central Park South," Ms. MacGraw remembered, "on one table there was a glass of milk spilled on the glass top. I don't know how many times I tried to clean that up before I realized it was a fake."

Ms. Bergen's most important relationship is with her daughter. "The birth of my daughter was the greatest event in my life," she said.

Some would argue, Ms. Malle said wryly, that the umbilical cord is still not severed. Ms. Bergen raised Chloe mostly on her own in Los Angeles, where she lived for the 10 years of "Murphy Brown." After Louis Malle lost the Oscar for Best Foreign Language Film for the 1987 film "Au Revoir Les Enfants," his dislike of Los Angeles deepened and he went back to France to work.

"I was very happy being married to Louis," Ms. Bergen said. "He was really a great love of my life and we had a great time together, but you're pulled in different directions and then you have a child and they become the love of your life and that's hard." She added, "The distance was very hard on the marriage and then the balance of power was in question," referring to her growing fame with "Murphy Brown."

Now she is focused on her 6-month-old grandson, Artie. "He's just the dumpling," she said. "He's just the best arrival of joy in one's life. I'm crying. I'm just looking forward to the future with Artie."

She asked her daughter if she could take over a dilapidated barn, one of two on the land that Chloe and her husband, Graham Albert, a financier, bought in Connecticut. "That's all I need," mother told daughter. "That's where I'm going to retire."

Now, said an amused Ms. Malle, "she has built a Gil Schafer minimanse on the site. She said it's the smallest project he's ever taken on."

I ask Ms. Bergen what she thought of Quentin Tarantino's "Once Upon a Time . . . in Hollywood," released last year.

"The feeling of it," she said, "was very close."

In the late 1960s, she and her boyfriend at the time, Terry Melcher, a record producer and the son of Doris Day, had lived in the house on Cielo Drive before Sharon Tate and Roman Polanski. It has been said that a reason Manson targeted that house was because he was angry Mr. Melcher didn't give him a record contract.

"Terry was very stupid and he went out there to record Manson's group singing," Ms. Bergen said. "He knew it was very loaded, and one of Manson's people came to the door once when I was at the house. Then one day, Terry just said, 'We're moving.' I said, 'When?' He said, 'Tomorrow.' His mother had a house in Malibu that became David Geffen's house where we went. Then they took the telescope off our balcony at the beach house. It was like Manson saying, 'Don't try to hide from me.'"

And about that famous date with Donald Trump, when she was at the University of Pennsylvania?

He was shy, quiet and introspective, one presumes?

"Yes, in fact his knowledge of philosophy goes way beyond," she said, laughing. "We went to, I think, a steakhouse but he picked me up from school in a limousine, which was unusual, and it was a burgundy limousine and he was wearing a burgundy suit and burgundy patent leather boots. I just thought, this guy can color coordinate with the best of them. I think I was home by 9. I remember it being just very slow going and heavy lifting, it was just like pulling a sledge. And then I was home early."

There was another renowned date in the 1970s, with Henry Kissinger, arranged by family friends. Ms. Bergen went ahead with it at the puckish urging of her counterculture boyfriend, Bert Schneider, and his pal, Abbie Hoffman, who wanted intel on the Vietnam War.

She said if it wasn't the best date she ever had, it was "certainly the best-guarded. Some family friends invited Frank Sinatra and a date and Henry Kissinger and me for dinner. I remember, when he was late, getting a call that the Secret Service couldn't find Beverly Hills. It was concerning. The whole dinner was just a mano-a-mano between Frank and Henry. I think Frank won."

When I noted that Ms. Bergen had to be the only person on earth who was friends with both Nancy Reagan and Huey Newton, she laughed and agreed.

I said it was surprising Mr. Sinatra did not woo her.

"He did ask a friend of mine for my contact but it wasn't given," she said, with a prim smile.

Charlie McCarthy is now in the Smithsonian. Ms. Bergen wrote about her shock when her father left money in his will to her "older, all-powerful brother"—the dummy—and not to her. She used to talk to a shrink about their relationship, which she calls the zaniest sibling rivalry ever, but she said it was too wacky even for a therapist.

She has reconciled her feelings toward her wooden "brother"—and her father, who was a loving but emotionally distant child of Swedish immigrants. She said that she has Charlie McCarthy memorabilia on display and her daughter has windup toys and salt and pepper shakers.

"The older I get, the more fierce I am about my pride in being a ventriloquist's daughter," Ms. Bergen said. "I just think it's the weirdest thing."

[Putting words in her mouth? No, just a holiday round of Confirm or Deny.]

Confirm or Deny

MAUREEN DOWD: *You would have loved to work with Alfred Hitchcock.*

CANDICE BERGEN: Yes. I would have been a Hitchcock blonde. I did have lunch with Grace and Prince Rainier at David Niven Jr.'s house in the South of France. David and I had grown up together. The Rainiers came for lunch, and we talked about this and that. It was fantastic. She was lovely. And afterward, an interviewer said, "Who will be the next Grace Kelly?" She said, "Perhaps it's Candice Bergen."

You used to figure out who you wanted to date with the help of a shoe code.

If you wanted to place really high on the board, Italian loafers. Any kind of loafer basically got you in the door, or sneakers. But no cordovans, no wingtips.

You've read Matthew McConaughey's memoir twice.

All right, all right, all right. No.

You love listening to the podcast "Call Her Daddy."

Here's the thing. I've never listened to a podcast because I don't know how. I know there's a podcast app someplace, so I'm going to do that. I have to find my earphones first.

You have James Bond's old couch.

Yes, Roger Moore's—because I once bought his house. My daughter has it.

You love practical jokes but it's harder in the woke culture.

I think you have to pick your subjects more carefully. It's a very structured moment in time.

Your biggest regret is missing the famous Diana and Charles dinner-dance at the Reagan White House.

I was pregnant with Chloe and she was two and a half weeks late. Mrs. Reagan was calling me and she said, "Candy, what's happening? We'd love you to be there." I couldn't go. Chloe was born the day before.

You miss sitting on the bed and watching bad TV and smoking pot with Sue Mengers.

Well, I do. That was fun.

You would like to die the way the Maasai do, where they just lay you out in the savanna as a buffet for the animals.

Exactly.

PART 2

Leading Men

RALPH FIENNES, MASTER OF MONSTERS

—OCTOBER 22, 2022

TORONTO—After 10 minutes sitting alone, I panicked. I was meeting Ralph Fiennes for dinner and suddenly realized I was in the wrong restaurant.

The 59-year-old actor is a confessed compulsive, always overly prepared, not the sort who would be late or appreciate lateness in others. So I began frantically running around Canada, a stranger in a strange land.

I was dreading that famous icy blue stare, the one that seems lit with darkness; the merciless glare that was so blood-chilling when Mr. Fiennes played a depraved Nazi commandant in "Schindler's List," a reptilian Lord Voldemort in "Harry Potter," and a psychopathic chef in his stylish new black comedy, "The Menu."

When I finally careered into the right place, 30 minutes late, he was sitting alone, looking sharp in a Timothy Everest navy wool suit, eating an appetizer, which he called "a chickpea thing," and drinking a glass of Sancerre. He did not give me a brooding Heathcliff look (though he perfected it in 1992's "Wuthering Heights").

Instead, Mr. Fiennes was charming, indulging my fan-girl questions about Shakespeare—his 1995 Broadway performance in "Hamlet," for which he won a Tony, and his blazing 2011 film version of "Coriolanus."

After eating "duck three ways," at Richmond Station, he suggested we start over the next morning because he was due on the red carpet at the Toronto International Film Festival for the premiere of "The Menu."

He was probably *acting* like he wasn't irritated by my tardiness, because he's an astonishing actor. He's that rare creature who's equally powerful in the classics and popular fare, who's dedicated to toggling between stage and screen. He is both prolific and enigmatic, disappearing into a dazzling range of characters.

When you watch or rewatch 20 of his movies, as I did, you think that the Oscars have no meaning because this guy doesn't have one. No offense to Tommy Lee Jones, who was great in "The Fugitive," and in 1994 beat out Mr. Fiennes for best supporting actor for his role in "Schindler's List," but . . . *Amon Goeth?* The scene in which the Nazi sets his sights on a Jewish prisoner in a death camp, played by a trembling Embeth Davidtz, and he's tempted to kiss her, even though, as he tells her, she's not "a person in the strictest sense of the word," is one of the best things ever put on film.

Now Mr. Fiennes is in New York, starring at the Shed in "Straight Line Crazy" as Robert Moses, the master builder who created, for better or worse, the New York of today.

"Ralph's good at monsters," said Nicholas Hytner, a director of the play. "He doesn't approach them sensationally. He tries to understand them."

It was Mr. Hytner who suggested that David Hare write the play about Moses for the theater he runs in London, the Bridge, where it opened this spring.

Moses was an American Caesar—a perfect barrel-chested, desk-slapping role for a leading Shakespeare interpreter like Mr. Fiennes.

"I've always loved a toxic male," Mr. Hare said, fondly recalling the 1985 Rupert Murdoch satire, "Pravda," that he wrote with Howard Brenton. "They're great for theater, aren't they?"

Mr. Fiennes likes them, too. Unlike some top American actors, who carefully curate heroic roles, the British actor relishes swimming in moral murkiness, "the gray areas where you can't easily put a definition."

Mr. Hytner said of his star: "With Robert Moses, the ability to subordinate his charm to a brutal megalomaniac to the extent that he's completely unafraid to alienate an audience. That doesn't go with being a movie star. He makes himself open but he never makes himself too open. He's one of those actors who is fascinating because he appears to be nursing a secret."

A DISCIPLINED HEDONIST

Mr. Fiennes has had a storied career, starting at the Royal Academy of Dramatic Art in London. He had a quartet of scorching roles that made him famous and a heartthrob by his early 30s: Steven Spielberg's "Schindler's List" in 1993, Robert Redford's "Quiz Show" in 1994, "Hamlet" on Broadway in 1995 and Anthony Minghella's "The English Patient" in 1996.

But he hasn't pursued fame so much as interesting work.

"Being a leading actor on the classical stage and a huge, great film star is an almost impossible double to straddle," Mr. Hare said. "Laurence Olivier could do that. Judi Dench could do that. And Ralph Fiennes is the only other one."

Just for fun, on a Monday night in December when he has the night off from playing Moses, he's doing a reading of T.S. Eliot's "The Waste Land" at the 92nd Street Y. (Don't bother: Tickets sold out within minutes of going on sale.) Coming out of Covid, Mr. Fiennes tried to revive England's regional theaters, touring with a recitation of Eliot's "Four Quartets."

"That's what he chose as a post-pandemic pick-me-up," Mr. Hare said dryly. "'Four Quartets' is about as difficult an evening as you can offer. The thing about Ralph is that he has the easiest, most relaxed relationship with high culture of anyone I know. He doesn't give a damn about whether things are too difficult for people. He just thinks difficult stuff is good."

Mr. Fiennes is democratic in his advisers. Two years ago, while he was rehearsing "Beat the Devil," Mr. Hare's monologue play about his own severe case of Covid, Mr. Fiennes went to a house he rents in the Umbria region of central Italy to prepare.

"He would find a stray shepherd and ask him to sit down and he would perform the monologue to the shepherd," said an amused Mr. Hytner, who also directed that show. "He was always calling me to say, 'There's this contessa who lives 10 miles up the road and she thought it was great!'"

Mr. Fiennes has a reputation for being tunnel-visioned about his work.

"When I worked with him 20 years ago, there was undoubtedly a nimbus of depression and intensity around him," Mr. Hare said. "That cloud has cleared with the years. His work process is just beautiful to observe because he's just very, very hard at work every minute of the day. Then he closes the door and puts it behind him."

When Mr. Fiennes was doing the Moses role in London, he listened to recordings of the builder hour after hour. But, worried about his New York accent, Mr. Fiennes would sometimes call a friend in Brooklyn, the actor and documentarian Fisher Stevens, just before curtain to ask him how to pronounce "Bronx" or "West Side Highway."

He was just as meticulous about his concierge uniform in "The Grand Budapest Hotel." When he first tried it on, Wes Anderson, the film's director, recalled, Mr. Fiennes bristled at the cut and materials, explaining that he wanted to move like Fred Astaire in the role and couldn't. Mr. Anderson let him redesign it.

Mark Mylod, the British director of "The Menu," said that Mr. Fiennes is rigorous but loose, like a free-form jazz musician.

"He's a sensualist and a hedonist on some level," the director said. "He'll tell you himself his idea of perfection is to go off to the place he rents in Italy in the middle of nowhere and dive naked into a lake."

Jessica Chastain, who played Mr. Fiennes's wife in "Coriolanus" (which Mr. Fiennes also directed) and in last year's "The Forgiven," said she was nervous when she first met him about filming Shakespeare opposite him, given his ferocity as an actor.

"But then I realized how fragile he was because the financing fell through and he called me and left me this message and it was so emotional," she said. "I remember listening to it, thinking, 'I'll love him forever because he trusts me with this vulnerability.'"

At one point during the filming of "Schindler's List," recalled Liam Neeson (who played Oskar Schindler), they were doing a scene and Mr. Fiennes, as the Nazi, let out an unearthly cry of hate and rage that gave Mr. Neeson goose bumps. (It was cut from the finished film.) When they announced best supporting actor at the Oscars, Mr. Neeson said, he was keeping his fingers crossed that his friend would not win for playing the Nazi officer, because Mr. Fiennes would be typecast forever like Tony Perkins was after "Psycho."

"He's terribly sweet, Ralph," Mr. Neeson said. "He almost belongs to another century." (So does his full name: Ralph—pronounced "Rafe"—Nathaniel Twisleton-Wykeham-Fiennes.)

He became close to Mr. Neeson and his wife, Natasha Richardson—who, before she died in 2009, made two movies with Mr. Fiennes—and they hung out at the farmhouse in the South of France that her father, the director and producer Tony Richardson, left her. They would turn the record player on and dance on the lawn in the moonlight on warm summer nights.

Andy Cohen, the Bravo impresario, who was there sometimes, said Mr. Fiennes would recite Beckett at 3 a.m. under the stars. Like Mr. Neeson, Mr. Cohen sees his friend as a throwback, "this amazing poetic soul from another time who's walking among us."

They got to be friends over the years, having nightcaps in Greenwich Village and going on what Mr. Cohen calls "bro-buddy adventures."

"He's very mischievous," Mr. Cohen said. "He loves women in the most beautiful way, in all forms. There's not a woman in front of him that he doesn't appreciate."

When fame hit in the early '90s, Mr. Fiennes's life erupted in a Harry Styles–style publicity blizzard. He was married to Alex Kingston (who later became a regular on "E.R.") when he fell in love with Francesca Annis, the beautiful British actress, nearly 18 years older, who played his mother, Gertrude, in "Hamlet." Ms. Annis and Mr. Fiennes split after 11 years.

The actor, who prizes mystery, hated being gossip fodder. "That was anathema to him," said his sister Martha Fiennes, a filmmaker, "and he just hated the curiosity into his life."

In contrast with his brother Joseph Fiennes, also a famous actor, who lives in Spain with his wife and family, Ralph is an adventurous free spirit in his love life and cherishes his solitude.

Sometimes, as he did when he was a child, Ralph likes to "separate himself from that rough and tumble," Martha said. Laughing, she added that Ralph prefers to live in beautiful, civilized places "where there are no dogs that are vomiting or kids that are screaming." Mr. Stevens, a father of two, drolly affirmed that Mr. Fiennes is skittish around diapers.

I told Mr. Fiennes I would respect his privacy, but he should tell me if he was engaged or having a baby.

"No, no, nothing," Mr. Fiennes told me, laughing.

As he once said about being the oldest of many siblings, "I had kids when I was a kid."

I CONFESS, I LIKE THE WEST SIDE HIGHWAY

When Mr. Fiennes played Moses in London, most English theatergoers were not familiar with the concrete potentate, knowing only that he had a thunderous Old Testament name. Now Mr. Fiennes is playing the role in the city that Moses shaped. In the preview audience I was in, the Jane Jacobs character—who describes herself as the woman who beat Robert Moses on his plan to put a highway through Greenwich Village—got a round of applause just for walking onstage.

Not since Ayn Rand has anyone tried so hard to make infrastructure so sexy. "I love mixing the concrete and driving in the stakes," the Moses character says.

As Robert Caro wrote in his magisterial biography of Moses, the visionary builder who hated public transport and loved cars (even though he didn't have a driver's license) conjured nearly all the major roads in the metro area today, determining how New Yorkers live and work.

"He would never admit the motor car was not the answer to mankind's problems," Mr. Hare said. "To me, he's an interesting figure because he's the prisoner of an ideal, but he can't change the ideal when the facts change and he becomes stuck in a dream, trapped in the ideas of his youth."

Working under six governors, Moses oversaw the building of Lincoln Center, the New York Coliseum and Shea Stadium; he vastly expanded the city's green space and constructed 673 baseball diamonds, 658 playgrounds and 288 tennis courts.

From 1946 to 1953, he approved countless public works projects and to clear the land, he evicted hundreds of thousands of New Yorkers, many of them minority residents, from their homes and tore the homes down. Perhaps his worst offense was the Cross-Bronx Expressway, which destroyed the borough, uprooting vibrant neighborhoods, and creating an eyesore that many New York commuters lament to this day.

The show is at the cultural center, the Shed, which might have been the one tiny part of the giant Moses-esque development that is Hudson Yards of which Jane Jacobs would have approved.

When I asked Mr. Fiennes if he was annoyed that his play wasn't running on Broadway, meaning he wouldn't be eligible for a Tony, he said, "What?" and I began to worry I had told him something he didn't know. But he shrugged. "Hasn't crossed my mind," he said.

As with many Shakespearean characters, Moses's arc is a fall from idealism to egotism.

The play depicts how at first, in 1928, he pushed to make Jones Beach accessible to the masses by building roads, so that Long Island wasn't a cloistered preserve of the Vanderbilts, the Whitneys and other aristocratic New York families. But as the master builder's power grows, his prejudice and intolerance are revealed. By 1955, after tearing up the Bronx, he wanted to build a four-lane highway through Greenwich Village that would bisect Washington Square Park; he was secretly planning to build three elevated expressways, a scheme that fell apart because of, as the Moses character says in the play, "a group of minstrels and artistic women with handbags."

Like Coriolanus, Moses's attitude toward "the people" is withering.

"We must advance their fortunes without having any respect for their opinions," Mr. Fiennes's Moses tells the young Irish woman working with him, adding: "To build a road, it may be that you need to knock down a house. What happens? A lot of screaming and shouting. 'That has always been there.' And then when the road is built? 'Oh my

God, how much better this is. How did we ever manage without this road?' They can't even remember the house. The people lack imagination. The job of the leader is to provide it."

Mr. Fiennes told me, "I've met people who say, 'You're doing a play about Moses? Oh, no, he's terrible.' And other people say, 'My parents love Moses. He gave them Jones Beach.'"

The actor added, "He gave you the West Side Highway, didn't he? I mean, you're kind of grateful for the West Side Highway on occasion, aren't you?"

The actor rejects the binary view, noting geniuses can be good and bad at the same time.

I noted that, with cancel culture, the arts have to deal with a more censorious world.

"Righteous anger is righteous," he said, "but often it becomes kind of dumb because it can't work its way through the gray areas. It has no nuance."

I wondered how he liked directing movies he was appearing in (including "Coriolanus," "The Invisible Woman" and "The White Crow," a movie about Rudolf Nureyev's life that was very difficult to get made).

"I don't like the money bit before," he said of procuring funding. "I find that very bruising. But the whole deciding of what it is you are going to show visually, I love that. Before I went to acting school, I went to art school for one year, thinking I would be a painter."

He said he loved making movies like Luca Guadagnino's "A Bigger Splash," in which his charismatic, obstreperous character, Harry Hawkes, a music producer described by the Italian director as "a pagan fawn," does a Dionysian dance to the Rolling Stones song "Emotional Rescue."

Mr. Fiennes liked that Harry would say outrageous things. "One of the attractions of being an actor," he said, is the freedom to say things "you don't say in life."

'A COILED TIGER IN AN ADOLESCENT FRAME'

Mr. Fiennes grew up mostly in southern England, one of six children; his father's income as a photographer was erratic. His mother was a writer, poet and painter. "I think it was a huge pressure on them both," Mr. Fiennes said. "Sometimes she would just explode. And often, the fact that she had so many children, she would literally vocalize it, 'Why do we have so many children?'"

Once, Mr. Fiennes said, he worked up "a little bit of courage" and said, 'Well, we didn't ask you and Dad to be born.' And that just made it worse—'Ah, don't speak to me like that.'"

The Fiennes lived on the west coast of Ireland for a time. Mr. Fiennes said his mother, a committed Catholic with some Irish ancestry, fell in love with the country. There, he said, the size of their family wasn't frowned on in the way it was in Britain.

His mother, Jennifer Lash, told him bedtime stories from Shakespeare, including "Henry V" and "Hamlet."

"I was on a top bunk and my mother said, 'I'll tell you a story. There was this young man and his father's died and he's a young prince.' And she told it to me in her own words. I think she saw the effect that it had on me. The next day she put on the vinyl record of Laurence Olivier, doing speeches from 'Hamlet' and 'Henry V.' And I sat there with a paperback, following this text as I listened to it, not knowing what it meant, but being thrilled by this voice of this actor doing this stuff."

Joseph Fiennes, who just finished five years in "The Handmaid's Tale," said that their mother taught them about "getting your guts into it, throwing yourself off the edge, mistakes and all, but being disciplined with it."

Martha Fiennes said that her brother was "completely self-contained" even at 5 or 6 years old. When Martha came along, she said, their mother would remark, "Oh, my God, I've got a sort of normally socializing child, thank God."

"She said she'd take him to a children's birthday party," Martha recalled, "and he'd go straight up to the mom and say, 'Do you have a puzzle I can do?' He wouldn't be the one to say, 'Let's all do this.'"

Joseph said his "lovely" big brother was not merely a bookworm as a youngster. "He was thinking about being a Marine and going to karate clubs."

"Maybe he wanted a sense of control," Joseph said. "There was this underlying physical tension. I remember being placed against a book-shelf and having punches and kicks thrown at me and asked, 'Can you feel the wind?' as he came within a millimeter of my nose. There was the sense of a coiled spring aching to release itself, a coiled tiger in an adolescent frame."

Ralph still seeks out physical release. Like Moses, he does his best thinking when he's swimming. "I think challenging yourself physically is a great way of getting all the crap out of your head," he said.

Mr. Hytner told me that Mr. Fiennes's one request for his rehearsal room, when "Straight Line Crazy" played at the Bridge Theater, was that it have a ballet barre, so he could do his ballet exercises.

"I arrived early one morning and crashed into the rehearsal room to find him with his ballet teacher at the barre," the director said. "Bare-foot, with a leotard. It was quite a sight."

A 'NAUGHTY' SENSE OF HUMOR

When Mr. Fiennes was starting out, he tried some Hugh Grant–ish parts to balance out the Shakespearean tragedies, but he said he felt uncomfortable in roles like the romantic lead opposite Jennifer Lopez in the Cinderella story "Maid in Manhattan."

"I can fit into comedy if the writing works for me, but I just felt that was a Prince Charming role," he said. "And Prince Charming's sort of a bland figure."

According to his sister Martha, the press often misses the fact that Mr. Fiennes isn't totally serious. "Ralph, he's got his naughty sense of humor, silly stories," she said. "He's unrepeatable."

That style of humor was clear when Mr. Fiennes suggested a "Harry Potter" spinoff called "Voldemort's Bride," starring him and Jessica Chastain, depicting a loving Voldemort marriage filled with sex, hate and spells.

He turned in a wonderful comic performance in Mr. Anderson's "The Grand Budapest Hotel" and he enjoyed playing Lord Voldemort, once Martha explained who the "Harry Potter" villain was and told him it was a "stonkingly vast, mega, mega part." Her middle son, Hero Fiennes Tiffin, plays a young Tom Riddle, who becomes Voldemort, in the films.

"I was a bit sniffy, I think, initially," Ralph said. "I thought, 'Oh, this is a children's fantasy thing. I'm not sure.'" (Martha noted that when Ralph was 7, he was reading T.E. Lawrence's "Seven Pillars of Wisdom.")

He said his proudest moment was when he walked past the 4-year-old son of the script supervisor on the "Harry Potter" set, as Voldemort, and the child burst into tears.

Mr. Fiennes bristles at the kerfuffle over J.K. Rowling.

"J.K. Rowling has written these great books about empowerment, about young children finding themselves as human beings. It's about how you become a better, stronger, more morally centered human being," he said. "The verbal abuse directed at her is disgusting, it's appalling. I mean, I can understand a viewpoint that might be angry at what she says about women. But it's not some obscene, über-right-wing fascist. It's just a woman saying, 'I'm a woman and I feel I'm a woman and I want to be able to say that I'm a woman.' And I understand where she's coming from. Even though I'm not a woman."

He's not angry that James Bond got killed off after 25 films, possibly putting Mr. Fiennes out of a job as M.

"I thought it was a bold and strong decision," Mr. Fiennes said. "You know, they might reboot everything and they might want a woman back as M. Every single film after I took over from Judi Dench, she upstaged me. They always had her voice, a recording or a portrait. I'm like, 'Look, can I be M, Judi?'"

When he was 14, he could name all the Bond girls. Can he still?

He rattles off the names, from Honey Ryder to Pussy Galore to Domino to Kissy Suzuki. He said he toyed with the idea of playing James Bond and had a conversation about it at one point, but he asked if it could be a black-and-white period piece set in the '50s.

Before we parted, I told him that I thought it would be fun if I asked him the four questions that Kristin Scott Thomas puts to him during an amorous bath in "The English Patient."

Mr. Fiennes, who was wearing a stylish denim jacket and jeans for our morning coffee, shot me a look as if to say "That would not be fun at all." But he was game.

When were you most happy?

He said that, after being "London-centric" for so long, his new place in Suffolk, with "the echo of my childhood," from a happy time when his parents were young and not so stressed out about money, "felt like a human coming home."

When were you least happy?

That, he said gingerly, is connected to his personal life. "If you are preoccupied with doing the right thing through the eyes of other people, what you think other people want to see, or you are locked into something that you haven't yet got the courage to say, 'This isn't working,' then I think you're unhappy."

What do you love?

"Swimming and Shakespeare," he said.

What do you hate?

"I try not to hate anything, but I think anything that feels like there's a phoniness," he said. "Funny, 'cause I'm in the business of pretending."

Confirm or Deny

MAUREEN DOWD: *Like Robert Moses, you prefer bridges to tunnels.*

RALPH FIENNES: Yes.

You always wonder what Othello saw in Desdemona.

No, I don't wonder.

You were jealous that your brother got to play Shakespeare in "Shakespeare in Love."

No, I wasn't jealous of Joe. I was thrilled for him. But a year or so before, I auditioned for Shakespeare for the same film, set up with Julia Roberts, and Ed Zwick directing. I don't think I did it for her.

When you worked as a valet at Brown's hotel in London in the '90s, you carried my bag when I came to cover Wimbledon.

No, I was there in the early '80s. I carried Jack Palance's bags.

You can't get enough Harry Styles gossip.

No, I can get enough. I'm not really into that.

You REALLY hate Harry Potter.

Yes.

Heathcliff was a jerk.

(Laughs.)

You hate having your Voldemort makeup done.

I want to correct that. The makeup guys were brilliant. It's a challenge, sure, to sit in the chair for three hours, but "The English Patient" was four hours. It was a lot of painting, and I shaved my head, and I had stuff to cover my eyebrows. But I didn't hate it.

You love Santa Maria Novella soap, shoes from Loeb and T-shirts from James Perse.

Yes.

"The Avengers" was your least favorite movie.

It did business, and I enjoyed making it, but I think it needed a particular style and very bold, stylish choices. It was trying to replicate that British series of the '60s, and it just didn't do it.

You are a Serbian citizen.

An honorary one.

You took inspiration for the obsessive chef in "The Menu" from Grant Achatz, who runs Alinea in Chicago and whose surreal techniques include encapsulation, pillows of scented air and an ingredient called Ultra-Tex 3.

Yes. I didn't even know what a s'more was.

In the classic "Seinfeld" episode when Elaine and Mr. Peterman go to see "The English Patient" and Elaine yells at your character, Count Laszlo Almasy, "I can't do this anymore. I can't. It's too long! Quit telling your stupid story about the stupid desert and just die already! Die!" she's right.

Yeah, yeah, yeah. Die—already.

YOU HAVE IDRIS ELBA'S FULL ATTENTION

—OCTOBER 4, 2017

I don't know how to break it to Idris Elba.

So I just say it. "Is Kate Winslet really the woman you want to be stuck with when disaster strikes in freezing weather? You do know that she didn't move over to make room on that door and Leo slipped into the icy Atlantic?"

The British actor laughs. He is sitting atop the New York skyline in a dining room at the Mandarin Oriental. "Kate Winslet is surprisingly resilient to almost anything," he says. "I mean, she is a *bruiser*. Tough. As. Nails. And if we were ever to fall off a real mountain, her and I, we would survive because she's not like a slouch in any shape or form."

And, to be fair, Ms. Winslet did hoist Richard Branson's mother down some stairs after a lightning bolt in a hurricane sparked a fire that engulfed the Branson holiday home on Necker Island, where she and her children were staying in 2011. That was when she met her husband, Mr. Branson's nephew, a.k.a. Ned Rocknroll, when he rushed into the burning house with a headlamp.

"She was just like, 'That guy's for me,'" Mr. Elba says.

The actor is starring with Ms. Winslet in the "The Mountain Between Us," based on a novel about strangers who struggle, snuggle and eat roasted mountain lion in the frigid Utah wilderness after their small plane crashes.

Mr. Elba often plays opposite very strong women, and he says that's fine with him.

His Ghana-born "Mum" is so into tough love, he says, that at his 45th birthday party recently, she turned her cheek away when he went to kiss her.

Mr. Elba also portrays the New York lawyer who defends Molly Bloom, the audacious poker madam to the stars played by a fiery Jessica Chastain in the Aaron Sorkin movie, "Molly's Game," out Nov. 22. And the actor created one of the most memorable romances in TV history in the popular BBC series "Luther," when his London homicide detective in the big tweed overcoat, known by his deputies as "his satanic majesty," gets in an erotic and psychopathic entanglement with a latter-day Lizzie Borden, played with film-noir panache by the flame-haired Ruth Wilson.

"I think powerful women are sexy," he says. "But powerful, dangerous women? It's like, *woooo*."

Mr. Elba confesses that he got jittery during his sex scene with Ms. Winslet because he hasn't done that many. "I was a bit nervous because it was Kate Winslet, number one," he says, slyly, and her breasts were exposed. "Do I look, do I not look? Am I supposed to kiss?"

In a world where most movies disappoint and true stars are rare, Mr. Elba is magnetic. He is tall and muscular, and before he hit the big time as the drug lord Stringer Bell in "The Wire," he was a bouncer (and pot dealer) at the comedy club Carolines on Broadway, sometimes living in his Chevy Astro van.

"Really nice velvety seats," he recalls. "I miss that little thing. Honestly, if I found one, I'd definitely buy it and ship it back to France to my little house out there."

He is leaner than he looks on screen, with a small hoop earring, a gray-flecked beard and elaborately tattooed arms. A tree climbs his upper arm. "I have a spiritual connection to trees," he says. "I kind of use trees as a place to pray."

His daughter's name, Isan, is also tattooed on his arm. (She is with him in New York, upstairs in his hotel suite.) And he has a line of a song inked: "This train carries no wrongdoers," to indicate that he does not want the people in his life to let him down. He is wearing a snug gray polo shirt and black jeans from his own clothing collection, with a small "IE" emblazoned.

When Amy Pascal was head of Sony, she suggested that Mr. Elba might take over the James Bond role if Daniel Craig ever "hung up his tuxedo." As a producer of "Molly's Game," Ms. Pascal said that they cast Mr. Elba as the lawyer because "if you had to put yourself in someone's hands, whose hands would you want? He is like the best version of masculinity. All his complicated contradictions make every character he plays fascinating. Maybe it's the way he walks, like his legs are more powerful than anyone else, like he is gravity. He always seems like he is in the midst of a moral struggle, but he is the calmest one in the room. It's rare, undeniable movie star stuff."

I remark to him that race seems beside the point in his romantic liaisons on screen.

"Yeah, my leading ladies have been both black and white and I haven't thought about it consciously," he says. "You know, a good friend of mine, a black producer, said to me, 'Are you sure about the "Mountain" movie, man? Do you think the black audience is going to go for that?'" (In the book, his character, a surgeon, was white.)

He said it had not come up except during a Facebook Live video, when a woman asked if the movie was advocating greater trust between the races during a divisive time in this country.

"If it does, fantastic, but we didn't think that," he says. "Hopefully, you just go and watch a movie about two people falling in love."

Noting that he has starred in several dystopian movies, including the ill-starred "The Dark Tower," I wonder if he thinks America is headed toward a racial dystopia under the stewardship of Donald Trump.

"I lived in New York before 9/11, and I never felt any real racial tension going on," he says. "It was like, 'You walk into a bar where everybody knows your name' type of thing. Then post-9/11, it was a very different tension. You know, you're fighting an invisible terrorist, so to speak, and now everyone was like, 'Who are you and where are you from?' I could feel the shift and that was part of the reason I moved to L.A., to be honest."

Mr. Elba, who played Nelson Mandela in a movie about the South African hero's life, said he views the racial tension as something "America has to deal with."

"I don't think Trump's going to change the whole world and make us all be racists," he says. "I think human beings are smart and freethinking."

Growing up poor as the son of African immigrants in a part of East London called Canning Town, he says, "it was common to be called a black bastard as you walked down the street. Did it make me a racist against white folks? Not really. The nationalist front had a strong hold in Canning Town, and it was a party that was very vocal about a sort of separatism. I hate to say it, but it was a little bit of a storm in a teacup. Here I am, a product of Canning Town and I'm not that guy that's like, 'Hey, let's all be separate because I was called a black bastard once.'"

I wonder what he thinks about the intense debate over the plans by the creators of "Game of Thrones"—two white men—to make "Confederate," a series envisioning a post–Civil War America in which the South won. (Husband and wife Nichelle Tramble Spellman and Malcolm Spellman, who are black, will write and produce.) Ta-Nehisi Coates, in The Atlantic, presented the case for HBO dropping the show: "the symbols point to something Confederate's creators don't seem to understand—the war is over for them, not us."

On the other hand, John Ridley, an African-American writer and producer who made "12 Years a Slave," brought up, in The Hollywood Reporter, Norman Jewison's "powerful stories about race and identity" in movies like "In the Heat of the Night." Mr. Ridley worried that the "litmus test" could be flipped and prevent him from making a movie about Hispanics, for instance.

"Actually," Mr. Elba says about the uproar, "I personally don't want to see any more slave films. I think it's a time that's been very well documented. '12 Years a Slave,' although a genius movie, I just found it really hard to watch and didn't want to go back down that road for the sake of entertainment. I think there are a lot more interesting stories that are less covered that we can spend our time on."

I also ask for his response to the kerfuffle when Samuel L. Jackson complained about black British actors getting leads in American movies, such as David Oyelowo playing Martin Luther King Jr. in "Selma" and Daniel Kaluuya in the Jordan Peele horror film, "Get Out."

"They think they're better trained, for some reason, than we are because they're classically trained," Mr. Jackson told Hot 97, the New York radio station, in March. "I don't know what the love affair is with all that." He said he thought that "Get Out," a movie about white liberal racism, should have featured "an American brother who really feels that."

Mr. Elba says: "I spoke on this and I spoke quite openly that I was disappointed." He got a standing ovation when he made a speech to British Parliament last year urging greater diversity in film and television because he could only play so many "best friends," "gang leaders" or "athletic types." (It was around the same time he got snubbed by the Oscars, failing to receive a nomination for his powerful performance as a brutal African warlord with a child army in "Beasts of No Nation," and wasn't even invited to the ceremony.)

He calls Mr. Jackson "a god" who gets respect "as an actor, black, white, whatever," but adds: "It felt like a very stupid thing to say, if I'm really honest and in a time where people are being marginalized, why marginalize us even further by going on about black Americans and English Americans? And to his credit, he read that and apologized. He called and said, 'Hey, man. I agree. You're right, black is black.' I respect him for actually acknowledging what I said and sort of rethinking it.

"Americans come into England to the theater and play English characters all day long and no one pipes up and says, 'Hey, you can't do that,' and no one should. It's called acting for a reason."

I wonder why it's harder for Americans to get a British accent right than vice versa.

"Something to do with the way the tongue sits in the mouth, believe it or not," he says. "But when the English speak, we speak more frontal and it's harder for Americans to get that sound because the tongue is so much more relaxed. I've studied it."

He did worry about the East Coast accents for "The Wire" and "Molly's Game," however.

Just as he was nervous to make love on screen with Ms. Winslet, he says he was nervous to speak the high-velocity words of "the oracle," as he calls Mr. Sorkin, especially since it was the writer's first directing gig.

"I thought he'd be super-pedantic and edgy but he was chill," Mr. Elba says. "Someone said to him, 'We're going to change lens,' and he'd say, 'Change lens? That's exactly what I was going to say, let's change the lens.' He didn't pretend to be like a technical genius. He just knows the drama. He really knows words. He knows emotion."

Mr. Sorkin also managed not to freak out with him when Mr. Elba engaged in a kickboxing competition in Thailand and England for a documentary days before he arrived, exhausted, in Toronto for shooting.

"Everyone was on a knife's edge, like come on," Mr. Elba says. "'The truth is, if Idris loses and he gets his face broken or his leg snapped in half, how do we make our movie?'"

He muses: "I think there's something to be had about testing your fear capacity, something that keeps you alive." He snaps his fingers. "Maybe it keeps me younger. I think they call that a midlife crisis."

I wonder, given his Parliament speech urging greater diversity in TV and film, including for women, what he made of the recent spat between the "Wonder Woman" director, Patty Jenkins, who now holds the record for the biggest United States opening for a film directed by a woman, and James Cameron, who called the movie "a step backward" because Wonder Woman is "an objectified icon, and it's just male Hollywood doing the same old thing."

Mr. Cameron got throttled, but he is right that it's easier for the suits who run Hollywood to accept a gorgeous young woman in a sexy costume than to make movies with middle-aged, non-cartoony heroines struggling with life, the kind Bette Davis and Joan Crawford used to do.

"Cameron has a point to some degree, but come on!" Mr. Elba says. "Let's be positive—it's a character created for TV in the '70s and she kicks ass in the movie. Change is incremental, O.K.? First you can't have a black guy kissing a white woman. But then you can have a light-skinned black kissing a white woman. And then it changes, you know. So first you can have a lead woman and she is the hero, but she has to be slightly sexualized. It's going to change."

I ask how he handled the critical drubbing given to "The Dark

Tower," based on the Stephen King magnum opus, in which he played the Gunslinger. The New York Times's Manohla Dargis called it "an unappealing hash of moviemaking clichés" but still praised Mr. Elba's "irrepressible magnetism and man-of-stone solidity."

"I don't tend to read reviews but this was inescapable," he says. "Cause it made such a big fanfare—'Dark Tower' is coming out!' And the reviews really beat it up. I didn't take it personally but I was like, ooof, that hurts."

But the Brit, who comes from a country with much tighter gun-control laws, agonized over taking the part of the interplanetary vigilante, telling Esquire, "I had a clash of conscience with my character. In America, there's a real awareness of gun culture." Luther, the London lawman, is about reasoning, not shooting.

(Mr. Elba revisited the subject when I reached him after the Las Vegas horror. "Yes, I had an internal struggle with the Gunslinger. Given his title, it was impossible to avoid. The human spirit took a meteor-sized hit yesterday, and the world of America is falling off its axis.")

His father once advised him to look people in the eyes. It was the same technique Alfred Hitchcock used when he directed the great actress Eva Marie Saint in her sultry performance opposite Cary Grant in "North by Northwest."

In our A.D.D. planet, it works. Mr. Elba does not look away at his phone, at the waitress when he asks for a knife, at his publicists trying to hustle him along or at his steak salad and steak and eggs. His expressive brown eyes are always on you.

His vibe is cool but his career is frenetic. When he's not starring in movies and "Luther," he's directing movies, designing clothes, D.J.-ing in London and Ibiza, and producing his own music, as well as making documentaries about his adventures kickboxing in Thailand and car racing in Ireland. Maybe that's why his personal life is so turbulent; he has vowed never to marry again.

He has had two children—a 15-year-old girl and a 3-year-old son—with two makeup artists, one of whom he married, and a brief second marriage to a lawyer. He publicly stepped out with his new girlfriend, Sabrina Dhowre, a former Miss Vancouver, at last month's debut of

"Molly's Game" at the Toronto International Film Festival. He met her when he went to Vancouver and British Columbia (standing in for Utah) to make "The Mountain Between Us."

"Falling in love while falling in love," he says, dreamily.

He also experienced that "You are not the father" moment that can either be the worst or best moment of a man's life. In a therapeutic moment four years ago, he told a GQ reporter the "tragic, punch-in-the-face" story of how he discovered that the son he thought he had had with a woman he was involved with in Florida was not his.

"It is definitely without a doubt one of the worst things to happen to any person, and I include her," he tells me about his ex. "Because whatever she went through and did, she was hoping that I would never find out, and I did. So for all three of us including the boy, it was. . . ." His voice gets softer with each word until he finally trails off.

How did he find out? I ask.

"My mom came and saw us and she said, 'That's not your son,'" he says, adding: "So I just did a paternity test."

I note that the lawyer has recently said in The Daily Mail that the marriage broke up because Mr. Elba's handlers thought it would be better, given his sex-symbol status, if he were single.

He shakes his head ruefully and says that was absolutely not true and that many stories about his relationships are "completely wrong," but that he doesn't like to fight back in public.

"I think I'm the most misunderstood partner ever," he says, looking distraught. "I've had many failed relationships but not because I'm an ass, just because there's so many complexities to relationships and perhaps I'm very guarded, just like Luther's guarded. And being guarded, people presume things and I often haven't corrected them.

"They just have so much of who I am wrong, they feel like I must be a playboy. I must be noncommittal. I must be the kind of guy that jumps in and out. And, you know, I suppose if you look at my history or you know anything about my history or you can read on Google who I was married to or what's happened, you know, it might appear that way. But it's completely misunderstood. People think they know about me and my past and my relationships and they don't. There's very few people that can say they really, really know me and I can say, 'Yes, you really, really know me.' Very few people. Very few."

I ask him about a rap lyric he wrote that fame brings you to the "devil's door."

"I live a duality, do you know what I mean?" he says. "I got an O.B.E. It's Officer of the British Empire, but I've always known it as a British sweetheart, treasured.

"But I'm a naughty boy. Do you know what I'm saying? I sort of live a full life, and naughty. And I'm one knock away from the devil's door. Because, you know, I'm human, man. But at the same time, I'm honored by my country and I'm like, yeah," as long as he doesn't mess up or be a jerk, he says, using raunchier words. "There's responsibility to be a leader on the right moral side. Don't go out there and get coked off your face and get caught in orgies. Not that I would."

I reassure him that Mick Jagger has been knighted, so other naughty boys are in the Queen's pack of aces. And I wonder if there's any other challenge on the horizon, noting that he would make a remarkable Othello.

"Don't like the story," he says brusquely.

But why?

"Jealousy's a real poison and I'm not into it," he says.

Is that because you get jealous?

"It's a poison," he repeats, laughing. As we get ready to leave, I pose the question I know Mr. Elba doesn't like: "I have to ask about James Bond because George Clooney has now said you would be a 'perfect James Bond and it would be a great step forward.'"

"George Clooney said that?" Mr. Elba asks with a skeptical grin.

"I don't know, man," he says. "It's interesting that the James Bond thing continues to go. I think it's more about, we just want to have a black guy play James Bond rather than Idris Elba the actor play James Bond. That's the part that I'm like, 'Ugh, come on.'"

So at long last, we need to know: Does he like martinis? Offering his most suave look, Mr. Elba murmurs: "I like them stirred. Not shaken. Jesus Christ, did I just say that out loud?"

Confirm or Deny

MAUREEN DOWD: *When you were a pot dealer, you only sold 10's and 20's.*
IDRIS ELBA: Yes, and the 20 bags went, the 10's not so much.

You once sold weed to Dave Chappelle.
   I don't want to name names because I'll get in trouble and they'll curse at me but yes, I sold to most of those comedians that walked in.

"The Wire" is the best TV show of all time.
   Confirm.

Your friends still call you "Moprah" when you're feeling down.
   Deny.

You gave Beyoncé acting tips for her first big starring role with you in "Obsessed."
   She was very receptive as a collaborator. I looked up and she was an actor. I have a lot of time for Beyoncé and Jay-Z.

Your fellow D.J. in Ibiza, Paris Hilton, is rocking Ibiza harder than you did.
   Pfffft! Deny.

Kendrick Lamar is the greatest rapper alive.
   Confirm.

New York is cooler than London.
   Deny.

Prince Harry should marry Meghan Markle.
   Confirm! He's in love. I'm happy for him.

Britain should Brexit.
   Deny. I don't think Britain should Brexit, no. I was disappointed in that decision.

Shonda Rhimes was smart to go to Netflix.
   Confirm. I think Shonda Rhimes could have made her own Netflix, if I'm honest.

Sex on the Beach is your drink of choice.

Deny. At the moment, it's Black Label and Coke.

Co-hosting the Met Gala was the most stressful night of your life.

Deny. It was great. I felt really famous that day. It was a bit awkward because Taylor Swift and I had to present an award. We were walking through the crowd and obviously, there was a little beef between Taylor and Kanye. I didn't know any of this. But I was there! And I was, like, "Oh, this is awks."

You've lost track of how many times you've appeared on the cover of men's magazines.

Confirm.

PAUL NEWMAN, RELUCTANT SEX SYMBOL

—SEPTEMBER 28, 1986

If you are meeting Paul Newman for the first time, he will have on his sunglasses. As he gets to know you, he will peek over the rims occasionally. As he gets to trust you, he will let the sunglasses hang from his left ear. The next time you meet, he will take them off.

To the public, the actor's cerulean eyes have become a symbol of his stardom. To Newman, they have become a symbol of his long struggle to be thought of as a craftsman. "To work as hard as I've worked to accomplish anything and then have some yo-yo come up and say, 'Take off those dark glasses and let's have a look at those blue eyes' is really discouraging.

"It's as though someone said, 'Open your mouth and let me see your gums,' or 'Open your blouse and let me see your chest.' The thing I've never figured out is, how do you present eyes? Do you present them coyly? Do you present them boldly? Usually, I just say, 'I would take off my sunglasses, madam, but my pants would fall down.'"

He wonders, looking in the mirror some mornings, can color be destiny? "I picture my epitaph: 'Here lies Paul Newman, who died a failure because his eyes turned brown.'"

He is one of the last great movie stars, a legend built up by the old Hollywood studio system at Warner Brothers and Metro-Goldwyn-Mayer and sustained by his magnetism and talent.

The name is a cultural reference point on several levels—on his own, for enduring sex appeal and fame; with Robert Redford, for male friendship, and with Joanne Woodward, for marital longevity.

His public biography is familiar. Paul Leonard Newman was born 61 years ago in Cleveland, the son of a Jewish sporting goods store owner, and was raised in the affluent suburb of Shaker Heights. He has appeared in 47 films and directed five. He has been nominated for an Oscar six times, and last year was awarded an honorary one recognizing his career and "his personal integrity and dedication to his craft." He lives with Joanne Woodward, his wife of 28 years, in a 200-year-old carriage house in Westport, Conn. He is a champion race-car driver, the founder of a successful food business, a political activist and a philanthropist.

And yet, though he is one of the most famous people in America, he remains curiously elusive. He exists in the public mind as bits and pieces of his characters—Butch Cassidy's charm, Ben Quick's machismo, Cool Hand Luke's defiance, Harper's irony, Hud's disdain.

Newman is an intensely private, even shy, man who does not like to talk about himself. Partly, this is because he hates answering the same questions over and over. (No, he did not start racing cars as a way of reclaiming his lost youth and no, he and Redford are not best friends, and yes, he's still crazy about his wife.) And partly, it is his way of holding the movie-star legend at bay.

On rare occasions, however, when he is in a movie that he likes or when there is a cause that he believes in, Newman allows a glimpse inside his life. Now, he is in a movie he likes very much indeed. In "The Color of Money," a Disney Touchstone picture that opens next month, Newman picks up the trail of Fast Eddie Felson, the cocky pool shark he created in the 1961 classic "The Hustler."

"The delight of a character like Eddie is that he's had an additional 25 years of hustling," Newman says, a low thrill in his voice. "He's so slick. He's pulling so many things. There are scenes in this movie an actor would kill for."

This time around, Tom Cruise is Vince Lauria, the young pool player who wants to be the best there is, and Newman is the Machiavellian manager who wants a piece of the action.

It turns out that Fast Eddie, who was supposed to have learned something about character at the end of "The Hustler," did not. "He's a guy," says Martin Scorsese, the movie's director, "who needs more than one lesson."

Gleaming with a cashmere coat and a white Cadillac and a diamond ring and a fancy line of patter, Fast Eddie sells liquor and manages a stable of young pool players in Chicago.

The new movie offers a vivid reminder that Newman, who created some of the screen's most memorable young men on the make, is now creating some of the screen's most memorable older characters. It is impossible, when Cruise calls Newman "Gramps" and Newman tells him to change his diapers, not to feel a small jolt at the passage of time as marked by the evolution of Newman's career. The film makes mocking note of that.

"C'mon, Fast Eddie," Vince says as the two shoot pool. "Let's see some heavy legend action here."

Not only is this "legend" aging gracefully; he is embracing this new phase of his career with adolescent abandon. "I was always a character actor," he says. "I just looked like Little Red Riding Hood."

After several years when he felt bored with acting and thought about "chucking it all and becoming a gentleman dairy farmer," he has come alive again with such challenging roles as Michael Gallagher, the victim of the press who turned the tables in "Absence of Malice"; Frank Galvin, the alcoholic, down-and-out lawyer in "The Verdict"; and now an older, faster Eddie Felson.

Although Eddie envies Vince, Newman feels no regret at turning over the young sexy role to Cruise. "I sort of like being a gray eminence," Newman says, popping a Budweiser in his Connecticut kitchen. "Except I can no longer take those five-foot fences."

Because of his happy-go-lucky nature and golden good looks, the actor always seemed the sort for whom things would come easily. But the key to understanding Newman is that nothing has come easily. He often describes himself as "a terrier."

"I always wanted to be an athlete, a football player or a baseball player," he says. "I tried skiing for 10 years. The only thing I ever felt graceful at was racing a car, and that took me 10 years to learn."

Even his famed masculine presence did not come naturally. In high school, he was a short scrawny kid who could not qualify to try out for the junior varsity football team, and in the Navy he was so small he was once mistaken for a Sea Scout. He grew six inches in one year in the service, took up acting at Kenyon College and later—leaving the family sporting-goods store behind—at Yale Drama School.

When he came to New York, he was not immediately regarded as leading-man material. In the original Broadway production of William Inge's "Picnic" in 1953, he played Alan Seymour, the well-meaning rich boy who loses his girl to a physically magnetic friend. He asked Joshua Logan, the director, if he could go on the road in the lead role.

"Josh told me no, because I didn't have any sexual threat," Newman recalls. "At that particular point, I probably didn't. That sort of thing has a lot to do with conviction."

Logan told Newman to get in shape. "The way I translated that was six hours in the gym every day," he says. He did move into the leading role and worked at his presence as well as his pectorals. "You can measure each woman," he says, "and find ways of being gallant, of listening, of crowding, of pursuing."

He studied under Lee Strasberg at the Actors Studio in New York with an extraordinary roster of classmates—Marlon Brando, James Dean, Karl Malden, Geraldine Page, Kim Stanley, Eli Wallach and Julie Harris. "It was monkey see, monkey do," he says. "Man, I just sat back there and watched how people did things and had enough sense not to open my big mouth."

Newman is a modest man who loves talking about the accomplishments of others, but hates talking about his own. He cannot remember any of his great movie lines, but he can remember his worst, from his first role as a toga-clad slave in a turgid Roman epic called "The Silver Chalice": "Helena, is it really you? What a joy!" He can even recite from memory The New Yorker magazine review of the 1954 movie: "Newman delivered his lines with the emotional fervor of a Putman Division conductor announcing local stops."

By the time he appeared in "The Long Hot Summer" and "Cat on a Hot Tin Roof," his smoky gaze and muscled chest adorned posters in the rooms of teen-age girls everywhere. The fame came with a beefcake stereotype. "There's something very corrupting about being an actor," he says. "It places a terrible premium on appearance."

He strived, as his career went on, not to play himself over and over again or to slide into familiar mannerisms. But he was often disturbed when the movies in which he felt he was doing his best work and moving furthest away from the stereotype—such as "The Outrage" in 1964, "Pocket Money" in 1971 and "The Life and Times of Judge Roy Bean" in 1972—were box-office bombs.

During the 1970's, he concentrated more on racing than acting, and even thought about quitting acting. But, somewhere along the line, his passion for racing revived his passion for acting.

Newman has dramatized this in "The Color of Money." Fast Eddie sees Vince's pure love of pool, and after years of thinking of the game as merely a hustle, the older man suddenly falls back in love with the game himself. "I'm hungry again," he tells Vince, "and you bled that back into me."

At one point, Eddie calls his girlfriend from the road and tells her that he is getting jumpy because things are going too well. The scene was drawn from an actual call Newman made to his wife from the Chicago set last winter. "I told Joanne I felt scared because there was a real feeling of community and it was so much fun to get up in the morning," Newman recalls.

For Newman, it all goes back to his image of himself as a terrier, keeping at it and at it until he wins. "I'm just now beginning to learn a little something about acting," he says. "I don't say that as a joke and I don't say it because I'm being modest. I don't think I ever had an immediate spontaneous gift to do anything right."

There is a sense that he has finally been liberated from the burden of his sex-symbol image. According to the director Sidney Lumet, when Robert Redford dropped out of the lead role in "The Verdict," after trying to have the drunken lawyer character made less gritty, Newman jumped at the chance to play the role that way.

"Paul's always been one of the best actors we've got, but there was that great stone face and those gorgeous blue eyes and a lot of people assumed he couldn't act," says Lumet, who directed Newman in "The Verdict." "He got relegated to leading-man parts and he wasn't using a quarter of his talent. Now he's able to cut loose and do sensational work."

It has been said that the actor's looks, rather than fading, have "purified." The same word could be used about his performances.

"There's a stillness in his acting now that is quite magnetic," says Sydney Pollack, the director of "Absence of Malice" who has known Newman since they worked on "The Alcoa Hour" for television 30 years ago. "You can feel his intelligence, you can see him thinking. He has the depth of a clear pool of water, not rippling or churning or tumbling."

Newman did not look at a tape of "The Hustler" before he began the sequel. "When I look at my old movies, I get gloomy because I can see myself consciously working to create the character," he says. "In the scene in 'Hud' when I was talking to my nephew and I said, 'My Mamma loved me but she died,' I was working too hard to find the emotions. I compare that to the summation scene at the end of 'The Verdict.' The emotions were there, but you couldn't see the machinery."

He says he has a more sophisticated understanding now of "how the strings are synchronized." "There are certain characteristics you carry with you. If I am being oily in a part, that is going to come across completely differently than Warren Beatty or Jack Nicholson being oily. If you get an actor who's angry at life, his machinery for manipulation will be entirely different than mine."

Just as Newman has streamlined his acting, he has streamlined his preparation. "My imagination appears to be more fertile," he says. "I don't really have to get down on my hands and knees and look under the rocks. I remember for 'Hombre' I went down to an Indian reservation for five days and brought back one thing. I drove past a general store and there was a guy standing there in front with one foot up and his arms crossed. He was in exactly the same position when I drove back four hours later. That whole character came out of that."

Now he can create a character, he says, "by finding his nerves." In the scene in "The Verdict" in which Frank Galvin follows a doctor down the street, desperate to get him to testify for his foundering case, Newman played it "the way a dog follows somebody that had a bone in his hand—sideways."

Newman gave Michael Gallagher in "Absence of Malice" his own physical traits but made them even more economical. "He knew a lot," Newman says. "And people who know a lot don't do very much with their bodies."

Scorsese recalls that as he sat in a cutting room in the Brill Building on Broadway two months ago, editing "The Color of Money," "The Long Hot Summer" came on the television set in the corner. In an odd double exposure, Scorsese watched the 33-year-old Newman on television and the 61-year-old Newman on his editing screen.

"I like him better now," says Scorsese. "He looks like he's been there and survived but taken something with him."

After decades of obsession with the color of those eyes, now people are talking about the expression in them. "There's so much information in his eyes about what they're seeing," Scorsese says.

Newman likes to test himself; he hates complacency. "You have to keep things off balance," he says, "or it's all over." That is why he looks for risky roles, why he started the Newman's Own food business—selling salad dressing, popcorn and "industrial strength" spaghetti sauce—and why he took up racing.

With his red, white and blue Nissan, Newman won the national championship in the Sports Car Club of America GT-1 class last year and is favored to win it again on Oct. 19 in Atlanta—and this at an age when most other drivers are long retired. He also picked up the $11,000 first-prize purse in the Bendix Trans Am race in Lime Rock, Conn., last month.

"A lot of drivers will find all kinds of fault with the car when they're not going as fast as they should be," said Gene Crowe, the director of Newman's racing team. "But Paul tends to blame himself, even when there is something wrong with the car."

On the movie set, as well as the track, his colleagues talk about his "sense of decency." He is always prepared and on time. He does not object to camera angles that make him look bad, and he is generous with everyone—offering blocking tips to a director, romantic advice to a leading lady and popcorn to the crew.

"Flattery will get you nowhere with Paul," says Sidney Lumet. "He doesn't want to hear what's good because, first of all, he knows, and second, if there's trouble he wants to know about it."

The actor, everyone agrees, does not suffer fools or phonies gladly. "Charm is not one of Paul's big points," says George Roy Hill. "He goes right for the essence."

The director recalls that while filming "Butch Cassidy and the Sundance Kid" the stunt man hired to double for Newman on the bicycle tricks refused to work on the appointed day—calling the tricks too dangerous. As the director tried to persuade him to work, they suddenly saw Newman riding down the road doing the most difficult stunt—standing on the seat of the bike with his leg stretched out in back. "I said two more words to the stunt man—'You're fired,'" Hill says.

Sally Field recalls that during the filming of "Absence of Malice" Newman had a very hard time when he was supposed to knock her down and rip her blouse. "He kept trying to fake it," she says.

Newman refuses to consider any film project that has what he considers mindless violence, and even turned down the lead in the popular adventure-comedy "Romancing the Stone."

Just as he does not have the violent edge of "Hud," he does not have the cool, darting wit associated with many of his characters. His humor is more, as he says, "weird." "We had a joke-off every day on the set to see who could tell the worst jokes," says Tom Cruise, who has developed a minor case of hero worship and gone to some of Newman's races.

Newman loves practical jokes. He once had Hill's desk sawed in half and during the filming of "Buffalo Bill and the Indians," he had Robert Altman's deerskin gauntlets dipped in batter and served to him for lunch.

At the Road America race in Elkhart Lake, Wis., Newman was quizzing his crew about where they could get some acetylene torches to cut the car of one of his young racing rivals in half. Maybe, someone suggested, it would be easier just to slice the roof off. "I don't mind paying to replace the car," Newman demurred. "But if I'm going to ruin it, I really want to ruin it."

He seems to regard his food business as a wonderful prank as well. He started the company in 1982 with his Westport neighbor, the author A. E. Hotchner, after the salad dressing he gave away at Christmas was so popular.

"I couldn't think of anything tackier than putting my name and reputation on a bottle of salad dressing, so I did it," Newman says. "No one expected it to be successful." He considered adding a line of men's cosmetics—"you know, like a heavy-duty men's cologne"—but decided to stick with food.

Newman's Own expects to gross about $26 million this year. Running it seems to consist of an occasional game of darts or Ping-Pong with Hotchner at the Westport office. The Ping-Pong table doubles as a conference table, and the rest of the office is decorated with Newman's old pool furniture. The president's desk has a striped beach umbrella attached, and there are two chaise longues for visitors.

All the profits (close to $9 million so far) are given to charities, including the Scott Newman Center at the University of Southern California in Pasadena, a drug-education foundation run by his daughter Susan. Newman and Hotchner just bought a lakefront property outside of Storrs, Conn., that will be the site of a Western-style camp called "The Hole in the Wall Gang" for children with life-threatening diseases.

Newman's favorite part of the business is writing the Joycean labels, such as the one on the spaghetti sauce that goes something like: "Working 12 hour days . . . wrecked . . . hungry . . . arrive home, deserted by wife and children . . . cursing! Cook-junk! YUCK! Lie down, snooze . . . yum, yum . . . slurp, slurp. . . . Terrifico! Magnifico! Bottle the sauce . . . share with guys on streetcar . . . ah, me, finally immortal!"

And nothing delights him more than when people tell him they don't like his politics or his acting but they like his food. He framed a letter from one Michael Sullivan from Rancho Cordova, Calif., complimenting the spaghetti sauce: "My girlfriend mentioned that you were a movie star and I would be interested to know what you've made.

If you act as well as you cook, your movies would be worth watching." There was a P.S.: "Are any of your movies in VCR?"

Paul Newman is, like his favorite characters, a nonconformist who has managed to reflect the tenor of the times—the indifference of the 1950's, the rebellion of the 60's, the softening of the 70's, the individualism of the 80's—even as he stuck with his own values. As society became more conservative, he stayed unabashedly liberal; as it became more materialistic, he got more altruistic; as it became more disposable, he worked harder at his marriage.

He is a man of extremes. On one level—in matters of work and politics and the environment and the arms race—Newman is intensely serious. On another level, he has a boyish delight in life, treating it as a great prank.

"He loves to have a good time," says his pal, Redford, laughing as he recalls how easily Newman is distracted. "He has the attention span of a bolt of lightning."

In a fickle industry, he has remained a top movie star for three decades. But Newman feels that he is just now entering his prime, and wants to be thought of as an actor, not a movie star. More than ever, he finds the adulation embarrassing. Hotchner recalls that at a Westport charity event where Newman was handing out punch, a dowager asked him to stir her drink with his finger. "I'd be glad to," the actor replied, "but I just took it out of a cyanide bottle."

In many ways, Newman's celebrity is a throwback to the sort of clamorous attention paid to Hollywood stars of the 1930's. Perhaps his friend Gore Vidal captures the intensity of it best with a story about a trip he took to the Gobi Desert in Mongolia two years ago to research a piece he was writing. "This K.G.B. agent from the Foreign Ministry who was following me around asked if he could see me privately because he had something very special to talk about," Vidal recalls. "When we were alone, he whispered, 'How tall is Paul Newman really?'"

This level of fame is a force that affects everything around it— Newman's personality, his lifestyle, his friendships, his family relationships.

Miss Woodward has talked frankly about "the tough fight" and many years of analysis involved in keeping her own identity.

Newman's only son, Scott, an actor who had to cope with his father's large shadow, died of an accidental drug and alcohol overdose in 1978, at the age of 28. He was one of three children from Newman's first marriage, to the actress Jacqueline Witte.

"There are times when you feel very trapped," says Susan Newman, 33, the oldest of the actor's five daughters. "At any given moment, maybe when you haven't seen your old man in a year and you're trying to tell him something important about your boyfriend, there are five ladies and gentlemen crowding around yelling, 'Paul, Paul, sign this!' And if he doesn't sign, they yell, 'I never want to see one of your movies again!'"

Newman has tried to shield the people he loves. "There are liabilities and assets," he says. "Some of my children have focused more on the liabilities and others have been able to enjoy the assets." He does not talk about his son's death. He says he did not draw on his relationship with Scott for his 1984 movie "Harry and Son," about a father and son struggling to communicate. "You can't fictionalize grief," he says.

The actor has a small, loyal circle of friends. But even when he is in a relaxed setting, cooking barbecue and making salad for the members of his racing crew, he seems to stand apart. Like Shakespeare's Prince Hal, he is often treated with deference even when he tries to be down to earth. His stance is often guarded and he uses his eyes to create a circle of privacy around his companions, shutting out others who stare and clamor for his attention.

He is nearly always polite, even when he is pushed to the limit, as he was one night last summer in Fond du Lac, Wis. He was having a nightcap in the deserted bar of his hotel with some racing buddies. Within a few moments, hundreds of people appeared—hanging from balconies, standing behind rails and crowding into the bar. As the room blazed with flashbulbs and people called out to Newman to "look pretty for the camera," the scene took on an eerie aspect reminiscent of Alfred Hitchcock's horror film "The Birds."

A woman wearing a slinky black dress wove her way through the crowd and knelt next to Newman's chair. "Hi, Paul," she said, setting her drink next to his. "Tell me how the race went today." He told her pleasantly that things had gone well, but that he was just about to say good night. As he left, the woman plopped into his chair, turned to his friends and demanded, "Is he always that rude?"

The next day, Newman laughed at the incident. "The thing I resent about this sex symbol thing is that writers create these sexy, flamboyant, aggressive characters who might have nothing to do with who you really are under the skin. You don't always have Tennessee Williams around to write glorious lines for you."

He has dealt with his fame, he says, by developing "selective insensitivities." "With film critics and fans, you have to be selectively insensitive to their insensitivities. If people start treating you like a piece of meat or a long-lost friend or feel they can become cuddly for the price of a $5 movie ticket, then you shut them out.

"The toughest part is not to let that insensitivity bleed into those areas where you want to be like a piece of litmus paper, in your personal life and in your work."

It is ironic that, while it bothers Newman that the public has endowed him with the attributes of his characters, he does the same thing himself. Over the years, he found that the lines began to blur between his roles and his own personality. He would wake up with hangovers from Hud or Fast Eddie. "You get to the point where it's much easier to play a role that has been examined and accepted on the screen than it is to play yourself," he says.

He began to adopt mannerisms in his life that were successful in his art. "I can listen better than anybody without hearing a thing," he says. "I can be completing a bridge hand in my head and be bidding four no trump at the moment that the other guy is saying, 'My god, he really listens quite attentively.'"

Even now, as he talks, the timbre of his voice seems different than it did a few years ago. It sounds as though it has been soaked in Jack Daniel's, and suddenly you recognize it as the voice of Frank Galvin in "The Verdict."

"You have such an investment in the roles you play," Newman says.

"You have to step back sometimes and figure out whether you're doing you or somebody else. Will the real Dustin Hoffman please stand up? Where is Jack Nicholson? Where is Marlon 'I could have been a contender' Brando? I have no idea who these guys really are. Do you?"

He grins. "That would be a good title for your article—'Will the Real Paul Newman Please Stand Up?'"

And who is the real Paul Newman?

"None of your business," he growls from behind his beer and sunglasses.

There are several clues to the real Paul Newman in his Fifth Avenue penthouse. Classical music fills the living room as the actor makes iced tea one afternoon. "Mozart's 29th," says Newman, who is really more of a Bach fan.

He is wearing jeans, a cotton sweater, sneakers and orange Polo socks. He sports a large diamond-studded racing ring and a silver neck chain with a beer tab made for him by Budweiser.

Paul Newman says he is a lean 5 foot 11. His entire summer wardrobe seems to consist of the ubiquitous jeans, some worn striped cotton pants and his old orange Navy flight suit—which has been stenciled on the back with "Coor Hand Ruke." Someone has penciled "I love you" below the stencil, and when Newman learns of it, he rushes off to a mirror to see if it is his wife's handwriting.

"Fashion bores the bejesus out of me," he says. Pointing to the small battered leather satchel that he carries on racing weekends, he demands proudly: "Would Sylvester Stallone have luggage like that?"

He does not, as his friend George Roy Hill suspects, have a Dorian Gray pact with the devil. He does not even soak his face in ice water every morning. He works out every day on an exercise bike and weight machines while watching cable news. He recently got a new slant board and did so many sit-ups he suffered a hernia.

His hobbies include poetry and painting. He writes verses like the one inscribed on the silver sherry cup he gave his wife as a wedding present: "So you wound up with Apollo / If he's sometimes hard to swallow / Use this."

In the bathroom there is a framed picture of a delicate flower, inked in shades of brown, violet and yellow. It is signed, "Paul Newman, 1982," and labeled "Self Portrait." However, when a friend arrives with a restored oil painting that Newman bought downtown for $200, the actor decides that this should be his self-portrait. It shows a Dutch nobleman looking out at the world with dark, watchful eyes. "I've been accused of being aloof," he says. "I'm not. I'm just wary."

The woman who knows Newman best is not available for consultation; she prefers not to discuss her husband for articles focusing on him. "Maybe familiarity breeds contempt," he says, apologetically. "We're equals, but sometimes I'll forget how incredible she is and then I'll see something that reminds me; like this room," he says, waving to the elegant array of antiques, chintz couches with embroidered pillows, and a baby grand piano. "If anyone had ever told me 20 years ago I'd be sitting in a room with peach walls, I would have told them to take a nap in a urinal."

Miss Georgia and Mr. Shaker Heights, as Gore Vidal calls them, met in 1952, during the run of "Picnic." Woodward, an intense young actress from the South, was an understudy for the two female roles. They were married in 1958, after Newman's divorce from his first wife. They have three children—Nell, 27, who is studying to be an ornithologist, and Lissy, 25, and Clea, 21, who are both in college. Newman's other daughter from his first marriage, Stephanie, 31, is also a student.

The Woodward-Newman alliance is a strong one, regarded with some awe by their friends. He is directing her this fall in a film version of Tennessee Williams's "The Glass Menagerie."

Although he once was chastised by his wife for explaining his fidelity to Playboy magazine by saying, "I have steak at home, why go out for hamburger?" (Woodward did not like being referred to as "Paul Newman's meat"), he does not seem to have learned his lesson. "She's like a classy '62 bordeaux," he says. "No, make it '59. That's a year that ages well in the bottle. Will I get in trouble for that?"

They have worked at their marriage—she has gone to the races he loves and he has gone to the operas and ballets she loves. "Joanne and I have had difficult, body bending confrontations, but we haven't surrendered," he says. "I've packed up and left a few times, and then I realize I have no place to go and I'm back in 10 minutes. Ultimately, I think we both delight in watching the progression. And we laugh a lot."

Like the apartment, the house in Westport is comfortable and filled with photographs of friends and family—including one in which the heads of Woodward and Newman have been transposed on the bodies of Margot Fonteyn and Rudolf Nureyev.

The Newmans seem like any upper middle class couple enjoying their "empty nest syndrome." As he goes out one morning, she is coming back from a ballet class. They kiss and he asks her to put gas in his car as she goes to clean the barn. When he returns, she is leaving to do some grocery shopping. She tells him that their daughter Clea has won a prize in a horse show and that she has forgotten to put gas in his car.

"Joanne and I live between two worlds and are accepted by neither," Newman says. "It's just like Thomas Mann's story, 'Tonio Kroger.' The bourgeois think we're revolutionaries and the bohemians see that we have a lot of Jell-O and don't wear neckerchiefs and they think we're bourgeois."

He thinks that his lifestyle—shunning Hollywood and the trappings of stardom—made many in the industry uncomfortable with him and cost him recognition he deserved. "Paul's done it without their rules," says Sidney Lumet. "And in Hollywood, they love labels and they love people who are beholden to them."

If you are "tagged" as a sex symbol, says Redford, "it stands to reason you're not a good actor. It's as though you can't have too many things or people get angry."

When Newman was awarded his honorary Oscar last year, he nearly decided to refuse it, according to his friend and lawyer, Irving I. Axelrad. "He said they'd always treated him as second," says Axelrad, "and now they were acting as if he was old and through."

Newman says only that he would have preferred getting it for a specific piece of work. "It did ruin a great moment," he jokes. "In my 87th year, having been denied an Oscar since 1952, I would have been carried up to the stage on a stretcher. Then, reaching my wizened hand out, I would have grabbed the statue and cackled, 'Thank you, finally.'"

In the middle of a conversation about acting, Newman interrupts with the tale of an unusual encounter. He seems, suddenly, to want to cut through the scrim of illusion and reality and explain the real Paul Newman.

He was strolling down Fifth Avenue one recent day when he saw a woman in a white dress who was causing something of a commotion. "A real stunner," he recalls. "Man, drivers were jumping the curb to get a better look." Their eyes met in a flicker of mutual appreciation, and Newman walked on to Lexington Avenue, stopping to look in the window of an antique shop. He felt a tap on his shoulder. The woman in white explained that she was a call girl but, for him, she would dispense with her usual fee. She waited for an answer. And waited some more.

The actor known for his cool was blushing. "You think about how you would play a moment like that," he says. "You want to send her off with something classy and stylish, the way Cary Grant would, or Clint Eastwood. You think, how would Hombre handle this?

"And when this woman came up to me—the guy who played Hud—what comes through? Laurel and Hardy. Both of them. All I could manage was this massive foot shuffling and dancing around, like a worm on the end of a hook."

He jumps up to illustrate, doing a little rain dance of embarrassment. "I was still shuffling," he says, grinning, "eight blocks later."

ROBERT REDFORD, THE SUNDANCE KID RIDING INTO THE SUNSET

—OCTOBER 9, 2013

SUNDANCE, Utah—Maybe when you play Death on "The Twilight Zone" at the start of your career, mortality doesn't faze you.

"It's all part of the deal," Robert Redford deadpanned.

He didn't think about dying while he was making his new movie about it, J. C. Chandor's melancholy mariner's tale, "All Is Lost." He thought about enduring.

"I'm interested in that thing that happens where there's a breaking point for some people and not for others," he said over morning coffee recently in the deserted Owl Bar at his resort here. "You go through such hardship, things that are almost impossibly difficult, and there's no sign that it's going to get any better, and that's the point when people quit. But some don't."

That's also what drew him to an earlier story: his 1972 tale about a 19th-century mountain man battling the wild, "Jeremiah Johnson," shot on Mount Timpanogos where we were sitting.

"You just continue," Mr. Redford said. "Because that's all there is to do."

Like Mr. Chandor's talky 2011 Wall Street drama, "Margin Call," set on the day a Lehman-type firm struggles not to go under, the taciturn "All Is Lost," due in theaters Oct. 18, is an existential horror story about trying to survive the worst moment of your life—in this case a crippled boat at sea—as panic rises.

Mr. Redford has made a career of playing what he calls "intrinsically American guys" going up against implacable forces: He battled the banks and Pinkertons in "Butch Cassidy and the Sundance Kid," Indians and grizzlies in "Jeremiah Johnson," a superficial political system in "The Candidate," the Irish mob in "The Sting," the C.I.A. in "Three Days of the Condor" and "Spy Game," Richard M. Nixon in "All the President's Men," big business in "The Electric Horseman," and, his most formidable adversary, Barbra Streisand, in "The Way We Were."

Hollywood is no country for old men. Yet at 77, the subject of considerable Oscar talk (David Thomson in The New Republic described his performance in "All Is Lost" as "noble, vulnerable and harrowed"), Mr. Redford is soaring as the solo star of a movie that evokes the elegiac spirit of "Sailing to Byzantium," by Yeats, one of his favorite poets. Yeats wrote about sailing "the mackerel-crowded seas," coming to terms with the agony of aging and contemplating how the soul can rise above a heart "fastened to a dying animal."

Mr. Redford likes to write poetic observations himself. Leaning back in his chair, slender and fit in jeans and Tony Lama cowboy boots, he recited one he had written: "You look up and you realize, what a beautiful day, the leaves are turning and you're starting to feel confident. You're feeling full of yourself until you realize you're drooling."

He laughed, that great Redford laugh. The thing that's easy to forget about Mr. Redford, with his serious pursuits and perfectionist strivings, is that he can be really fun. We talked for three hours next to the 1890s rosewood bar from Ireland commissioned by the real Hole-in-the-Wall gang. Sitting beneath a sepia picture of him and his pal Paul Newman glowing as Sundance and Butch Cassidy, he tells a story about fame.

"It's right around the time where I'm beginning to think I'm a pretty big deal," he said. At a curb in Beverly Hills, "there's a car coming with a bunch of teenage kids in it. I see they're freaking out inside and trying to get their windows rolled down. I step back. I'm ready for it. 'Robert Redford!' they scream. 'You are such an'"—here he drops in a vulgarity for jerk. He grinned. "That's probably what I would have done at that age."

Mr. Redford grew up in Los Angeles, a wild child breaking away from a remote, hard-to-please father, the real Rebel Without a Cause caught up in drinking and drag races. (He even went to the same high school as Natalie Wood.) Breaking into Bel-Air mansions, he and a friend were the Bling Ring before the word bling entered the popular lexicon.

Bob Redford was popular with girls early, winning a Charleston contest at 13, but the other boys grew jealous and "vicious."

"Pretty soon it became a regular thing where guys would pass me when I was with a girl and say 'ARF! ARF! ARF!,' and I could see that the girls were bothered," he said. Finally one of his friends explained that ARF was the Anti-Redford Federation.

"I was so hurt and shocked," he said. "From that point in my life, I retreated into a more loner place. I was then forever shy of going out and expressing myself, and I would do it in my art."

After his mother died when he was 18, he left the University of Colorado and went off to be a starving art student in Italy and France. The girls he met in Paris in 1957 did not find him attractive; he was mocked for knowing nothing about the Suez Canal and American politics.

"I got kicked in the teeth by Paris," he said.

He started to read the newspaper, trying to see beyond American sloganeering and explore "the gray area that was underneath the red, white and blue." Just so, his longtime collaborator, Sydney Pollack, said that the actor's allure came from the darker shades lurking beneath his golden facade.

Still, he has been criticized for not taking grittier roles over the years. But he demurs that he enjoyed his reign as a matinee idol. "I loved working with Jane, I loved working with Natalie, I loved working with Barbra," he said, referring to Ms. Fonda, Ms. Wood and Ms. Streisand. "I loved the body language, the mystery, the sexual chemistry."

Was it hard, after decades as a top screen babe, to spend every moment with Mr. Chandor shooting so close to his weather-beaten face as it was getting more beaten by the weather?

"Well, let's get something straight," Mr. Redford replied. "I don't see myself as beautiful. I was a kid who was freckle-faced, and they used to call me 'hay head.'"

When he turned into a sex symbol after "Butch Cassidy" and "The Way We Were," he said, he thought: "This feels great. I think I'll roll with this for a while." But "out of whack" fan experiences made him withdraw.

"It got harder and harder, and then it got exhausting," he said. "And I guess the nice thing about getting older is that you don't have that quite so much anymore. I never had a problem with my face on screen. I thought it is what it is, and I was turned off by actors and actresses that tried to keep themselves young."

Mr. Redford has always been a minimalist, luring audiences in by seeming "unpossessable," as Pollack put it. But in "All Is Lost," Mr. Redford takes that to new heights, speaking only a handful of words, the loudest one unprintable here.

The script was a scanty 31 pages. A character known only as Our Man is sailing on his 39-foot yacht in the Indian Ocean when a foreign shipping container filled with children's sneakers gashes the boat, swamping the communications devices. Our Man spends the rest of the film improvising to save his life, learning how to desalinate water and navigate celestially. Mr. Redford, who ended "Downhill Racer" and "The Candidate" with a question, likes the ambiguous ending, which has divided audiences.

He said that during the Sundance Kid's silences, he would look at other men, thinking, "Can I kill you or not?" But this role was different; Mr. Redford did not bother to think like someone else. "There was so little described of the guy that, of course, it had to be me," he said. He wore his own turquoise and silver ring and displayed his own stubborn perseverance.

"He has got a conscience," Mr. Redford said of his character. "Clearly he has a family. He's not a bad person, but he's failed in some way. So maybe this journey has to do with him sorting all that out."

Films about being adrift seem to suit the national mood: "All Is Lost" is one of a spate of movies this season, including "Gravity," about Americans unmoored.

Mr. Chandor, 39, got the idea when he was living in Providence, R.I., and commuting by train to New York to edit "Margin Call." He would stare out the window at the sailboats stored for the winter and wonder about adventures never undertaken. His parents had raced sailboats as newlyweds, and he had spent summers in Rhode Island as a junior sailing instructor. He was also thinking about end-of-life issues watching his two grandmothers die. (The film's yacht, the Virginia Jean, is named after them.)

Then Mr. Chandor went to the Sundance Film Festival in 2011 for the premiere of "Margin Call" and attended a brunch for filmmakers. Mr. Redford got up to talk, but the audio system was not plugged in. "When you couldn't hear that buttery voice, it was almost like it wasn't Redford," Mr. Chandor said. "I started thinking about a film with no dialogue, because it seemed really cool to take that tool away from him as an actor and see what he could do."

Mr. Chandor asked Mr. Redford about the role, and the star was jolted.

"In 30 years of supporting new artists and Sundance labs and the festival, no one ever came to me and asked me to be in a film," Mr. Redford said. "Maybe they thought I was above it. And when I realized J.C. was ferocious in his focus and devotion to detail, I thought, this is a guy who I can give myself over to as an actor, which I was longing for. It was like coming full circle."

The reserved actor with the loner tendencies said he loved working with the exuberant extrovert of a director and teased him about making a film with no chat when he's so chatty. (Mr. Chandor is still a bit in awe, referring to his star at times as Mr. Redford.)

They filmed on the ocean around Los Angeles and spent two months in Mexico shooting with three massive water tanks that James Cameron built for "Titanic."

The plan called for a stunt double, "but we get down there and, of course, my ego kicks in," Mr. Redford said, grimacing. "I started saying: 'I think I can try that. Let me see what I can do.' And I realized that my doing that stuff was really a big part of the character, and that it would be much better for the film if he didn't have to cut and slice."

He grew up "a California water guy," as he put it, but was more of a surfer and swimmer than sailor. He's in great shape from horseback riding, hiking, skiing and tennis. Even spending all his time getting dunked in water in Mexico, Mr. Redford still sometimes did morning laps in the Rosarito Beach Hotel pool, an astonished Mr. Chandor reported.

Still, Mr. Redford admitted, "they beat the hell out of me." There were wave, wind and rain machines and a crew member with a giant hose spraying water at his head, leading to an infection that cost him 60 percent of his hearing in his left ear.

Mr. Chandor said the grips were agog. "They were looking at me, like, 'Am I really going to spray Robert Redford with a big power hose?'"

With a tight schedule and a budget of less than $10 million to make the film, Mr. Redford said, "I was so tired of being wet and there was no time not to be wet except at night, and so then it was tequila."

Mr. Redford has talked about how the constant references to his looks early in his career made him feel as if he were in a cage.

"So I think he found this very liberating," Mr. Chandor said. "The face at this point is a story in itself. That face is a thing of beauty but in a different way."

And Mr. Chandor can verify to skeptics Mr. Redford's claim that his hair remains naturally Hubbell strawberry blond. His locks survived the months of sun and chlorine, with no colorist in sight.

"No one believes me," Mr. Redford said. "Even my kids didn't believe me. I keep thinking of Reagan. It's freaking me out."

The New York Times critic A. O. Scott described "All Is Lost" as a "haunting allegory of environmental and economic hubris," depicting unfettered global capitalism as the Chinese container gouges the sailboat and a cargo ship and oil freighter pass by, oblivious to Our Man's plight.

But Mr. Redford, an earnest environmentalist, said he didn't think about any allegories; his character even throws a piece of plastic into the ocean. Mr. Chandor said he winced when he realized the environmental faux pas, but his star did not object. "I wasn't thinking of symbolism when I was doing it," Mr. Redford said. "I was thinking about surviving." On the plus side, Our Man eats organic soup.

Though Mr. Redford has plenty to occupy him, including turns next year in "Captain America" (chosen because it's "so different and a little weird") and filming "A Walk in the Woods," based on the Bill Bryson book (with Nick Nolte in the role originally envisioned for Newman), he's still passionately interested in the world. But he says he's no longer sure how to critique politics, when "the center is not holding, when everything's spinning and spinning, and when you can't beat 'Saturday Night Live.'"

When I noted that the glossy Bill McKay from "The Candidate" would now be as weighty as Pat Moynihan, given the childish display in Washington, he agreed. "I'm shocked at how dumbed down the process is," he said, "Looney Tunes without the Merrie Melodies."

He seldom watches his movies. He didn't see "The Sting," a smash hit in 1973, until 2004 when his grandson suggested it at Christmastime. "I thought it was a really good movie," Mr. Redford marveled. And he hadn't seen "All Is Lost" until May when he and Mr. Chandor got to Cannes, where it played out of competition. Mr. Chandor said Mr. Redford never even checked the monitor during filming.

At Cannes, "we walk in and we sit down front and center and that made me nervous," Mr. Redford recalled. "Where do you escape? How do you get out of here? And then the film plays, and it was hard for me to watch it."

Mr. Redford, who has never won an Oscar for acting, braced himself for boos and received a nine-minute standing ovation.

"It just threw me completely," he said. "I felt self-conscious and awkward and shy, and I didn't know what to do." He remembers saying to his wife, the German artist Sibylle Szaggars, and his director, "Hey, let's go." He said he also told Mr. Chandor, "Enjoy this moment because it will probably never come again," acknowledging with a laugh that he might have been a damper on the party. "I'm a great partner to have."

He says he has grown more comfortable in himself as he gets older, and abides by his favorite T. S. Eliot line: "There is only the trying. The rest is not our business."

"To me, it was always to climb up the hill," said the man sitting on his own mountain. "Not standing at the top."

SEAN PENN, REBEL WITH MANY CAUSES

—JUNE 22, 2024

MALIBU, Calif.—Don't mellow my harsh, dude.

I was coming to talk to Sean Penn, the notorious Hollywood hot-head who helped launch the word "dude" into the American blood-stream when he played stoner surfer Jeff Spicoli in the 1982 classic "Fast Times at Ridgemont High."

I was nervous because the Times photographer was already inside the Spanish-style ranch house with Penn, who has a history of throwing punches at paparazzi. I hurried past Penn's three surfboards and silver Airstream in the front yard, half expecting to see the un-pacific denizen of the Pacific Coast wrestling on the floor with the photographer.

Nah. Penn, in dark T-shirt, Columbia utility pants and sneakers, was charming, trailed by his adoring dogs, a golden retriever and a German shepherd rescue puppy.

When I joked that I was relieved to see him treating the photographer sweetly, he laughed. "When I did my 23andMe," he said, "I thought I might be part Hopi because they don't like to be photographed."

Penn, a lifelong Malibu resident, pointed in the direction of his old grade school in the days of a more rural Malibu. He said he gets up at 5:30 a.m. and goes, barefoot, out to his wood shop. "I even forget to smoke for five hours."

As it turns out, Penn has finally mellowed.

At 63, the weathered, tattooed rebel with many causes is a certified humanitarian—riding the crest into dangerous crises around the globe and saving lives in New Orleans and Haiti after disasters—and a crusading documentarian. He started out making the documentary "Superpower," thinking it would be a story of how Volodymyr Zelensky, a comedian, ascended to Ukraine's presidency. But then Vladimir Putin pounced.

Penn ignored the warning of his friend Robert O'Brien, a national security adviser for former President Donald Trump, to "get the heck out of there," and interviewed Zelensky in his bunker, hours after the invasion started. He also went to the front lines to dramatize for Americans the story of a young country protecting its democracy against an oppressor, to persuade them to help.

In 2013, Penn executed a rescue of Jacob Ostreicher, an American businessman rotting in a Bolivian prison after what Penn called a "corrupt prosecution."

He went all Batman again when the Covid vaccines became available. His organization, CORE (Community Organized Relief Effort), set up a huge vaccine administration site outside Dodger Stadium.

Penn, still wiry but now sporting a shock of natural white hair with the sides shaved—a do he has for a Paul Thomas Anderson movie with Leonardo DiCaprio—took me on a tour of his house. On prominent display is a painting by Hunter Biden called "The Map," the black outline of a head with colorful, detailed brushstrokes all around it. It's a gift from the president's son. Hunter, his wife, Melissa, and their son, Beau, had been over the night before.

Hunter painted it, Penn said, when he was "in pieces" and trying "to put the pieces back together." Penn could relate.

He said the two met in 2022 when Penn gave a speech in honor of U2 at the Kennedy Center Honors. He had read an interview with Hunter, the first "since the chips were rolling down, and I was really taken with him and I told him." Then last fall, after a screening of his Ukraine film with big shots on Capitol Hill, Penn had dinner with his friend Representative Eric Swalwell of California, who suggested he look up Hunter in Malibu.

"I had no idea he lived down here," said Penn, adding dryly: "I thought he was off in some judicial-focused place that we see on TV."

He called Hunter "a very, very insightful guy."

Penn also showed me the pump and hoses he keeps next to the pool. He has been en garde since the Malibu house he had shared with Madonna burned down in 1993.

We did the interview in his man cave, where he likes to serve vodka and talk about the world with his friends. There's a cozy circle of blue chairs and a sofa and a plywood coffee table Penn made. The walls are chockablock with pictures and letters, including one from his friend Marlon Brando. There's also a photo of Brando marching for civil rights.

The beach house is not your typical professionally decorated movie star manse. Penn has hung up photos of friends and his kids, actors Dylan, 33, and Hopper, 30, with his ex-wife Robin Wright; watercolors by Jack Nicholson; medals that belonged to his dad, Leo Penn, who flew 37 missions in World War II and got shot down twice; and paintings by his mother, Eileen, an artist and actress, and Hopper. He has a series of head shots above the fireplace of his brother Chris Penn, the actor, who died in 2006. There are vintage posters of the movies of his father, an actor and director who was blacklisted (turned in by Clifford Odets).

And there's a picture of Andriy Pilshchikov, known as "Juice" and the "Ghost of Kyiv," a member of a unit defending Ukraine from the air. The charismatic pilot, who was killed in a training accident, was featured in Penn's documentary.

There are several clocks set to different times around the world, including Ukrainian time.

The room is wreathed in smoke, as Penn alternates between chain-smoking American Spirits and noodling around his mouth with a dental pick. In the bathroom, he displays pictures of his friends smoking, including Dennis Hopper and Harry Dean Stanton and, justifying his cigarette addiction, the Charles Bukowski quote "Find what you love and let it kill you."

The peppery Penn knows a lot of people don't like him "out of the gate." He also knows people do not want to be lectured on global ills—and hectored for donations—by celebrities. He knows a lot of fans and fellow artists think he's a show-off and he should just focus on fulfilling his early promise as one of the great American actors and hone his talent as a director, and stop dancing on the world stage with leaders, dictators (Hugo Chávez and Raúl Castro) and even one infamous drug lord (El Chapo, whom he interviewed for Rolling Stone in a wild adventure Penn later conceded was a failure because it failed to spark a conversation on America's drug policies).

Penn has been mocked and satirized for some of his escapades, but his friend Bill Maher says he's the "real deal" in a town full of "phonies."

"Sean could search the rest of his life for a script that was even half as interesting as his real life and he'd never find it," Maher told me. "The rowboat during Katrina, the political prisoners he's gotten sprung from jail, the years of personally going to Haiti and unloading the food and supplies and getting it to the people. John and Yoko were 'activists'? Why, they spent a week in bed once? Please, if you look up 'walking the walk' in the dictionary, it's Sean's picture.

"I didn't want to get the Covid vaccine, but when I did, it was Sean's organization that had the whole city coming to the parking lot at Dodger Stadium!"

Doug Brinkley, the presidential historian who worked side by side with Penn during Katrina and went on humanitarian missions to Venezuela, Cuba and Haiti, called his friend "the rebel shaking the rafters on behalf of the underdog."

He added that what's easy to forget about Penn, given how serious his pursuits are, is how much fun he can be. "There is no better raconteur around," Brinkley said. "There is never a dull moment around Sean. He is all forward motion."

Penn wasn't at the splashy Hollywood fund-raiser for President Biden, hosted by George Clooney, Julia Roberts and Jimmy Kimmel. But he was photographed walking barefoot out of the White House state dinner for President William Ruto of Kenya last month. (He's not a tuxedo type, and his dress shoes pinched.)

"Hunter invited me," Penn said, noting that he was happy for the chance to talk to Ruto about how Kenyan peacekeeping troops could combat the gangs that have overrun Haiti. He told me that violence-ravaged Sudan will be the next country his organization tries to help.

But Penn did not press the president on any of his causes.

"I left the president alone because there were opportunities for that when everyone is not tapping his shoulder," the actor said. He thinks Biden should "take it slow" in the campaign, leaning into an elder statesman role, doing fireside-chat kind of talks, not getting into nasty spats with Trump but giving the nation a sense that red and blue can be united.

He showed me a medallion with the CORE motto: "Slow is smooth, smooth is fast, and blood is slippery."

Of Trump, he said dismissively: "He's shameful as an art and as a way of life."

Penn said that the more time he spent in Ukraine, the more he was able to accept people with different political views in our fractured country. He went on Sean Hannity's show in 2022 to push support of Ukraine, even though Hannity had named him an "enemy of the state" in 2007, back when Penn was lambasting the Bush administration for its Iraq debacle. Penn also did a panel in 2022 with the Fox News anchor Bret Baier and O'Brien at the Nixon Library in Yorba Linda, Calif.

Ukrainians also have political divisions, Penn told me, but he was blown away by their "unbreakable" unity in the face of tragedy.

"It's like breathing a different kind of air there," he said. "I really had a sensation of what I've been missing here. It's really abnormal what we're doing."

Penn escaped more and more into his gonzo journalism and global swashbuckling because he was disillusioned with Hollywood.

"I went 15 years miserable on sets," he said. "'Milk' was the last time I had a good time." That 2008 movie about the murder of Harvey Milk, the first openly gay elected public official in California, earned Penn his second Oscar. (His first was for "Mystic River" in 2003.)

At the time, he got credit for being a straight man playing a gay one; but now there is sometimes an outcry when straight actors get cast as gay characters. I wondered if he could even play Milk now.

"No," he replied. "It could not happen in a time like this. It's a time of tremendous overreach. It's a timid and artless policy toward the human imagination."

He vigorously rubbed his face to show how he felt on sets, even with good actors and producers, as if he was trying to rub out the experience.

"I feel like an actor who is playing a leading role and is a known actor and is being paid well has a leadership position on a film and you've got to show up with energy and be a bodyguard for the director in some way," he said. "I was faking my way through that stuff and that was exhausting. Mostly what I thought was just, 'What time is it? When are we going to get off?'"

"I was sure it was done, but I didn't know how I was going to keep my house running or travel freely or things like that if I stopped."

Then his friend and neighbor (and fellow talented nepo baby) Dakota Johnson dropped by with an indie script, "Daddio," by Christy Hall, who was also going to direct. It featured only two actors, an enigmatic young woman who gets in a cab at J.F.K. Airport with a driver who's a street philosopher raised in a hardscrabble Hell's Kitchen.

"I felt like this could be a pleasant experience and that's gonna matter to me now, maybe more than in the past," Penn said.

The first-time director recalled on the third day of shooting that she got a message Penn wanted to see her. "My heart was pounding," she said. "He just looked at me and said, 'Am I giving you everything that you're looking for?' I was so blown away by it. For someone of his caliber to care so much about a tiny, little indie two-hander."

"He's quite known for being tough and intimidating," Johnson said, "but there's a sweet boy in there."

"There's a real tenderness in him," she added.

The driver and passenger engage in erotic taxicab confessions about their personal lives, with Penn's character sharing some blunt observations. He warns Johnson's character, a computer programmer coming back from a visit to her small hometown in Oklahoma, sexting with her famous, married boyfriend, that men don't like to hear the word "love" from their mistresses because the L-word is "not their function." He notes that "men, we want to look good for other men" and that, for men, "looking like a family man is more important than being one."

Penn said that when guys come over to his man cave, they make the same sort of blunt judgments about relationships with women that

Hall's cabdriver does. Penn's own feeling is that some feminists still want to be feminine, and some men are "getting feminized." He thinks dating is getting more transactional for both men and women.

I wondered if Penn, who has been formally coupled and uncoupled with three women—first Madonna, then Robin Wright and, briefly, the Australian actress Leila George, the daughter of Greta Scacchi and Vincent D'Onofrio—and dated several other celebrities, had improvised from his own vivid experiences. (Jewel, an ex girlfriend, called him "a fantastic flirt.")

He said he just said the dialogue as it was written.

He said that he once loved drama in romance. But now, even if he's madly in love with someone, he said, if there's any unnecessary drama and visits from "the trauma gods," his feelings evaporate, like they never existed.

"I look at my dogs and say, 'Hey, it's us again.'"

He has experienced a fair number of relationships where "the first thing I see in the morning are eyes wondering what I'm going to do to make them happy that day. Rarely reciprocated," he said.

"On one of my marriages, the background noise of life was a 'Housewives of Beverly Hills' or another thing called 'Love Island,'" he said. "Not even being in the room—I'm not saying this to be cute—I was dying. I felt my heart, my brain shrinking. It was an assault."

He sees his "friends in the female department"—"Beautiful, wonderful people, wonderful with their partners or wonderful on their own"—who show him that relationships don't have to be dramatic or draining.

He's not in a serious relationship now and feels "thrilled every day."

"I'm just free," he said. "If I'm going to be in a relationship, I'm still going to be free, or I'm not going to be in it, and I'm not going to be hurting. I don't sense I'll have my heart broken by romance again."

Speaking of which, I wondered, what was the truth about the epic fights that devoured his turbulent marriage to Madonna?

"I had a freaking SWAT team come into my house," he said, sipping his Diet Coke. Madonna told the police she was worried because there were guns in the house. "I said: 'I'm not coming out. I'm going to finish my breakfast.' The next thing I knew, windows were being broken all around the house and they came in." Then, he added, "they had me in handcuffs."

He said he belatedly realized there were stories circulating that he had "trussed her up like a turkey. I didn't know what 'trussed up' meant, first." He said he was dating one woman who confronted him the morning after "a lovely night" when he was on the back porch smoking a cigarette. "She's looking at me like I killed her dog," he said, asking him "about this hitting Madonna in the head with a baseball bat."

"I didn't know what the hell she was talking about," he said. "Now I think it's fair to say that I'm not the biggest guy in the world. But if I hit Mike Tyson in the head with a baseball bat, he's going to the hospital."

Madonna herself cleared up the matter in 2015. When the director Lee Daniels defended the star of his show "Empire," Terrence Howard, saying that Howard's admission that he had hit his wife was no different from what Penn had done, Penn sued Daniels for $10 million, charging defamation.

Madonna provided an affidavit, saying that the baseball-bat and "tied me up" rumors were false and that Penn had never struck her.

"Not only did we win the case," Penn said about the settlement, "but Daniels wrote a public letter and he had to contribute to CORE."

About Madonna, Penn says simply: "She's someone I love." He said he worked with her on raising funds for Haiti and she recently agreed to do "a really terrific" video for a peace summit about Ukraine.

"It turns out it's a lot quicker to repair a friendship after divorce if there are not kids involved," he said. "It took Robin and I quite a while. There was a lot of drama." He added: "Much more important to repair it if there are kids involved, but no easy swing, right?"

Funnily enough, given how much time he spends helping humans, he once told The Times: "I don't like humans. I don't get along well with people."

When I asked him about that quote, he chuckled and said of people, "They should suck less."

Despite the encounter with a dread journalist, Penn was in a good mood as I left.

"Happy hour starts at 5:30," he said with a grin.

KEVIN COSTNER, GROUCHY SUPERHUNK

Kevin Costner is in a bad mood. He does not want to be trivialized. He does not want to be analyzed. He does not want to be criticized. He does not want to be "titillized," as he puts it, much less titillated.

He stalks down a street on the cusp of the French Quarter, wearing jeans and a bright green shirt, his hair slicked back and his scorching blue eyes shaded behind dark sunglasses. The heels of his brown cowboy boots tap an impatient tattoo, and he is annoyed when a group of middle-aged women hesitantly beg him to pose for a photograph while he waits at a red light.

"O.K.," he says, glowering at them and gesturing to a reporter who has moved out of the shot, "but can't you see I'm being interviewed?"

The highly anticipated $40 million to $50 million epic produced by Morgan Creek Productions and distributed by Warner Brothers, "Robin Hood: Prince of Thieves," opens on Friday. Mr. Costner seems nervous about how "Raiders of the Lost Sherwood Forest," as some of the stars are calling the movie, will be received.

He is still adjusting to superstardom, to the blessings and burdens that come with inheriting both Paul Newman's mantle as Hollywood's "head hunk" and Orson Welles's mantle as a quirky acting-directing prodigy. "Orson Welles with no belly," Pauline Kael, the New Yorker movie critic, wrote sarcastically in a scalding review of "Dances With Wolves" that contains the now famous line, "Costner has feathers in his hair and feathers in his head."

Despite what Ms. Kael wrote about Mr. Costner's "New Age Gary Cooper" act and his "bland megalomania," the public embraced his innocent daydream of the West, just as they had embraced his innocent daydream about baseball, "Field of Dreams." "Dances With Wolves" received seven Academy Awards and vaulted Mr. Costner into Hollywood heaven.

Others may still be debating whether he is a lucky naif or a brilliant visionary, but Mr. Costner feels at home at the top. "I wanted to operate in the highest circle," he says, as he settled in his elegant hotel suite for a lunch of club sandwich, potato chips and a beer, as a radio played easy-listening music in the background.

The 36-year-old has, however, been taken aback by the wind shear of his stardom. "I have tried not to get caught off guard and to be kind of prudent in anticipating the stuff to try to understand the good and the bad and the success," he says. "I've tried to monitor my life that way, not just in terms of Hollywood, for a long time. But 'Dances' did catch me by surprise, the leap, the kind of quantum leap that occurred with the public. Things have changed, and changed for me in ways that were difficult to anticipate.

"Personally, I don't know if people think I suddenly can think now, or I'm smarter than I ever was. And you're more vulnerable."

It has been said that Mr. Costner is worried about his thinning hair. His hair looks O.K. It's his thinning skin he should be worried about. Almost every question evokes a prickly response from the once-breezy actor.

He feels defensive about several things at the moment: his strange, now-you-see-it-now-you-don't English accent in "Robin Hood." His penchant for "politically correct" scripts with an anti–white male twist. Criticism that he has lost the roguish gleam exhibited in early interviews and in early films such as "Silverado" and "No Way Out," in favor of a tiresome thirtysomething earnestness and smugness. Controversy over whether he is lending his prestige to the dubious conspiracy theory of former New Orleans District Attorney Jim Garrison, whom he plays in the Oliver Stone movie "JFK," now being filmed here.

Like other movie stars who capture the public's attention through their looks, Mr. Costner is both pleased and tetchy about his image as sex symbol and stresses that he prefers riding horses to kissing leading ladies. "Oh, God, the horses are always fun; the fights are fun," he says of "Robin Hood."

At one point, with a self-conscious cockiness, he points at the reporter's tape recorder and asks, "So who hears this tape, your girlfriends?" (He is assured that the tape will be used for professional purposes only.)

At the moment, what is bothering Mr. Costner most on this score is a nude swimming scene that the "Robin Hood" producers have played up in the film's trailer. The scene shows Mary Elizabeth Mastrantonio, who portrays Maid Marian, experiencing a flash of desire as she watches Mr. Costner swim in a pond below.

Mr. Costner, who had a similar nude scene in "Dances With Wolves," offers a long, exceedingly earnest explanation, saying he agreed to the swimming scene only because it was integral to the original script. He says he feels a little used now because the "meaning" of the nudity was left on the cutting-room floor. To make it even more absurd, it's not even his derriere. It belongs to his double.

"There was a reason for that scene that's not there anymore, so it seems maybe gratuitous or seems like all this is an opportunity to titillize— what is the word, titillate?" he says. "But it's not. The whole point of that scene was when she sees him, he has tremendous scars on his back from prison, and the camera never picked it up; and out of that she begins to change. It puts another interesting spin on the movie, that he's been disfigured a little bit, violated that way. So the device of swimming was a device to see that. This wasn't something that I invented and thought, 'Oh, boy, that works.' When I see the horses, I think, 'Oh, boy!'"

He dismisses questions about such "gratuitous stuff." "Aren't you trying to completely trivialize my life?" he snaps.

But Mr. Costner has bigger problems with this movie. There is, for starters, his accent.

The star says that the director, his friend Kevin Reynolds, who gave Mr. Costner a start in the 1985 movie "Fandango," and the Morgan Creek producer James Robinson were wary about his trying a British accent. He started out with an accent coach, but, he says, before he felt he had perfected the accent, the coach was gone and he was left to his own devices. He says he thought it was important for the movie's reality to sharpen his relaxed California surfer drawl with an English accent, but it comes out sounding like Moondoggie goes Nottingham as Mr. Costner drops his "r's" in words like "armor," "fear" and "sworn."

The accent problem is underscored by the stilted dialogue, which runs along the lines of "I'm swahhn to protect you" and "Please allow that yeahs of wah and prison may change a mahn." Ms. Mastrantonio, who does better with her British accent, is stuck with lines like "How did a once arrogant young nobleman find contentment living with the salt of the earth?"

Despite the standards set for speaking in tongues by Meryl Streep, there is still a school in Hollywood that believes that some popular stars are better off not trying accents. Robert Redford, for instance, did not attempt Denys Finch Hatton's clipped Eton accent in "Out of Africa." The makers of "Robin Hood" may be assumed to be in this school, since the trailer for the two-and-a-half-hour movie, and almost the entire second half of the film, find Mr. Costner bounding about "buckling swash," as his co-star Alan Rickman puts it, with flaming bow and arrow and flashing sword, but little dialogue.

Asked if he was feeling defensive about the accent, Mr. Costner replies: "I'm going to have to answer questions about it. So you can choose what you think my posturing is. You know about it. You have to answer questions about it. So if you're asking questions about it, you're being offensive about it. Are you being offensive about it by asking about it?"

There is also bound to be much comment about the awkward addition to the Robin Hood myth of Morgan Freeman, an Oscar nominee for best actor for "Driving Miss Daisy" in 1989. Mr. Freeman plays Azeem, a Moor rescued by Robin Hood during the Crusades in Jerusalem. Mr. Freeman's character follows Robin to Sherwood Forest, where he uses the skills of a higher civilization to teach the racist Merry Men some lessons in loyalty, gunpowder and delivering a breech baby.

Critics will no doubt draw parallels to Mr. Costner's treatment of the Sioux in "Dances With Wolves," a movie that glorified the Indians while presenting the white soldiers as cruel louts.

"I didn't write the piece," Mr. Costner says of the new movie. "But I wouldn't have done 'Robin Hood' unless it leaped forward in terms of genre. I saw the humor in it. And it seemed exotic that Robin Hood start in Jerusalem and how he behaved not as a boy but as a man, not as a rascal but as a person who's been through some things, as a hired trained soldier who's capable of fighting, as opposed to guys who've been killing deer illegally."

Since Mr. Costner is "a Robin Hood for the 90's," as the producers proclaim, this version of the medieval fable is violent, even though it has received a PG-13 rating. Mr. Costner is proud of the fact that his Robin Hood is grittier than Errol Flynn's, in 1938. He wears studs on his jacket instead of sequins and brown pants instead of tights, and there's no cunning green hat with a feather. Mr. Costner also dispensed with Mr. Flynn's tongue-in-cheek derring-do, because it did not fit with the brooding new Freudian twists in the plot—young Robin's refusal to accept his widowed father's affair with a peasant woman, and the murder of his father by the Sheriff of Nottingham.

"You tell me my father just died, and I can't do the next scene tongue-in-cheek; I can't get all revved up; that's not really real behavior," he explains. "If I do that, I'm going to spin you out of the movie." On the other hand, he notes, it is a fairy tale. "I mean, it's not Virginia Woolf; it's not heavy, heavy, heavy drama. C'mon, look at me, how deep could I get with stuff like that, for crying out loud?"

Asked about the backlash of fame, asked how he feels when he is criticized for being too self-righteous, he goes on a lengthy, bitter and largely unprintable rampage against critics like Ms. Kael and Tom Shales of The Washington Post, who has dubbed Mr. Costner "the Prince of Sanctimony."

Asked what he thought of his less-than-flattering cameo appearance in "Truth or Dare," in which Madonna makes a gagging motion after Mr. Costner comes backstage looking strangely dweebish and praises her show as "neat," the actor looks daggers but says: "I didn't see it, and I'm not going to give you a quote on it." He adds a sarcastic "Wow" when asked if he wished he had chosen another word besides "neat."

The Warner Brothers press agents, realizing what a touchy subject the new "JFK" movie is, have warned against asking Mr. Costner too many questions about the Oliver Stone film. But the actor seems quite ready to rebut suggestions that he may be putting his prestige on the line with this saga. Mr. Garrison's theory holds that Lee Harvard Oswald was merely a C.I.A. fall guy for a plot to assassinate President Kennedy that involved the highest levels of the United States Government.

Mr. Costner says "incredibly honorable men" lent their credibility to the Warren Commission Report, which concludes that Lee Harvey Oswald acted alone, a finding Mr. Costner regards as "unbelievable, like one bullet causing seven different wounds, like one man doing all that himself."

He added: "It's easy to poke fun at Garrison because he can be made to appear a Southern caricature, but he was asking some very, very important questions."

He says he admires Oliver Stone for being "bold" enough to make the movie. "You know, movies have to take leaps of faith. Just like Robin Hood can't beat up 50 guys, but he does. And just like in this movie, it shouldn't be thought of as a factual kind of thing. But it should be pretty thought provoking and fall into the guise of entertaining and some real things. For those who would paint Garrison as a complete kook, they're missing the point. There is within all of us an ambiguity that exists within all people. But that's not what we're discussing. We're discussing complete blockages of justice."

Mr. Costner says he is trying to "fight my way back to the 20th century and a tie" and plans to stay away from period pieces for a while. He worries about the effects of fame on his wife, Cindy, and their three young children, but he is not worried about his professional future in Hollywood.

"I always felt armed with the one thing that they value, which was good stories, you know, because, like, basically, that's what they're in business for."

About his nettlesome new stature, he concludes: "Are you kidding? I would trade it all for anonymity again." Asked if there were any good things, he replies: "I just can't think of any. Those things don't help you get up in the morning. Fame doesn't help clear your mind. Fame doesn't tell you when you're right or wrong. I can't think of anything good that comes out of it. Let's modify that. There's not anything that comes out of it that I really need."

And with that, the Prince of Thieves and Sanctimony stalks off, surrounded by publicists-in-waiting.

AL PACINO, HOW "THE GODFATHER" MADE THE SHY STAR "NOTORIOUS"

SEPTEMBER 1992

Al is not easy.

At least, that's what everyone will tell you.

It's not easy to persuade him to do interviews to promote his movies. It's not easy to do love scenes with him. It's not easy to understand what the hell he's talking about, because he can be so inarticulate at times. It's not easy to get him to commit to an acting project, and it's not easy to understand all his choices. He's not easy to work with, because he always wants just one more rehearsal or one more take or one more test screening.

This is not the sort of star who makes voice-over commercials for Japanese cars or glitters at fund-raisers for politically correct candidates or yaks about his love life on Arsenio Hall's couch. We're talking here about a guy who rereads Chekhov and Emily Dickinson for fun. A guy who writes poetry and, mercifully, loses it.

So it is with some trepidation that I walk up to Al Pacino's table in the back of Joe Allen, a pub in New York's theater district, and shake hands. The 52-year-old actor, who in performance is often compared to a hand grenade, seems a gentle soul in person, with a soft, gravelly voice and a courtly manner. Although he sometimes makes odd fashion statements with scarves used as headbands, tonight he looks rather stylish, in a black silk shirt, a black sport coat and a green-and-black

Forties-style tie. There is a glint at his neck, a long gold chain with a primitive cross.

Although interviews rank somewhere below root canal on Pacino's favorite-things list, he seems to want to make this work. We chat for a bit about his new movie, *Glengarry Glen Ross*, and where he might go from here. I want to ask him something profound, something that will make him respect me. But before I can stop myself, I blurt out "So, do you regret not taking the Richard Gere role in *Pretty Woman*?"

He turns those mournful basset-hound eyes on me, the ones director Garry Marshall calls, "the best eyes in the world," and gives me a look of amused disdain.

"No, the only movie I wished I could have done was *Lenny*," he says, referring to the blistering 1974 Bob Fosse film about comedian Lenny Bruce, in which Dustin Hoffman starred.

The finicky Pacino, who has turned down more hits than he has made, then allows that he also might have liked to have played the Paul Newman part in the 1977 George Roy Hill comedy about hockey players, *Slap Shot*.

"I told Hill that I was interested, if they could fix the problems with the script, and all he wanted to know was 'Mr. Pacino, do you ice-skate?'"

Pacino laughs.

That is not as strange a thing to say as "Garbo talks," by the way. Pacino laughs fairly often.

He says he did not picture himself as Michael Corleone when he got the role in *The Godfather*.

Though he is a genuine American film icon, Al Pacino cannot "open" a movie in the way that Arnold Schwarzenegger and Eddie Murphy can. He went for a decade without a hit movie, between *And Justice for All*, in 1979, and *Sea of Love*, in 1989. So he has gingerly agreed to this interview to reap some attention for *Glengarry Glen Ross*, an independent production, directed by James Foley, that does not offer the usual blandishments of sex and violence. The film version of David Mamet's Pulitzer Prize–winning play about cutthroat real-estate salesmen is a scalding, syncopated ensemble piece featuring Jack Lemmon,

Alec Baldwin, Alan Arkin, Ed Harris and Kevin Spacey. Pacino gets to curse and charm, wear a diamond pinkie ring as Ricky Roma, a wired purveyor of "choice parcels" in a world where only one thing counts: getting them to sign on the line which is dotted.

He will also star this fall in Universal's *Scent of a Woman*, playing Lieutenant Colonel Frank Slade, a blind, bitter army veteran living in New England who decides to go on a weekend jaunt to New York City, with the teenage boy hired to care for him reluctantly in tow.

Pacino has a lot of nervous energy. At the restaurant, he drinks cappuccino and chews gum and constantly runs his fingers through his thick hair. He gave up alcohol fifteen years ago, after friends suggested that he had a problem. Lately, he has gotten a bit pudgy around the middle and is supposed to be on a diet. His assistant has been fixing him bean dishes from the actor's grandmother's Sicilian recipes and quizzing his companions to see if he's cheating.

He's cheating. "Do you want to split a hot-fudge cake?"

It's an offer I can't refuse. After polishing off dessert, we get up to go. "Leave a big tip," he instructs, suggesting I offer 80 percent of the bill. He was once a struggling actor working odd jobs in Manhattan, so he identifies with the kids waiting tables at Broadway restaurants. (Pacino is also generous with his own money. He quietly contributes, through a foundation he has set up, to hungry children, AIDS research and other causes.) He checks out the Knicks game on the bar television, then, outside, climbs into his jeep and heads uptown. When he stops at a red light across from Lincoln Center, a street hustler comes up to talk. Pacino lowers the window and chats with the guy until the light changes, handing him a five-dollar bill from a stack of crisp ones and fives that's spilling out of his glove compartment. He is accustomed to strangers on the streets of New York calling him "Al" and tossing him a favorite line from *Scarface*—"Can I go now?"—or chanting "At-ti-ca! At-ti-ca!" from *Dog Day Afternoon*.

Born in Harlem, Alfredo James Pacino grew up in a small apartment in the South Bronx with his mother, her parents and various cousins. One grandfather was a plasterer, the other a house painter. His father, an insurance agent, left home when Al was 2 and, while

Pacino sees him occasionally, he says they "don't have any real relationship."

Although his childhood had its dark moments—"Living in three rooms with a bunch of Sicilians is not easy"—he remembers it as happy. As a child, he was encouraged to act out movie roles (like the drunken Ray Milland looking for a hidden bottle in *The Lost Weekend*) and was eventually accepted at the High School of Performing Arts. But he had to drop out at 16 in order to help support his mother, who had become ill, and the next year, he moved to Greenwich Village and began auditioning for plays. He worked a series of odd jobs, from building superintendent to movie usher to messenger.

"I know every street in this city," he says, driving past packed restaurants on the Upper West Side. "I never thought about moving to Hollywood. Not for a single moment. I have always been a kind of a homeboy."

And as much as a quirky millionaire movie star who dates beautiful women, hangs out with the likes of Michelle Pfeiffer and Ellen Barkin, lives in a trendy suburb on the Hudson River called Sneden's Landing and ponders buying a farm so that his daughter can have "horsies," as much as this guy can still be a homeboy, Pacino probably is.

"It's hard for people to believe that actors can be shy, but Al is shy," says Sidney Lumet, who directed Pacino in *Dog Day Afternoon* and *Serpico*. "In his acting, his instrument is himself, his emotional nakedness. So other than acting, he tries his damnedest not to bare himself."

Garry Marshall, who directed *Frankie and Johnny*, agrees that Pacino will curl into his shell if he has the slightest suspicion that someone is mocking him. "In a way, he's extremely naive," Marshall says. "It's strange to talk about vulnerability and innocence with a guy who's played the foremost killers on the American screen. But he's so pure and honest and artistic, it's a little like Don Quixote walking through Hollywood."

Ellen Barkin, who slammed Pacino around the bedroom in their steamy scenes in *Sea of Love*, says with mock bravado that she deserves all the credit she got for those scenes. One of Hollywood's most famous tough guys, it turns out, had a tough time feigning lust.

"It's hard for him to do it unless he means it," Barkin says. "Lovemaking is an intimate gesture, and you don't do it with people you're not intimate with. That's what's sexy about him. It's real. He's not a seducer."

When shooting the bedroom scenes for *Frankie and Johnny*, Michelle Pfeiffer loosened up her costar by giggling and being, as she puts it, "immature." "I'd conjure up the meanest things to say to him just before we would start a love scene, like 'You really bore me,'" she recalls. "He'd be on the floor, laughing."

Pacino hates to talk about his personal life, even though he has been involved in high-profile relationships with a flock of famous actresses, including Kathleen Quinlan, Tuesday Weld, Jill Clayburgh, Marthe Keller and Diane Keaton. He has said that he has spent a lot of time hiding and withdrawing from stardom and from women.

His friend James Caan says he thinks Pacino's reclusiveness, which extends to wearing disguises, is an affectation. "Al hiding under a hat and a mustache and saying 'I vant to be alone' is full of shit, and you tell him I said so. I told him to his face," Caan says. "You go in the business to get recognition and then you refuse recognition? Who are you bullshitting with that?"

For Pacino, fame is an unfortunate by-product of his brilliance as an actor. From the beginning, his intensity for "the work" has been legend.

"Everything stems from some incredible core inside of him that I wouldn't think of trying to get near, because it would be like getting somewhere near the center of the earth," Lumet says. "What comes out of his core is so uniquely his own. It's the only thing he can trust. It is quite clear that Al is a loner."

Unlike actors who are trained to find the truth of the character in the moment and switch it off when the scene is over, Pacino stuck with the emotion twenty-four hours a day during *Dog Day Afternoon*. "He was never really light in spirit. It's a very tough way to work. The cost has to be enormous, really nightmarish and horrendous," said Sidney Lumet.

Even Lee Strasberg, the head of the Actors Studio and Pacino's Method guru, a man not known for his frivolity, warned him to lighten up. "Strasberg said to me, 'Darling, you know, you have to let it go sometimes,'" Pacino recalls.

Pacino remembers that in 1983's *Scarface*, he was so deeply into the role of Tony Montana, the foul-mouthed, murderous Cuban drug kingpin, that when a neighbor's attack dog lunged at him—an action that he says normally would have scared him to death—he yelled "Back off!" and the dog scurried away in fear.

Pacino has always done exhaustive preparation for the roles. For *The Godfather*, he met with Mafia chieftains. For *Scarface*, he met drug dealers. He learned Benihana-style chopping from short-order cooks for *Frankie and Johnny* and got so involved in it that Michelle Pfeiffer finally had to tell him to chop softer so she could hear herself speak.

But lately, he has developed a sense of humor about his perfectionism. At one point, he told the crew of *Frankie and Johnny*, "I know you guys have a pool on how many takes I'm going to do here, and I say that the one who bet over twenty has the best shot."

And he tries to be polite about it. "He'd say, 'You're the director and I'm the actor. But I'm imploring you to do one more take,'" say James Foley. "As if I would say no."

At the heart of Pacino's talent is his ability to tear down the wall between reality and illusion. Arvin Brown, who directed the actor on stage in *American Buffalo* and *Chinese Coffee*, was literally afraid when he first saw Pacino, in *The Indian Wants the Bronx*, in the late Sixties. "He had so much violence in him that he shattered the mystical line that allows the audience to feel comfortable," Brown says. "Intellectually, I know he was an actor and he was not going to jump off the stage and attack me. But he scared the shit out of me."

Barkin describes a similar experience while shooting *Sea of Love*, during a scene in which Pacino gets drunk and yells at her. "We did three or four takes, and there was this weird clacking noise. I was terrified. I felt like he might lose it and strangle me right there. Then Al suddenly turned to me and said, 'Could you be, like less . . . ?' and I realized that my hands were shaking so hard that my rings were clacking away."

But now he seems able to flip off the emotional switch. Pfeiffer noticed a dramatic difference between Pacino's temperament when they worked together on *Scarface* and then, eight years later, on *Frankie and Johnny*. "He's a happier person," she says.

Pacino says that getting older has helped. "As you do this more and more, you don't mix up your parts and yourself as much."

And life is not so serious anymore.

Barkin recalls how Pacino broke up a tense *Sea of Love* production meeting one night by bursting into an imitation of Barbra Streisand singing "And we've got nothing to be guilty of/Our love is one in a million...."

Pacino used to be touchy about being lumped with the group of intense ethnic actors who changes Hollywood's image of leading men in the Sixties and Seventies. Asked in a 1979 "Playboy" interview about the comment in Pauline Kael's review of *Serpico* that, with a beard, he was indistinguishable from Dustin Hoffman, Pacino snapped "Is that after she had the shot glass removed from her throat?"

Last year, a mellower Pacino told Garry Marshal that his real name is Al De Niro: "Yeah, we're all the same guy."

Some of the worst times of Al Pacino's life were spent working on the *Godfather* movies.

When Francis Ford Coppola began shooting *The Godfather*, the studio chiefs weren't buying Pacino, then a 31-year-old New York stage actor. They made Coppola test dozens of others for the role of Michael, including Robert De Niro and James Caan. Pacino seemed so deadpan, so passive. Everyone thought the young actor was being self-destructive.

Pacino says he was unhappy but trying. "Here I was, this kid, and all of a sudden I was thrown into an environment that was pressured, to say the least. Francis was worried about his job every day. He was young, too, up there for the first time. And he had been given this mountain to climb. And there I was, I just wanted to quit and go back to something else. I was having to do film acting, which I wasn't used to. And I was playing a leading man and everyone kept telling me I wasn't a leading man.

"Word kept coming down from the studio: 'Well, when is this kid going to deliver?' And I'd just say 'I need a drink.'" Finally, the studio relaxed, but Pacino didn't. "Movies were difficult things for the first ten years of my career," he observes. "I kept feeling as though this was not the medium for me."

When *The Godfather* came out, in 1972, celebrity hit Pacino hard. His life was suddenly filled with booze, tranquilizers, women, deals, money and sycophants.

"When you become visible and notorious, you start accepting people into your world that you wouldn't normally be associated with," he says. "That was what got me in some trouble. I started to get involved in situations that came readily to me, where I didn't have to earn it. Especially if you're a shy person to start with, what happens is, now you are accepted. You become unduly suspicious."

He also struggled with darker emotions: selfishness, loneliness, isolation, depression. "It was like the scene out of *Dr. Strangelove* when Slim Pickins rode the bomb down," Pacino says. "It was anarchy. I didn't feel a rush. I just felt chaos when I was younger. I say 'What is going on? Give me another drink.'"

During this period, he lived with actress Jill Clayburgh, and he remembers soaking in the bathtub for hours, drinking and talking on the phone. Clayburgh even got him a plastic tub tray to hold a drink and a phone. "As long as I was home, it was all right for her, even if I was in the bathroom. She should have turned off the plumbing." He used the tray in a scene in *Bobby Deerfield*, a movie that marked the nadir of his noncommunicative, melancholy, out-of-it phase.

There was a scary incident before *Dog Day Afternoon* began shooting, in 1974, when Pacino dropped out briefly, sick with exhaustion and drink. Dustin Hoffman was waiting in the wings, but Pacino beat back his demons and returned. After the movie came out, he was bigger than ever, but he didn't do much with his life except drink and indulge his melancholia about the meaning of celebrity and existence. When friends insisted, he went to AA meetings and stopped drinking and smoking.

I ask Pacino whether he considered himself an alcoholic.

"I still don't know, frankly how far or how deep my problem goes," he says. "I had some very close friends who were concerned about it. I was not as aware of my drinking as I guess other people were. Because I was always functioning, really. I didn't ever use drugs. I did the tranquilizers, that type of thing. I don't think I was doing a wise thing doing it while I drank."

He looks out the window at darkness for a moment, then continues. "I don't have any desire for the hard stuff. But wine, it's warming, mellow, takes the edge off after having had a tough time; it's kind of a reward for having made it through the day.

"It's a struggle. I wish it wasn't. Sometimes it isn't. My hope is, having stopped, that it made whatever is positive in my life, it gave me more of a chance to have that."

If making *The Godfather* was hard, shooting *The Godfather, Part III*, on location for six months in Sicily, was a nightmare.

Caan recalls that Pacino called him from Italy, "screaming and yelling about what Francis was doing. Francis was still mourning the death of his son. It was not the Francis who did the first *Godfather*. He even thought he could make George Hamilton an actor."

Pacino says that once Robert Duvall dropped out of the cast due to a money dispute, the script had to be substantially rewritten: "When Duvall wouldn't do the movie, I thought we were in trouble."

Then an exhausted Winona Ryder left the film and was replaced by Sofia Coppola, the director's daughter. "I think it's difficult when you cast your own kid," Pacino says. "It was a strain. The film developed a strain. I think there was a problem in the fabric of the story, but I wish that we'd had the complete cast."

Pacino, who has been nominated six times for an Oscar but has never won, says he was disappointed that he did not get nominated for *Godfather III*, which received seven nominations. (He was however, nominated for best supporting actor for his hilarious turn as Big Boy Caprice in *Dick Tracy* but lost to Joe Pesci.) "As I get older, I think about it more," he says.

Roy Orbison is crooning on the box, and Herb Ritts, photographer to the stars, is chatting with Pacino at a West Side studio. The actor has donned a gray Armani suit, the trousers puddling around his ankles, for a photo shoot.

"So, you're dating Lyndall Hobbs?" Ritts asks, referring to the tall, slim blonde Australian woman who has been Pacino's companion for the past year and a half. Hobbs, a former London television reporter who specialized in fashion, directed Annette Funicello and Frankie

Avalon in *Back to the Beach*, in 1987. She moved to Manhattan with her young daughter last year to be closer to Pacino. Those who know her say she is as outgoing and interested in parties and celebrities as he is reclusive. Some have noticed a resemblance to Diane Keaton in Hobbs, with her nervous energy and eclectic wardrobe of vintage menswear and high fashion.

Pacino, who looks like he'd rather have a horse's head in his bed than confide anything about his love life, is glancing around the room skittishly.

"Lyndall's great," Ritts says affably. "She has that great smile. And she's really *there*. So how did you two get together?"

Pacino, his private side and his polite side visibly warring, goes with the polite. "We met a long time ago, but it didn't go anywhere. Then we ran into each other again." Ritts notes that it is unusual to return to a relationship years later.

"No, it's happened to me before," Pacino says with a wry grin. "It happens more as you get older."

A few nights later, as we drive back from the Long Wharf Theater in New Haven, Connecticut, where Pacino went to see a friend's production of *A Touch of the Poet*, it seems like a good time to slip in some questions about romance. I pop the question: Why has he never married?

When he feels comfortable with a subject, Pacino can be an eloquent conversationalist, but when the talk turns to love, he is instantly elliptic.

"I guess there comes a point where one defines marriage for oneself and what does it mean," he answers, finally. "I have just not come to that point yet."

Has he ever come close?

"Not really."

Will he ever?

"I think so. If I could relate to its relevancy."

He observes that "sharing your life with someone is a kind of wedding, in a way."

What attracts him in a woman?

"It takes more than one encounter."

A sense of humor? A literary bent?

"It's no one thing," he says. "But I remember once having fallen in love instantly. I won't say who, but it did happen to me once. Who knows with those things? They must have something to do with some unconscious precepts. Before it happened, I would have said there was no such thing."

He swears he is easy to live with. "I'm not that demanding," he says, adding that he believes in "a certain amount of freedom, come and go" in relationships.

Is he the jealous type?

"I wouldn't say I'm the jealous type, no," he says, smiling.

He feels the most important thing in a relationship is to have an understanding of why you are together and what you are together. "It's always best when you know what the rules are," he says. "Otherwise, it starts to go like a house of cards."

Does he prefer strong, successful women like Diane Keaton, one of his most prominent romances?

"I was very close to Diane Keaton before she or I made a movie; I knew her when she was very young," he replies. But she got involved with Woody Allen and then Warren Beatty, and then, many years later, she and Pacino picked up where they had left off.

Although Keaton told *Mirabella* that working with Pacino in *The Godfather* movies was exciting "'because you really know him and he can't trick you, and you can't trick him,'" Pacino says of working with a lover: "I prefer not, frankly.

"It's wonderful when it's working," he says. "But you also have to know there are times when little things happen in day-to-day life that will affect your working life. Being in close quarters so long, the least little thing might upset you. A lot of people think that it allows you to bring personal things to the work, but it isn't true. For the most part, you don't really use it — it's an interference. In order to work, you need objectivity and you have to be able to use your imagination. And you need a little peace." Keaton said that making *Godfather III* "'was so bittersweet'" because it was "'the end of the trail for us.'"

Andy Garcia, who helped nurse Pacino through the bad professional and personal moments of the film, says of the Keaton-Pacino romance: "I liked them together. I think they're destined for one another."

Although Pacino has lived with women in the past, he lives alone now—with five dogs—in his book-filled house in Sneden's Landing.

"Sometimes, living together puts a strain on it," says Pacino, not sounding too interested in the idea of settling down. "Sometimes you're better off living apart and being together. I've found that to be very effective, especially if you like each other a great deal and enjoy each other's company. Having time alone is important to me, but not too much—that gets tiring. When Bette Davis was asked what makes a marriage successful, she said 'Separate bedrooms.'"

Pacino's approach to fatherhood is similarly unconventional. A brief romantic interlude in 1989 produced a daughter named Julie, now 3, whom he kept a secret for a while before publicly incorporating her into his life.

"When she and her mother went to a video store, in the days when nobody knew that I had a child, Julie would point to videos, going 'Dada, Dada,'" Pacino says, grinning. Now he goes to the movies, Central Park and Playland with her; he keeps her toys, finger paintings and photographs in his midtown office; and he has a room for her at his house. In one picture in the office, Julie, a brunette heartbreaker, sports pink heart-shaped sunglasses and a pink bottle. Pacino observes that when he doesn't see her, he misses her in a way that is entirely new to him.

Pacino has always been more interested in art than in money, which has caused him to make some strange career choices. He recently took about a $4.9 million pay cut to star in two one-act plays at New York's Circle in the Square, as part of a fundraising drive for the theater. The critics praised Pacino's acting in Ira Lewis's *Chinese Coffee*, in which he played a scuzzy, washed-up Greenwich Village writer, and in Oscar Wilde's *Salome*, in which he played a campy Herod, but they argued that he was wasting his time in second-rate vehicles and that the ornate language of *Salome*, full of "thine"s and "thou"s, was ill suited to him. Nor have they been kind about his forays into Shakespeare, in *Richard*

III and *Julius Caesar*. Some observers think that Lee Strasberg encouraged Pacino to take on the kind of highbrow roles that are a bad fit for this quintessentially urban, American actor.

"He has all the ability in the world, but sometimes his head gets in the way of his ass—it's like Jon Lovitz's thing about 'ahc-ting,'" says Caan, referring to the *Saturday Night Live* spoof of the windy Master Thespian. "After *Revolution*, Al shouldn't do another thing that requires an accent."

Following the disastrous 1965 British-made costume epic about the American Revolution ("Mr. Pacino has never been more intense to such little effect," Vincent Canby wrote. "It's like watching someone walk around in a chicken costume"), Pacino burrowed out of sight for four years. He refreshed his interest in acting by giving readings at colleges, doing workshops and obsessively editing his own fifty-two-minute film, *The Local Stigmatic*, from the 1965 Heathcote Williams play about two cockney thugs gripped by class envy who brutalize an actor they meet in a pub because "fame is the first disgrace—because God knows who you are."

The movie is required viewing, preferably twice, for those who would interview Pacino. He said he likes it because it is "bottomless," like the classics.

Maybe the work speaks to Pacino on a subject close to his heart: the dark side of celebrity. Still, it is hard to understand his preoccupation with this play or why he has spent seven years and a small fortune filming it, editing it and screening it at colleges and museums and for small groups. the piece is a stale mix of John Osborne's working-class rage and Herold Pinter's anomie, and the Alfie-goes-to-the-Bronx accent Pacino affects in it is distracting.

Pacino feels strongly that the movie is too raw, too difficult, to ever be released commercially. But even Williams, something of an eccentric himself, begged Pacino to make *The Local Stigmatic* more accessible; he suggested changing the title to Fans and adding some scenes to clarify the class conflict. But, after years of debating, Pacino refused, thinking that would sully the work's purity. So it remains an expensive hobby. (Not one to walk away from an obsession, Pacino is thinking of editing down about five hours of tape from college lectures on *Stigmatic* to make a short documentary about the film.)

One night this past May, Pacino and Hobbs attended screening of the movie for a group of Whitney Museum contributors. Explaining why the movie has never been released, Pacino told the audience that "it needs a controlled environment." And the whole group was about as controlled as it gets—a veritable New Yorker cartoon of Dan Quayle's dread cultural elite.

The evening had an emperor's-new-clothes feel: The audience knew its task was to "get it." After the screening, guests murmured knowingly to one another about how powerful the film was. And no one walked out in disgust at the violence, as has happened on occasion.

Certainly, the group was thrilled to see Pacino standing on tiptoe to kiss the cheek of his girlfriend, who was wearing a black miniskirt and granny glasses and briskly drumming her fingers on various surfaces. But when asked, some guests quietly conceded that they didn't really understand the movie at all. Were the men supposed to be gay? Why did they beat up the actor? What was the message?

In a question-and-answer session following the screening, Pacino looked out over the blanched faces in the audience and commented, "This reminds me of a man outside a movie theater who saw an audience coming out of *Scarface* and said, 'What did you do to these people?'"

One man asked Pacino why he has bothered with his exercise in terror when he had done something so similar at the start of his career, in *The Indian Wants the Bronx*. (Pacino won an Obie Award in 1968 for the Off-Broadway play in which two toughs beat up an East Indian on a Bronx street corner.)

"Naturally, it has the violence, but I think it's saying something different," he replied.

Another man in the audience raised his hand: "Wasn't Heathcote Williams married to Twiggy?"

Pacino, very artsy in a blue jacket, with a scarf around his neck, seemed a bit fatigued at the nature of the questions.

"No," Pacino said. "He was involved with Jean Shrimpton."

When you spend some time with him, you understand what a

good match Pacino and Keaton must have been. He is much more like Woody Allen than Michael Corleone. Ellen Barkin notes with affection that "Al is not the most optimistic person in the world." And Michelle Pfeiffer does a wonderful imitation of Pacino whining about how burned-out he is: "'Oh, I'm so tired, I can't possibly do another movie. Oh, I'm so old.' He's kvetching all the time, when really he has boundless energy."

Pacino is talking to Tri-Star Pictures about financing a theater space downtown, but the project its all very fuzzy and even his partner, Michael Hadge, laments that "no one understands what we're doing." And there has been some talk of a movie about the life of the artist Modigliani. But it's no surprise when, one night, Pacino begins moaning gently about how tired he is and maybe he needs a change and maybe he should move to Paris or London for a year and maybe he should just chuck acting and retire.

"I keep envisioning myself sitting around the duomo, sipping anisette and watching the girls and having a great life not acting," he says with moody grandeur.

No one believes him of course. Because he is a man addicted to the high wire and the process of acting and the sound of words.

"Did you hear what I sad about the duomo?" he asks a little while later.

Sure, Al.

BONDING WITH DANIEL CRAIG

—SEPTEMBER 5, 2013/SEPTEMBER 6, 2013

James Bond is slipping into a room at the louche Bowery Hotel. Naturally, I follow.

When I knock, he opens the door.

"Are you lurking out there?" Daniel Craig asks, looking at me with ice-blue eyes.

Those eyes are now as famous as those of Paul Newman—who played his father in the Irish gangster yarn "Road to Perdition"—but they're very different. Newman's were a warmer, cerulean blue, with a guarded expression. Mr. Craig's are openly appraising:

What do you want? What is he willing to give?

I've come to interview him about "Betrayal," the Harold Pinter play directed by Mike Nichols in which Mr. Craig and Rachel Weisz will reprise their real-life roles as husband and wife—except with more sadism and pauses.

Will audiences be able to wrap their heads around James Bond as a cuckold?

"I hope they won't be able to," Mr. Craig says, appearing delighted at the thought. "I hope they'll get unnerved by it."

The 45-year-old Mr. Craig is notoriously private about his romance with the 43-year-old Ms. Weisz: They wouldn't be interviewed as a pair; when I talk to them and their fellow Briton and co-star, Rafe Spall, they avoid sitting next to each other; when the photos are taken, Mr. Craig chafes at looking too lovey-dovey.

"Someone called us a power couple the other day," he marvels. "I was like, what the"—he drops in an expletive—"does that mean? We just keep ourselves to ourselves."

The two fell in love in 2010 while making the movie "Dream House," which was, like "Betrayal," a domestic horror story. The movie sank, but they sparked. Bond put the gold on her finger quietly two years ago in New York after they disentangled themselves from long relationships with others. Mr. Craig was engaged to the producer Satsuki Mitchell; Ms. Weisz had lived for nine years with the director Darren Aronofsky, with whom she now shares custody of their 7-year-old son, Henry.

The newlyweds settled in the East Village and put a "Do Not Disturb" sign on the relationship. But then they decided to star in a revival of "Betrayal" on Broadway, where previews begin on Oct. 1.

So now they're stuck answering questions about why they chose to play an unhappy husband and wife if it makes them unhappy to talk about being a husband and wife.

"It's a play about" sex, Mr. Nichols says, instead using a vulgarity, "with two sexy stars."

Mr. Nichols recalls working with the newlywed Richard Burton and Elizabeth Taylor in 1966 on the first movie he directed, "Who's Afraid of Virginia Woolf?" They were a "giant worldwide circus," he says fondly, with "absolute freedom about using their relationship in the work."

"This is the reverse," he says of Mr. Craig and Ms. Weisz. "They are completely private. What they have in common is a kind of grace, an adroitness with people. It's very rare."

Mr. Nichols, who won the Tony for best director last year for "Death of a Salesman," was friends with Pinter; he courted Mr. Craig, who describes himself as "a Pinter virgin," for two years. The director had been taken by gritty performances Mr. Craig had given in British indies like "Love Is the Devil," as a small-time crook who's the lover of the artist Francis Bacon, and "Mother," about a cocaine-snorting construction worker who reawakens passion in the widowed mother of his girlfriend.

In 2009, Mr. Craig proved that joining another star on Broadway could generate record ticket sales—even if they had merely recited "the alphabet in counterpoint," as Ben Brantley put it in The New York Times—when he and Hugh Jackman starred as Chicago policemen in Keith Huff's melodrama "A Steady Rain."

Written with a reverse chronology, "Betrayal" begins with the end of an affair between Emma and Jerry, a book agent who is also the best friend of Robert, Emma's husband. Mr. Nichols initially talked to Mr. Craig about playing Jerry. But the actor decided he wanted the smaller but more potent role of Robert, and his wife wanted to come along to play Emma.

"It seemed like an obvious thing to do; if it feels stunt-y, it wasn't," Mr. Craig says. They had been looking for a play to do together for some time, he said, adding that they met 20 years ago doing a workshop at the National Studio Theater in London.

In our interview, I had been prepared for Pinteresque silences and indirection; Mr. Craig has been known to play the sulky brute with interrogators. But instead, he's funny, smart, charming and, for him, remarkably open. He even seems a bit shy, admitting he's afraid of extemporaneous public speaking because, he says, "I lose verbs."

The residue of smoke in the room puts the occasional smoker in a good mood. He's dressed in jeans and a polo shirt, with tattoos peaking beneath the sleeves, and sporting a salt-and-pepper beard he's grown for the part.

Did the personal nature of the play give the press-averse actor pause, so to speak?

"Maybe it's a contradiction," he says. "I suppose the idea that we're sort of exposing ourselves, you do that anyway onstage. We're not exposing our marriage onstage." They have only one scene by themselves, midway through. When Emma confesses the affair, Robert says he likes Jerry better than Emma and suggests perhaps Robert and Jerry should have had the affair.

Asked about Pinter's dictum that the two male friends not be played homoerotically, Mr. Craig deadpans: "Well, he's dead now, so he can't stop this. I can't tell you how much homoeroticism we're going to squeeze into this play."

There was no romance back when "the world's hottest couple," as

British tabloids call them, met in 1994. Mr. Craig was the son of a pub landlord and an art teacher, raised near Liverpool, who dropped out of school at 16 to act. He was briefly married to the actress Fiona Loudon, a union that produced Ella, now 20, one of the few guests at his upstate New York wedding to Ms. Weisz, the Cambridge-educated daughter of Jewish intellectuals from Austria and Hungary. In your 20s, Mr. Craig observes, it's hard to find love that offers "a kind of stability," and "it's very hard to make it stick, especially if you're an actor."

Does he recall a glimmer in 1994 when they acted in the steamy play "Les Grandes Horizontales," about a 19th-century Communard lolling about with four French courtesans, one of them played by Ms. Weisz?

"I'd rather not say," he replies. "But we're together, so maybe there's a clue in that."

(Later, Ms. Weisz offers a radiant yes, adding that because the cast members improvised the play, "we would have to literally spend the day trying to seduce him." She goes on, "It was really hard work, as you can imagine.")

I ask him if his marriage to Ms. Weisz has changed him. "Yeah, for the better," he says. "I'm far happier than I've been for many years. I think finding the right person and being with the right person is probably the answer to most things."

Can he envision himself in the position of Robert in the play, knowing his wife was having an affair with his best friend and allowing it to continue without confronting the friend?

"I don't think so, no," he says. "It's that weird thing, like Roger Vadim having all his ex-wives round for dinner, that kind of thing of going, 'Oh, I can deal with everything.' I'm not carved out of that cloth. I'm too working class, or middle class. I think when a marriage is that broken, you need to walk away."

Mr. Craig and Ms. Weisz, who also have a house in upstate New York, are moving into their own place in the East Village after renting there; he's been busy unpacking his books, including poetry collections by E. E. Cummings and Ted Hughes. (He played Hughes in the movie "Sylvia," and notes that a bathroom at Cambridge bears the scrawl "Sylvia Plath, psychopath.")

In the "Stars are just like us" category, they loved watching their fellow Briton John Oliver host "The Daily Show." They went to see John Waters's one-man Christmas comedy show in Poughkeepsie. Ms. Weisz confides that her husband is a great cook of classic bistro food who is finicky about doing his own shopping. Mr. Craig reveals that, while they ordinarily like to keep it very simple, they occasionally spoil themselves with luxury trips.

As for bonding in an industry swirling with insecurity and narcissism, he knows there are pitfalls. "But I don't see them," he says. "There will be problems, and they'll be no bigger or less. We'll have to figure it out like any other married couple, to the benefit of both of us, not just one."

Would he and Ms. Weisz ever want to do a Jennifer Aniston–style comedy?

"Does it have to be a Jennifer Aniston comedy?" he asks mordantly.

Later, over a pot of green tea at a Moroccan restaurant in the East Village, Ms. Weisz says she prefers something darker for them to bat around. "I'd love to do, in a decade, 'Who's Afraid of Virginia Woolf?'"

Like her husband, Ms. Weisz is funny and self-effacing, casually ravishing in a 10-year-old Narciso Rodriguez emerald dress. I note that the inspiration for Emma, Joan Bakewell—who seemed to regard her seven-year affair with Pinter as more fun than tragic—was a Cambridge graduate called "the thinking man's crumpet."

"In England, a lot of people get called that," Ms. Weisz says, smiling. "Helen Mirren is called that. I myself have been called that."

She says she doesn't find it sad, as someone who seems madly in love, to be in a play that's mad at love, with a structure that underscores that passion wanes even as it blooms. "Happiness writes white, someone told me that," she says, adding that drama needs edge.

I ask how marriage has changed her. She hesitates a bit, saying it's made her happier and a better person and mom. But she keeps gnawing on the question, musing that she never thought her life was heading toward marriage, noting softly (and incredibly), "It's not like there were that many people asking."

"It's a contract, marriage," she says finally. "There's something very certain about the word 'husband.' There are infinite ways to interpret Emma. But husband is husband."

And with her luminous smile, she concludes about marriage, "I love it."

In London, Ms. Weisz broke through in 1994 playing a "chubbier," as she describes it, Gilda in Noel Coward's "Design for Living," and in 2009 she was Blanche in "A Streetcar Named Desire." She sees Emma as honorable, as Antonia Fraser put it, and Mr. Craig notes that Emma, possibly because Pinter wrote "Betrayal" soon after moving in with Ms. Fraser, was one of his first positive female characters.

But Emma is still a Pinter woman, a dangerous Eve who disrupts the male Eden of camaraderie. When I ask Ms. Weisz if Pinter wrote so many sexually rapacious and manipulative female characters because he was scared of women, she laughs and says:

"He was right to be. We're a scary lot."

Her dark, sensual looks and easy empathy will be a change for her character, often played by cool, unreadable blondes. "She is the sort you have to have when you see her."

It's funny how our emblems of cool can be so unsure underneath.

Steve McQueen was a mass of insecurities, even refusing to hang his wardrobe next to that of a taller co-star. Paul Newman fretted that Marlon Brando was so brilliant, he made other actors pale by comparison. Kirk Douglas, Spartacus, no less, wrote recently in The Huffington Post about auditioning with Mae West to be a strongman for her stage show and being rejected after she took just one look at him.

Even Craig, who plays the classic symbol of cool, James Bond, has had moments of feeling shaken and stirred.

"Look, I was scared" silly "when I started doing it," he recalled, using a coarser word than silly, which befits the man who made Bond, as A. O. Scott of The New York Times wrote, "rougher and more soulful."

Mr. Craig said he was on the set of "Casino Royale" in the Bahamas, just starting to relax in his new role, when he got a call from his representatives, warning, "There may be trouble." There was a press backlash and a grass-roots campaign in Britain to boycott the movie by those who deemed him James Bland: not tall, dark and handsome enough.

There were even breathless—and false—rumors that he didn't know how to drive the Aston Martin stick shift.

"And that's the first time I experienced the Internet," he said. "And did that thing, sort of stayed up all night, going, 'Oh my God.'"

"There's nothing to prepare you," he said. "You can't win—that was a lesson in itself, how much of that you can fight."

The belittling digerati, blazing fame and "paps," as he calls the paparazzi, were a tough adjustment for someone who had mostly played character roles, reflecting what John Naughton, writing for British GQ, called "glamorous gloom."

"There's a weird thing, there's no one really to turn to," Mr. Craig said. First, "your pride kicks in, and you go, 'I can handle this.'" Then, he decided he needed some advice but wasn't sure whom to ask. "I didn't hang around with movie stars or famous people, so I couldn't get someone on the phone and go, 'What's going on?'" he said. "And the times I'd meet people and either be drunk enough or get the courage enough to go, 'What the [expletive] is this about, because I have no idea what's going on in my life? I'm paranoid, I'm looking behind curtains, because I think people are following me.'

"And they'd just look at you with a wry smile and say, 'Yep, well, that's what it is.' And it's like, really? You mean there isn't an answer?"

He gave up self-Googling after his all-nighter with the online craignotbond crowd. "I don't look at myself on the Internet," he says. "I'm so much happier."

So he hasn't seen the nicer chatter about how he and Rachel Weisz, his wife and co-star in "Betrayal," are "the world's hottest couple," as they've been described in the tabloids.

"I think there are far hotter couples out there than Rachel and I," he said, laughing, "not putting Rachel down in any way, shape or form."

Hollywood, in his view, sees the Internet as "the oracle," to its own detriment.

The Internet has been integral to the Arab spring, he said, but "it's not a particularly useful tool" for the film industry. "Certainly, when I grew up, what everybody else was thinking was not what I wanted to think," Mr. Craig said. "I mean, not that that made me cool, but that's how I thought cool people thought. Lou Reed didn't worry about what people were thinking on Twitter when Lou Reed was just the coolest human being around. Or David Bowie. They cared, but they cared in a way that was so ahead of the curve because they weren't interested in what people were thinking. And to now have this whole thing of being completely worried of what everybody's thinking. Even people who are not famous, they're worried about what their followers think, what their Facebook people think. It's just, you're chasing your tail. And the creativity, I think, just gets stifled.

"With studios—I may be completely wrong, and I don't care if I am—but so much credence is being given to what is being said by a relatively small group of people that studios keep on making huge mistakes. They think they're making a movie that's going to be hugely successful, and it's a failure. The movies that make it—and it's always been that way, and it always will be—are the good movies. Yes, good advertising and good publicity is always going to help. But if the movie's a dog, and I've been in a few, they don't work." (He used to hide "A Kid in King Arthur's Court" at Blockbuster.)

Mr. Craig thinks the fight against devices consuming your life "is a good fight to have, as far as I'm concerned."

"There's nothing technological allowed in the bedroom," he said. "If the iPad goes to bed, I mean, unless you're both watching porn on the Internet, it's a killer. We have a ban on it."

Mr. Craig says he thinks the era of "Betrayal"—about an affair and its aftermath that goes from 1968 to 1977 in reverse—was a sexier time, before the world was full of leering smartphone cameras and people staring at little screens, when they still had the "pip pip pips" talked about in the play: the coins dropping into a phone booth for a "crafty telephone call," as Harold Pinter wrote, from a pub or restaurant to make an excuse about coming home late.

All the constant updates now, calling and texting from the tarmac about when you'll be home, are not sexy, he believes, adding, "Just turn up when you turn up." Too much "extraneous" information, Mr. Craig said, is "putting us on edge all the time."

He imagines that adulterers like those in the play would get caught a lot faster these days: "If you're on the phone and making phone calls and popping up in the middle of dinner and kind of going, 'Oh, look, a text,' you're rubbing it in my face. If you're rubbing it in my face, maybe it's impossible for me, or us, to do this."

The man who plays a spy thinks it's a turnoff that average citizens are all turning into spies, awash in tracking and video technology.

"It's a complete anti-aphrodisiac," Mr. Craig said. "It's like we've had bromide put in our tea."

He credits the Broccoli family, producers of the 51-year-old Bond franchise, on its sixth 007 actor, with saving the character from becoming a Mike Myers lampoon and macho cliché, letting Bond evolve while keeping his essence. Mr. Craig considers the alternative: trying to keep Bond frozen in time, like that superannuated symbol of virility, the founder of "Playboy."

"Hugh Hefner still remains Hugh Hefner; Hefner's essence is a little bit tired," Mr. Craig said, cracking up. "It's probably by his bed."

Since the dazzling "Skyfall"—which earned $1.1 billion worldwide, making it the highest-grossing Bond film ever and the most profitable movie in British history—Mr. Craig is enjoying the role more. He, the director Sam Mendes (an ex-boyfriend of Ms. Weisz's) and one of the "Skyfall" screenwriters, John Logan, are all on board for the 24th Bond film, due out in the fall of 2015.

Mr. Craig hopes that, without returning to Pink Pantherville, they can start to instill a bit of the arch humor of Roger Moore, the first Bond he saw at the age of 7.

"We've got it all to play with, and we should play with it, and we should have some fun with it," he said.

He draws a distinction between acting and modeling (though he concedes that he does both as Bond). "There's a lot of modeling in films now," he said, adding wryly: "I do a movie where I have to turn around a lot. I want to kill myself sometimes, but sometimes you have to go, O.K., right, this is the moment when I have to turn around."

Mike Nichols was struck by Mr. Craig's co-starring role with Queen Elizabeth in Danny Boyle's opening show for the Olympics in 2012, because he was able to act as if Bond were the queen's equal.

"I'm probably a republican at heart," Mr. Craig said, grinning. "I probably want to abolish the monarchy deep down inside."

He called it "surreal" to be suddenly thrust into a scene with the queen in her chambers, adding: "She improvised. She sat down at the desk and said, 'Would you like me to pretend to be writing something?' Took out a piece of paper. Did some business. Completely got it."

Was she as good as Helen Mirren?

"Better," he said.

Maybe the queen could play M, I suggested, now that Judi Dench (who has played many queens) has been killed off.

He demurred, noting, "There's high maintenance, and there's high maintenance."

British reporters love to write about Mr. Craig, the highest-paid Bond ever, living in the "grimy" East Village, as The Daily Mail put it, amid the tattoo parlors and head shops.

"I know where to get two hash pipes for the price of one—I can always get a deal," he said dryly, adding that the allure of the neighborhood isn't in case he needs an emergency tattoo.

When he gets his tattoos, he said, he likes going alone, going through the pain of having it, and then having something indelible that's "not for anybody else" emblazoned on his body. "If it is for somebody else," he said, "that's where you make the mistake." (Ms. Weisz said she also has a tattoo, a small ladder, on her hip, a reminder of an award-winning play she wrote and starred in at Cambridge.)

Mr. Craig is more like Bond than like Pinter when it comes to male friends. "I don't have a whole host of friends," he said. "I don't have a gang of guys who are friends. I have two or three very close friends, all of whom are male," he said. "They're all kind of scattered all over the globe."

How does Ms. Weisz, a feminist who helped found a fringe theater group while at Cambridge, feel about being christened "Bond's babe" and Mrs. James Bond? No one calls Mr. Craig Mr. Hester Collyer (the character she played so dazzlingly in Terence Rattigan's "The Deep Blue Sea").

"Because you and three other people saw it," she said, laughing.

Ms. Weisz said it's important to remember that she knew Mr. Craig pre-Bond.

"I don't see him in that way," she said. "I grew up in England, watching him work. I saw him as a fellow actor. I love him, he's my husband. I think of him as a great, a really great, actor."

She said there is nothing (yet) to rumors that she might play a Bond villainess. She once toyed, for professional reasons, with changing her name to how it's pronounced, to Vice or Vyce, which sounds like a perfect Bond babe name. "Yes," she agreed. "But Rachel's too Old Testament. Maybe Roxy. I love that name. Roxy Vice."

I asked Mr. Craig if he had any workout tips from his Bond training, which has been written up in the press as entailing seven hours a day with three trainers.

"None of that is true, no," Mr. Craig scoffed. "I train as little as I possibly can."

Referring to Mr. Craig's tight inner circle, Ms. Weisz said playfully to her husband, "There are things people have to get through before they can be your friend."

Feats of strength, I wondered?

"Yeah," Mr. Craig said, laughing. "You have to lift 150 pounds above your head. It's your challenge."

EDDIE MURPHY: HE'S NEVER BEEN HAPPIER, OR MORE GLUM

—JUNE 28, 1992

LOS ANGELES—Eddie Murphy glides in, looking like he wants to slug someone. Black wraparound sunglasses. Black jeans and black T-shirt with a picture of Sarah Vaughan. Black cap emblazoned with the word "Yeah," the name of a song he wrote for his latest album. A small gold hoop in his left ear.

With "Boomerang," his new romantic comedy about a playboy who gets his comeuppance, the 31-year-old actor hopes to change his fortunes. His goal is to climb out of a professional slough and graduate from playing the street kid in male buddy movies to portraying more sophisticated leading men. He also hopes to put some salve on a reputation rubbed raw by reports of lateness, ego trips, materialism and an Elvis-style entourage.

"The perception that people have of me as Eddie with the leather suit on and chicks and the bodyguards and all that stuff, that's something from a nine-year-old image," says Mr. Murphy, sipping a Dr. Brown's black cherry soda during an interview in a suite at the Four Seasons Hotel. The actor is soft-spoken and low-key amid Paramount Pictures' full-court press for "Boomerang," which opens Wednesday.

"That's from back when I did 'Raw' and 'Delirious,'" the actor continues. "I haven't been that guy in almost 10 years, and people still think of me as that image."

Asked about Paramount's hope that "Boomerang" will give him a "Cary Grant image," Mr. Murphy seems pleased by the notion: "Cary Grant is bad, you know, so I guess that's flattering to be compared to a cat as cool as Cary Grant.

"I'm not saying that I won't do a mindless comedy again," he says. "I still think that kind of stuff is cool. But when you get older, your tastes change. I wanted to do something where it wasn't just a cat jumping over a car, talking real fast and laughing."

The question about Mr. Murphy's career now is whether the rascally persona that won him stardom is being submerged in the effort to re-make his image. Part of the problem is that his comic talent depends on an edge of hostility that risks crossing the line into unpleasantness.

There is not much evidence—either in person or in "Boomerang"—of the brash style and breakaway grin that turned Mr. Murphy into "Mr. Box Office," as Newsweek called him in a 1985 cover story. He had dazzled audiences in the early 80's on "Saturday Night Live" as a grouchy Gumby and the procurer Velvet Jones hawking his book, "I Wanna Be a Ho," and in blockbuster movies such as "Beverly Hills Cop," "48 Hours" and "Trading Places."

Wanting to star in a romance, Mr. Murphy conceived the idea for "Boomerang," in which he plays Marcus Graham, a Manhattan market-ing executive and a rake who falls in love with his boss (Robin Givens) and gets a dose of his own medicine.

"It's a movie about how a dog becomes a man," says Reginald Hudlin, the director. "It's personal for Eddie in the same way that 'Annie Hall' was for Woody Allen."

Reginald and his producer brother, Warrington, the hot black film makers who made the 1990 hit "House Party," say they studied classic screwball comedies such as "Adam's Rib" and "His Girl Friday" before embarking on this movie, which also features Halle Berry, Eartha Kitt, Grace Jones and David Alan Grier.

Mr. Murphy, who has been chided by friends like Spike Lee for not using his studio clout to help blacks more, joined with the Hudlin brothers to help get Paramount to agree to help train 10 young black filmmakers on the set of "Boomerang."

Most of the cast members of "Boomerang"—and even the extras—are black, and some of the humor has an angry edge. A supercilious white salesman at a chic men's store tries to shoo Eddie Murphy out by telling him, "We don't have layaway, and we don't keep cash in the store." Later, Ms. Berry says something to her date in a foreign tongue, then explains that it is Korean for: "I'm sorry I shot you, but I thought you were robbing my store."

All in all, the star says he has never been happier. On his left wrist, he wears a gold charm bracelet with small locks and keys—"To my heart," he says. There are an "N" charm and a "B" charm on the bracelet, given to him at Christmas by Nicole Mitchell, a 24-year-old model who is the mother of his 2-year-old daughter, Bria.

In November, the couple are expecting a son, whom Mr. Murphy plans to name after Miles Davis. Although Mr. Murphy and Ms. Mitchell were engaged at Christmas, he is coy about a possible marriage.

Mr. Murphy wears totems of his success (a ring studded with diamonds) and his spirituality (a large rose quartz heart that dangles at waist level). Still, behind his sunglasses he seems guarded.

Asked about Dan Quayle's recent attacks on Hollywood morality, the star seems unsure about what the Vice President said.

Mr. Murphy says he has never registered to vote because "white, powerful, rich men rule the world" and "you don't know who counts the votes." It was, he says, merely a matter of whose foot was on your back. "What size are Ross Perot's feet?" he asks. "I know George Bush is wearing some size 13 triple E, the way it feels."

UNEASY LIES THE HEAD FIRING BACK AT THE CRITICS

Mr. Murphy's critics have suggested that the actor, a great admirer of Elvis Presley who has enshrined photographs of "the King" at his home in Englewood, N.J., has become isolated behind a cordon of cronies, just as Presley did.

The star mocks the comparison: "They'll see me with people, and then they go, 'He's an Elvis Presley fan. Ahhhh, he likes Elvis. He thinks he's Elvis. HE THINKS HE'S ELVIS! That's what it is. He's paranoid like Elvis. That's why he has all those people around him. He's going crazy.' That's their trip."

Mr. Murphy also says he detects an element of racism in the way he is perceived, suggesting that sometimes white people would judge five black men to be a gang or "entourage," whereas five white men would just be a dinner party.

"I walk into a room with my cousin and my brother and Ken Frith, a guy I went to school with, and one security person," he says. "That's five cats, O.K.? But it's me and my friends, and we're walking into Spago's or Morton's or any of these trendy white restaurants. You tell me where I got the reputation that I have a bunch of bodyguards. I'm not lying— there's a bodyguard there—but the rest of the people are relatives or my buddies.

"They call my friends and relatives my 'entourage' and my 'hangers on,' and I get upset because I think, wait a second, I'm doing what any successful person would do. If I got successful because I owned a plumbing company, and I had all my friends and relatives working with me, nobody would be tripping on it."

The last few years have been difficult for Mr. Murphy, the son of a New York City policeman who became very rich, very fast, very young. The reception for his two most recent movies, "Harlem Nights" (1989) and "Another 48 Hours" (1990), was tepid. Reviewing "Harlem Nights," which Mr. Murphy produced, directed, wrote and starred in, The Los Angeles Times suggested: "Like many superstars, Eddie Murphy may have gotten so tangled up in the myths and myopia of high-power movie making that he can't get back to the gritty, pungent, kick-in-the-throat awareness earlier audiences loved."

Mr. Murphy concedes that he did both movies "for the wrong reasons" and lost his focus. "All my peers started doing movies where they were directing and producing and starring," he says of "Harlem Nights." "So I said, let me see what it's like. And I didn't dig it and I hated doing it throughout the whole trip, and it affected my performance."

ON PARAMOUNT EQUAL PAY FOR EQUAL BOX OFFICE?

Mr. Murphy, whose nickname in Hollywood is Money, was reportedly upset at Paramount, where he has been under contract, for not giving him more grown-up roles and for not paying him as much as Arnold Schwarzenegger and Sylvester Stallone, who can command up to $20 million a picture.

"If my movies are performing like this person's movies, or better than that person's movies, I want to be compensated the same way they are," he says. Mr. Murphy reportedly has a new deal with Paramount that will allow him to earn at least $12 million for each film.

The star was also hurt by Art Buchwald's successful suit claiming that Paramount had stolen his idea for "Coming to America," the story of an African prince who searches New York for a wife. The splashy trial revealed financial arrangements that stars usually manage to keep private.

The Wall Street Journal reported that Paramount paid "the year-round salaries of the 50-plus employees of Murphy's movie and television companies," and, for "Coming to America," "spent an additional $600,000 or so on the salaries and living expenses of a half-dozen relatives and cronies, a valet, a personal trainer, a 24-hour limousine and driver and a luxury motor home and driver for Murphy, not to mention such sundry items as a $235.33 tab at McDonald's."

Mr. Murphy continues to maintain that the story for "Coming to America" was his own idea. "The court made a ruling that someone told me the story, and that influenced my subconscious to write it," he says. "But when you get off into my subconscious being influenced, that's in a weird area. There are nine other people who say they wrote it, too, but Buchwald's the intellectual, the writer and the journalist, so he can't possibly be wrong."

Mr. Murphy has said he was the "whipping boy" for a movie industry where he is far from the only person who likes cars, clothes and women. He sees a racial angle to the trial.

"I think they wanted to open up my whole life anyway," he says. "I was this odd nigger they didn't know anything about, so let's open up the nigger's books and see what he makes. I knew that's what it was, so I didn't trip on it."

'BOOMERANG' BETTER LATE THAN NEVER?

There has been bad press about the making of "Boomerang." Variety has reported that Mr. Murphy was self-indulgent and constantly late. Warrington Hudlin defends his star, saying, "We'd rather have a comic genius like Eddie Murphy late than another actor on time."

Mr. Murphy's defenders say he was overscheduled because he was also recording an album called "Love's Alright," to be released by Motown, with such guest vocalists as Michael Jackson, Hammer and Bon Jovi, and was involved in production meetings for the movie he is now making, a Disney film about a con man turned Congressman, called "The Distinguished Gentleman."

And the Hudlins suggest that the bad publicity about Mr. Murphy may have been spread by other studios with their own pictures coming out this summer and possibly by white studio executives threatened by a movie that represents so much black clout. They also contend that what is seen as a charming eccentricity in a white may be perceived as a character flaw in a black.

"In the 60's, a lot of Congressmen behaved in certain ways, but Adam Clayton Powell was the one they wanted to censure," says Warrington Hudlin. "Take some stars like Tom Cruise, Harrison Ford and Arnold Schwarzenegger, and then take Eddie Murphy and put them side by side on the subject of how many people they have for security and other things."

Brian Grazer, another producer of "Boomerang" who is white, disagrees. "I don't think there's a white conspiracy to hurt Eddie—that's completely false," he says. "Harrison Ford does not have five family members and bodyguards around him. He drives himself to work. Steve Martin rode a bike to the set."

But Mr. Grazer also defends Mr. Murphy. "A lot of famous actors get there right on time and struggle through the performance, eating up an entire half day. Eddie might show up two hours late, but he contributes to rewriting the script and does brilliant things."

For his part, Mr. Murphy sees it this way: "Every time they write that I'm late, they should also write that my movies have made $2 billion."

ON WOMEN: FROM HEARTBREAK TO PANCAKES

While the Hudlins suggest that "Boomerang" traces Mr. Murphy's personal progress toward maturity in his relationships with women, it is hard to imagine that he has received similar demeaning treatment at the hands of a woman.

Indeed, Mr. Murphy has shown he can play rough in the romance department, according to a new book, "Fatal Subtraction: How Hollywood Really Does Business," by Pierce O'Donnell, Art Buchwald's attorney, and Dennis McDougal, a Los Angeles Times reporter.

The book reports that during his bitter breakup with Lisa Figueroa, a college student, Mr. Murphy switched her pleading message from his answering machine to his answer tape so callers were greeted with her cries: "Please, Eddie! Please! I love you, Eddie! Take me back!"

But Mr. Murphy says that Ms. Figueroa broke his heart and that he knows about such things. "I've had girls dis me, I'm telling you; it's true. Maybe not as much as the next cat. But I haven't always been famous, you know. I've been obsessed with a chick who was immune to my dimples and lips," he says, finally emitting his braying laugh.

He seems amused at the idea that a lot of women will be happy to see him squirm, even cinematically, in "Boomerang." "This is the first time that I've done a movie where I think women get the upper hand, which is cool because it's probably something that a lot of women will respond to because probably chicks have been going to the movies, saying, 'When is this cat going to do a movie that I can really dig?' There's a scene in the movie where Halle slaps me, and the audience cheers like, somebody finally slapped him for all those years."

The star, who once said he could never get married or live with anyone because his credo with women was "my way or the highway," now says he wants to get married. He seems less afraid that all women are gold diggers.

"But if I ever get married I will have a prenuptial agreement," he says. "I'm not, like, a lunatic."

Although in the past Mr. Murphy has said all he wants is a woman who will cook him breakfast, now he says he is willing to return the favor.

"Even if you're a successful man with millions of dollars, if I'm in love with somebody and she's laying in the bed and don't feel like getting up, I'd get up and cook. There's nothing punkish about that; you're still macho. I can cook some crazy, fluffy scrambled eggs, and pancakes that look like off the box. Yes, I will."

WARREN BEATTY IN LOVE, ON STAGE AND OFF

—DECEMBER 8, 1991

LOS ANGELES—Warren Beatty is tooling through the Beverly Hills night, looking the picture of Hollywood cool with his brown leather jacket and his black Mercedes convertible and his car phone on the dash.

He stops at a large, dramatic-looking white house at 810 Linden Street. "This was the house Virginia Hill rented, the one where Bugsy Siegel was killed," he says. "Every time I drove past here while we were making the movie, my car phone would go out."

Mr. Beatty is not the mystical type, collecting crystals and claiming past lives, like his older sister, the New Age guru Shirley MacLaine. But his third obsession, after women and movies, is the telephone, so any disconnection, no matter how temporary, is a serious matter.

Mr. Beatty has moved from one of America's most famous fictional detectives in last year's "Dick Tracy," to one of America's most famous real-life gangsters in his new movie, "Bugsy," which opens on Friday.

And he has moved from Madonna, his leading lady in "Dick Tracy," to Annette Bening, his leading lady in "Bugsy." Ms. Bening and Mr. Beatty, who live together in what looks to be genuine domestic bliss at his starkly elegant home high on Mulholland Drive, are expecting their first baby, a girl, this winter. Though they are both ordinarily guarded about personal matters, they talked with some candor and humor about their highly publicized union.

Just to clear this up quickly, Mr. Beatty denies gossip items that he built a birthing tank and fainted while watching birthing instruction videos with his pal, Jack Nicholson, who is expecting his second late-in-life baby with his girlfriend Rebecca Broussard. Neither is he planning, as the tabloids have suggested, to name his daughter Warnell, after himself.

"War-nell, War-nel-la," he says, rolling the syllables around on his tongue. "No, that I can assure you."

There is talk in Hollywood that people are sick of gangster movies. And Mr. Beatty, a co-producer of "Bugsy," and Barry Levinson, the director, have been upset that the studio, Tri-Star, has been devoting more time and money to promoting another of its Christmas releases, "Hook," the Steven Spielberg extravaganza about a grown-up Peter Pan, which opens about the same time.

But Mr. Beatty believes that if you tell a good story, they will come, and he is excited about "Bugsy," calling his character "a good outlaw hero for the 90's." The stylish, fast-paced film, set in the gold-lamé glamour of 40's Hollywood, focuses on the volatile relationship between Benjamin Siegel—who founded modern Las Vegas and punched out anyone who called him Bugsy—and his girlfriend, Virginia Hill, a starlet and mob moll with a penchant for throwing glass objects when she was mad.

In "Bugsy," Hill tells Siegel: "All we're going to do is give each other misery and torment because we both want whatever we want whenever we want it and we both want everything."

Mr. Beatty describes the affair with similar 40's patter: "His passion and his obsession with Virginia Hill had a lot to do with the fact that he didn't have to pretend for her, that she knew his milieu. She had known gangsters, and she knew who he was. He knew that she knew. He knew who she was, and she knew that he knew. And they fell in love."

Comparing her last bad girl, Myra in "The Grifters," a role for which she won an Academy Award nomination, with this bad girl, Ms. Bening says: "Myra is a woman who doesn't have many resources. She has an emotional hungriness for men. Virginia is a wild, promiscuous, good-time girl, but she's self-sufficient. She falls in love with Ben and experiences what a lot of us experience: being very vulnerable."

Except for a couple of early erotic scenes, the off-screen lovers get to do more sparring than smooching on screen. The affair between Hill and Siegel was soured by the gangster's obsessive jealousy about Gene Krupa, bullfighters, wise guys, Latin entertainers and assorted other former Hill boyfriends.

Ms. Bening says that while she has "certainly touched on it and felt feelings of jealousy, I haven't experienced it in the wild, crazy way that Ben and Virginia do."

Mr. Beatty is asked if, in the course of his many romances, he has ever felt such obsessive jealousy. "I wouldn't tell you if I had," he says. "Orson Welles said a great thing to me once: 'Jealousy is the seasickness of emotions. You think you're going to die, and everyone else thinks it's funny.'"

Ms. Bening notes that, while they are not Lunt and Fontaine, she thinks their real relationship spices up their celluloid one. "It's hard to be objective, but, yeah, there's this great chemistry there," she says. "There's something going on."

Mr. Beatty, who commissioned a script on Bugsy Siegel from James Toback seven years ago, was drawn to the character because he was not a cardboard gangster. Mr. Toback says the character taps into dark feelings that Mr. Beatty has held in check in his own life.

"It's revolutionary for Warren," Mr. Toback says. "In 'Bugsy,' he shows sexual frenzy, homicidal violence and overall psychopathy encased in a very stylized, elegant veneer."

Sent by the mob to Los Angeles to seize control of the West Coast rackets, Siegel hung out at Ciro's and made friends with Gary Cooper, Cary Grant (who reportedly based his portrayal of "Mr. Lucky" on Siegel) and George Raft (played in the movie by Joe Mantegna). He even made a screen test of himself.

Was it a stretch, Mr. Beatty is asked, to play a character who is vain, glamorous, promiscuous and a perfectionist?

"You're speaking, of course, of Dick Tracy," he says, laughing. After a pause, he adds: "I've had my moments."

The reports of Mr. Beatty's charm are not greatly exaggerated. He is considerate, pulls out chairs, fetches sodas and expresses more interest in others than in himself. He is discreet and says nice things about people who have said barbed things about him. In "Truth or Dare," the documentary about Madonna, the singer mocked Mr. Beatty about his preference for flattering lighting, and, in interviews on a Friday night at his production office and home, he did seem to like dim lamps, candlelight and firelight, using a small flashlight if he needed to read something at the dinner table.

Mr. Beatty, who got in his own dig about Madonna in "Truth or Dare"—"She doesn't want to live off camera, much less talk"—says he hasn't seen the movie. "I want to see it," he said not very convincingly.

The dashing Siegel was also concerned with his appearance, but he was not a nice guy. He killed strangers and friends and once plotted to assassinate Mussolini. In one harrowing scene, Mr. Beatty's Siegel humiliates a wise guy who skimmed money by making him crawl and bark like a dog and oink like a pig.

With money-driven Hollywood swept up in the cachet of Kevin Costner's politically correct films and movies aimed to appeal to the younger set, Mr. Beatty knows he is going against the grain, playing a sympathetic psychopath.

"Politically correct never interested me," he says simply. He is interested in character, not moralizing. "Gangsters and outlaws do provide, very often, very dramatic plots."

Mr. Beatty was drawn to the humorous aspects of Siegel's persona, even though he knows that some will be concerned about the blend of comedy and violence.

"They beat the hell out of us on 'Bonnie and Clyde,' because we did something not permitted so often and not so easy to do," he says. "I think we've done it again with this. These guys can be funny. Bonnie and Clyde were funny, and I think Bugsy Siegel and Virginia Hill were hilarious."

Mr. Beatty gets mileage out of Siegel's primping. A fastidious dresser, with monogrammed Sulka shirts and manicures, Mr. Beatty's Bugsy works constantly to improve his appearance and practices his elocution by repeating the phrase: "Twenty dwarves took turns doing handstands on the carpet." He is seen wearing goggles under the sun lamp and lying on a chaise longue at the health club with a hairnet, a face mask and cucumbers on his eyes.

While in jail on charges that he murdered one of his best friends, Siegel is concerned only that his newspaper picture might not accurately convey his deep tan.

At another point, he complains to a friend when a newspaper story has him "brandishing a .45" at one of Hill's dates in Ciro's. "It was a .30, not a .45, and I was not brandishing it. I was concealing it subtly to make a point."

Although some might not call the man who founded modern Las Vegas a visionary, Siegel fought with the intensity of a true romantic for his dream of a palmy oasis where people could get everything they fantasized about: sex, money, romance and adventure. He gave Virginia Hill a cut of the profits and named his casino after her: Her nickname was Flamingo, because of her long, thin legs.

"Bernie's always put women first, only this time it's one woman that's got him instead of the whole female race," his mentor, Meyer Lansky (played by Ben Kingsley), sadly tells the other mobsters. It is one of several lines in the movie that have a humorous echo with the star's real life. But though he is playing the father of Las Vegas, Mr. Beatty, a man interested in control, has never bet a nickel. "I got hot flashes once when I lost a Monopoly game," he says.

Ms. Bening says Mr. Beatty is like the title character in his intensity about his work, in his desire to push things to the limit of his imagination. She thinks "Reds," Mr. Beatty's epic movie about the early-20th-century Communist John Reed, was his Flamingo Hotel.

"I think they both have the ability to envision something and follow it through in a kind of crazy, passionate, tenacious way where they don't let anything stop them," she says. "Warren is an individual thinker. He doesn't follow the crowd, and I really like that about him."

Like Woody Allen, Mr. Beatty tends to make movies with women he is involved with, or get involved with women with whom he makes movies.

As he told Norman Mailer in the November issue of Vanity Fair, "After I got established in films, it sometimes seemed I had very little interest in making a movie until I was romantically motivated." In terms of artistic inspiration, he told Mr. Mailer, it would have been hard for him to make "Reds" without his love of that time, Diane Keaton, or "Heaven Can Wait" without his onetime girlfriend Julie Christie.

Sitting before the crackling fire in a house of curving unadorned white walls and glass panels overlooking the valleys and the ocean, Mr. Beatty muses that he has never produced a movie that did not have a romantic theme between a man and a woman—"Bonnie and Clyde," "Shampoo," "Heaven Can Wait," "Reds," "Dick Tracy" and "Bugsy."

He is asked how he felt about all the publicity dubbing it the end of an era—or as The Washington Post called it, "the watershed moment in the history of American civilization"—when he and Ms. Bening announced last July that they were expecting.

After all, Mr. Beatty has been a throwback to Erroll Flynn, one of the few Hollywood sex symbols who embraced the role off screen. His sister said he couldn't even commit to dinner, and Woody Allen said he'd like to be reincarnated as Warren Beatty's fingertips.

The actor smiles about all the end-of-an-era stories. "I would be lying to you if I didn't confess that I liked it," he says. "I also liked all the cartoons. One related it to the fall of Cuba. Nice to be noticed."

Told that one paper headlined his news "From Cad to Dad," he seems pleased and asks slyly, "What page was it on?"

Although he says his sister and mother were surprised and delighted— "My mother has been on an unmitigated high ever since"—he says the pregnancy was not out of line with his plans for his life.

"I do know something of what I've aspired to and tried to make room for in my life," he says. "So I was a little surprised at the surprise."

He says all the reports of his nervousness are "fabricated." Pointing in the direction of the bedroom to which Ms. Bening has long since retired, Mr. Beatty confides: "When I designed this house, I put a little room right off the master bedroom. That was designed for a baby." Mr. Beatty, who built his house 12 years ago, worries that this revelation will sound "corny."

But his feeling about fatherhood is, the 54-year-old bachelor observes, different. "There's no doubt about it," he says slowly. "It does, ummm, fill you with a kind of optimism that nothing else quite equals."

He says he first got to know Ms. Bening through her work in "Valmont" and "The Grifters," and he and Barry Levinson asked to meet with her to discuss the role of Virginia Hill.

"I knew immediately that she was a long-ball hitter, emotionally, intellectually and artistically—and by the way, physically, too—and it was hard to see where the limitations were," he says. "I thought I had some objectivity. Now, I'm just completely nonobjective about her. She's the Michael Jordan of actresses. She just has it."

Many of the others working on the film, including Mr. Levinson, say they never realized that Mr. Beatty and Ms. Bening had become involved during the shooting. "I simply thought they were working very, very well together," the director recalled. Mr. Toback says he heard some gossip during the second month of filming but discounted it until he saw the pair talking at midnight after a day's shooting on the lot and realized there were some "vibes" between them.

Mr. Beatty is asked how far into the film his feelings for Ms. Bening changed. "My feelings didn't really change," he said, with his soft, knowing laugh. "But the question is, when did my actions change? And that I won't tell you."

Told that some crew members said they had noticed a moment in the daily rushes when they felt that the two had become infatuated, Mr. Beatty laughs and replies: "Then they'd have had to be shooting rushes 15 seconds after I met her. Because my feelings never changed. I met her and I thought, 'Wo-o-o-o-o! Wait a minute.'"

Although Mr. Beatty is secretive about his private life—he once avoided interviews for 12 years—his on-screen, off-screen romances always seem to fuel the publicity for his films.

One writer noted that Mr. Beatty and his former girlfriend, Madonna, were "cozy in a prickly way." Mr. Beatty and Ms. Bening are cozy in a cozy way. Over a casual Friday night dinner of salad and a rice dish at his house, in a room with glass walls and a glass table, overlooking a small curved swimming pool, they are lightly affectionate and solicitous of each other, talking easily and engagingly about subjects ranging from Tennessee Williams to the birth of a friend's baby to the state of Democratic politics.

The 33-year-old actress, wearing no makeup, her light brown hair pulled back in a ponytail, and very pregnant in an oversized sweater and long, filmy skirt, bears little resemblance to the high-tempered, immoral vixens she has played on screen. She seems clean-cut and level-headed, more like a graduate student in drama school from Kansas—her native state.

In contrast to the tempestuous lovers they play on screen, their life seems serene and devoid of flying ashtrays. They had had lunch by the pool that day with Mr. Beatty's mother, who, he says, "is completely crazy about Annette."

The next day, in a phone conversation, Ms. Bening notes that it's wonderful, after several years of being absorbed in the creative passion of her work, to have a creative passion in her personal life as well.

"I always felt lost if I didn't feel connected to the heartbeat of some role," she says. "Now I've come to a time in my life when I have something else to focus on in a rich way.

"It's thrilling to share this great moment with him. It's something I've wanted to do since I was a little kid. I've always had a strong desire to have a family."

She says she does not worry about the next step—"I've already been married"—and that she does not worry about Mr. Beatty's reputation as a Lothario, reluctant to commit.

"I can't control that," she says. "It has nothing to do with us. I'm just very happy. It's certainly the most remarkable time of my life. We are not so unusual. We are just two people doing this together because we want to."

Asked if the "M" word is in their future, Mr. Beatty replies: "Annette and I are in complete agreement on the subject." Then he smiles. Enigmatically, naturally.

PART 3

Funny People

WHATEVER TINA FEY WANTS, TINA FEY GETS

—JANUARY 2009

Tina Fey has never dated a bad boy.

She didn't even let boys she dated do anything bad.

"I remember the biggest trouble I ever got into—" says her husband, Jeff Richmond, a short, puckish man of 48 in jeans and a T-shirt, cutting himself off mid-thought at the mere memory of Tina's wrath. "Oh, my God." (He calls himself "the Joe Biden of husbands" because he's prone to "drop the bomb" in interviews.)

Fey is sitting across from Richmond in their comfy, vintage-y Upper West Side apartment, where a lavender exercise ball lolls next to the flat-screen TV, a pink tricycle is parked under a black grand piano, and golden award statuettes abound. When I arrived, at 9:30 P.M., Fey had already put her three-year-old daughter, Alice, to bed and was tapping away on a silver Mac laptop at the kitchen counter on a script for *30 Rock*, her slyly hilarious NBC comedy about an NBC comedy. She'll return to the script when I leave, near midnight.

Fey shoots Richmond a warning look. It's undercut by the fact that she's wedged into her daughter's miniature red armchair, joking about squeezing her butt in and looking like Alice in Wonderland grown big in navy velour sweatpants and pink slippers.

The 38-year-old Fey sips a glass of white wine and eats some cheese and crackers—all her food-obsessed doppelgänger on *30 Rock*, Liz Lemon, longs to do is go home and eat a big block of cheese—while Richmond and I drink vodka martinis he has made.

"What are you gonna tell?" she teases her husband. "Think this through."

Richmond wades in. "When we were first dating," he says, harking back to Chicago in 1994, "some of the guys at Second City said, 'Hey, wouldn't it be a hoot if we go over—'"

"'—over to the Doll House,'" Fey finishes. "'We'll go to this strip club *ironically*:' I was like, 'The fuck you will.'"

Their conversation is woven with intimacy, the easy banter of a couple who knew each other long before fame hit. They fell in love quickly, soon after a Sunday afternoon spent together at Chicago's Museum of Science and Industry. ("We walked into a model of the human heart," Fey deadpans.) The writer-comedian and the musician-director dated for seven years, have been married for another seven, and have worked together in improv theater in Chicago, on *Saturday Night Live*, and on *30 Rock*. (He composed the bouncy retro theme music.) Richmond still reassures her, all these years later: "Nothing happened. We were there for like an hour. We ate chicken, really good pasta."

And Fey still recoils. "It didn't go great when you came back, did it? I was very angry. It was disrespectful."

I mention that in the pilot of *30 Rock* Liz Lemon puts on a Laura Bush–style pink suit from her show-within-a-show's wardrobe department to go to lunch with Tracy Jordan (Tracy Morgan), to try to sign him, and he takes her to a strip club in the Bronx, where she gets drunk and dances onstage with a stripper named Charisma.

"I love to play strippers and to imitate them," says Fey. "I love using that idea for comedy, but the idea of actually going there? I feel like we all need to be better than that. That industry needs to die, by all of us being a little bit better than that."

There's a reason her former *S.N.L.* pal Colin Quinn dubbed Tina Fey "Herman the German." She's a sprite with a Rommel battle plan.

Elizabeth Stamatina Fey started as a writer and performer with a bad short haircut in Chicago improv. Then she retreated backstage at *S.N.L.*, wore a ski hat, and gained weight writing sharp, funny jokes and eating junk food. Then she lost 30 pounds, fixed her hair, put on a pair of hot-teacher glasses, and made her name throwing lightning-bolt zingers on "Weekend Update." Speeding through the comedy galaxy, she wrote the hit *Mean Girls* and created her own show based on an *S.N.L.*-type show: *30 Rock*. The comedy struggled in the ratings for two years but was a critical success, winning seven Emmys last fall and catapulting Fey into red-hot territory. Before she even had a chance to take a breath, a freakish twist of fate turned her from red- to white-hot, and enabled her, at long last, to boost the ratings of *30 Rock*: Fey was a ringer for another hot-teacher-in-glasses, Sarah Palin, the comely but woefully unprepared Alaska governor, who bounded out of the woods with her own special language to become not only the first Republican woman to run on a national ticket but also God's gift to comedy and journalism. So where does Fey go from white-hot?

"Tina is not clay," says Lorne Michaels, the impresario of *Saturday Night Live*, *Mean Girls*, and *30 Rock*, when I ask him how he helped shape her career. Steve Higgins, an *S.N.L.* producer, observes, "When she got here she was kind of goofy-looking, but everyone had a crush on her because she was so funny and bitingly mean. How did she go from ugly duckling into swan? It's the Leni Riefenstahl in her. She has such a German work ethic even though she's half Greek. It's superhuman, the German thing of 'This will happen and I am going to make this happen.' It's just sheer force of will."

As it turns out, the 669-page autobiography of Leni Riefenstahl—chronicling her time as Hitler's favorite filmmaker and the creation of the propaganda movie *Triumph of the Will*—is one of Fey's favorite (cautionary) books. "If she hadn't been so brilliant at what she did, she wouldn't have been so evil," Fey says. "She was like, in the book, 'He was the leader of the country. Who was I not to go?' And it's like, Note to self: Think through the invite from the leader of your country."

Tina Fey speaks what she calls "less than first-grade" German and so does Liz Lemon of *30 Rock*, which Fey thinks is fun because German is "so uncool." (Lemon's cell-phone ring is the Wagnerian "Kill da Wabbit" from Bugs Bunny's *What's Opera, Doc?*) Fey is a rules girl—"I don't like assertions of status or line cutting"—and she's made Lemon one, too. Far from the John Belushi model—the only drug packets scattered around *S.N.L.* these days are Emergen-C—Fey drinks sparingly, is proud that she has never taken drugs, and calls her husband's ex-smoking habit "disgusting."

Her true vice is cupcakes. I've brought her a box, including one frosted with the face of Sarah Palin. She chooses that one, which is bigger, joking that it's O.K. if she gains weight before her Annie Leibovitz photo shoot in a few days, because "Annie's going to photograph my soul, right?" When it comes to her looks, she's both forgiving and self-deprecating. "The most I've changed pictures out of vanity was to edit around any shot where you can see my butt," she says. "I like to look goofy, but I also don't want to get canceled because of my big old butt." Frowning and rubbing the lines between her eyes, she adds that she might also tell the *30 Rock* postproduction team, "'Can you digitally take this out?' Because I don't have Botox or anything."

Fey's friend Kay Cannon, a *30 Rock* writer, says that Tina has remained self-deprecating even as she has glammed up. "She'll always see herself as that other, the thing she came from."

Rules are Tina's "Achilles' heel in some ways," Richmond says. "She's half German, half Greek. That is just like loosey-goosey-crazy, and then you get, 'Do the trains run on time?'" It is Fey's fierce clarity about rules that allows Richmond to feel secure now that he's suddenly in celebrity-magazine features with titles such as "I Married a Star" and is living with the woman the *New Yorker* staff writer Michael Specter calls "the sex symbol for every man who reads without moving his lips."

"I know how she feels about some things," Richmond tells me over coffee one day at an Italian place around the corner from his house. "Like, we never had to deal with any of this, but: adultery. Just looking at examples from other people's lives, we know that anything like that, messing around, is just such a complete 'No' to her. And she has her principles and she sticks to her principles more than anybody I've ever met in my life. Like that whole idea of, if you are in a relationship, there are deal breakers. There's not a lot of gray area in being flirty with somebody. She's very black-and-white: 'We're married—you can't.'" He calls their marriage "borderline boring—in a good way." And she concurs: "I don't enjoy any kind of danger or volatility. I don't have that kind of 'I love the bad guys' thing. No, no thank you. I like nice people."

Rip Torn, the wonderful 77-year-old actor who plays the C.E.O. of G.E. on *30 Rock*, told me he was "gazing admiringly" at Fey one day, and she said, "I'm married, you know. I love my husband and I have a child."

S.N.L.'s Amy Poehler has described Fey as "monastic," the type who sits on the side and watches everybody else belly-flop in the pool, and then writes about it.

During cocktails at her apartment, I ask Fey, What's the wildest thing you've ever done?

"Nothing," she replies blithely.

Did she ever use the Sarah Palin voice to entice her own First Dude?

No, she said, but once, when she did a voice-over for a pinball machine in Chicago, she used an Elly May Clampett voice. "These critters need some attention," she says in a soft southern drawl, giving her husband a sexy glance. She's as pitch-perfect channeling Elly May as she is channeling Palin. "And that was the only time Jeff has kind of hinted that maybe I should talk like that all the time."

Last September, when Fey saw Mary Tyler Moore and Betty White giving out the Emmy for outstanding comedy series, she says, "I had this visceral thing of, like, I want them to gimme that! I want to get that from those ladies!"

And within moments *30 Rock* was called and she went up onstage, glowing in a strapless eggplant mermaid David Meister gown, to take the Emmy from the two women who had provided the template for her own show. In fact, *30 Rock* would rock the Emmys, tying the record held by *All in the Family*. Given her frumpy start in comedy and her wooden start on *30 Rock*, it was a dazzling Cinderella moment (except for Fey's purse getting stolen while she was onstage). She got her own slipper, writing and willing herself into the role, and the shoe wasn't glass. It was a silver Manolo Blahnik.

"I don't like my feet," she says. "I'm not crazy about anybody's feet. But I have flat feet."

Liz Lemon sleeps in socks and tells Oprah she hates her feet. Robert Carlock, who wrote for *S.N.L.* and now is co-showrunner of *30 Rock*, told me that Fey, too, is "not willing to have people see her feet. I come in to talk about scripts when she's getting pedicures and have been summarily dismissed." Jack McBrayer, the former Second City comic who plays Kenneth, the Goody Two-Shoes NBC page, laughs: "They're normal feet. She's just a loony bird."

Fey has unleashed her inner Sally Bowles, the role she played in a student production of *Cabaret* at the University of Virginia. (Yes, she sings too, with what she calls "a birthday-party-quality voice.") Her makeover is the stuff of legend. The Hollywood agent Sue Mengers warned her pal Lorne Michaels that he simply could not bring Fey out of the writers' room and put her on-air for "Weekend Update."

"She doesn't have the looks," Mengers told him.

"Lorne brought her over to my house when she was head writer," Mengers recalls. "She was very mousy. I thought, Well, they gotta be having an affair. But they weren't. He just appreciated her talent. And now, suddenly, she's become this sexy, showing-tit, hot-looking woman. I said to Lorne, 'What the fuck did she do?'"

Far from holding Mengers's brutal candor against her, Tina spent the Friday night before the Emmys hanging at Mengers's house, thanked her when she won, and came back with Jeff the next day for a celebratory brunch. "She's quietly smart," Mengers says. "You know that she doesn't miss anything, right down to the buckle on your shoe."

Fey's father (the German side) is an affable Clint Eastwood lookalike who loves reading books about comedy and often drives up from the Philly area to visit Tina and Alice on the set. (His artwork fills their apartment.) Fey's acerbity comes from her mother (the Greek side), who has what Richmond calls "drag-queen humor—that bitter, extremely caustic kind of stab-you-in-the-heart humor." Mrs. Fey played a weekly poker game with her friends. "I loved hanging out with the ladies, because they were very funny, and a little bit mean, and had lots of Entenmann's products," Fey says. There's an additional legacy: "Because of the Greek-girl thing, I have, like, boobs and butt," so "I only have two speeds—either matronly or a little too slutty. I have to be steered away from cheetah print."

30 Rock features many shots of Liz Lemon's younger life, when she looks like a nerd in goofy clothes and frizzy hair. "I really wasn't heavy in high school," Fey recalls over lunch one afternoon at Cafe Luxembourg, where she dutifully switches her order from a B.L.T. to a salad. "But no one feels right in their own skin, particularly in high school." Her love life in school was, she says, a "famine": "I really didn't have very many dates at all. And that's not an exaggeration. But also, I don't think we should discount the fact that unplucked eyebrows and short hair with a perm may not have been the best offering, either." Liz Lemon tells Oprah on *30 Rock* that she was a virgin until she was 25. Tina Fey confesses much the same to me, noting, "I remember bringing people over in high school to play—that's how cool I am—that game Celebrity. That's how I successfully remained a virgin well into my 20s, bringing gay boys over to play Celebrity."

Adam McKay, the former *S.N.L.* head writer who hired Fey and taught her first improv class in Chicago, remembers one night when a bunch of comics were having drinks after a performance at the Upright Citizens Brigade. "I asked her who she lost her virginity to and she blushed, and I said, 'Tina, I'm really surprised, who cares?'" He loved her "prim and proper" Philly reserve combined with the "chord of anger running through her humor," the way she could throw down the fastest, meanest joke referencing everything from Allen Ginsberg to poop and still be shy.

That prude/lewd split personality had already been defined during her adolescence in Upper Darby, a suburb of Philadelphia, where, Fey says, she had "a dash of high-school bitchy," as one of her *S.N.L.* skits described Palin. Her friend Damian Holbrook, a *TV Guide* writer who attended a nearby high school and whose first name she took for the gay character in *Mean Girls*, says she was like the Janis character in that movie, the sweet girl in an oversize Shaker sweater who didn't run with the cool crowd or strut around to get guys, yet had the wit to burn the mean girls if she wanted to. Fey liked to watch *The Love Boat* and old Gene Kelly movies; she was involved in choir, theater, and the newspaper, for which she wrote a tart, anonymous column under the byline "The Colonel." In middle school, she was a flutist, which came in handy for her imitation of Sarah Palin's beauty-contest skills. She didn't have great athletic ability but played tennis, and, citing Kay

Cannon, says that team sports breed "a different kind of woman," with a "game-on, let's-do-it work ethic"; she hopes her daughter will grow up to play sports. ("I want Alice to play professional football.") She also wants her daughter to go through "a character-building puberty" with some frizzy, zit-filled years. ("It's going to be heartbreaking when we have to see that kid with a unibrow, when all that Greek stuff kicks in," Richmond observes.)

Liz Lemon favors her right side. That's because a faint scar runs across Tina Fey's left cheek, the result of a violent cutting attack by a stranger when Fey was five. Her husband says, "It was in, like, the front yard of her house, and somebody who just came up, and she just thought somebody marked her with a pen." You can hardly see the scar in person. But I agree with Richmond that it makes Fey more lovely, like a hint of Marlene Dietrich *noir* glamour in a Preston Sturges heroine.

"That scar was fascinating to me," Richmond recalls. "This is somebody who, no matter what it was, has gone through something. And I think it really informs the way she thinks about her life. When you have that kind of thing happen to you, that makes you scared of certain things, that makes you frightened of different things, your comedy comes out in a different kind of way, and it also makes you feel for people."

I wonder how the scar affected Fey in high school. "She wasn't Rocky Dennis developing a sense of humor because of her looks, like in *Mask*," says Damian Holbrook, laughing. Liz Lemon's blustery Republican boss, Jack Donaghy, played with comic genius by Alec Baldwin, tells Lemon, "I don't know what happened in your life that caused you to develop a sense of humor as a coping mechanism. Maybe it was some sort of brace or corrective boot you wore during childhood, but in any case I'm glad you're on my team."

Marci Klein—the cool, tall, blonde executive producer of *30 Rock* and producer of *S.N.L.*, and the daughter of Calvin Klein—who was kidnapped for 10 hours when she was 11, remembers, "Tina said to me, 'Well, you know, Marci, we had the Bad Thing happen to us. We know what it's like.'"

Fey herself rarely mentions the episode. "It's impossible to talk about it without somehow seemingly exploiting it and glorifying it," she says. Did she feel less attractive growing up because of it? "I don't think so," she says. "Because I proceeded unaware of it. I was a very confident little kid. It's really almost like I'm kind of able to forget about it, until I was on-camera, and it became a thing of 'Oh, I guess we should use this side' or whatever. Everybody's got a better side."

She used therapy to cope with her extremely fearful reaction to the anthrax attack at 30 Rock shortly after 9/11—the first time her co-workers had seen her vulnerable. The therapist talked to her about 9/11 and the anthrax delivered to Tom Brokaw's office, linking them to the crime against her when she was little. "It's the attack out of nowhere," Fey says. "Something comes out of nowhere, it's horrifying."

I asked her how the childhood attack affected her as a mother.

"Supposedly, I will go crazy," she replies evenly. "My therapist says, 'When Alice is the age that you were, you may go crazy.'"

Over coffee with Richmond, I ask him to describe Fey in her pre-glamour-puss days, back in Chicago. "She was quite round," he says, "in a lovely, turn-of-the-century kind of round—that beautiful, Ruben-esque kind of beauty." And as for her clothes: "Things that didn't match. She used to wear crazy boots. She would wear just a lot of knee-length frumpy dresses with thrift-store sweaters and kind of what was comfortable. It still looked kind of cool on her. I used to get all my suits in thrift stores, because I realized I was the size of little old men who were dying." The five-foot-three-and-a-half Richmond says they bonded over hot veal sandwiches and their appreciation of "sarcastic humor and Garry Shandling shows."

Fey recalls she was at her heaviest in Chicago and, later, sitting at a desk at *S.N.L.* "I'm five four and a half, and I think I was maxing out at just short of 150 pounds, which isn't so big. But when you move to New York from Chicago, you feel really big. Because everyone is pulled together, small, and Asian. Everyone's Asian."

She saw herself on an *S.N.L.* monitor as an extra, "and I was like, 'Ooogh.' I was starting to look unhealthy. I looked like a behemoth, a little bit. It was probably a bad sweater or something. Maybe cutting from Gwyneth Paltrow to me." She wanted to be "PBS pretty"—pretty for a smart writer. She called Jeff, who was directing a show at Second City in Chicago, and said, "O.K., I'm starting Weight Watchers."

Fey says, "I got to that thing that's so enjoyable where people tell you, 'Oh, you're thin, you've gotten too thin.' Lorne was like, 'Please, please make sure you're eating.'" McKay recalls Fey telling a story about her heavier days. "Steve Martin walked right past her at the coffee table, and then, after the makeover, he was like, 'Well, hel-looo—who are you?'"

The newly svelte Fey took over the "Weekend Update" anchor desk with Jimmy Fallon and made her name writing zingers for herself and jokes for Fallon, like this one about Demi Moore going with Ashton Kutcher: "Actress Demi Moore turned 40 on Tuesday, but she feels like a 25-year-old inside."

30 Rock made its debut in 2006, with *Washington Post* critic Tom Shales acidly noting that Fey was "not Orson Welles." I ask Baldwin if he coached Fey, whose acting background was improv and "Weekend Update," on how to do longer-form comedy. No, he says, only on what Richmond dryly calls "knockers shots." "I would say things to her, never giving advice: she's a woman you don't easily give advice to— she's very self-reliant. I'd say to her, 'You know, you're a really beautiful girl. You've got to play that. It's a visual medium. This is not Upright Citizens Brigade, where we're doing sketch comedy at nine o'clock at night on a Sunday for a bunch of drunken college graduate students. You are a very attractive woman and you've got to work that. You've got to pop one more button on that blouse and you've got to get that hair done and you've got to go! Glamour it up.'"

Ah, I say, so you're the one who encouraged Fey to wear so many low-cut tops, even though Lemon seems like the crewneck-sweater type. "There is Liz Lemon and there is Liz Lemon as portrayed by a leading actress in a TV show," Baldwin responds with amused and amusing disdain. "It's not a documentary. Tina's a beautiful girl. We needed to get the pillows fluffed on the sofa and we needed to get the drapes steamed, and we needed to get everything all nice and get the presentation just right. Tina always played the cute, nerdy girl. Tina on the news, the glasses. There was not a big glamour quotient for her. Now there is.

"The collective consciousness has said, 'Tina, *dahling,* where have you been? Where on earth have you been?'"

30 Rock struggled at first. The network made Fey drop her old friend Rachel Dratch from one of the leads, and the show was locked in a sibling rivalry with NBC's other show-within-a-show, Aaron Sorkin's *Studio 60 on the Sunset Strip.* Fey lured the viewers she craved only when she started moonlighting on *S.N.L.* as the look-alike Alaska governor who sometimes talks, as Fey puts it, as if she's lost in a corn maze. Sarah Palin's debut left conservative men salivating— "Babies, guns, Jesus: hot damn!" Rush Limbaugh thundered—and left Fey little choice. There had not been such a unanimous national casting decision since Clark Gable as Rhett Butler in *Gone with the Wind.* Besides, she and Michaels knew it could be good for *30 Rock* and *S.N.L.* Her Palin mimicry—with sketches written mainly by Seth Meyers—convulsed the nation and propelled *S.N.L.* into relevance again. The show got its biggest ratings since Nancy Kerrigan hosted in 1994, after having had her leg busted up by Tonya Harding's henchman.

Even the pros were blown away by Fey. "I've never seen a better impression," the *S.N.L.* master of the art, Darrell Hammond, says. "If they put those two on a sonar, they would match up electronically." Jon Stewart—her "Dear Diary," as she calls it, teenage crush (replacing Danny Kaye) from his days at *Short Attention Span Theater* on Comedy Central—told *The New York Times*'s Bill Carter that Fey "had the single best line of this campaign year," one she wrote herself and delivered in the role of Palin during the debate: "I believe marriage is a sacred institution between two unwilling teenagers."

In October, it seemed that Tina Fey *was* the campaign, with journalists writing that she had "swift-butted" Palin and derailed her future. Two weeks before the election, Fey's Palin and Palin's Palin met cute: the two women walked past each other wordlessly in *S.N.L.*'s opening sketch. As cast member Casey Wilson, standing next to a giggling Secret Service agent backstage, looked at Palin on a monitor raising the roof to Amy Poehler's racy Wasilla rap, she blurted out, "Oh, my God!" Watching a parade consisting of Mark Wahlberg, a donkey, Palin, and her Secret Service agents, a visiting screenwriter observed, "This is like a Fellini movie."

The McCain camp was on hand to ride herd, cutting out Poehler's rap line about how, in the Palins' bedroom, it's "drill, baby, drilla."

There were passionate arguments leading up to Palin's appearance. Some connected with the show did not want to give the Alaska governor a platform. Neither did bloggers on the Huffington Post. "The people on the left were like, 'No, you can't do that!'" Fey recalls. "And it's like, 'We don't work for you.'" The famously liberal Baldwin also found that line of liberal reasoning silly, saying he was outraged that commenters on the Huffington Post compared Palin to David Duke: "Palin came there to get thrown in the dunk tank. She knew it and she was gracious."

Still, the debate raged about the politics of Sarah Palin's appearance on *S.N.L.* Did it help her? Did it hurt her? Was it demeaning to politics? Were late-night shows determining the election? Should a comedian care? (Similar questions had arisen after Fey's "Weekend Update" comment about Hillary Clinton: "Bitch is the new black.") After weeks of appearing on *S.N.L.* as Palin, Fey opted to minimize the onstage interaction when the real Palin finally showed up, and despite reams of speculation the reason wasn't fundamentally political. "Tina was agonizing about it, and I'm drawn to anybody who agonizes about things," says her friend Conan O'Brien. "She told me, 'When I fly, I don't like to meet the pilot.' On the one hand, she knew: It's my job to sort of go after this person in a way, but at the same time I know when I meet her, she's a human being and a mom. She's not the Devil incarnate or Antichrist."

After the mock and real Palins do their walk-by—in identical red jackets and black skirts the *S.N.L.* seamstresses whipped up for the two women, with flag pins provided by Palin—Fey seems relieved. She changes and comes back to the small room offstage where Lorne Michaels's guests are hanging out. There are some drinks on ice by the monitor in Lorne's cubbyhole, and Fey has a glass of white wine in a plastic cup. "At least I can have one of these now," she says, smiling, to Jeff Zucker, the NBC president, who crows that she is "the hottest thing in American culture." She's wearing a purple-and-white checked Steven Alan shirt, and black Seven for All Mankind pants. She has taken off her

Palin-streaked beehive wig, and her dark-brown hair is pulled back in a thick ponytail. She looks like a really pretty graduate student, and she has a soft voice and reserve that Matthew Broderick says cause people to "lean in to her." (Like Daisy Buchanan, except her voice is full of funny rather than money.) She says the moments with Palin—which she has been dreading because it has been an ugly week on the Republican campaign, and because you don't like to meet someone you're "goofing" on—have gone fine. "She asked me where my daughter was," Fey says. (Alice had been there earlier at the rehearsal, pointing at the monitor showing Palin and thinking it was somehow her mommy, even though Mommy was with her.) "She said Bristol could have babysat."

Fey chats about the election for a moment, wondering if Obama could be "another Jimmy Carter." She tells Zucker, who is leaning against the wall, taking it all in, that she hasn't yet called her "Republican parents" to see how they feel about tonight's skit. Later, she tells me, "I grew up in a family of Republicans. And when I was 18 and registering to vote, my mom's only instruction was 'You just go in and pull the big Republican lever.' That's my welcome to adulthood. She's like, 'No, don't even read it. Just pull the Republican lever.'" (Fey made a call to arrange for Richmond's excited Republican parents and sister to meet Palin at a rally in Erie, Pennsylvania.)

Although some considered it a missed comedic opportunity, Fey says she didn't want to do what Jim Downey, the burly writer who has done many of *S.N.L.*'s renowned political skits, calls "a classic sneaker-upper" with Palin. "I just didn't want to have to do the impression at the same time with her," she said. "One, it would shine a light on the inaccuracies of the impression, and, two, it's just always . . . the only word I can think of is 'sweaty.' It just always feels sweaty."

Two weeks after the appearance with Palin, Fey does another scorchingly funny Palin skit, this time with John McCain, a bit where Fey's Palin goes "rogue" and starts selling "Palin in 2012" T-shirts on QVC. "A man running for president of the United States onstage with a woman playing his running mate—isn't that a great moment in our country's history?" Lorne Michaels says in wonder as he leaves 30 Rock, wading through a throng of reporters, at 1:30 A.M. Adam McKay, Will

Ferrell's writing partner in Hollywood, wrote the *S.N.L.* sketch where Ferrell's fumbling W. gives Fey's flirtatious Palin an endorsement. "It is the most ridiculous, borderline-dangerous thing that the Republican vice-presidential nominee happened to look like the funniest woman working in America," McKay says. "What if the next Republican presidential nominee looks exactly like Seth Rogen?"

Around the same time, Fey saw an entertainment reporter on TV say that Palin had been gracious toward Fey, but Fey hadn't been gracious toward Palin. "What made me super-mad about it," Fey says later, "was that it seemed very sexist toward me and her. The implication was that she's so fragile, which she is not. She's a strong woman. And then, also, it was sexist because, like, who would ever go on the news and say, 'Well, I thought it was sort of mean to Richard Nixon when Dan Aykroyd played him,' and 'That seemed awful mean to George Bush when Will Ferrell did it.' And it's like, No, that's not the thing. This is a comedy sketch on a comedy show." "Mean," we agreed, was a word that tends to get used on women who do satirical humor and, as she says, "gay guys."

"I feel clean about it," she says. "All these jokes were fair hits."

When Fey and her clever band of writers conjure up Liz Lemon, her 21st-century Mary Tyler Moore New York career girl, they put in a lot of Rhoda-like neuroses and insecurity about looks and food jokes and epically bad dates—though this season she's upgraded to *Mad Men*'s sexy Jon Hamm, who plays a pediatrician who impresses Lemon with his love of pie-making documentaries and ice-cream makers. Liz is more like *Seinfeld*'s Elaine—bossy/awkward on the outside and meek/insecure at her core—than *The Mary Tyler Moore Show*'s poised Mary Richards. Fey borrows much of the material from her own life and her writers' and actors' lives, and then heightens it. Baldwin's character has an obsessive relationship with an ex, and hers dates a little person she had initially mistaken for a child. Richmond wonders serenely if he inspired it.

Lemon noshes on "off-brand" Mexican cheese curls called "Sabor de Soledad"—"Taste of solitude." When forced to choose between a great man and a great sandwich, she puts the sandwich first. "No one has it harder in this country today than women," Liz complains to her friend

Jenna. "It turns out we can't be president. We can't be network news anchors. Madonna's arms look crazy."

But in her own life, Fey is the stable one, just as Mary Richards was on TV, anchored among oddballs in her Minneapolis newsroom. Outside her comedy, Fey does not want drama. When I ask her if she ever gets the urge to straighten out Lindsay Lohan, who starred in Fey's movie *Mean Girls*, or to counsel Tracy Morgan or Alec Baldwin when they hit tempestuous passages in their personal lives, she says, "I have no enabler bone in my body—not one. I'm sort of like, 'Oh, are you going crazy? I'll be back in an hour.'" She is the Obedient Daughter, the German taskmistress, the kind but firm maker and keeper of rules. And what Tina wants, Tina gets, sooner or later, because she works and works and works for it. So what does she do with what she calls her "15 minutes," now that she's got America's attention and a $5 million deal for a humor book?

Her manager, David Miner, whom she met when he was in the coatroom at Second City, has no doubt she'll continue to call on the way up to his office and get a latte for his assistant. "She never looks at the world and says, 'Give me this,'" he says. "She adapts and rolls up her sleeves."

She'd like to "mono-task" for a change and pull *30 Rock* into syndication. She'd like a slightly bigger apartment, so they can entertain more. (Jeff cooks *and* sews.) "I feel like the window is closing—I'm 38," she says about having more kids. "Obviously you want the best chance of the baby being healthy, and I think with our life and jobs right as they are at this moment, it doesn't seem possible. It's the year after the baby comes that is like someone hitting you every day in the face with a hammer."

Fey's idea of an ideal day off is still the same: she and Jeff take Alice to the playground and go to the Neptune Room, a fish place around the corner, or the Shake Shack on the Upper West Side for shakes and burgers and fries.

Everybody wants to be Tina Fey, I tell her. Who do you want to be?

"I don't want to be somebody else," she says.

And why would she?

LARRY DAVID, MASTER OF HIS QUARANTINE

—APRIL 4, 2020

Our lives now depend on staying home and doing nothing.

We are cooped up with no end in sight, getting increasingly irascible.

So I thought I would reach out to the world's leading expert on the art of nothing: the endlessly irascible man whose mantra has always been: "It doesn't pay to leave your house—what's the point?"

I found Larry David barricaded in his home in the Pacific Palisades in Los Angeles. "No one gets in here," America's most famous misanthrope said. "Only in an emergency plumbing catastrophe would I open the door."

I asked what he fears most and he replied: "Anarchy and a potential dental emergency—and not necessarily in that order."

Long ago, when he was a miserable stand-up comic in New York, he would sometimes abruptly stop his act, telling the audience, "This is what happens when you run out of nothing." Then he made two of the best shows in TV history, "Seinfeld" and "Curb Your Enthusiasm," about . . . nothing.

And now, in this plague season, Mr. David's odes to trivial pursuits are providing relief to some of us who are nostalgic for the days when we had the bandwidth to focus on trivia, when our lives weren't blighted and freighted.

"It's an escapist pleasure," said Daniel D'Addario, the chief TV critic of Variety, who has been watching one episode of "Curb" at lunchtime and one before bed. He does not think Mr. David will be a target of the class rage hitting Hollywood, pillorying tone-deaf celebrities who blanketed Instagram with their cringe-worthy "Imagine" video and glamour shots of their posh quarantine compounds and yachts and petal-strewn baths.

"Larry David is saying you can have as much money as you want and not only are you still unhappy but you're still unhappy about the most picayune things—jealousy and envy and all these venial sins," Mr. D'Addario said. "That is something that puts a smile on my face, as opposed to celebrities telling you to be happy from inside their gated communities, which engenders rage."

I asked Mr. David, a social critic of Hollywood mores who has been called "a savage Edith Wharton" by his friend Larry Charles, why all these celebrities seemed so devoid of self-awareness.

"I don't know, that's the $64,000 question," he said. "I guess their instinct is to help, their motives are good, and they don't consider how it might come off." But, he added, "I think it's a complete lack of judgment to talk about your lifestyle at this time, it's crazy. Of course other people are going to react like that."

Mr. David only popped his head up to make a P.S.A. for the governor of California, Gavin Newsom, asking people to not be "covidiots," to stay home and not hurt "old people like me." He was a little embarrassed when news leaked that he had set up a GoFundMe page for the golf caddies at his beloved Riviera Golf Course adjacent to his home.

We're FaceTiming—something Mr. David has grown to like in quarantine—and he picks up his iPad to walk me around and show me the view of the deserted golf course from his bedroom window.

It's my first FaceTime, and I'm nervous, having watched all week as even the glossiest cable news shows have downshifted into low-tech "Wayne's World" basement productions. To shore up confidence beforehand I asked my lighting sensei, Tom Ford, for some tips and he kindly sent these instructions, which you all are welcome to use:

"Put the computer up on a stack of books so the camera is slightly higher than your head. Say, about the top of your head. And then point it down into your eyes. Then take a tall lamp and set it next to the computer on the side of your face you feel is best. The lamp should be in line with and slightly behind the computer so the light falls nicely on your face. Then put a piece of white paper or a white tablecloth on the table you are sitting at but make sure it can't be seen in the frame. It will give you a bit of fill and bounce. And lots of powder, et voilà!"

A GERMOPHOBE VINDICATED

The crane-like Mr. David, in a dark blue Zegna pullover, rust-colored pants and sneakers, is sporting a scruffy beard. "Any facial hair is very beneficial for the bald man," he said. "It really enhances the bald man's appearance." He looked snug in a blue wing chair in a corner of his house. I was less comfortable.

"I'm only seeing half your face," he complained. "Do you know that?"

When I ask if he is hoarding anything, he is outraged. "Not a hoarder," he said. "In fact, in a few months, if I walk into someone's house and stumble onto 50 rolls of toilet paper in a closet somewhere, I will end the friendship. It's tantamount to being a horse thief in the Old West."

"I never could have lived in the Old West," he added parenthetically. "I would have been completely paranoid about someone stealing my horse. No locks. You tie them to a post! How could you go into a saloon and enjoy yourself knowing your horse could get taken any moment? I would be so distracted. Constantly checking to see if he was still there."

Jerry Seinfeld has observed that Larry David is the greatest proof that "you are what you are," given the fact that he remained a curmudgeon even once he got rich and popular.

Though, at 72, Mr. David does seem more comfortable in his skin. His outlook used to be so dark that Mr. Charles, one of the original writers of "Seinfeld," said that if he thought he could get away with it, Mr. David would have put out contracts to kill people.

Now, however, he is contentedly holed up with the older of his two daughters, Cazzie, 25; an Australian shepherd puppy named Bernie (after Sanders, whom Mr. David embodies with uncanny likeness on "Saturday Night Live"); a cat; and his girlfriend, Ashley Underwood, who worked as a producer of Sacha Baron Cohen's Showtime satire,

"Who Is America?" Ms. Underwood is friends with Isla Fisher, Mr. Cohen's wife, who had a hilarious role in this season's "Curb" as a professional crier who manipulates Larry into handing over his mother's mink stole.

Mr. David met Ms. Underwood at Mr. Cohen's birthday party in 2017. "We were seated next to each other, I think with that in mind," he said of the fix-up. "Much to her surprise I left before dessert. I was doing so well, banter-wise, I didn't want to risk staying too long and blowing the good impression."

Mr. David and Cazzie, who writes wry columns for Graydon Carter's digital weekly, Air Mail, are both lifelong germophobes. "This might be the only thing I've ever agreed with Trump about, we should put an end to the shake," Mr. David said. "You know, we might as well end intercourse while we're at it. That's always been a lot of trouble."

He also agrees with the president about the allure of hand sanitizer, which was a pivotal plot point in this season of "Curb." "Who can resist Purell?" he said. "Anytime you see it, you're drawn to it."

Now that Mr. David can't go out and argue with friends, neighbors, strangers and staffers over stuff like whether he can clean his glasses on a woman's blouse or the regulation shape for a putter, he must do his bickering inside his own home.

"There's not a moment in the day when there isn't friction between at least two of us," he said of the trapped troika. "Then when that gets resolved, two others are at each other's throats and it's invariably about dishes. 'You didn't do the dishes!' Or 'You didn't help with the dishes!' I think that is being screamed all over the world now.

"Another issue is the business of one of us starting a show and not waiting for the other. Huge problem! You at least have to ask. Ashley does not ask. She starts and then it's impossible to catch up. And I'll catch her. I'll walk into the room, and she'll instantly click off the TV."

Cazzie David said that the real Larry David does not constantly start fights. In fact, it is just the opposite. "I guess this is kind of ironic, considering his character on TV, but he can't stand having any animosity with anyone," she told me.

She said that if she gets into an argument with someone in the house, "he cannot stand it for a second. It just pains him. I remember when my sister and I were growing up, we would whisper-fight because if he heard us fighting, he would just get so upset, like it was the end of the world that two people were angry with each other. And it was just kind of a crime to stress him out because he's really just so gentle and nice, so we always avoid upsetting him at all costs."

Even though Mr. David's iconic shows are all about whining, he doesn't tolerate it at home.

"If anyone can make you feel stupid for complaining, it's him," Ms. David said. "If I complain even a little bit about anything, he'll ask me 'How old are you?' and I'll be like, '25,' and he does that thing all parents and grandparents do and be like 'You want to know where I was at 25? In a subway station selling magazines. In the Army reserves.' He cannot stand hearing complaints of any kind, especially right now when a lot of us are lucky enough to be cozy in our homes.

"He's super against any self-pity. He thinks it's the most disgusting thing in the world. So there's no wallowing allowed, even when we were growing up. In the house, you're not allowed to feel bad about yourself or be depressed. He just has no sympathy for it. So if you're depressed or feeling bad about something, he'll just tell you to take a shower. That's like his cure for mental stress. And if it doesn't work, he'll be like, 'Just take another one.'"

She, too, thinks that her father is "less grumpy."

THE POWER OF NO

Mr. David ventures out for solo walks in the deserted neighborhood. "I cross the street when I see someone coming, like I used to do when I was a kid in Brooklyn and the Italian kids would shake me down for change," he said. "And when someone crosses first, I know I shouldn't take it personally but I can't help it. How dare they?"

I wonder how he's faring without restaurants, which provide much of the fodder for his shows.

"The one positive thing to come out of this for me is the lunch decision, which in normal times takes me at least 15 minutes," he said.

"Now there's nothing to it. It's turkey or tuna. There's nothing else in the house."

There is another positive, which I point out to the antisocial Mr. David: Social life has skidded to a halt. "I will say that the lack of invitations, OK, that's been fantastic," he agreed. "Yeah, that I love. You don't have to make up any excuses." In "Curb," Mr. David's namesake character—a more obnoxious, fortissimo version of himself—is constantly lying to get out of going places. "Saying 'no' is such a skill in and of itself because the no's are rarely direct," he said. "There's a lot of thought that's put into the no and those emails or texts when you are saying no really do take a lot of time and effort to get the wording exactly right."

Cheryl Hines, who plays his ex-wife on "Curb," observed: "I bet Larry's in heaven. He's been trying to social-distance for years."

Mr. David said the best way to stay away from self-destructive behavior in quarantine is to think of it "like quitting smoking. You wake up and you say, 'I'm not going to smoke today.' 'I'm not going to freak out today.' That's the only way you can do it."

The crisis has coined a mordant new vocabulary: covidivorce, corona babies, isolationship. And in Hollywood, there's "pandemic nice guys," a term being thrown around by high-strung types who suddenly find themselves engaging in shocking niceties, like waving out their car windows at pedestrians and thanking the garbage collectors and police officers.

During what he called his "chaos break," Mr. David was making notes on his phone, as he always does, about this dark chapter for sunny California, in case it can inspire him, even just as a flashback in "Curb."

The show just finished its 10th season over two decades. Mr. David said that this season, a gleeful barbecue of P.C. culture, may be his favorite. As usual, his character roams around town, getting into big, self-defeating tangles about minor issues.

After buying cold coffee and a scone that tasted more like a muffin at Mocha Joe's coffee shop, Larry opens up a "spite store," a competing coffee shop next door called Latte Larry's. This spurs Sean Penn to open up an exotic bird store next to a bird store that dissed him and Mila Kunis to open up a jewelry store next to a jewelry store she wants to put out of business.

It was, typically, inspired by a real-life incident. "I went into this store on the Vineyard and I got a cup of coffee and it was a little cold and I said, 'You know, this coffee's a little cold' and they didn't give me satisfaction. I walked out of the store and across the street was a shack. And of course, I was pissed off and I said, 'I'd like to buy that shack and build the exact same store but with lower prices and take them out of business.'"

But he didn't?

"Oh, no," he said. "God, no."

Mr. David was stunned when President Trump retweeted a scene from the episode where Larry wears a MAGA hat to get out of commitments in liberal Hollywood, and ends up using it to assuage a Trumpster on a motorcycle with road rage. Mr. Trump tweeted a clip of the fight with the motorcycle guy with the message: "TOUGH GUYS FOR TRUMP!"

"What in God's name was that?" Mr. David asked me. "That was crazy, crazy. I don't understand it. I still don't get it."

Mr. David's show is beloved by some Trumpsters because it is so anti P.C. and because Larry is always raging against the machine. But he told an audience at the 92nd Street Y that he didn't care if he alienated Trump voters with his MAGA hat episode. "Alienate yourselves! Go! Go and alienate! You have my blessing."

When we speak about the president, Mr. David marveled, "You know, it's an amazing thing. The man has not one redeeming quality. You could take some of the worst dictators in history and I'm sure that all of them, you could find one decent quality. Stalin could have had one decent quality, we don't know!"

He said he gets mad at Mr. Trump's briefings, where he contradicts his own scientists in real time. "That's the hardest thing about the day, watching what comes out of this guy's mouth," he said. "It turns you into a maniac because you're yelling at the television. All of a sudden, you find yourself screaming, like I used to do on the streets of New York, pre-'Seinfeld,' when I saw happy couples on the street."

Does he ever think Trump can be funny?

"He's like a bad Catskills comic," Mr. David replied.

Idris Elba, who has more charm than the law should allow.

Sean Penn in his yard in Malibu, smoking and abiding by his favorite
Charles Bukowski quote: "Find what you love and let it kill you."

Mel Brooks, cracking an egg during breakfast as he prepares to crack more of his cherished fart jokes.

The man you most want to spend Halloween with:
the diabolically entertaining Ryan Murphy.

Tom Ford, a sweetheart who proves having the best taste
in the world can be oppressive.

Diane von Furstenberg, sleek as a panther, lounging on her favorite chaise in her Venice palazzo.

Ann Roth, lounging amid her sketches—blueprints for some of
the most iconic looks in Hollywood history.

André Leon Talley, a man who allowed no dreckitude, on a sentimental journey home to Durham, North Carolina.

He said he's been watching the Hillary Clinton documentary on Hulu. "I'm not the first person to say this, obviously, but you never got the feeling that you were really seeing her. There was a problem warming up to her. But you see her in this documentary and you love her."

The Hillary moment he can't stop thinking about is when she didn't wheel on the lurking Trump in the debate and tell him to get the hell out of her frame.

"I have literally gone over that moment in my basement so many times, pretending to be her, trying out different lines to say something to him," Mr. David said. "I'll say, 'WHAT in God's name are you doing?' 'What the *hell* are you doing?' 'Back up, man, what are you doing?'"

He is relieved not to be flying back and forth to New York on weekends to do his Sanders imitation for "SNL."

"Imagine if he had become president, what would have happened to my life?" he said.

After he learned on Henry Louis Gates Jr.'s PBS show, "Finding Your Roots," that Mr. Sanders was a distant cousin, he ran into the pol at the "Today" show and Bernie greeted him with a big "Cousin!"

"When I see him, it does feel like I'm talking to somebody in my family," he said.

I wondered if he took it personally when Mrs. Clinton said of Mr. Sanders's reputation in Congress: "Nobody likes him, nobody wants to work with him."

"It was a little harsh, yeah," he said.

Does he think it's time for his doppelgänger to drop out?

"I feel he should drop out," Mr. David said. "Because he's too far behind. He can't get the nomination. And I think, you know, it's no time to fool around here. Everybody's got to support Biden."

How else is he spending his time in lockdown?

Mr. David said he's watching "Ozark" and "Unorthodox" on Netflix. He tried to watch America's favorite distraction, "Tiger King," but couldn't get past the first episode. "I found it so disturbing," he said. "The lions and the tigers just really scared the hell out of me. They were going to attack somebody. They were going to kill somebody. I didn't want to see them attack and those people were just so insane, I couldn't watch it."

Mr. David, who starred in Woody Allen's 2009 movie, "Whatever Works," also said he is reading Mr. Allen's memoir, "Apropos of Nothing," which was picked up by Arcade Publishing after Hachette Book Group dropped it following pressure from another one of its authors, Mr. Allen's son Ronan Farrow, and protests.

"Yeah, it's pretty great, it's a fantastic book, so funny," Mr. David said. "You feel like you're in the room with him and yeah, it's just a great book and it's hard to walk away after reading that book thinking that this guy did anything wrong."

I told Mr. David I disagree with his remarks in the past that people don't like to see neurotic single guys or older guys onscreen after a certain age. I could watch "Curb" ad infinitum.

"I can only think about when Buster Keaton got old," he said. "I don't know, he was such a great comedian and then he just—you didn't want to see him. Even old people don't want to watch old people."

It was time for Mr. David to hang up. He had to get back to doing nothing.

Confirm or Deny

MAUREEN DOWD: *Michael Kay is a much better radio host than Mike Francesa ever was.*

LARRY DAVID: Confirm.

The best bagels in New York are Absolute Bagels, off 110th Street.

Never had 'em. I wouldn't go to 110th Street for a bagel. That's just way too far to go for a bagel. Who's going to 110th Street for a bagel? That's crazy.

You carry loose dental floss in your pocket.

Deny. I carry brush picks.

You swear on your children's lives that you've never carried loose dental floss.

I'm not saying it didn't happen at some point. Yeah, I may have pulled out a piece of floss from my pocket. But I can say categorically that I have not had a piece of dental floss in any pocket in at least seven years.

You like to throw your gum into the fireplace.

Confirm. I also really like to throw anything—paper and gum— into baskets that are like 10 feet away to see if I can throw it in. I think I'm going to do a show about it.

Kanye invited you to a Sunday service.

Deny. Where'd you get that from? Is that true?

You owned a Porsche for an hour and then you returned it.

It was a week.

You don't like it when stars doing guest spots on "Curb" touch your face.

Confirm!

During "Curb" filming, you trained the camera on Richard Lewis's grow- ing bald spot to get back at him for having such great hair (that he said looked like challah bread) when you were young comics in New York.

It wasn't positioned there purposely but when I noticed it, I didn't say anything!

You have never put money in a jukebox.

Confirm.

You've never owned a camera.

Yes, other than a cellphone. I have no interest in taking pictures. Who cares? What's the point?

When you gave a fund-raiser for Bill Clinton, you were asked if you wanted to go in a room to meet the president and you said, "Nah, I'm good."

I don't remember. But sure, yeah, it's good for the brand.

When you were a teenager, your mother was so worried about your future prospects that she wrote a letter to The New York Post advice columnist seeking counsel.

Yeah, she did. I always read Dr. Rose Franzblau's column and then this one time I read the column and it was about me. It was me! I wish I had cut out the article and saved it.

You do a great imitation of Raymond Massey as Lincoln.

"A house divided against itself cannot stand!"

You're meditating a lot lately.

Oh, God no. I find that's an extreme waste of time. I'm supposed to be sitting here repeating this thing over and over again. Toward what end?

MEL BROOKS ISN'T DONE PUNCHING UP THE HISTORY OF THE WORLD

—MARCH 11, 2023

Mel Brooks is a sophisticated guy. He collected fancy French wines and did a tasting on Johnny Carson's show. He drops references to Nikolai Gogol's "Dead Souls." He was married for 40 years to that epitome of elegance, Anne Bancroft. He was a favorite lunch companion of Cary Grant, the suavest man who ever lived.

But in the new Hulu show "History of the World, Part II," you can still find all the Mel Brooks signature comedy stylings: penis jokes, puke jokes and fart jokes.

"I like fart jokes," he said, Zooming from his home in Santa Monica, Calif. "It adds some *je ne sais quoi* to the comedy. A touch of sophistication for the smarter people helps move the show along."

After all, with the percussive campfire scene in his 1974 comedy classic, "Blazing Saddles," where the cowhands sit around eating beans and passing wind, he elevated flatulence to cinematic history.

The comedy legend, 96, preferred to meet on Zoom because he's wary of Covid. Strangers love to hug him and say, "Mel, I love you!" he said, adding, "I'm a target."

The man behind outlandish, hilarious movies like "The Producers," "Young Frankenstein," "Spaceballs," "High Anxiety," "Robin Hood: Men in Tights" and "History of the World, Part I," along with the hit TV spy comedy "Get Smart," no longer lives in a time where he can have "absolutely no restrictions on any and all subjects," as he said about writing "Blazing Saddles" (which was slapped with its own content warning in 2020 when it was on HBO Max). And he lost the two loves of his life, Ms. Bancroft and Carl Reiner. But Mel Brooks is still a ball of fire.

Having lived through nearly a century of history, Mr. Brooks is sneaking up on his famous character, the 2,000 Year Old Man. But his taste in comedy is still as merrily immature as ever. He has sharp takes on world history, greed and hypocrisy. He knows who the villains are and what the stakes are, and yet he's not afraid of the lowbrow.

Max Brooks, his son with Ms. Bancroft, said his father's mantra is: "If you're going to climb the tower, ring the bell."

"He believes if you're going to make a piece of art, don't be safe, don't be careful, don't pander to a certain group to win their favor."

Mel Brooks is still making fun of Hitler. The new show has a sketch called "Hitler on Ice," with three TV commentators savaging an ice-skating Führer who falls. One sniffs, "I've said it before and I'll say it again: If you put concentration camps in people's countries, you better be flawless on the ice."

USING COMEDY AS A WEAPON

Mr. Brooks's parents were immigrants, his mother from Ukraine and his father from Germany. His father died of tuberculosis when Mr. Brooks was 2; there was no money to send him to a sanitarium, Max Brooks said. When the little boy, born Melvin Kaminsky, needed fillings for his teeth that would have cost a dollar apiece, his mother could not afford it, so she had to let the dentist rip them out for half price.

He fought in the U.S. Army against the Nazis, and dealt with antisemitism among some of his fellow soldiers. He said he felt like Errol Flynn when he got instruction on cavalry charges with horses and sabers. He was a corporal, a combat engineer who defused land mines and cleared booby-trapped buildings in France and Germany. (He was in the German town of Baumholder on V.E. Day.) His three other brothers also fought in the war and one, Lenny, an Air Force pilot, ended up a prisoner in a Nazi P.O.W. camp for 19 months, where he had to pretend he wasn't Jewish.

"I was on a troop ship, and I paid a sailor on deck $50 to let me sleep under a lifeboat in case we were torpedoed," Mr. Brooks recalled. "The smells were dreadful, 500 guys on a ship. It was 16 or 17 days from the Navy yard in Brooklyn to Le Havre, France, zigzagging and trying not to get torpedoed."

And ever since the war, he said, "I've tried to get even with Hitler by taking the Mickey out of him, making fun, but it's difficult."

Mr. Brooks, who was sometimes bullied as a child, learned to use comedy as a weapon. When his musical version of "The Producers" in 2001—with a swanning, singing and dancing Hitler—held a preview in Chicago, "some big guy kept storming up the aisle and saying, 'How dare you have Hitler, how dare you have the swastika? I was in World War II risking my life and you do this on a stage?' I said, 'I was in World War II and I didn't see you there.'"

"History of the World, Part I," the 1981 movie on which the Hulu series is riffing, was a raunchy romp through different eras, from the Stone Age to the French Revolution. It featured the peerless Madeline Kahn as Empress Nympho, Nero's wife; Sid Caesar as the cave man who invented music and the spear but could not quite figure out fire; and Mr. Brooks in multiple roles. He played Comicus, the stand-up philosopher; a singing Torquemada with a bevy of synchronized swimmers; and a libidinous Louis XVI, having his way with women and crowing, "It's good to be the king."

It was chockablock with puns, including the classic in which Harvey Korman, as the Count de Monet, chastised his impudent companion, "Don't be saucy with me, Béarnaise."

Mr. Brooks tacked on "Part I" to the title as a joke, he said, but then "I was plagued with about a billion calls, 'Where's Part II?' I never intended to do Part II."

But he and his producing partner, Kevin Salter, eventually gave in to popular demand. Mr. Brooks said he thought, "What the hell? Let's try Part II." They reached out to the comedian Nick Kroll in 2020. He recruited Wanda Sykes, Ike Barinholtz and the showrunner David

Stassen. "I've been laughing at comedy, some of which I didn't create," Mr. Brooks said, "which is very weird for me." The writers did remind themselves, though, as Ms. Sykes said, to "Mel it up."

Once the ball got rolling, all the comedians who idolized Mr. Brooks wanted in—from Johnny Knoxville (who plays Rasputin getting his attenuated member cut off) to Sarah Silverman (who is in a "Jews in Space" skit previewed in Part I with the song "Jews, out in space, we're zooming along, protecting the Hebrew race") to Jack Black (a sneaky Stalin).

Mr. Knoxville said that Mr. Brooks is "the legend of legends," who pushes things as far as possible (which is also the "Jackass" way). He got to talk to his idol on the phone one night. "I was shaking before and during and after," Mr. Knoxville said. "I don't know if he got a word in edgewise."

Mr. Knoxville thinks that he actually saw Rasputin's "Jim Dog," as he called the body part, pronouncing it "Dawg," in a jar in St. Petersburg, Russia, at the Museum of Erotica. It's not clear if the castration of the concupiscent mystic was mere legend, but in the "History of the World" universe, Mr. Brooks is happy to go with the legend.

"Before Mel, I don't think movies were hilarious," Mr. Barinholtz said. "Before 'Blazing Saddles,' regular people were not going to the movie theater and laughing so hard they were hyperventilating. Mel, I think, really ushered that in." He and some of the other comedians who worked on the show had not met Mr. Brooks before, Mr. Barinholtz said, adding: "He inspected our teeth and could tell that we were strong."

Mr. Brooks himself narrates the film, with a muscly C.G.I. body. I asked how he compared with the original narrator, Orson Welles. Mr. Brooks gave the contest to Mr. Welles: "He said, 'I want $25,000 in a paper bag and please don't mention it to my agent.' I said, 'What are you going to do with that $25,000 in the paper bag?' He said, 'Beluga caviar and the finest Cuban cigars.'"

GALILEO ON SOCIAL MEDIA

Mr. Brooks helped the comedians decide which slices of history to explore in the sequel, and joined the Zoom writers' room sometimes to weigh pitches or offer jokes from his vault of unused material.

"The first time we talked, he was like, 'I have an idea for this joke where Robert E. Lee is at Appomattox and he turns to sign and his sword knocks his guys in the balls,'" Mr. Kroll said. "Then when we decided to do a whole section on Ulysses S. Grant and the signing at Appomattox, we were like, 'Perfect. We can do that joke.'"

And like Part I, in which Comicus pulls up in a chariot to Caesar's palace during the Roman Empire but it turns out to be the Vegas Caesar's Palace, Part II has plenty of fun anachronisms, like Galileo on "TicciTocci" or Harriet Tubman's Underground Railroad morphing into the New York subway.

Mr. Barinholtz said Mr. Brooks's instruction was: "Don't get too esoteric. Play the hits." He said they didn't use the racial and sexual epithets that peppered Mr. Brooks's movies in the 1960s, '70s and '80s, but they stuck to the same themes.

In one episode, a Native American Civil War soldier played by Zahn McClarnon has to do a standup routine to distract a bunch of West Virginia racists who are trying to hang General Grant, played by Mr. Barinholtz. Noting that the colonizers had built Ohio on top of his razed family home, the soldier advised: "If you're going to genocide a people, you should get something better out of it than Cleveland."

Mr. Brooks, too, said he would no longer use the inflammatory words he used so freely back in the day. I asked him about his fellow comics, like Chris Rock, Bill Maher and Jerry Seinfeld, who worry that wokeness is neutering comedy.

He looked over at Mr. Salter, who was sitting beside him. "I had a talk with Kevin before this," he told me. "He said, 'If Maureen, for some reason, brings up woke and woke comedy, stay off it. Stay away.'"

Laughing, I conceded, "I'm so obvious."

"Yes," he replied. "Absolutely."

(When I pressed about the commotions around Dave Chappelle and Ricky Gervais, who were accused of being insensitive to transgender people, Mr. Brooks again glided away.)

He endorsed Joe Biden in 2020 but he said he doesn't like to do political comedy because then, "half the audience is going to be angry at me." He prefers jokes like this one from the new show about the Virgin Mary: "She thinks her son is God. The mother's definitely Jewish."

Why are so many of the most storied comedians Jewish?

"Well, I don't think they let them into railroads," he said, laughing. "If you were a Jew, you couldn't own a railroad."

Is he surprised antisemitism is on the rise?

"Why would you want to be anti-Jewish after those stories about concentration camps?" he said. "How could you be?"

I asked Larry David, who did a whole season of "Curb Your Enthusiasm" revolving around "The Producers"—with cameos by Mr. Brooks and Ms. Bancroft—why Mr. Brooks sits atop the comedy pantheon.

"It's almost as if he was designed in Silicon Valley," Mr. David said. "What would the funniest man in the world look and sound like? And they came up with Mel."

THE GREATEST WRITERS' ROOMS IN HISTORY

My first memory of laughing until I cried was sitting on Saturday nights watching Sid Caesar cavort on "Caesar's Hour," the sequel to "Your Show of Shows." Mr. Brooks wrote for both, as part of the most famous writers' rooms in TV history.

(The new "History of the World" depicts Shakespeare's writers' room, with Francis Bacon toiling away. Someone pitches "Othello," an interracial love story about a white woman and a Black man that's not about race, and Shakespeare replies: "I am an ally but I don't think it's my story to tell.")

Mr. Brooks worked in those rooms with Mel Tolkin, the head writer; Carl Reiner; Neil Simon; Larry Gelbart ("the fastest mouth and brain in the West," as Mr. Brooks called him, who went on to do "MASH" and "Tootsie"); Lucille Kallen, one of the first women writing for television, who did the domestic sketches for "Your Show of Shows"; Aaron Ruben (who later produced "The Andy Griffith Show"); and a very young Woody Allen.

Was he jealous of the prelapsarian Allen?

"I was, but this is the first time I've ever mentioned it," he said, with a mock grimace. "I said, 'That little mouse. That little rat. How did he come up with that?' Woody would come up with a lot of stuff. He was sly and he was a brilliant writer."

He said that Mr. Simon, known as Doc Simon, "had a very pale, light, little voice, which sometimes drove us crazy. Carl Reiner would sit next to him and Doc would whisper his jokes into Carl's left ear, and Carl would stand up and say, 'Doc has it!' And it would be wonderful."

I asked him about an interview I saw in which he and Mr. Reiner talked about which numbers are funny.

"We once had a sketch on 'Show of Shows' where Imogene Coca was playing roulette," he recalled. "She's going to win but we have to figure out the number. We asked her to read some different numbers, like 16 and 28. When she read 32, we all broke into great laughter. The last sound has to zoom up. Eight doesn't zoom up. But two does zoom. I was very disappointed because my birthday is June 28."

Mr. Brooks said that Mr. Tolkin was a "flat-out intellectual" and got him into Gogol. But Mr. Tolkin relished jokes like "She would not have anything to do with him because he was beneath her. He got off at 116th Street and she got off at 125th Street."

When Mr. Brooks was working on "Your Show of Shows," and married to his first wife, a former Broadway dancer named Florence Baum, with three small children, he had anxiety attacks so severe that he was throwing up between parked cars.

Mr. Tolkin told Mr. Brooks about "the talking cure," and sent him to a psychiatrist, who offered some career advice, too.

"I told the guy that I felt I couldn't go in every day," he said about the writers' room. "I felt I'd have to quit. It was too much, that they'd say, 'OK, the little dude from Brooklyn, fire him.' He said, 'No, you're Mel Brooks and you're probably the best writer on the show. I want you to go in there and not worry about being fired and ask for a raise. Say, "If I don't get a raise, I'm quitting."'"

I wanted to know what the titanic, mercurial Sid Caesar was like. I said that Mr. Caesar looked remarkably buff playing a cave man in "History of the World, Part I," even though he was in his late 50s.

"Sid was an animal," Mr. Brooks said. "He had instinctual feelings about comedy, and they were always correct. He was the strongest man on earth. He was a big, tall, giant of a guy with muscles."

In his 2021 memoir, "All About Me!," Mr. Brooks describes how Mr. Caesar grabbed his collar and belt and hung him out the window of a Chicago hotel room after the writer complained about Mr. Caesar's cigar smoke.

"Got enough air?" Mr. Caesar asked his dangling writer.

Mr. Brooks told me about another terrifying night in Chicago when Mr. Caesar's car grazed a taxi and the taxi driver yelled a vulgarity at the TV star. Mr. Brooks shivered, knowing what was coming.

"Sid got out of his car, went over to the cabdriver, who wore a yellow cap and black leather bow tie, and yelled, 'Do you remember your birth? Do you remember being born? Think back. You're going to enter the world, what are your thoughts?' Then Mr. Caesar reached in, grabbed the driver by the bow tie and started pulling his head through the little clipper window and said, 'We're going to re-enact it.' I had to bite Sid's hand to let him go. He would have made a snake out of that guy."

When Mr. Brooks switched to the big screen, he thought his movie career was over before it got off the ground.

In 1968, Renata Adler reviewed "The Producers" for The New York Times and called it "a violently mixed bag. Some of it is shoddy and gross and cruel; the rest is funny in an entirely unexpected way." She said she was torn between leaving and laughing.

"I said, 'The New York Times didn't like it, so maybe I should go back to television where they liked everything I did,'" Mr. Brooks recalled. By then, he had gotten divorced and remarried to Ms. Bancroft. He remembers her telling him, "No, you were born to make movies, and you just keep making them."

Now, "The Producers," "Blazing Saddles" and "Young Frankenstein" are all on the Library of Congress's National Film Registry of cherished American films. He not only has an EGOT but President Barack Obama awarded him the National Medal of Arts in 2016. At the ceremony, Mr. Brooks pretended to pants the president as the crowd howled.

When Mr. Brooks became a successful writer and director of movies, he was working at Universal and he saw Cary Grant step out of a Rolls-Royce. "Who wears a double-breasted chalk stripe suit in the '80s?" he said. "It's ridiculous."

Mr. Grant began asking Mr. Brooks to lunch at the commissary. They ordered boiled eggs (Mr. Grant) and a tuna fish sandwich (Mr. Brooks), traded favorite colors (yellow for Mr. Grant and blue for Mr. Brooks) and favorite shoes ("I said, 'I like black and white shoes' and he said 'Never'"). Mr. Brooks turned the odd-couple bromance into a renowned comedy bit, saying that by the end of the week, they had run out of things to talk about, so Mr. Brooks stopped taking Mr. Grant's calls.

But in real life, Mr. Brooks said, "I certainly was hanging on every word" when Mr. Grant told stories about his beginnings as Archie Leach in England.

Was he the best-looking man Mr. Brooks ever saw in Hollywood?

"I was in an elevator at the William Morris office once," he replied, "and Tyrone Power"—the darkly handsome actor who was a swashbuckling romantic lead in the '30s and '40s—"got in and I said to him, 'Oh, it's going to be hard for me to say who's better looking, you or Cary Grant.'"

LIFE WITH ANNE BANCROFT

Certainly, Mr. Brooks and Ms. Bancroft are one of Hollywood's greatest love stories. People considered them an odd couple, the short comic with the funny mug and Brooklyn accent, and the gorgeous actress who created the indelible portrait of the panther-like seductress and pre-cougar, Mrs. Robinson, in "The Graduate," even though she was only 35 to Dustin Hoffman's 30.

But they fell in love nearly instantly after meeting on the set of "The Perry Como Show." Mr. Brooks compares his wooing style to Pepper Martin, a St. Louis Cardinals player in the '30s who was famous for stealing bases. She was also really impressed with his taxi whistle, he said.

They soon learned that they loved all the same things, from baseball to foreign movies to Chinese food. And if Anne loved something Mel didn't know about, like opera, he decided to love it, too. "Anne was Catholic, a good Catholic," Mr. Brooks said. "I lived with her for so long, I started crossing myself." There was none of the A-lister married to A-lister angst that Paul Newman and Joanne Woodward experienced.

He was broke, so it was tough to court the more famous actress, who had already been in a spate of movies and had won two Tonys for "Two for the Seesaw" and "The Miracle Worker."

"We'd go to a restaurant and she would slip me a couple of $20 bills under the table so it looked like I was paying for the meal," he said. Once, when he told the waiter to keep the change, he said, "We got outside, she hit me with her purse as hard as she could. She said, 'Are you crazy? As long as I'm paying for it, be careful with the tipping.'"

Even after they had been married for about 35 years, the thrill was still there. As she put it to The New York Daily News: "I get excited when I hear his key in the door. It's like, 'Ooh! The party's going to start!'"

After she died in 2005, felled by uterine cancer, Mr. Brooks never dated again.

"Once you are married to Anne Bancroft, others don't seem to be appealing," he said. "It's as simple as that."

After they became widowers, Mr. Brooks and Mr. Reiner often had dinner together on tray tables and watched TV at the Reiner hacienda on Rodeo Drive. In his memoir, Mr. Brooks called Mr. Reiner, who died in 2020, not only the best friend he ever had but "the best friend *anyone* ever had."

They talked and napped and watched "Wheel of Fortune" and then "Jeopardy," arguing over the answers. Sometimes, they watched old movies. "Once a week, I had to watch 'Random Harvest' with Ronald Colman," Mr. Brooks recalled dryly. "Carl always said, 'If you don't cry watching the end, you're not alive.'"

Proudly, Mr. Brooks noted that their chairs and tray tables are now on display in the National Comedy Center in Jamestown, N.Y.

He is happy, as we end our 90-minute interview, because we have laughed a lot, and laughter, he said, is the most important thing to him.

"Money is honey, funny is money," he said blithely, echoing a Max Bialystock line from "The Producers." "I really care about saying things that make people roar with laughter. I was on the stage at Radio City Music Hall and we took questions in the last part of my standup. One of the questions was, 'What do you wear—long shorts or briefs?' I yelled, 'Depends!' It's a thrill to get a big laugh."

Confirm or Deny

MAUREEN DOWD: *You love schwanzstucker jokes.*

MEL BROOKS: Actually, Gene Wilder came up with that word while we were writing "Young Frankenstein" together.

You still like to do your wolf howl from "Young Frankenstein."

You're all wet. It's not a wolf howl. It's a cat yowl. I'll do it for you. [He does a cat yowl, based on the big alley cats he knew in Brooklyn.] Nobody does a better cat yowl than me. I could do that for a living.

You like to set the mood when you're writing.

When we were writing "Blazing Saddles," I actually wore a war bonnet. Just to stay with it, and get everybody crazy.

You preserved your hearing during the war by shoving cigarettes in your ears, but you ended up with yellow ears.

True story. When I did my first movie, "The Producers," the insurance nurse looked me over and said, "Did you have yellow fever?"

Richard Pryor, who worked on the script of "Blazing Saddles" with you, was the greatest standup comedian who ever lived.

He was. One time on a Friday night, he said, "Mel, go over to the Bitter End and sub for me, do my act. I have to be in Chicago." I found out later he had a girlfriend in Chicago. I said, "All right, what do you want me to do?" He said, "Be funny. Do my act." I went to the Bitter End and I said, "Richard couldn't make it but I'm doing his act for you. I was born in Kansas City to a big Black woman who ran a cat house and she took care of me and she taught me how to play the piano. I used to pee out the windows." I was doing his act. Afterward, he said, "Are you crazy?"

You almost cast Dustin Hoffman as the Nazi playwright in "The Producers."

I did cast him. He put that helmet on with the pigeon doody and he looked exactly like a good Nazi. Anyway, he couldn't do it because he got another job.

You have some final words from the 2,000 Year Old Man.

As the 2,000 Year Old Man, I would say be nice to everyone around you because you never know where they're going to end up. Even if you don't like them, don't let them know because they're liable to one day run a studio. They're liable to be Harry Cohn.

Your Hollywood star has one six-fingered hand.

It's true. I did it with a plaster mold just so that somebody from Idaho would scream, "Henry, come over here! Look at this. Mel Brooks has six fingers."

PART 4

Creative Class

GRETA GERWIG, IN THE PINK

—DECEMBER 4, 2022

Greta Gerwig can be scattered. But she likes to say that the greater the chaos and uncertainty, the calmer she gets.

When I met her at her office in Chelsea, she was very calm. This, despite the whirlwind: She's six months pregnant with her second child, another boy. She's promoting her star turn in a Netflix black comedy with Adam Driver and Don Cheadle—an adaptation of Don DeLillo's 1985 novel, "White Noise," directed by her partner, Noah Baumbach. And she's editing a movie due out in July that she directed—and she and Mr. Baumbach wrote—that has generated giddy excitement, along with intense curiosity about Ms. Gerwig's approach: "Barbie," a cotton-candy-pink extravaganza starring Margot Robbie and, as the living doll's consort, Ken, a platinum Ryan Gosling.

"I've just got to finish 'Barbie,'" said Ms. Gerwig, 39, who was wearing a plaid shirtdress, black leggings and some black ankle boots she got at Liberty's in London, the city where "Barbie" was mostly filmed. "I'm bad at focusing on too many things at once. I don't have that kind of bandwidth."

She sheepishly confessed that she was so busy that she had used dry shampoo that morning instead of taking a shower. But it's hard to believe that Ms. Gerwig is a bad multitasker, given how many things she is juggling, including, on the day after we talked in her Chelsea office, hosting a big family Thanksgiving dinner for 20 in her downtown Manhattan apartment.

She has collected so many hyphens in her résumé that even Barbra Streisand would be impressed: actor-writer-director-producer and multiple Oscar nominee for the critical darlings she wrote and directed, "Lady Bird" and "Little Women."

I had heard Ms. Gerwig was a great eater, so, even though we were lunching dutifully on Sweetgreen salads, we started off talking about one of her culinary delights: doughnuts.

"I think, particularly on film sets, I become the child version of myself that wants just junk food," she said. She read that Steven Spielberg had wooed a reluctant David Lynch to play a cameo as John Ford in "The Fabelmans" by acceding to his request for Cheetos on the set. "Then I felt like a kindred spirit with David Lynch, since we have the same addiction to the salty, cheesy goodness of Cheetos."

INSIDE THE DREAMHOUSE

Will Ferrell, who plays the Mattel C.E.O. in "Barbie," has said the movie is a homage and a satire. But details are scarce about how Ms. Gerwig solves the sticky issue of Barbie. Feminists have had their issues over the decades, saying the doll offered a superficial, beauty-centric view of women—in 1992, a talking Barbie burbled, "Math class is tough!" Under pressure, Mattel added different shapes and races and professions to the line. "Barbie believes in the power of representation," the doll's Instagram account boasted.

"My mom was a feminist, and I think there was some resistance to all of it and eventually there was relenting," Ms. Gerwig recalled, describing hand-me-down dolls. "I think I was totally compelled by hair that was 10 times bigger than your body."

Her own childhood hair, she recalled, was thin, which made Barbie's all the more an object of fascination. Ms. Gerwig said she wanted the movie "to be something that is both able to come from the adult part of your brain and also remember what it was like to be a little girl just looking at a beautiful Barbie."

She said the main draw for her in taking on the project was Ms. Robbie, who is starring and producing. "She's so fearless," Ms. Gerwig said. "There's something really infectious about that. For some reason, I thought, 'Yes, I would love to write this and Noah would love to write it, too.' I don't think I really checked with him. At first he was like, 'What? What are we going to do?' He was not sure. Then we both got really excited and fell in love with the project."

In London, Ms. Gerwig and Ms. Robbie kicked off filming with a "Barbie sleepover" with some of the other women and men working on the movie (alas, Mr. Gosling didn't participate)—complete with games, goody bags and pink sleepover outfits.

"I really love building companies of actors almost like a theater troupe," Ms. Gerwig said. "I wanted that kind of energy because it was a really big cast. It was like, well, let's do something totally girly."

The director also showed movies every Sunday at the Electric Cinema in Notting Hill for the cast and crew, hoping to provide some style or comedy inspiration for the shoot: "His Girl Friday" for the manic pacing and "The Red Shoes" for the saturation of color. Ms. Gerwig said the message was: "Don't worry. People have made really wild movies before."

Even Ms. Gerwig seemed startled by the pictures of Ms. Robbie and Mr. Gosling as Barbie and Ken on a beach in Los Angeles that broke the Internet in June. "I couldn't believe Ryan and Margot were just out there in full neon," she said. "It was like we were in this bubble, and all of a sudden they were doing it in public in front of everyone. Everything was so extreme and they were really going for it. Just 100 percent commitment."

Ms. Robbie recalled that, in order not to "waste brain power" on her wardrobe, Ms. Gerwig wore the same boiler suit, in different colors, every day of the shoot. "We did pink on Wednesdays," Ms. Gerwig said.

Laurie Metcalf, who played the mother in "Lady Bird," said that, on that shoot, Ms. Gerwig told people to wear a name tag revealing a movie that everyone else loved but you just didn't get. Ms. Gerwig's was "Breakfast at Tiffany's."

It's funny, I noted, since she played free-spirited young women not unlike Holly Golightly earlier in her career, ones whose brio masked their vulnerability as they tried to make it in New York.

"I just never liked it," she said of the Audrey Hepburn classic. "It made me uncomfortable. There's something at its core I just don't like."

THE FIRST COUPLE OF FILM

In her early career, Ms. Gerwig's quirky, wobbly, lovable persona in "mumblecore" films, then later in "Greenberg," "Frances Ha" and "Mistress America"—she wrote the latter two with Mr. Baumbach and he directed both—made her the indie "It girl," a successor to Diane Keaton in "Annie Hall."

"She was a wonderful combination of an actress who can embody the character naturally but at the same time keep half of her brain working as a writer inside of the scene," said Mark Duplass, who made mumblecore movies with her. He recalled directing her in "Baghead" in 2008, as she was putting a suitor in the friend zone; she improvised and put tiny hair clips in the young man's hair while she was letting him down, as a way of letting him know.

It's a shock to see Ms. Gerwig in "White Noise," looking almost unrecognizable as Babette Gladney, the permed, sweatsuited wife of a Hitler-studies professor at a small liberal arts college in the Midwest.

"It was strange for our 3-year-old, who was 2 at the time, because he would come to the set and look at her and he had a hard time processing it," Mr. Baumbach said.

Ms. Gerwig was thinking Teri Garr and Dee Wallace, as well as women she had seen in her hometown, Sacramento, as a child. "I got a really early, quick picture of Babette in my mind, and I saw her hair and I saw her in a lavender sweater," she said. "I saw acrylic nails that were mauve. I was born in '83. I have sense memories of being in the grocery store and the color of certain women's nails."

She worked out the look with Ann Roth, the Oscar- and Tony-winning 91-year-old costume designer who worked on the movie. "She would call me sometimes and say, 'Gret, do you think that Babette is the kind of woman who has only red underwear or does she have a few other colors?' I said, 'I think she only has red underwear.' Ann said, 'That's exactly right, red.'"

She cast herself in the role. "When Noah said, 'Who do you think should play Babette?' I said, 'Me.'"

Since the first time she was directed by Mr. Baumbach a dozen years ago, Ms. Gerwig has become an acclaimed director herself. Did she ever want to correct him on how he was directing a scene?

"No, I think I only did it once on the set," she said. "He's incredibly open to suggestion. The truth is, I think if I had wanted to sit there all day, every day, even when I wasn't on the set, he'd be happy to ask what I thought of every shot. I think also, as a director, there's a certain loneliness. Mike Nichols said directors need a buddy. So someone who has a thought or a point of view or is looking over your shoulder makes you feel less like you're having an isolated existential crisis every day."

Was it uncomfortable when the two had to go up against each other at the Oscars for Best Picture of 2019, he with "Marriage Story," she with "Little Women"?

"It was so weird in the moment when we actually were there," she said. "It's very funny, but we did actually vote for ourselves. We were at our computers and I was like, 'Just so you know, I'm going to vote for myself,' and he said, 'OK, I'm going to vote for myself, too.'"

Mr. Baumbach told me that the Oscar face-off was "easier" because they both lost. "We could celebrate that together."

Having been in competitive situations with journalists I was dating, I was impressed with their equanimity, especially with Mr. Baumbach's apparent lack of an overweening male ego. Ms. Gerwig has addressed this in her work; in "Mistress America," Lola Kirke's Barnard student is interested in a guy in her class, even as the two compete against each other to get into a prestigious writing club and she wins a spot. He gets involved with another young woman and dismisses Ms. Kirke's character, saying: "I need someone I can love, not keep up with."

"I feel like it must be hard if you're 25," Ms. Gerwig said. "I think as you get older, things work, things don't work. You're up, you're down."

I explained that my illusions about the glamour of being "the first couple of film"—as The Hollywood Reporter called Ms. Gerwig and Mr. Baumbach in 2019—was shattered long ago when I interviewed Paul Newman and Joanne Woodward, that earlier first couple of film. Ms. Woodward said she would not participate in the 1986 New York Times Magazine cover story about Mr. Newman because she did not give quotes for stories that were focused on him, rather than on her or both of them. Mr. Newman appealed to her but was rebuffed. Later, I interviewed them both for the cover of a women's magazine, and Ms. Woodward was charming.

Ms. Woodward had talked about "the tough fight" and many years of analysis involved in keeping her own identity, and I was left wondering: How many hours with a psychiatrist did it take to work those rules out? Clearly, even in this most enduring of Hollywood marriages, careful ego management was required.

Even though Ms. Gerwig seems more excited to take on big commercial projects and Mr. Baumbach seems more fixated on capital-A Art, they make their collaboration seem suspiciously easy and fun. (Perhaps it has something to do with Ms. Gerwig's high school obsession with the sport of fencing.)

She is hesitant to say this on the record because "it feels very cheesy to me," but finally it tumbles out: "He's my favorite person ever to talk to and I think I might be his favorite person to talk to."

She recalled a time in the early pandemic when they were still in isolation. "I was in the kitchen and he hadn't woken up yet. I had a thought and I thought to myself, 'I can't wait until Noah wakes up and then I can tell him this.' I thought, 'He's the only person I see and I was still excited to talk to him.'"

Ms. Kirke said that Ms. Gerwig, who co-wrote and acted in "Mistress America," and Mr. Baumbach, who co-wrote and directed, presented "a united front on set together. You can see how inspired by and respectful they are of one another."

Ms. Kirke never saw them fight, she said, adding that she had been in situations with other husband-and-wife teams and thought they must "hate each other."

A WORKING ROMANTIC PARTNERSHIP

Mr. Baumbach first worked with Ms. Gerwig on the 2010 movie "Greenberg," starring Ben Stiller. Mr. Baumbach directed the movie, and wrote it with Jennifer Jason Leigh, then his wife, who also acted in it and served as a producer.

Clearly, some life-altering alchemy was at work between the 40-year-old Mr. Baumbach and the 26-year-old newcomer Ms. Gerwig, who played a personal assistant. (She trained for her role by working as a personal assistant for a month to Ms. Leigh's mother, Barbara Turner, a screenwriter.)

I told Ms. Gerwig it's easy to see now, rewatching their first movies together, that the director was infatuated with her. "I'm turning red," she said, a blush spreading over her ivory skin. Mr. Baumbach midwifed Ms. Gerwig's stardom; in the Times review of the film, A.O. Scott declared that she "may well be the definitive screen actress of her generation."

Ms. Leigh filed for divorce eight months after the birth of her son with Mr. Baumbach, who was born just before "Greenberg" came out. The divorce was not finalized until 2013. This bitter, chaotic time informed Mr. Baumbach's "Marriage Story."

Was it difficult establishing a relationship with Ms. Gerwig amid the wreckage?

"I was going through a hard time in my life, and she was going through a different time in her life," he said. "We really wanted to make it work together, we really wanted to be together, and we were both drawn by that. That's how we still feel about each other."

He said that he and Ms. Leigh—who has stayed publicly silent about the dissolution of the marriage and her opinion about "Marriage Story" (although Mr. Baumbach told The Wall Street Journal that he screened it for his ex-wife and she liked it)—co-parent their 12-year-old son, Rohmer. "In another completely different way," he said, "you have to work together on that so that you can be the best parents you can to your great kid."

His partnership with Ms. Gerwig—they are not married but she wears an engagement ring—has changed him, he said. "I feel like I'm a better artist because of it," he said. "I know I am. I think a lot about 'Marriage Story,' which she didn't write with me, but the things I was able to do with that movie as a direct influence of just being in a relationship with her and being around her, and things that she's brought out in me that I was maybe sitting on."

Like what?

"I think a joy of looseness," he said. "I'm less afraid of being embarrassed."

Mr. Baumbach said he's not immune to competitive feelings, but dryly noted: "I've been in a ton of therapy." He continued, "If I show her something I'm writing, or I show her a cut or something I'm working on that she's not directly involved in, the highest compliment she pays is, she says, 'I'm jealous.'" He mused, laughing and echoing Ms. Gerwig: "Maybe if I was 25 and met her, I wouldn't have been able to handle it."

In a way, the couple's early collaboration replicated the dynamic between Woody Allen, Mr. Baumbach's early idol, and Diane Keaton, an idol for Ms. Gerwig. Ms. Gerwig brought a kooky, boho California lightness to Mr. Baumbach's darker coiled, neurotic Jewish New York sensibility.

In the beginning, did people think she was the Hollywood ingénue riding on Mr. Baumbach's reputation? I remind her of the time Barbra Streisand asked Steven Spielberg to watch an early cut of "Yentl," and then a lot of people falsely assumed he had directed it. Ms. Gerwig grinned and said she showed Mr. Spielberg an early cut of "Little Women" to get his notes, and no one assumed he had directed it.

Ms. Gerwig said that before she started directing, some people assumed that she was just contributing some extemporaneous lines to films she was starring in and Mr. Baumbach was directing, like "Frances Ha" and "Mistress America."

"People would say things like, 'Did you help to write the script?'"

she recalled. "I was like 'No, I co-wrote it.' I think the more work I did and the more authorship I took on, the less that was something that was a question mark. People are more like, 'Oh, she probably did write those with him because now we can see this work or that.' That assumption of 'Oh, you probably didn't do this really,' that's gone away."

Mr. Baumbach wryly said it goes the other way now, with people talking about "Frances Ha" as though it's Ms. Gerwig's sole creation.

'HER AMBITION IS TO CONQUER AMERICAN CINEMA'

Saoirse Ronan, a star of "Lady Bird" and "Little Women," said that Ms. Gerwig, like the director Steve McQueen, was "a bundle of energy, ideas and inspiration. She was constantly rewriting scenes to make the script as tight as she could. She'll work all the hours that God sends."

Ms. Ronan said that in "Lady Bird," a nun tells her character that the greatest form of love is to pay attention. "That came from Greta directly," she said. "She pays absolutely incredibly sharp attention to everyone and everything around her."

Amy Pascal, a producer of "Little Women," was equally effusive. "She barged into my office and said, 'You have to hire me to write "Little Women," and I want to direct it, and here's why. I want to tell the story in a completely different way.'" She told Ms. Pascal: "It's about money."

"She was able to decipher the book to tell it in a really modern way," Ms. Pascal said. "Her ambition is to conquer American cinema."

Ms. Metcalf said the key to Ms. Gerwig's success as a director is dogged preparation. "She does all of the homework before anybody gets to the set," she said, eschewing the usual mad scramble. "There's a lightness there. She takes away all the pressure." Instead of being the type of director who withholds praise from "the children" and whispers about the actors behind the monitor to make them paranoid, Ms. Metcalf said, Ms. Gerwig "keeps a bubble around you, so no negative feelings are allowed in."

Before they began filming "Lady Bird," Ms. Gerwig brought the cast over to her New York apartment and showed them a shoe box of mementos she had kept from high school, saying, "Here's how I see the character."

"That clicked with me in a way that was rare," Ms. Metcalf said. "That made it so real to me. It was the first time I was playing a fictional character where I actually was able to think of it as a real woman."

Ms. Gerwig and Mr. Baumbach both like to blend autobiographical elements into some of their movies. Does it ever feel like you're sucking out each other's emotional DNA, I asked her, or studying each other for good material?

"He's working on something right now, and I've been reading it as he's working on it and I said, 'You know what?' and I gave him this little story and a good line and then he put it in," she said. "And then I read another draft and I was like, 'Listen, if you're not going to use that line, I'm going to use it.' He said, 'No, no, no, I'm going to use it. Don't worry.'

"Some little things are flattering," she continued. "There was something in 'Marriage Story' with the Scarlett Johansson character, Nicole," who was widely understood to be a stand-in for Ms. Jason Leigh but shared some of Ms. Gerwig's traits. "In the beginning, when Charlie and Nicole are talking about each other and he says, 'She makes tea and leaves it all over the apartment and she leaves the cabinets open.' And my friends watched it and were like, 'That's you. You do those things.' I was like, 'It's true. It is me.'"

Mr. Baumbach laughed when I asked him about it. "She pours herself water, then puts it down somewhere and then never drinks it," he said. "There are usually five of them around."

As sunset neared and New Yorkers scurried off to trains, planes and automobiles, getting ready for Thanksgiving, Ms. Gerwig cleared our plates from lunch and went to the fridge in the kitchen to make herself some yogurt with honey and cinnamon. Then she got back to work, cutting "Barbie." After writing for so long about the paucity of women directors, I tell her as I leave, it's great to see a woman behind the camera smashing it, and doing it like a woman, not a man.

"I hope to continue to do so," she said, as she disappeared into an editing room. "I hope I make movies all the way through my 70s, maybe my 80s. We'll see how I go."

Confirm or Deny

MAUREEN DOWD: *You threw up on a yacht in front of the Kardashians.*

GRETA GERWIG: It's true. I had never been on a yacht and I was so excited to, and then five minutes after being on one, I threw up in front of two Kardashians. I haven't been on a yacht since. I don't think this is a big memory for them. Only for me.

Your greatest accomplishment was forcing hipsters to like the Dave Matthews Band after "Lady Bird."

I don't think I had to force anyone to do anything. I think they all secretly loved it just like I do, and they just had to admit it to themselves.

Your favorite sex scene is Donald Sutherland and Julie Christie in "Don't Look Now."

Yes, I stand by that.

You avoid sex scenes when you write your own movies.

I'm not interested in the sex scene just for the sex scene of it. It would have to be something where it felt part of the story. I might write one eventually.

You want to make a musical.

Musicals are always top of mind for me. I would love there to be a musical in my future.

You forbid cellphones on the set.

Yes.

Your favorite place to eat in Brooklyn is Court Street Grocers.

Yes. They actually have one now in Manhattan.

You make your own baby food.

(Laughing) Not anymore. It's a lot of puréeing. I've forgotten all of this. I'm going to have to remember how to do all this stuff.

You grew up in a house without a television.

There was a little black-and-white set that they plugged in, they kept it in the closet. My parents were hippies a bit. They didn't really want us to be inundated. We weren't allowed to wear logos on our clothes. My mom felt that it was turning us into billboards.

You said your fallback career is tutoring "rich, stupid kids."

No, my fallback career is being a step aerobics instructor, which I'm certified in.

You bring a posse of college friends to the Vanity Fair Oscar party and they all dress alike.

Those are my best friends. One's a nurse, one's a social worker, one's a lawyer, one's an actor. It was their idea because I was like, "I don't know if I can get everybody into the Vanity Fair party." And they said, "If we all wear the same outfit, they'll think we're part of something and then we'll be able to find each other easily." They wore a print from a designer in Brooklyn the first time and five different yellow dresses the next time. It's going to get weird as we get older.

RYAN MURPHY IS HAVING A VERY HAPPY HALLOWEEN

—OCTOBER 29, 2022

When he was 14, Ryan Murphy made a cigarette holder out of paper clips so he could pretend he was Norma Desmond and smoke "Sunset Boulevard" style.

The television auteur is glad Norma killed her young screenwriter lover and left him floating facedown in the pool.

"One of my idols," Mr. Murphy said of the fictional, homicidal and histrionic silent screen star.

We are talking here about someone who knows that he is big, even when others think he's small.

We are also talking about a man who is ready for his close-up.

The night I had a five-hour dinner of pasta with red sauce and white wine at the Mercer Hotel in New York with the king of Grand Guignol, Netflix had just called to tell him he was in a fierce competition with himself: his latest drop, the mini-series "The Watcher," about a New Jersey couple (played by Naomi Watts and Bobby Cannavale) tormented by a threatening, anonymous pen pal, was vying with his "Monster: The Jeffrey Dahmer Story" for the top spot in TV shows. Both shows were created with his longtime collaborator, Ian Brennan.

Mr. Murphy has, in the last decade, conjured what Jon Robin Baitz, who is writing Mr. Murphy's forthcoming FX series on Truman Capote, described as "a strange alternate history of America here. It's the 'American Berserk,' as Philip Roth called it. Nobody has captured that intersection between beauty, death, horror and corruption the same way."

Mr. Murphy, America's most productive producer, who likes to say he has reinvented himself as often as Madonna, has reinvented the TV landscape with transgressive hits that disrupt norms and bring outsiders into American homes. Exploring taboos and temptations, Mr. Murphy, known for hits like "Glee" and the series "American Horror Story," earns his eyeballs and gazillions by creating shows that no one knew they wanted, as he slyly mixes social justice messages with lusty and macabre spectacles.

He created "a mythos and a kind of line of production that's branded and wildly successful, like Disney and Spielberg," Mr. Baitz said.

But for the last four years, many in Hollywood whispered (loudly) that Mr. Murphy's best days were behind him, casting him as the loser in the Shonda Rhimes vs. Ryan Murphy contest drummed up by the press.

Ms. Rhimes got a $100 million deal with Netflix in 2017. Then Mr. Murphy got a $300 million deal in 2018 and was declared "King of the Streaming Boom" in a Time cover story, "TV's First $300M Man" in a Hollywood Reporter story and "The Most Powerful Man in TV" by The New Yorker.

The deals were closely watched, with many hoping they would fail—both to prove the invalidity of the new streaming economy, which had upended the old Hollywood economic and power structure, and as punishment for those reaping its spoils.

Mr. Murphy had a patchy initial run at Netflix—with the streamer judging shows like "The Politician," "Hollywood," and "The Prom" as underperforming—while Ms. Rhimes hit it big with "Bridgerton," which debuted in 2020.

"Hollywood, since its origins, has attracted broken-toy people looking to lord it over someone even more broken," said Janice Min, the chief executive of the Ankler. A lot of writers (and a lot of unemployed writers) who were jealous of Mr. Murphy's jackpot with Netflix were "smacking their lips," Ms. Min said, at the idea that "the so-called mad genius had lost his grip on the zeitgeist." But then, she said, "the guy only striking out and hitting singles hit a home run in the ninth inning."

The silvery-blond-haired Mr. Murphy roared back on a Targaryen dragon by Beyoncé-dropping, with no advance notice, "Dahmer" in September.

The mini-series—about the serial killer who preyed on predominantly young gay men from 1978 to 1991—has become the biggest hit of his career and the second biggest smash in Netflix history, after the fourth season of "Stranger Things."

"Mr. Harrigan's Phone," a Stephen King adaptation that Mr. Murphy produced with Jason Blum, is also floating in the top tier on Netflix. On top of all that, Mr. Murphy's 11th installment of "American Horror Story" has started on FX, starring Joe Mantello and Patti LuPone in another harrowing tale set on the cusp of the AIDS crisis and about a serial killer of gay men, this one a fictional story about the "Mai Tai killer."

And so the man who loves gasp-inducing twists in his TV narratives created his own. Soon, there were headlines like this one in the Decider: "Netflix Bet $300 Million on Ryan Murphy—They'd Be Fools Not to Give Him Even More."

Before his latest fireworks display, it seemed like a good bet that Mr. Murphy and Netflix, which is now more careful with nine-figure paychecks, would have a conscious uncoupling when his contract is up in five months and the producer would make a full-time commitment to FX and its parent company, Disney.

Now it looks like Hollywood streamers will be competing over Mr. Murphy.

"Look, the reason why I wanted to do this deal with Ryan back when we did, there's very few people capable of doing what he ultimately did at Netflix, producing something on this scope and scale and buzz level of 'Monster: the Jeffrey Dahmer Story,'" Ted Sarandos, the co-C.E.O. of Netflix, said, adding that his streamer can get "a huge, global audience" for Mr. Murphy's shows.

"Everyone knew about Versace," Mr. Sarandos said. "Everybody knew about O.J. Everybody knows about Jeffrey Dahmer and yet he takes these stories that are so familiar and makes them completely fresh."

He does not fault Mr. Murphy for an uneven start, noting: "I don't think it's possible, not just for Ryan but for anyone, to achieve the levels that they achieve without having a couple of misses under their belt while they figure out 'How do I adapt my storytelling to this platform? How do I connect it with this audience?'"

A TRIPLE SCORPIO WHO DOESN'T WANT TO BE EVIL

Mr. Murphy's old friend Greg Berlanti, another very successful producer who once, long ago, was so broke that he had to borrow money from the equally struggling Mr. Murphy to get the boot off his car, said that when people ask him what Ryan is like, he answers: "If you mixed Hitchcock with Madonna."

"I've watched him over 30 years and he has created himself over and over again, across platforms and genres," Mr. Berlanti said. "He's always loved classic Hollywood icons and now he's made himself one."

Jason Blum agreed: "God—or someone—sends him what's going to be the big hot next thing. He's consistently ahead of the curve." (Billie Lourd thinks he's a witch.)

Mr. Murphy can create with old friends, elevate new writing talent, anoint actors, producers and even directors, but no one makes any mistake about who's running the show. To paraphrase a line about the Susan Hayward character, Helen Lawson, from "Valley of the Dolls," a camp-classic film Mr. Murphy loves: "There's only *one star* in a Ryan Murphy production and that's Ryan Murphy."

He has his own personal style, looking modish at the Mercer in Rick Owens black pants, 20-year-old Ann Demeulemeester boots and a long-sleeved James Perse shirt. "I do believe past 45, you should not show your elbows," he said. "People always describe me looking like an orphan and I'm like, 'OK, I'll take it.'" He also sported a vest he found in a used clothing store and what he calls his "Dracula Comme des Garçons coat."

Mr. Murphy said he never lost faith in himself, despite the Hollywood schadenfreude.

He did, however, do a couple years of intensive therapy to figure out what was noise he should tune out and what were his own behavior patterns that he could change to get a better result. When he feels cornered, he stings, and he said he'd like to curb that tendency.

He said his friends laugh about his story of a trip to an astrologer years ago who said "Ugh, you're a lot," when she learned that he was a triple Scorpio.

"She said, 'You are so extreme.' I said, 'That's true.' She said, 'You have the capacity for great good and great *evil*.' I said, 'OK, well, I don't want the evil.'"

Despite what he calls his "Danish bitch face," he said that "ultimately, I think I'm a real softy. I'm like an ice cream cone."

Still, he is such a perfectionist that he uses a ruler when he makes his bed to make sure his sheets are even. "You want to make sure the line is straight, especially with a print," he said, adding, "I like right angles."

He has held up production to have a picture on set raised an inch and a half on a wall. If he gets obsessed with something—like the garden at the farm in Bedford, N.Y., that he just bought from Richard Gere—he goes deep.

"I decided that I wanted to do 5,000 daffodil bulbs around this memorial that the Dalai Lama built for Richard Gere," he said. "I'll research random daffodil bulbs for a year before I will buy them. I can tell you everything you would want to know about a daffodil bulb called the Dutch Master."

Pruning, he said, is one of his favorite things to do with his 100 different kinds of boxwoods—to make order out of chaos.

"Everyone in my life thinks I'm insane," he said. "I think it's a form of O.C.D., clearly. It's meditation—the same reason I still go into a church sometimes. I like being lost in a task."

He said that one of his psychiatrists persuaded him that he was allowed to fail. "I just think there was a rigidity to me as an artist and a person that has gone away," he said. "A lot of that has been fatherhood. A lot of that has been dealing with my child's health issues."

Mr. Murphy and his husband, the photographer David Miller, have three sons, Logan, 9, Ford, 8, and Griffin, 2.

Ford was diagnosed with neuroblastoma when he was 18 months old (and later, diabetes). The toddler had surgery to remove the tumor.

"To walk in and see your baby who's not talking yet hooked up to 15 tubes was very, very upsetting and hard," he said. (In 2018, Mr. Murphy donated a wing of Children's Hospital Los Angeles in his son's name with a $10 million gift.)

He thought the experience of his son's illness would make him slow down. But instead, the opposite happened. "I realized, like, wow, you've got one life, you've got one shot."

His father, who worked in newspaper distribution, never got up the nerve to take the bar exam. His mother, who wrote books, would have liked to be in show business. "I was like, I don't want to have any regrets," Mr. Murphy said. "The saddest thing in the world is lost potential."

He continued: "People always ask me, 'How do you do so many things?' I micromanage my day down to 15-minute increments. I stay up until 2 or 3 a.m., after putting my kids to bed at 9. I feel guilty sleeping, like there's something I should be doing. I have a little black leather-bound book that no one in my life has seen that has ideas, like 'Maybe this would be good.'"

Mr. Murphy has a reputation for being taciturn and demanding. He says that because his shyness can be mistaken for aloofness, he prefers to work with the same collaborators and stars over and over, like a repertory company, including Joe Mantello, Evan Peters, Darren Criss, Billie Lourd and Sarah Paulson.

His intensity can leave some who work with him feeling off-kilter if he withdraws his attention without explanation. It is like the sun shining and then he disappears, giving people whiplash. Mr. Murphy seems to enjoy the fact that he leaves people off-balance, fixated on why he's gone cold.

"He's certainly not easy," Mr. Baitz said. "But that's part of his odd magic. He's very hard on himself. It's as though he's got Wernher von Braun, Grace Coddington and Edgar Allan Poe in his head."

CHER SET HIM ON THIS PATH

The producer-director-writer started out as a journalist.

At his first internship at the Knoxville News Sentinel in Tennessee, he wore a vintage white three-piece suit to cover his first crime scene, a robbery at a liquor store, where the perp tripped and shot himself in the face.

"As I looked at this person whose jaw was dangling by a thread, I excused myself and threw up," Mr. Murphy said. "Then the photographer said, 'I don't think you'd want to be wearing white on this job.'"

He went on to an internship at The Washington Post along with Kara Swisher, who recalled him as "brilliant and a handful. The same as he is now." The editors tried to send him to cover the suburbs and he told them no, that he wanted to meet Bob Woodward.

He ended up with an entertainment column syndicated by Knight Ridder, specializing in female movie stars. The stars were impressed with his detailed knowledge.

"With Jessica Lange, it wasn't somebody saying, 'What was it like to kiss Jack Nicholson?'" he recalled. "It was like, 'OK, you did that one scene as Frances Farmer and you had to do the lobotomy. How did you do that weird twitch with your left eye?' They liked me for that.

"I thought that I was going to be like a Rex Reed sort of person. I kept interviewing Cher. Then when she said, 'You've got to do something else. You can't interview me again,' I was like, 'You're probably right.'"

In the 1990s, when Mr. Murphy was still a journalist, he lived for six years with Bill Condon, a director a decade older who went on to make "Gods and Monsters," "Dreamgirls" and two "Twilight" films. Writing about the relationship in a profile of Mr. Murphy in The New Yorker, Emily Nussbaum told the story of how the pair went to Laguna Niguel beach one weekend for Memorial Day: "Condon got caught in a riptide—and when he thought he saw a flash of hesitation on Murphy's face, as if he might let him drown, he knew that the relationship was over."

Mr. Murphy said he was hurt by the characterization because, from his point of view, he was scared and trying to help save Mr. Condon, who got pulled out of the riptide by a lifeguard.

Mr. Condon reiterated to me that he thought he saw a flicker of hesitation that he interpreted as a signal that they had "no future." But he said he never intended it to be read as accusation of murderous intent akin to Bette Davis as Regina Hubbard Giddens in "The Little Foxes," letting her husband die by refusing to get his medicine.

The pair continued their holiday weekend at the Ritz Carlton. "It was a moment that we both laughed about because it's grimly funny," Mr. Condon said. Even after they broke up, they remained friends for 14 years, with Mr. Condon inviting Mr. Murphy into his writers' group.

Mr. Murphy said some people, and some in the press, liked to believe the caricature. "In my work, I elicit very strong feelings in people, *good and bad*," Mr. Murphy said. "I have a lot of friends and I have a lot of joy, but I think people want to write about this ruthless, cold, gay person with no feelings, who's ambitious at any cost. That's a character that they've made up, but that's not me."

The 5-foot-10 Mr. Murphy felt like an alien when he was growing up in Indianapolis, a towhead in a family of very tall, dark-haired Danish-Irish who called themselves Vikings.

"I was alone a lot as a kid," he said. "I wrote plays, my father wanted me to be on the baseball team. I wanted to read 'Little House on the Prairie' in the library. I just learned to retreat, and some people find that to be calculated, mysterious, but it's not."

His grandmother helped shape his obsessions. She took him to Vincent Price movies and the original "Dracula" with Bela Lugosi, and it colored his world. He decided he wanted to decorate his bedroom in red, as "the portal to hell," a homage to Diana Vreeland and John Milton. (Later in childhood, he had a Studio 54 theme, complete with disco ball and a chocolate shag rug. When Grace Kelly died, he took a picture of her to the paint store so they could make an ice-blue paint to match her eyes, for his bedroom.)

His grandmother also gave him a love of gardening. When the nuns let their yard at his Catholic grade school go to seed, he spent five years restoring it.

"By the time I left that Catholic school, it looked like Martha Stewart had been there for years," he said, grinning.

His career in Hollywood is strangely similar to his life in high school, "because I was attacked and persecuted, slammed into a locker, punched in the head, and in equal measure, popular," he said. (Mr. Murphy has returned to high school several times in his work, including on his early show "Popular"; his first breakthrough hit, "Glee"; and "The Politician.")

"Football players loved me," he said. "How many football players was I sleeping with on the side? I had the lead in all the musicals. I was president of every club, dated the homecoming queens for three years in a row and gave them all makeovers and ran their campaigns."

"It wasn't like they were highly sexualized relationships," he continued. "It was like, 'OK, do you want to win homecoming queen? This is what we're going to do.'"

His family would take a different nun each year on vacation with them to St. Petersburg, Fla., and young Ryan (who aspired to be pope at that point) and his brother had to take turns sharing a bed with the religious guest.

"They loved me," he said of the nuns, "because I would talk to them about their skin care and sometimes I would help them out. I had an allowance, and I spent all my money on Noxzema and Sea Breeze for them and gave them tutorials."

"I remember being obsessed with the idea of like, 'Are you OK that you're never going to be in love?'" he recalled. One nun confessed to him that she was a lesbian but was too afraid to come out.

Asked how his parents handled his sexuality, he replied that he felt "unloved" as a child; his father struck him at times. "It was not something they liked and they did not want that."

His parents sent him to a therapist "to be changed and converted, not a conversion therapy but close." By the time his parents "got there" in accepting him, he said, "it had created such huge problems in my life, trouble with intimacy, trouble with trusting, trouble with love."

It left him guarded. "I thought I would be over my childhood wounds by now, to be honest with you, but I guess I'm not. I'm trying."

He said he couldn't abide anything puritanical but admits to being something of a prude.

"I am Victorian, almost," he said. "Sometimes, I'll be squeamish or prudish and my friends will be like, 'You do realize what you just aired last night on television, right?'" His work has sex and violence, but at home, "If I had pearls, I'd be clutching them at all times."

IS THERE STILL BIAS AGAINST GAY MEN IN HOLLYWOOD?

Some of his friends think that part of the schadenfreude aimed at Mr. Murphy stems from a lingering bias in Hollywood about gay men getting very powerful.

"I think my dad gets that, too," said Billie Lourd, the daughter of Carrie Fisher and Bryan Lourd, Mr. Murphy's agent, who is now married to Bruce Bozzi. "Even though it's 2022 and everybody says it's OK, he's still a really powerful gay man and I think that's hard for some straight men to stomach, which is so sad and weird. And Ryan is the proudest out, most powerful gay man in the bunch." (Mr. Murphy has grown so close to Ms. Lourd that he is giving her baby shower.)

Mr. Murphy said that when he took a bow on some magazine covers when he got the Netflix deal, thinking he would be an inspiration to other gay people, instead, it ruffled feathers. "I used to be the underdog"—he moved to Los Angeles with $56 in his pocket, he said—"and then I became the establishment. Nobody roots for the Yankees."

His production company has 302 Emmy nominations and 51 wins; Mr. Murphy personally has had 37 nominations and won six Emmys, and a Tony for his "Boys in the Band" revival and two Grammy nominations for "Glee."

He recalled that when he started out in 1995, "Those early years were very, very, very hard because I would want to write gay characters or women, other marginalized groups, and straight men wearing Dockers in power would say, 'No, people don't want to see that.'"

He recalled that one male executive imitated his voice and hand mannerisms to be a Paul Lynde–like gay caricature—even though he has a basso profundo voice, unlike Lynde's.

"I was just absolutely shocked," Mr. Murphy said, adding that "the true joy of the arc of my life" is that it's not even a conversation with the executives he works with now.

In 2016, Mr. Murphy began the Half Initiative, seeking to ensure that at least half the directing jobs on average for his shows were filled by women.

Mr. Murphy says his vision has always been "to take the people that in another person's work would have been the sidekicks, the misfits, the marginalized people you laugh at, and to center the story around them."

He also writes many parts for women over 40, debunking the old idea that women should vanish from the screen after a certain age. His first FX hit, "Nip/Tuck," was about plastic surgery and he created a love letter to faded movie queens in their 50s in "Feud: Bette and Joan," about the dueling Mesdames Davis and Crawford during the filming of "What Ever Happened to Baby Jane?"

Naomi Watts, the 54-year-old star of "The Watcher," said she was grateful to be a part of the club. "It doesn't matter to him that we're not at the tippy top this second," she said. "He knows and recognizes that we've had great moments and we've proved ourselves as artists."

Ms. Watts will also be playing the socialite Babe Paley in Mr. Murphy's next installment of "Feud," set for next year, about the cafe society battle royale that resulted when Truman Capote wrote a book, "Answered Prayers," dishing about his swans and they dropped him like a hot tiara. Tom Hollander will play Capote, with Diane Lane as Slim Keith, Demi Moore as Ann Woodward, Calista Flockhart as Lee Radziwill and Chloë Sevigny as C.Z. Guest.

Mr. Murphy used to get upset when his style was called "camp." "I thought that was a way to pigeonhole gay people: 'You didn't write a drama. You wrote a camp drama,'" he said. "Now, I'm like, if you want to call it camp, yes, maybe 'American Horror Story' is camp. I don't think it is, but if you want to, OK, I get it."

"The rule of my career has been: The more specific you are, the more universal you can become," he said. "I also don't think that all gay stories have to be happy stories. There was a moment on Netflix where they removed the L.G.B.T.Q. tag from 'Dahmer,' and I didn't like it and I asked why they did that and they said because people were upset because it was an upsetting story. I was, like, 'Well, yeah.' But it was a story of a gay man and more importantly, his gay victims."

He said he is most proud of an episode about one of Dahmer's victims, a charming Black deaf man named Tony Hughes. "There's a five-minute scene of three gay deaf men at a pizza parlor talking in sign language about dating, gay life and how hard is it for them," he said. "I could not believe that I was getting the gift of putting it on television."

Why did he think it became such a big cultural phenomenon, with Jeffrey Dahmer Halloween costumes trending to the point that eBay banned them?

"The world is a dark place and getting darker, and people are looking for a place to put their anxieties," he said.

Some on social media were quick to accuse the show of exploiting the trauma the victims' families had suffered. Mr. Murphy said he did the story to shed light on the racism and homophobia that pervaded the case, at the victims' expense, and because "it was the biggest thing I've ever seen that really sort of examines how easy it is to get away with things with the white privilege aspects."

He asked: "What are the rules now? Should we never do a movie about a tyrant?"

He said they spent three and a half years researching the story, and reached out to at least 20 friends or family members of the victims trying to get input. "I think when you make something like this, you have an obligation to history," he said.

Mr. Murphy said that President Barack Obama called him after he watched his 2014 film adaptation of "The Normal Heart," about Larry Kramer's crusade to have doctors and politicians acknowledge the AIDS epidemic, and told him to keep being a historian. "That was a lightbulb moment," Mr. Murphy said. "What I try to do regularly is unearth buried history."

And what does he have planned after his autumnal triumph?

He had a commercial, if not a critical, success in directing Julia Roberts in "Eat, Pray, Love," but he says he doesn't want to do any more movies. "I like the energy of the long-form television series," he said.

And he's working on a book about famous women and how they informed his life, called "Ladies and Gentleman."

"I might not do anything," he said dryly. "I might retire and launch a line of beeswax products. I would not be surprised if I moved to the East Coast and changed my life completely. I just bought a farm and I've always wanted to be a farmer. I grew up in Indiana. My backyard was a cornfield."

I said that I thought he was dying to get away from all things Indiana.

"You always just end up being the person you ran away from," he said, smiling.

Confirm or Deny

MAUREEN DOWD: *The next season of "Feud" will be Harry and Meghan vs. Charles and William.*

RYAN MURPHY: No. I actually love Harry and Meghan. I was doing a season of "Feud" about Diana and Charles, and I abandoned it because I'm not British. Also, I wanted to see it on "The Crown." I'm like, "They're going to do it so much better than me."

The Kardashians are dragging down culture.

I think they're brilliant and also very misunderstood. These are women who are working their asses off and doing businesses and they're also unapologetic about, "This is who I am." One of my most fun nights ever was I had dinner at Kris Jenner's house. Kim came unannounced and we just hung out and talked about furniture. They are cheerleaders for other people. I would love to work with Kim in an acting part. I might hire Kris to be my manager.

Your biggest regret is approving the "Glee" rendition of the "Alvin and the Chipmunks" song.

That's actually my biggest triumph.

You interviewed Bette Davis.

She said, "I'll give you 20 minutes." She was wearing a Patrick Kelly suit and a pillbox hat. She was shrouded in this thick cloud of cigarette smoke and she looked like Yoda. The first thing she said is, "Do you want to hold my Oscars?" I said, "Yes, I do." She ended up giving me two and a half hours and I still have the tapes. I chain-smoked with her. She died three months later.

Warren Beatty once gave you this directing advice: "It's all about the wigs."
He was making a joke, but I took it as Bible because he's right. I build that into my contracts that I must have wig budgets to make sure they look perfect.

You can spot any plastic surgery at 10 paces.
Absolutely. I never judge anybody for doing it. I don't like the hypocrisy of someone saying, 'Look at me, I'm aging so beautifully and naturally,' and then it turns out they've had a brow lift, a forehead lift and an eyelift.

You have come around to the Tom Ford theory that houses are calmer without color.
I tend to create environments now that you feel like you're in a bowl of oatmeal. But for the farm, I've been researching all these plaids and what countries and families they came from. Death by plaid.

On one of your first dates with your future husband, he took you to a U.S.C. football game and you wore a fake fur coat and read Vogue the whole time.
Actually, I got a lot of compliments by the people on the stands.

You love bidding on Karl Lagerfeld at auctions.
I bid on one specific thing: a couple of candlesticks in the shape of Karl Lagerfeld's head.

When your friends go out to dance in Provincetown, you stay home with 1stdibs and Sotheby's.
Usually, I'll just stay home because I want to be with my children. I'm a nester now and I want to be with my babies and I want to be with my Karl Lagerfeld candlesticks.

TOM STOPPARD FINALLY LOOKS INTO HIS SHADOW

—SEPTEMBER 7, 2022

DORSET, England—Long before he became the august Sir Tom Stoppard, hailed by some as the greatest British playwright since Shakespeare, Stoppard was a teenage journalist in Bristol, making a few pounds a week covering lawn tennis, flower shows and traffic problems. He loved wearing a mackintosh and flashing his press pass, operating in the spirit of a British contemporary, Nicholas Tomalin, who wrote: "The only qualities essential for real success in journalism are ratlike cunning, a plausible manner, and a little literary ability."

So Stoppard was ready to lend a hand when I arrived at his dreamy 1790s stone house called "The Rectory" (because it once was one) to talk about the Broadway debut of his heart-rending epic, "Leopoldstadt," which begins previews Sept. 14 at the Longacre Theater and opens Oct. 2.

"I thought about you coming, and I thought I must try and help you be a success at this interviewing thing," he said, in his seductively dry tone. "And I thought, oh, I'll show her my cigarette box. That would definitely be worth a couple lines."

He held up the elegant silver box, and as long as he was at it, took out a cigarette, the first of many he'd smoke over the next three hours. (He used to write by cigarette time, laying out a row of matches with his smokes and saying, "Tonight I shall write 12 matches.")

"This says, 'Christmas, 1967. Affectionately, David Merrick,'" Stoppard said. The big Broadway producer was "fearsome," as Stoppard put it. He brought the young writer to New York that year with "Rosencrantz and Guildenstern Are Dead," the darkly funny worm's-eye view of "Hamlet" that transformed Stoppard's life, imbuing him with an image as the Mick Jagger of theater, a dashing icon of '60s Swinging London. As his friend and fellow playwright Simon Gray said, Stoppard was a magnetic figure blessed with so many enviable gifts—talent, riches, looks, luck—that it was futile to envy him.

When Stoppard landed in New York that year he was the toast of the town, as his biographer, Hermione Lee, writes in "Tom Stoppard: A Life." Marlene Dietrich came to see his play; Walter Winchell drove him around to crime scenes in a car with a siren. New Yorkers began asking him whether he was Jewish. He would respond vaguely that there must be "some Jewish somewhere." Borrowing an old Jonathan Miller line, he would say he was "Jew-ish." He breezily called himself "a bounced Czech."

Fifty-five years later, Stoppard is returning to New York with "Leopoldstadt," a play inspired by his belated reckoning with his Jewish roots.

The man who writes so brilliantly about time travel was ready to time-travel with me. He settled back on the couch in his sitting room, wearing a green sweater and khakis, still lanky and still with a tousled—but more silvery—mane. At 85, he retains, as Daphne Merkin once wrote in The New York Times, a louche glamour, "like a lounge lizard who reads Flaubert." The house Stoppard shares with his third wife, the charming Sabrina Guinness, is exactly what you would expect: elegant, erudite, fey and library-quiet. No tapping, since Sir Tom has no computer and is not on social media. He lets Guinness email for him, and he still writes with a Caran d'Ache fountain pen with a six-sided barrel.

There is a bookcase full of first editions of Jane Austen and Charles Dickens, which gets raided by "American burglars," as he calls his novel-purloining friends. In the hall hang framed letters Stoppard has collected, including one from A.E. Housman (the subject of his play "The Invention of Love") to the Warden of The Fishmongers' Company and another from Albert Einstein to the National Labor Committee for Palestine. The most cherished one, dated 1895 and composed on stationery from the Albemarle Hotel in Piccadilly, is a flinty put-down

Stoppard bought at auction as soon as he had money: "Sir, I have read your letter, and I see that to the brazen everything is brass. Your obedient servant Oscar Wilde."

The bathroom features another whimsical collection, which Stoppard ordered from autograph collectors and booksellers in the '70s: small, framed, signed publicity stills of Mae West, Marlon Brando, Elvis, Brigitte Bardot and others. Pointing out Frank Sinatra, Stoppard said regretfully that the signature had faded from too much sunlight.

Once or twice, when Stoppard was working on the arts page of the Western Daily Press and had more than one story to write, he used a different byline on the second one, so as not to look "too provincial." It was Tomáš Sträussler, his own name before his widowed mother remarried a British army major she had met in India named Kenneth Stoppard.

Tommy immigrated to England at 8, assuming an identity as British as white flannel cricket pants. It was a duality he did not dwell on for decades. Even when he was eventually prodded in his 50s into examining the identity of his Eastern European family and their fate in the Holocaust, it would take him six more years to write a magazine piece about it, and then two more decades for the play to gestate.

"I think he'd already faced it, but he hadn't faced it all the way through his body to be sufficiently able to write it," said Patrick Marber, the playwright ("Closer") who directed "Leopoldstadt" as well as the successful revival of Stoppard's "Travesties" a few years ago in London and on Broadway. "It's looking at his Jewishness, but it's Tom looking at death and his own mortality and everyone's mortality as well."

Stoppard's early life was defined by a series of escapes, and those escapes led to elisions. He showed me a painting of a sepia photo of his mother, Marta, when she was young, giving a fetching smile, flashing her son's brown eyes, wearing a coat with a fur collar. "When you look closely," he said, "it was a cheap coat."

She married Eugen Sträussler, a doctor working in Zlín in Moravia, Czechoslovakia, for a shoemaking company called Bata, which ran the town. In 1939, after Hitler invaded Czechoslovakia, the Sträusslers fled to Singapore, where Bata executives had arranged a new job for Eugen. Tomáš was 18 months old.

Singapore fell to the Japanese when Stoppard was 4. He and his older brother, Petr (later Peter), and Marta were put on a ship that she thought was headed for Australia but turned out to be steaming toward India. His father tried to follow them but never made it; Stoppard would later learn that his ship had been bombed and sunk. (He has nothing his father owned or touched.) With her future uncertain, Marta made her third and final escape to England by marrying Major Stoppard.

Tomas fell in love with all things English and followed his mother's lead in not looking back. She played down her history and Jewishness, thinking she had delivered her boys to safe harbor.

The cascading escapes made Stoppard feel as though he had "this charmed life."

"I was scooped up out of the world of the Nazis," he said. "I was scooped up out of the way of the Japanese, when women and children were put on boats as we were being bombed. I was just put down in India where there was no war. The war ended, my mother married a British army officer and so instead of ending up back in Czechoslovakia in time for Communism—they took over in 1948 when I was 11—here I was, turned into a privileged boarding-school boy. I was just going on, saying 'Lucky me.'"

Eventually he was scooped up by the London theater world. But at some point, after some backlash, he turned the concept inside out. What about those who hadn't been lucky?

"I remember very clearly saying to my mother, 'Well, how Jewish were we?' and she didn't come clean at all," Stoppard told me. "She said, 'Well, in 1939, just to have a Jewish grandparent was dangerous.' I just thought, 'Oh, I see. OK.'

"My mother essentially drew a line and didn't look back. My name was changed, I was British, and I really began to love England in every sense— the landscape, the literature. I don't recall ever consciously resisting finding out about myself. It's worse than that. I wasn't actually interested. I was never curious enough. I just looked in one direction: forward."

He came to think of himself as "Anglo-Saxon," he said: "Church of England is barely a religion if you don't want it to be one. You go to church every Sunday with the rest of the school. I'm not sure when I first was inside a synagogue, but it was years and years and years later."

As he wrote about his mother in a searing 1999 Talk Magazine article, "'being Jewish' didn't figure in her life until it disrupted it, and then it set her on a course of displacement, chaos, bereavement and—finally—sanctuary in a foreign country, England, thankful at least that her boys were now safe. Hitler made her Jewish in 1939."

Stoppard told me, "Obviously, I knew that there was a reason why we'd fled from the Nazis, but I didn't quite join the dots. My mother was always terribly nervous about my Czech past catching up with me."

As he ascended to be the new prince of London and New York theater with "Rosencrantz and Guildenstern Are Dead," his mother was fretting. "When I was about 30, people were writing about me being from Czechoslovakia, and so on," he recalled. "It made her very uneasy, and she thought there was surely some way I could do these interviews without letting on that my name wasn't really Stoppard, and that kind of thing."

In 1993, a cousin, Sarka Gauglitz, who lived in Germany, got in touch. She came to the National Theater in London for lunch to talk to him and his mother about their Jewish family history.

"There was this weird scene where I said to Sarka, 'How Jewish are we?' and then she said, 'What? You're Jewish.' I said, 'Yes, yes.' I was embarrassed. So I'm kind of going, 'Yes, I know I'm Jewish, but how?' So she then drew this family tree."

She told him how his four grandparents had perished at the hands of the Nazis and how his mother's three sisters had died in Auschwitz and another camp—a horrific litany that is echoed in "Leopoldstadt."

"I was totally poleaxed," he said. "I was in my 50s. I'd had this entire life. I couldn't change it retroactively even in my mind. So it wasn't like some kind of new start. I just carried on being the person I was."

The next year, when he went to Prague for a PEN conference and to see his friend, President Václav Havel, he visited the synagogue where the names of his grandparents were inscribed as Holocaust victims.

When his mother died in 1996, his stepfather—who had not welcomed her Czech family in their home, and whom Stoppard and his brother had come to see as xenophobic and antisemitic—asked Tom to renounce his last name. Stoppard told me he was "shocked" by the request, which he ignored, chalking it up to his stepfather's grief.

Stoppard was later moved by a novel called "Trieste" by the Croatian writer Daša Drndić. One of the characters rips into real-life people, including Stoppard and Madeleine Albright, saying they took too long to discover their family history, calling them "blind observers" who played it safe.

"Basically, she was saying, enough already with the charmed life, you had this family, which you seem to have forgotten," Stoppard said. "And I thought that was completely legitimate and an intelligible thing to say. And I think it had a lot to do with choosing to write about it."

Marber called the novel "an intense bee sting" for Stoppard, adding: "Tom is a ruthlessly truthful man in private."

Stoppard wrote another play first, "The Hard Problem," about human consciousness and the question of whether people can be genuinely good. The final spur for his most serious, personal play came, oddly enough, when he was joking around with his longtime producer Sonia Friedman several years ago.

He told Friedman he needed six impossible-to-get tickets for "Harry Potter and the Cursed Child," which she produced, for his niece. "She said, 'OK, if you write me a play,' and I said, 'OK.'" When he was forced to think about it, he realized that he had a play all along. He had to break the news to Friedman that they would need a company of about 40 actors.

"Of course, it's autobiographical without really being an autobiographical piece," he told me. "But elements of it are completely taken from life."

He said he had "displaced" the enormity of learning about his family by reading a lot about Auschwitz, and other people's stories. He wanted to set the story in Vienna, which he had visited in other plays.

"It was because I personally didn't have the background I wanted to write about—bourgeois, cultured, the city of Klimt and Mahler and Freud," Stoppard said. "Where better than Vienna? It's got an incredibly rich society."

Lee, his biographer, noted that Stoppard was particularly influenced while researching "Leopoldstadt" by Alexander Waugh's book, "The House of Wittgenstein: A Family at War," about the wealthy, sophisticated Viennese family that produced the philosopher Ludwig Wittgenstein and his brother Paul, who continued to be a concert pianist after losing an arm in World War I. The family had been Catholic for two generations, but when Hitler annexed Austria, they were stunned to learn they counted as Jews.

This is what happens in "Leopoldstadt" to the Merz family, a clan of businessmen, professors and musicians who become prosperous and bourgeois in Vienna, leaving behind the Jewish quarter, Leopoldstadt, and presiding in a large apartment on the desirable Ringstrasse. They intermarry and convert into an uneasy blend of Jewish, Protestant and Catholic, celebrating Christmas and gathering for a Seder. They argue about the merits of a Jewish homeland versus assimilation.

"So don't fall for this Judenstaat idiocy," one character declares. "Do you want to do mathematics in the desert or in the city where Haydn, Mozart and Beethoven overlapped, and Brahms used to come to our house? We're Austrians. Viennese."

When the dreadful knock on the door comes, they are stunned.

Stoppard does something unusual, ending his play with three characters who have barely appeared. In 1955, a young Englishman shows up named Leonard Chamberlain, who was born Leopold Rosenbaum. He immigrated to England at 8 (as Stoppard did), took his stepfather's name (as Stoppard did), has grown up to be a witty British writer (as Stoppard did) and had "a charmed life" (as Stoppard did). It is an unflattering self-portrait. Leo, contentedly vague about his identity, must listen to the litany of Holocaust deaths recited to him by his cousin, just as Stoppard did with his cousin.

His cousin Nathan tries to get through to Leo, speaking what Stoppard says is the essential line in the play: "You live as if without history, as if you throw no shadow behind you."

The Leo character, Stoppard told me, was "written out of a kind of guilt."

Stoppard, who was raised knowing little about Judaism, turned to friends while writing the play, seeking advice for a scene involving a bris and discussing Seders with Fran Lebowitz. ("Only compared to Tom Stoppard am I a knowledgeable Jew," she said.) When Stoppard threw in an "Oy, vey," Marber cut it back to "Oy."

"I think there's a way of being consciously in denial, I guess, but also there's a way of being unconsciously in denial," Stoppard said. "You don't know that you're in denial, so you're quite happy about being in denial. You think that's your kind of resting place."

He knows he can't change things by agonizing, so he doesn't.

"I don't take things very hard," he said. "Death, for example. People die, and I sidestep the moment in some way. Or if you just say something embarrassingly dumb to someone or you think you're talking to one person but he's actually somebody else. I'm vaguely aware that I have a capacity not to dwell on this. I can see that there's another way to live where you're lying awake about it. I just think, 'Move on and to hell with it.'"

Critics have long debated whether Stoppard's verbal acrobatics and cerebral obsessions have deflected emotion in many of his plays, but Lee thinks this is misleading, that sadness, mortality, melancholy, vulnerability, the sense of being an outsider thread through his work.

At first, Stoppard resisted the idea that his work should have a moral or political message—"The whiff of social application." As the Malquist character in his novel, "Lord Malquist and Mr. Moon," said, "Since we cannot hope for order, let us withdraw with style from the chaos." Stoppard himself liked to say, in Wildean style, "I should have the courage of my lack of convictions." But history drew the onetime "apostle of detachment," as the drama critic Kenneth Tynan called him, into more intense commitments. In 2013, he shared the PEN Pinter Prize for his work opposing human rights abuses.

"'Leopoldstadt,'" Marber said, "is a really angry play. It's a play about murder, a terrible, terrible state murder, and how did this crime happen?"

Stoppard told me that when he started his career, he did not want to appear in his work "in any guise." He gradually grew less bottled up.

"Then, I think, with 'The Real Thing,' I didn't care so much," he said of his play about a dazzling playwright's affair with an actress, a topic Stoppard would come to know something about, given his liaisons with Felicity Kendal and Sinéad Cusack. "Now, with the last few plays, I really want to encourage the play to be emotional. A woman reviewing 'Rock 'n' Roll' wrote that she started crying when the love story got together at the end, just in time. I was aware that I was more pleased by that than any number of people telling me that I was too clever by half or intellectual.

"In fact, the reason I liked it so much was that I was two-thirds of the way through writing it before I began to understand that there was a love story in it. I'm very much in favor of love."

We had moved to the big country kitchen to eat a lunch Guinness had prepared: niçoise salad, a platter of cheese, dry rosé, and a blackberry and apple tart. Sabrina beamed at her husband's remark about love. Even though they have been married for eight years, and even though she was linked to celebrated men before Stoppard—including Prince Charles and Mick Jagger—she told me that she feels so lucky in this relationship, her first marriage, she has to keep pinching herself.

She confessed to Lee that she worried she was too "dim" for Tom, and I admitted I knew how she felt.

"I just wait for the day when you and others see through that," Stoppard murmured.

I asked him how he liked Guinness calling him "drop dead gorgeous" in the biography.

"I never felt even remotely good-looking for my entire life," he protested, always wary about being "over-esteemed."

Friedman, his producer, said that, despite Marber's description of Stoppard's air of "kingly bonhomie," the playwright is the most democratic person she knows. "Tom is as interested in the young child at the stage door who wants to ask how to become a writer," she said, "as he is sitting next to a member of the royal family."

He showed me some pince-nez reading glasses that Guinness has gotten for him, which make him look even more like an 18th-century European count. "I thought these were great," he said, "because glasses sometimes interfere with my hearing aid."

I talked with Stoppard—who wrote "The Coast of Utopia," about Russian radicals in the 19th century, and "Every Good Boy Deserves Favor" about the psychiatric abuse of political dissidents in the Soviet Union—about the war in Ukraine.

"This wonderful nation of Russians, a superb, amazing country, has got into the hands of the wrong people, and I would love them to be defeated," he said. He had worked for a year on a screenplay about Los Alamos, so he said the power of atom bombs was on his mind. "If I were prime minister or president and there was no nuclear weapon, I would've liked to have piled into Ukraine and made war. Because we are now all Neville Chamberlains—appeasement, appeasement."

Is Stoppard surprised about the ascendancy of authoritarianism in Central and Eastern Europe?

"The very concept of an idealistic democracy is beginning to sound quaint," he said. "Where is it now? It doesn't feel like England, let alone Poland. The English are the most surveilled people anywhere."

The man who once caused waves in the London theater community by praising Margaret Thatcher's early tenure said he is "horrified" at the idea of former President Donald J. Trump coming back. "Whatever the shortcomings are of a liberal democracy, you have to live with the shortcomings and not use them as a reason to grab the steering wheel and just go somewhere else," he said. "Because there is nowhere else which is as good. Nowhere else which is as humane."

After "Leopoldstadt" opened in London, Stoppard said that he was deluged with messages. "It was just rather extraordinary how many people had families with similar stories," he said.

His favorite anecdote: A bookseller he buys from in London told him about another customer, an Oxford academic in his 90s, who said he needed to change his shipping information because he now had a different name, a Jewish name.

"OK, fine," the bookseller replied. "Do you mind me asking why you've changed your name?"

The academic replied, "Because I went to see 'Leopoldstadt' and decided to go back to my real name."

I said that the Oscar-winning "Shakespeare in Love," which he co-wrote, was one of my favorite movies and he thanked me and said it was a great experience. But he added that he did not want to work on any more movies "because I'm a playwright, and if I have a play to write, that's all I want to do."

He said he had often done script doctoring when actors, sometimes friends, requested that Stoppardian polish, like Glenn Close in "102 Dalmatians" ("You've won the battle, but I'm about to win the wardrobe") and Sean Connery in "Indiana Jones and the Last Crusade." (A hilarious section in Lee's biography describes Stoppard's notes on scripts for producers, which are surely like no other notes Hollywood has ever seen: he called one line "otiose and hi-faluting," another "fudgy," and christened one cut to a script "the Portia Note" because it was like saying "Let's lose this pound of flesh.")

I wondered what the couple do for fun, way out here in Arden, besides looking after Guinness's garden of geraniums and daisies? Given that Stoppard told me he "adores" the Queen and living in a constitutional monarchy, and given Guinness's friendship with Prince Charles, I wondered if they watched "The Crown"?

"I watched the first series of 'The Crown,' which I thought was pretty good, but in the end, I began to see that there was what you might call dramatic license," Stoppard said. He thought it was "incredible arrogance and bad manners to dramatize people who are still around." Guinness, protective of Charles, agreed, saying, "I think it's so appalling."

There was a stir—and a shudder—when Stoppard told the BBC, before "Leopoldstadt" opened in London's West End in 2020, that he was slowing down and this might be his last play. But the world-class workaholic has, of course, taken it back.

Now Stoppard is mulling a play on moral realism, whether good and bad are objective truths, rather than subjective attitudes. Talking point: Is God a verb?

"I did think I could stop after 'Leopoldstadt,'" he said wryly. "That feeling didn't last long at all."

ROCKSTAR PATTI SMITH, MAKING PARIS SWOON

—SEPTEMBER 19, 2019

PARIS—The more Patti Smith rips her French audience, the more they love her.

She tells the crowd at the Olympia music hall, the scene of concerts by Édith Piaf, Marlene Dietrich and the Beatles, that they should show more appreciation for their beleaguered president because at least he cares about the environment.

Five hundred miles south that same day, at the Group of 7 summit in Biarritz, Emmanuel Macron had held a climate change meeting for world leaders and President Trump left his chair empty.

There were scattered boos at the mention of Mr. Macron, and Ms. Smith isn't having it. With her South Jersey accent gloriously intact, she lets loose.

"You should have Trump as your president," she tells the pack of Parisians. "Then you'd know what it's like to wake up every day with a president who doesn't give a"—and here Ms. Smith uses one of several vulgarities—"about living things, about trees, about animals, about the air we breathe or the water we drink. We have to give our leaders a chance who are trying to do something because our president in America does *nothing*."

She rocks them with "People Have the Power" ("The people have the power / To redeem the work of fools"), periodically spitting on the stage, and Neil Young's "After the Gold Rush," her wavy silver hair hanging in her face as she fiercely plays guitar and howls, "Look at Mother Nature on the run / In the 21st century."

Thinking of the Amazon fires, she feels herself starting to cry as she sings and then realizes that will make her pitchy, so she gets it together.

Ms. Smith drolly informs the audience that they should be applauding more when she name checks Sly Stone. "If I was in the audience and somebody mentioned Sly, I would go out of my mind," she says. "You know, he was with the Family Stone." (She has said she learned to spar with audiences by watching Johnny Carson.)

The next night, as she gets ready to sing "My Blakean Year," she is disappointed by the tepid applause that greets her dedication of her song to "the great ranks of the unappreciated," including Vincent Van Gogh.

"You know what?" she taunts. "If you're only going to give him a lame response, don't respond at all, because in his lifetime, he didn't sell a painting so he doesn't need a few accolades. Either he needs all or nothing cause that's all he ever had."

Wearing her tour uniform of black Ann Demeulemeester jacket and vest, old black dungarees, black Jimmy Choo motorcycle boots, an Electric Lady T-shirt and her St. Francis tau cross, Ms. Smith reminds her bewitched fans that the date of her first sold-out Paris concert, Aug. 26, is the 49th anniversary of the founding of Jimi Hendrix's Electric Lady Studios in Greenwich Village. She tells how she met Mr. Hendrix there once when he was leaving a party.

"All I can say is," she says with a grin, "he was really cute." The crowd goes wild, screaming "Pah-teee!!!" and sparking lighters. (Yes, they still have lighters.) She blows kisses back. The punk poet laureate is no longer scrawny and her dark hair is gray, but she is every inch the glam "gothic crow" Salvador Dalí once described her as.

She is thrilled to be in the land of her literary heroes Genet, Baudelaire and Rimbaud. At 16, working in a nonunion factory inspecting handlebars for tricycles, an experience immortalized in her protopunk song "Piss Factory," she shoplifted a book about Rimbaud and made him her imaginary boyfriend because she felt she wasn't attractive enough to get a real one. (Her father had warned her that she'd have to get a career because she wouldn't be able to nab a husband.)

When a man yells "Read some poetry, Pah-tee!" Ms. Smith offers an epic hippie-chick response: "It's all poetry, mannn!"

THE MEN IN HER LIFE

When Ms. Smith strolls with her band down the Rue des Capucines to her hotel, the narrow street is filled with Parisians smoking and drinking wine at cafes, sitting outside in rattan seats. They tumble out all along the block to applaud her.

She gazes back at them with a mystical smile, looking, as Rolling Stone once described her, like "a charismatic sect leader who has convinced her followers that she alone has the secret of life."

Jimmy Iovine, who produced her biggest hit, in 1977, "Because the Night," a collaboration with Bruce Springsteen, says her fire still burns bright at 72.

"Patti is a magical, magical, magical woman," he says. "What's missing today in music is everything that she brought as a voice to the world since she burst on the scene as a younger contemporary to Dylan. Where are the young people? Where are their voices? They're watching all this stuff go down. Why aren't they writing powerful lyrics just speaking the truth? That's the reason I've left the music business. These kids who are getting famous, going on Instagram and making money—what they're doing doesn't speak to me."

"The real Renaissance woman," as Mr. Iovine calls her, also has a book out next week: "Year of the Monkey," a picaresque voyage through her dreams and life as she faced 70, dealing with flashes of "sorrow's vertigo" as she remembers all the loves and rock contemporaries who are gone.

She believes that when people close to you die, you absorb what you most admire in them. "It's like they leave a little gift," she says.

About aging, she writes: "Seventy. Merely a number but one indicating the passing of a significant percentage of the allotted sand in an egg timer, with oneself the darn egg. The grains pour and I find myself missing the dead more than usual." Ms. Smith has a kaleidoscope of references, from "Mr. Robot" to Marcus Aurelius to Martin Beck mysteries to Maria Callas's Medea.

She writes of making herself a sardine and onion sandwich, and seeing her image reflected on the surface of the toaster: "I noticed I looked young and old simultaneously." That describes her spirit perfectly, too.

In this book, Ms. Smith, who is working her way to novels, blends fiction and reality, conjured characters and actual ones. It's not always clear when you're in her imagination or out of it. Her prose is, as always, gorgeous. She writes poignantly about her "sense of everyone gone," and her trips to see her old flame Sam Shepard in Kentucky and California when he was in a mortal battle with Lou Gehrig's disease. She slept on couches and helped him edit his last two books.

We have a three-hour lunch at a bistro next to Ms. Smith's hotel. She has no airs—she washes her clothes in the hotel sink—and is polite to everyone, including autograph hunters and servers. She gives our waitress a ticket to her concert, and later I spot the young woman sensually dancing all through the set.

Ms. Smith is "somewhat walleyed," as she writes in her new book, with shining gray eyes. She is wearing another Electric Lady T-shirt ("I don't like the new feeling so I keep recycling them"), this time with silk butterfly pants and some men's black Versace sandals that her daughter, Jesse, got her.

"I don't have to look nice for anybody," she says. "I feel like at my age I can do whatever I want, pretty much, as long as I don't hurt anybody and that includes dressing the way I want, everywhere I go."

She pulls up her pant leg ("sorry about my hair today," she says re the stubble beneath) to show me the lightning bolt tattoo on her knee that she got from an Australian artist when she was living in the Chelsea Hotel, at the same time Mr. Shepard got a crescent moon.

"I remember once in 1970 or something, I was such a scraggly thing, but I was in this bar waiting for him and he was late," she says. "And some guy, and he was a big guy, kept bugging me, semi-hitting on me. I just told him to leave me alone. Sam walked in and he just walked up, took the guy by the scruff of the neck and the guy went right up the bar, just like in the movies. And Sam wasn't a movie star then. He was just a guy."

I asked why the two split, after appearing in a play they wrote about themselves called "Cowboy Mouth."

"Well, he was married and he had a child and it was sad, but it was just the right thing to do," she says.

I wonder if she was surprised when Mr. Shepard made it big as a leading man in Hollywood.

"No, because first of all he was a really great actor in plays and theater," she says. "He had a magnetism. He was one of the most handsomest guys you would ever see, more even in person than in film. But that isn't even what I liked about him, which was funny because it was so obvious that he was so handsome. People were just drawn to him. We'd walk down the street and women would come up, hit on him and they'd just say right in front of me, 'Get rid of the kid.'"

I noted that Robert Mapplethorpe had charisma, too.

"Well, Robert was totally different," she says. "Robert was very shy. I met Robert when he was 20 and we were both wallflowers, but he was even more awkward than me. The beautiful thing about our relationship and what saved it for all the years is, it was based more on how we believed in each other when no one else believed in us, our trust in one another and respect for one another."

I ask about the recent New York Times essay by Arthur Lubow about a Guggenheim exhibit with the headline "Has Robert Mapplethorpe's Moment Passed?," suggesting that the photographer's images, so taboo in the 1970s and '80s, were no longer shocking and played into sexual stereotypes about black men.

At first, Ms. Smith says she has nothing to say about it. But soon, a defense of Mr. Mapplethorpe pours out:

"The idea of Robert exploiting people is ridiculous," she says. "He wasn't exploiting anyone, racially, physically, any more than Michelangelo was. To analyze and scrutinize him without him being able to speak for himself, I find heartbreaking. He liked that muscular kind of body as a photographer. He loved sculpture. He loved Michelangelo. He often said if he had lived in the Renaissance, he would have been a sculptor."

Of his critics: "They're overthinking. They're overanalyzing. Robert was not analytical. He was all visual. And when he was taking a photograph, it was because that is what he found beauty in."

She continues: "When he did those S-and-M pictures, he told me he refused to be voyeuristic and he had participated in certain things, which I found horrifying, frightening, but he was not a voyeuristic kind of person. I'm just saying that he got to know these people. He got to know his subjects, and I think they had mutual trust."

Harking back to Senator Jesse Helms's 1989 criticism of Mr. Mapplethorpe's pictures of semi-clothed children as exploitative, Ms. Smith notes: "Robert loved children. Robert even mourned that we didn't have children before the end of his life. And it would have killed him to see Jesse Helms say that his pictures were pedophilic or something."

Referring to Mr. Mapplethorpe's death of AIDS in 1989, she adds: "Robert only lived till he was 42 years old, and was a late bloomer. His work really only spanned less than two decades and not even that, because the first years, when we were together in semi-poverty, was without him having the tools to do the things he wanted to do. I've done my best work, really, my most important work, from the ages of maybe 57 to now.

"He had passed through photography. He had one more project he wanted to do, photographing animals, and then he wanted to go back to sculpture. He wanted to design big installations. He wanted to do film. Unfortunately, some of his work you have to look at in a context of when it was done and the fact that he had a stilted lifeline."

I ask why she didn't participate in the recent film "Mapplethorpe," starring Matt Smith, who played Prince Philip in "The Crown," even though she was a major character. "People cannot only portray you," Ms. Smith says. "They can make stuff up."

She has not cooperated with Mr. Shepard's biographers and scoffs at "stories about me being carried out of Max's Kansas City drunk and sobbing and screaming Sam's name. I mean, first all, it just never happened. I could laugh at it because it's so stupid but they keep repeating it."

She is also asked about a story about another famous singer, she says, "that I walk into a dressing room, slap some singer across the face and tell them, 'Rock 'n' roll doesn't have a place for both of us.' They just keep printing this stuff. But then you get into things that personally hurt."

She was not enamored of the famous "Saturday Night Live" impersonation, with Gilda Radner playing Candy Slice, clearly based on Ms. Smith, as a drunk and drug-addled screaming banshee with hairy armpits.

"I liked Gilda Radner," Ms. Smith says. "The only difficult thing was, it was very heavy cocaine oriented, which I didn't indulge in. I think I had taken acid with Robert once. It was '77 or '78. I had tried coke once or twice. I don't deny. I'm just saying that, 1), who had the money for that stuff? And 2), I like being in control of myself. I'm very happy with who I am. I know it wasn't her intent or anything like that. It's not that I lack a sense of humor, and comedians have to have some kind of leeway." But, she concludes, "the coke thing damaged my reputation and I still have to deal with it."

Ms. Smith was touring Europe over the summer with her band, her incantatory voice strong, her needs simple. She doesn't have any publicist or personal assistant or makeup artist with her. And her rock-star rider asks only for peanut butter, brown bread, ginger, lemon and honey.

She supplements that with a small plastic container of flaxseeds that her daughter has packed for her. After her show, she surfs the adrenaline, ignoring the bottle of champagne on ice by the makeup mirror. She says she has never overindulged, in part because she was a sickly kid, allergic to smoke and prone to bronchitis.

She has the occasional tequila shot or sake, and she writes in her book that she had a glass of vodka after Mr. Trump won the election.

Lenny Kaye, her guitarist who has been at her side for 48 years, from her very first night at St. Mark's Church, fusing poetry and music, with Lou Reed and Andy Warhol in the audience, says, "I've never heard her sing a false note." He says the coolest experience you can have is going into a bookstore with Patti Smith.

'I DON'T RECANT'

Her previous memoirs, both New York Times best sellers, were "Just Kids," her luminous reminiscence about her New York romance with

Mr. Mapplethorpe in the 1960s, and "M Train," about the period after she moved back to New York from Detroit, where she dropped out just as she was breaking out, shocking the music world and offending some feminists.

She moved to St. Clair Shores, Mich., north of Detroit, to marry the musician Fred Smith, known as "Sonic," and spent 16 years there, raising their two children, writing some unpublished novels. She worked with her husband to make her voice less nasal; he taught her to play the clarinet and they did one album together, "Dream of Life." The couple lived simply and mostly out of the public eye.

"It was 1979, and all I saw in my future was a series of tours, concerts, interviews, videos, fancy cars," she recalls. "I wasn't doing any art. I wasn't writing." Fame and fortune were escalating, but "it's such a stressful life and you find yourself getting more demanding about things that you never were demanding about, like, 'Why isn't my car here?'

"I don't have any aspirations to be rich. I came from a lower-middle-class background. Even when I've had prosperity, I just share it."

I ask about the feminist criticism about her semiretirement.

"Yeah, they got really upset with me, like I broke some kind of bond," she says. "I left the world of rock 'n' roll. I left my so-called career, you know, fame and fortune. But what I did do is, I saved myself as a worker, as a writer and as an evolving human being." (She says that even before that, she had lost out on being featured in a feminist magazine because the writer was dismayed to see her washing and folding a boyfriend's laundry.)

After her husband died, in 1994, she returned to New York, with places in downtown Manhattan and Rockaway Beach, and picked up her career. She still wears her wedding ring and even once bought her husband a mauve iridescent Valentino shirt because she missed him so much and knew he would have loved it.

Ms. Smith did not perform her famous 1978 song with the N-word in the title during her tour. Can she still sing it?

"No," she says simply, recalling that when she wrote it more than four decades ago, "I was fighting to take a term that was used in such a defamatory way and to take it as a badge for outsiders, artists, of any gender, any color. So, you know, a task that took a lot of hubris. But an absolutely pure heart. The real important phrase in the song is 'outside of society, that's where I want to be.' I've been asked to recant the song and it's like, I'm not recanting the song. I don't recant anything that I do. I mean, I've done it, I believed in it. It's still to me an awesome song.

"People want to embrace one as the godmother of punk, but her anthem? They don't want that. They want you to go far but not too far." She says the song has been "misconstrued" but she knows that also, "the pain that people feel because of past injustice is real."

"I miss doing it," she says. "But my son, he's opposed to doing it, out of respect to people. So I look at the younger generation and I think, O.K. I'm living in their time. This is not my time. So, in terms of younger people's time, it's not the right song right now."

She admits that "there's a part of me that's defiant. I was like that as a child. I can't help it. I'm a punk rocker who loves Maria Callas, you know?" But, she added, "I'm not going to shove it down anybody's throat. It's on a record, if they want to hear it."

She does worry about censorship in the age of cancellation, though. "We're moving more and more back to intense censorship," she says, citing the removal of paintings from museums. "More censorship than people like William Burroughs and Allen Ginsberg and Brancusi were fighting."

On the subject of #MeToo, she looks at the big picture: "I find myself more concerned about the terrible atrocities against women globally. I just think, again, we have to examine what is an atrocity and what is an insult and what is somebody being a pain in the ass."

She gets emotional when I ask her about Trump turning the so-called Squad into his 2020 foils.

"I felt almost like there was a tape around my ribs and somebody pulled it off and some skin went with it," she says. "All those girls are good people. We are a democracy, and it's all right for them to question how we're dealing with the Gaza Strip and how we're treating the Palestinians. It's not anti-American, it's not anti-Israel. It's the American way."

Weirdly, she says, she encountered Mr. Trump when they were young. Mr. Mapplethorpe took her to a dinner, when they were together and she was still working at Scribner's, where a young Mr. Trump pitched Trump Tower.

"I didn't know who this guy was, he was with his wife, Ivana, except he was the most obnoxious person I have ever experienced in my life," she says. "All he talked about was how it was going to be the greatest thing ever in New York City and anyone who bought into this was going to be part of the most important thing. Me and Robert left and I thought, 'I wouldn't live in his tower for free.' I can't believe that fate would let that guy . . ." She shudders.

I tell her what Mr. Iovine said about his disillusionment with young musicians for not being more political. Indeed, the night before, at the Video Music Awards, Taylor Swift, whose critics have dinged her for staying mostly mum in this era of political outrage, offered some mild, oblique criticism of the president.

"She's a pop star who's under tremendous scrutiny all the time, and one can't imagine what that's like," Ms. Smith says sympathetically. "It's unbelievable to not be able to go anywhere, do anything, have messy hair. And I'm sure that she's trying to do something good. She's not trying to do something bad. And if it influences some of her avid fans to open up their thoughts, what does it matter? Are we going to start measuring who's more authentic than who?

"I don't agree that artists and musicians have more responsibility to speak out than anyone else. I think everybody has to be more active. Art is inspiring and art can really bring people together. A song can rally people, but it's not going to make change."

She says she got punished for speaking out against the Iraq invasion: "All of a sudden, no radio play, couldn't get into festivals. People, even cool people—I'm sorry to say that, but some people that I really loved and respected and still love and respect—they were so frightened by this infusion of patriotism that they weren't able to see the whole picture. To me, patriotism is just a few steps away from nationalism if you're not careful."

She is not rooting for Joe Biden to be the nominee. "I would rather see a younger person make some mistakes than to have the petrified forest come in," she says.

She doesn't like labels, and she doesn't want to feel hemmed in to any movement. She doesn't like confinement of any kind; it's why she scorns high heels and makeup. She doesn't want to be hailed as the godmother of younger women in rock or a feminist icon or a political activist.

"If they want to call me a writer, an artist, I'm really happy with that, or a mother," she says. "But I don't really need more than that because I don't really qualify."

After her last Paris concert, we hang out in her hotel room at midnight overlooking the Place Vendôme. Her son, Jackson, a guitarist who often plays with her, calls and she tells him how much she loves him.

In her new book, and on Instagram, she has pictures of what she calls her "treasures," eclectic items that she travels with or gathers on her trips. I ask her to make a Polaroid picture of some now.

We sit on her bed as she spreads out her T-shirt, cross, her flaxseeds, her toothbrush, Weleda Salt toothpaste, stones she has gathered along the tour, a vintage photo of Antonin Artaud, a Nicholas Roerich postcard and a book she is reading, "The Book of Monelle" by Marcel Schwob.

We talk some more about the men she loved, all gone, and she suddenly smiled, radiantly, and says, "I've had some cool boyfriends."

Bonus track!

Confirm or Deny

MAUREEN DOWD: *You light candles in churches for your late cat.*

PATTI SMITH: I light candles in churches for everybody.

You love "Aqua Teen Hunger Force" on "Adult Swim," a late-night show about a milk shake, a box of French fries and a wad of meat named Meatwad, because it's set in Jersey.

South Jersey, actually. Yes, I do. It was love at first sight. I have socks with Meatwad on them. Did you know that I did their closing song?

My son is always turning me on to cool cartoons. I like all the "Ghost in the Shell" films and "Dragon Ball."

In 1977, you had your producer drive in from Brooklyn at 2 a.m. and the first thing you asked him was to take you to a newsstand to buy Italian Vogue and go straight to C.B.G.B.

True.

You dragged your feet on doing "Because the Night" because Bruce Springsteen was from Central New Jersey, not South Jersey.

Well, there was a little of the Jersey thing. But also, I just want to write my own songs. Even when I listened to it, finally, I thought, "It's one of those darn hits, it's going to be a hit, and if I sing this song, it'll probably be popular because it's a Bruce song." I mean, I couldn't write a song like that.

You know you're a good dancer.

It's my Philly upbringing. Philly and South Jersey have the best dancers. It comes from mimicking R&B songs from when I was young. When I moved to New York and I watched Long Island people or even New York people dance, I'd go, "They aren't even close." Robert was from Long Island and we fought about this all the time, about who was the best dancer.

Bob Dylan called to thank you after you accepted the Nobel Prize for Literature for him and sang "A Hard Rain's A-Gonna Fall."

No. I don't have that kind of relationship with Bob. For the canon of work that he's given us, he can do what he wants. That's how I feel. He can conduct himself the way that he wants.

You still feel bad that you forgot the words to the song and had to start over.

I had a white-out. Ralph Fiennes told me it was called a white-out. There was an orchestra, there's global TV, there's the king and queen, all the Nobel people. I mean, I've loved Bob Dylan since I was 15, 16. The funniest thing, the next day all the Nobel winners came up to take selfies with me. And I was saying, I wish I would have been better. And they said, "No, no, don't wish that." They told me that they were all so nervous, too, all these great scientists and thinkers.

You don't drive. You don't like utensils. And you can't tune a guitar.
They're all true.

You can't swim.
I don't know how to swim. I'm a goat. I'm a Capricorn.

In the '70s, you would refuse Novocain at the dentist on the grounds that it was un-American because they didn't have it during the Civil War.
That's something I would say, yeah.

You can't smoke because of a bronchial condition.
It's really funny, when young kids come up to me and they want to talk to me and there's a cigarette I will say, "You can talk to me but you have to put out your cigarette."

The night you met Jimi Hendrix, you had a ribbon in your hair with musical notes and you were wearing a polka-dot dress.
It was my "East of Eden" outfit. We talked about shyness. He said, "I'm shy, too." He said he was going to create a new language of music. "The language of peace, you dig?"

You want to live to be 100.
Well, I've pushed it up to 102.

PART 5

Fashion Savants

TOM FORD, FRAGRANT VEGAN VAMPIRE

—APRIL 20, 2019

HOLLYWOOD—Tom Ford has come early to rearrange the furniture.

He thinks that the already stylish room in the hottest new private club in town, the San Vicente Bungalows, could be even more captivating. So a team of eight club staffers gets busy under his direction, pulling a potted plant from the terrace for one corner and setting up two dozen glowing amber votive candles.

Mr. Ford himself redoes the white flowers, plucking out the roses and leaving in the ranunculus, because he doesn't like mixed blooms.

The Murphy bed he can do nothing about.

As I enter, the designer is lost in thought, still fantasizing about redoing the room in his own preferred palette, draping chocolate brown velvet on the walls.

Everything in life can always be more sensual and beautiful, if you think about it. And Mr. Ford is always thinking about it.

From the time he was big enough to push furniture, at 6 years old, he was rearranging it in his house, sometimes swapping his for his sister's. And giving his mother critiques on her hair and shoes.

And that's why being Tom Ford is awful, in a way.

He always sees what's wrong. And you can't help but feel bad for him because you know his flawless flaw detector is always on.

"I am a hyper-hyper Virgo," he said. "Perfectionist, anal-retentive, supposedly. Seemingly uptight, seemingly aloof. We're definitely homebodies also. We love the home." (Or in his case, six.)

Mr. Ford has been known to go to a movie in the middle of the day wearing a suit, and to make hospital corners with other people's slip-covers.

"I don't know if it's a blessing or a curse, but he actually can make things better," said the actress Rita Wilson, a friend. "He's not afraid to say you need to cut three inches off your hair or lose weight."

Even on vacations in the tropics or river rafting, she said, Mr. Ford looks eerily perfect. He used to tailor white T-shirts he bought at La Rinascente in Milan, but now he wears his own brand. "The cut of the sleeve has to be just right if you want your biceps to look right," he said.

In 2003, as the creative director of Gucci, he personally shaved a "G" in a model's pubic hair for an ad, adding definition with an eyebrow pencil.

Lisa Eisner, who has done jewelry collaborations with Mr. Ford and inspired the Alessia character in his 2016 film, "Nocturnal Animals," said that he doesn't expect everyone to be as persnickety as he is.

"At Graydon Carter's wedding, I drank way too much and ran out to go to the bathroom and got sick on his shoes—really good Tom Ford shoes," she recalled. "He just laughed and wiped it off."

And his friends praise his fierce loyalty.

Ms. Wilson recalled that after her breast cancer diagnosis in 2015, when she had to present at the Tonys feeling vulnerable because "you have had part of your body removed," Mr. Ford designed her a beautiful dress to wear that "made my shape look like a normal shape. And he did it with such sensitivity, generosity and love."

Mr. Ford did not check his phone during the three hours we spent together. He has perfect posture and lovely Southern manners and stands up when you return to the table from the bathroom. His voice, as one fan wrote in a YouTube comment, sounds like what melted chocolate tastes like.

Admiring the votives' golden aura, I confessed that I'm obsessed with lighting and have been known to unscrew bulbs in restaurant booths or flip off lights at parties.

"Oh, I do that," Mr. Ford said. "At Tower Bar, if you go to my table, the corner table at the back, there are these overhead spots and on mine it's blacked out, because I told them, 'You have to get rid of that spot or I'm not going to come here. No overhead lights.'"

Jeff Klein, Mr. Ford's friend who is the hotelier behind both the bungalows and the Sunset Tower hotel where the Tower Bar is, called an electrician to put in a special switch for Mr. Ford's table, which can be flipped off when he's on his way.

"Why, oh my God, overhead light," Mr. Ford continued, warming to the subject, "where your brow is going to create shadow right there, your nose is going to create a shadow like this, you look like hell, you look like you have no hair, even if you have a lot of hair. Nobody looks good in overhead lighting.

"That's why I don't go to Barry and Diane's lunch party," he confided, referring to one of the most coveted invitations in Hollywood, on Oscar weekend at the Coldwater Canyon mansion of Barry Diller and Diane von Furstenberg. "I don't like the middle of the day. Take a picture at noon, anywhere in the world. You're going to look like hell—*hell*. Everybody looks like hell. Unless you're 18, maybe, or under. Even then you don't look your best. I like daylight, but not to go out in public."

'PAINFULLY SHY'

Mr. Ford cloaks himself in black, planted a black garden in London of black tulips and black calla lilies, contemplates death constantly and plans on designing a black sarcophagus. He is 57 but for decades has not seemed to get any older. And he's wearing Beau de Jour (one of 39 Tom Ford fragrances), a scent meant to evoke the allure of Cary Grant's neck.

I told him that all this makes him a member of my favorite cult: sexy vampires.

His face lit up. "A vampire cape was one of the first things I got when I could tell my mother to make something for me, and it was black satin on the outside and red satin on the inside," he said. "And I had the vampire teeth and I had the LP with the music from 'Dark Shadows.' I was obsessed and I wanted to be a vampire because vampires are sexy. They don't age. Talk about seductive. I'm not talking about Nosferatu, you know. But vampires were usually rich, they lived in a fabulous house or castle. Wore black. Vampires are great."

Ms. Eisner demurred: "Tom smells too good to be a vampire."

She said that those who know Mr. Ford simply through the famous shots of him with naked models and actresses probably think he's "a sex pervert, someone who thinks about sex 24–7. Nope, he's not that guy at all. He's very loyal to his friends. Very married."

Richard Buckley, Mr. Ford's husband since 2013, confirmed that the facade of gleaming black lacquer is deceiving.

"The one misconception I think most people have of Tom is that he is some kind of press whore who loves to have his picture taken," said Mr. Buckley, a longtime fashion journalist with whom Mr. Ford had a coup de foudre during an elevator ride 32 years ago.

"He is, and always has been, *painfully* shy," Mr. Buckley said. "He did acting when he was in his early 20s, so he is able to 'turn on' for interviews." Referring to their 6-year-old son, he added: "And Jack has never been photographed. In London, we have a court injunction to keep any newspaper or magazine from running pictures of him. In Los Angeles, there is a law."

(The designer takes Jack—who already prefers black despite drawers filled with colorful clothes—every day to school, where "the mothers have to see Tom Ford looking great at 8 in the morning while they look like hell," an amused Ms. Eisner noted.)

Mr. Buckley, 70, said dryly that their lives are not "all champagne and caviar," opening up about his nightmarish struggle with the after-effects of radiation for the throat cancer which he had surgery for in 1989, three years after the men became involved.

"Tom has seen me through so much, from throat cancer to my brother and mother dying 48 hours apart, to more bouts of pneumonia than I can count," Mr. Buckley said.

Mr. Ford made his husband gray merino wool turtleneck dickeys with keyhole slits for his tracheotomy tube, and, for formal events, a black silk scarf with slits.

"Tom is actually quite good at sewing," Mr. Buckley said. (These days, a designer need not be.)

Recently, it was announced that Mr. Ford will succeed Ms. von Furstenberg as the head of the Council of Fashion Designers of America, a job he was persuaded to take by her and Anna Wintour.

"He's a cross between a Rolls-Royce and the Marlboro Man," Ms. von Furstenberg told me. At a time when Donald Trump's America is turning away from the rest of the world, Mr. Ford, who has spent half his life working and studying in Europe, says he will reach out because "if American fashion is going to flourish, it has got to drop the idea that it's American fashion and become global."

"It's a turbulent time in some ways for fashion, which has been rightly criticized for its lack of inclusivity, for not having enough women in C.E.O. positions," Ms. Wintour said. "These are things Tom cares about."

Indeed, back in the Gucci days, Mr. Ford was one of the first designers to prominently feature African-American and Asian models on the runway and in ad campaigns.

André Leon Talley said that Mr. Ford stands out because he's "not like most of the cruel snakes in fashion and in cutthroat business. His is an unapologetic universe of sultry, melting-pot sexuality, often fusing or blurring the genders."

Virgil Abloh, the creator of Off-White and the artistic director of men's wear at Louis Vuitton, said that, at the C.F.D.A., Mr. Ford will not be "just a puppet of the industry going with the flow. He has rigor in his work and his personality, and he will bring challenging ideas."

Mr. Abloh said that Mr. Ford's provocative Gucci ads inspired him when he was a teenager in Illinois, into skateboarding, hip-hop and normcore. "I was an outsider," he said, "and he made me believe in fashion."

WARHOL NIGHTS

Women's Wear Daily sleuthed out the news that Mr. Ford was the buyer, for $18 million, of the Paul Rudolph modernist four-story townhouse on 63rd Street in Manhattan where Halston once lived, hosting some of the wildest parties of the 1970s (Mr. Ford's favorite decade) for glitterati like Truman Capote, Jackie Kennedy Onassis and Liza Minnelli.

In Los Angeles, Mr. Ford lives in a $39 million Holmby Hills mansion, formerly owned by Betsy Bloomingdale, that is a study in black and white, complete with a Scottish butler named Angus.

He also has property in Santa Fe, where his family moved when he was 11, including a $75 million ranch, which he's selling, that includes a Western movie town used to shoot such movies as "Cowboys and Aliens" and "All the Pretty Horses." When a colleague told him that the Rudolph place had been on sale for eight years, he snapped it up.

"I've kind of lived in that house in my mind for many years," Mr. Ford said. "It has dark brown glass, it has a garage, it has a legal curb cut." There are 32-foot-high ceilings, skylights galore and a roof garden.

New York had long seemed stressful. "It felt like all work, if I walked down the street and somebody saw me, they would get on the phone and call so-and-so and then so-and-so would say, 'You need to come to my party,' and 'You need to go to her opening,' and 'So-and-so needs to see you,' and it just wasn't fun."

But then he thought about his son. "I love L.A.," he said, "but I do want Jack to know how to put on a jacket, go to a restaurant, go to a museum, walk on the street, go to a play."

Mr. Ford first visited his new house in the heyday of Studio 54, which is where, after years of dating women, he realized he was gay.

He was studying art history in his freshman dorm room one night, feeling disoriented about the move to New York. "I just said, 'Oh my God, please, please, please let something happen to me.' Knock, knock, knock. I went to the door and there was Ian Falconer, this guy from art history class, in a little blue blazer, and he said, 'Do you want to go to Studio?' And I said, 'Are you kidding me, Studio 54?' And he said, 'Yeah, I'm going with some friends.'"

One of the friends was Andy Warhol, who picked them up in a Cadillac limousine. "The stretch Cadillacs were fabulous. There were two jump seats in the back. And it was literally like a movie, everyone got pushed aside and we walked right in the door. 'Oh my God, here

I am, Studio 54 for the very first time' and I drank a lot, did a lot of coke."

Even back then, he always visualized the sort of cinematic life he has now, with several Warhols on the wall, including a triptych of vulvas and a "Big Electric Chair." He sold a fright-wig self-portrait of the artist at Sotheby's for $32.6 million to pay for his stores in China.

That night at Studio 54 was the first night he ended up with a man, and it "freaked" him out. "And I said to him, 'This was great but this isn't really what I do or who I am' and I went back to my dorm room. And I tried to sort of deny that, and then I remember friends that were gay saying, 'Why are you dating a girl? You're really gay.' I suppose I struggled with it for maybe six months. Maybe it was coming from my family background in Texas where, you know, guys are guys. I was nervous about telling my parents, but they're liberal Democrats who met at the University of Texas and it was pre-AIDS and they were totally cool with it." (His parents were real estate agents.)

"And I learned later on that it was a plus because people thought if you weren't gay, you couldn't possibly be a good designer."

'I NEED MY ARMOR'

Tom Ford is elegantly dressed, naturally, all in Tom Ford: a black double 002 watch with a removable woven leather band; a white cotton French cuff shirt ("because it's one of the only things a man can have, a pair of cuff links"); trousers, plain-weave; the black velvet peak lapel jacket favored by Hollywood moguls; and a pair of black cap-toe Chelsea boots. Men in Los Angeles never wear the proper shoes, in his opinion.

"I don't feel secure in a slip-on or a tennis shoe," he said. "I think it's the Texan in me. I could never go to a business meeting in a tennis shoe. You feel soft, bouncy, not in control. I don't feel good in sweaters either, when I'm out. I feel soft and mushy and vulnerable. I need my armor."

What about that time in St. Barts when he was nude on the beach and Anna Wintour happened to walk by?

A talented mimic, Mr. Ford describes the awkward moment: "'Hi,

Richard. Hi, Tom.' And I'm like, 'Oh, hi, Anna!' Oh, I'm naked! It was a wake-up call."

(When I asked Ms. Wintour about it, she answered breezily: "Everyone was naked in St. Barts in those days. And *if* it happened, I'm sure Tom looked as perfect as he always does.")

Politicians also need their armor, and Mr. Ford, who toggles from Turner Classic Movies to MSNBC to CNN to the BBC, was happy to muse about makeovers for them.

On Hillary Clinton: "I supported Hillary but when she talks to a camera she lifts her chin and all of the sudden, it's a haughty pose. Now Princess Diana, when she answered a question, she would look up at you from underneath doe eyes, which made you go, 'awww.'"

On Elizabeth Warren: "She needs shoulder pads!"

On Kamala Harris: "She looks great."

On Pete Buttigieg: "I started thinking of advice for Mayor Pete and Chasten, but then I realized what's so great about them is that they're so natural."

On President Trump: "He's a very tall man, but he's also not the slimmest thing. The elongated ties, it's one more vertical that could, in his head, make him feel slimmer. He also never buttons his jacket, which I find very odd. I've run around rooms at a party buttoning people's jackets because it gives you a waist."

And what about the time Mr. Trump Scotch-taped the back of his tie? "Well, Scotch tape *is* a miracle," Mr. Ford allowed.

He was drinking a Coke with his grilled artichoke and cauliflower steak, having become vegan, allowing himself the occasional piece of salmon, after watching the documentary "What the Health." He cheats with baked goods, jelly beans, Starbursts and Skittles. "Sugar is my weakness," he said. He weighs himself daily, holding at 165 pounds, and hasn't had a drink for 10 years.

"For several years leading up to stopping drinking—because I drank a lot—on the mornings after, I would have to send flowers to this one and flowers to that one and, 'Oh, I can't believe I did that' and 'I can't believe I said that,' and I told Richard for at least a year, 'Oh my God, I wish I could just not drink at all.' And the drinking was the open door for the drugs. Three drinks"—he mimes sniffing a line—"and anything I could hoover, anything was going to happen."

Living in London for 17 years didn't help. "You go to lunch there, you have two or three drinks," he said. "In my office at 5 o'clock, cocktail hour started, because we work in fashion until 8 or 9, so you're drinking, so now we're up to five drinks." By day's end he might be up to a dozen.

When Mr. Ford moved to the land of green juice and kind bud, culture shock ensued. "I was at an afternoon party at a friend's house, and Martin Short said to me, 'Do you think you might have a drinking problem?' Because it was lunch and I was just kicking back the vodka tonics and I didn't think anything of it. It was the first indication I had that, 'oh, maybe this isn't normal.'"

He worked with a therapist for a year, tapered off and then one weekend just stopped.

'AN UNSUSTAINABLE THING'

Mr. Ford's critically acclaimed movies, "Nocturnal Animals" and "A Single Man" (2009), are so drenched in color that they bring to mind the mesmerizing luminosities of Venetian painting.

"I don't allow the cinematographer to see the film until I'm finished with it because I have very specific ideas and I sit there, frame by frame, on the computer and color-correct every scene," Mr. Ford said. "And I have the ability to take those mandarin oranges and pop them and then desaturate the rest of the image. And you can manipulate the colors, so it is really like painting."

He had a new film deal fall apart on him last summer, and he has just bought the rights to a 600-page book he won't name but has been wanting to adapt for 12 years.

Naturally, he's looking for more control. "In fashion, we would never design something and then hand it off to somebody else to advertise it," he pointed out. "All movie trailers sound the same and look the same. I guess what I've learned is that there's this sort of myth that it's a magic thing that only professionals know how to do and I just don't buy into that anymore because I feel like I know how to do it better."

I was surprised to learn he has an aversion to color in his clothes and homes. He tried some, aside from the art, in his Santa Fe home but quickly backtracked because it was too "challenging." He even painted the bright yellow tractors on the ranch black, to go along with his black Angus cattle, black horses and black backhoes.

"I don't like color on me because I don't like to scream, I like to recede in a way," he said. "I was always shy and so I would feel silly in a bright color."

He said he feels enormous empathy for women who get frightened about their looks fading. "There's nothing more powerful in our culture than a beautiful woman," he said. But "it's an unsustainable thing. One day it stops. And I have lived through it with so many female friends and part of my job is to imagine myself, the female version of myself, would I want to wear that? Where would I go in it? How would I feel in it? Would I feel vulnerable?" (Mr. Ford said if he were a woman, he would be Ali MacGraw.)

He confessed that his hair "is a little more salt and pepper than it looks. I mean, Diana Vreeland stayed with black hair all the way until the end.

"I've been open about using Botox and fillers, although I can move. You have to be very careful with it. I do it about once every eight months. When I go to the dermatologist, I get a hand mirror, I take a white pencil and I say, 'Right there.' If I could do it myself, I would."

Now that he is a parent (and no longer walking naked around the house, as he once did), does he feel the need to tone down the sexuality of his fashion ads?

"Oh, yes, absolutely," he said, adding that it may also be because of "the hyper-politically correct culture. I mean, you can't say anything anymore. I was shooting an ad campaign last week, and the guy came up behind the girl and was kissing her on the neck and he was holding her wrists from the back and I said, 'No, no, we have to change that. Put his hand in her hand.' I don't know that any of us will survive this scrutiny."

His friend and collaborator, the photographer Terry Richardson, was banned from Condé Nast and several fashion houses as part of a wave of #MeToo accusations.

"Ugh! I love Terry," he said. "And I have to say that I never in my entire life saw any of that with Terry. One of my assistants went out with Terry for two years and he was the kindest, gentlest person in the relationship."

I wondered about the fracases over cultural appropriation. "Two shows ago, I showed the girls with scarves on their head, which were not durags and that was not where that idea came from," he said, adding that it came from the '70s, which I know to be true, because I wore them in college. "And a couple of people wrote that it was durags and appropriation. Well, first of all, if you're appropriating something, why isn't that great? You're celebrating it."

After we split a lemon meringue pie, the designer dropped me at my hotel in his chauffeured Range Rover.

The next day I flew home. On the plane, I saw a picture of Priyanka Chopra on Page Six, the gossip section of The New York Post.

She was wearing the same Tom Ford red ruched tulle dress that I wore for the interview. With horror, I realized that I had been wearing my velvet corset belt backward all night, with the hooks behind and laces in front.

Mr. Ford was too polite to mention it.

Confirm or Deny

MAUREEN DOWD: *You don't pop Molly, you rock Tom Ford.*

TOM FORD: (Laughs) Jay-Z's song called "Tom Ford." I had to go on a rap translator online to actually understand the lyrics. I always loved that disco song with the lyric "Halston, Gucci, Fiorucci." I'm such a lucky person. It's a wild thing seeing 60,000 people in a stadium chanting your name.

When you were in grade school, you carried a black attaché case instead of a book bag.

Confirm.

A few years back, you had both a butler and a fox terrier named Angus and a nanny and a fox terrier named India.
Confirm.

You shouldn't design underwear if you don't wear it.
I don't wear dresses and I design those too. And it's true, I don't wear underwear.

You won't design for Melania Trump.
I have said that, given Melania's husband's beliefs, she should be wearing "made in America." I think my clothes would be too expensive for the president or the first lady—and they're all made in Italy. I would also not have designed for Hillary. They shouldn't be wearing clothes that the major part of America couldn't relate to in terms of price.

You love slapstick.
Richard Buckley tried to teach me an appreciation of slapstick, but that is something I will never have. Once, we were leaving our apartment and I opened the door right into my head and it really hurt and he laughed and laughed. The quickest way to get Richard to laugh is to cut off your finger, trip and fall on your face or break something. He's evil.

You have your own swans, a posse of attractive, wealthy women in Los Angeles.
I don't think of them as swans, no, because swans can bite. And Truman Capote found that out.

There are 20 shades of black.
Confirm. At least.

Men should never wear shorts unless they're three feet from the pool.
Confirm. Or unless they're on the tennis court.

Never use the word "awesome," even when something is awesome.
Confirm. Do not use the word "awesome."

In New Mexico, you've shot 50 rattlesnakes.
Yeah, I usually kill about four or five every summer.

You think champagne breath is the worst.

I hate champagne breath. Confirm. It's like vomit. It is! White wine and champagne give you terrible breath. It's like bulimic breath.

You think famous parents let their kids be photographed too much.

Confirm. Absolutely. You will not find a picture of Jack anywhere.

You are no longer bothered by thumbprints on stainless steel.

Deny. I am bothered by thumbprints on stainless steel.

You now refuse to design wedding dresses.

Confirm, because every girl has an idea of their wedding and what they want to wear is in their head and so essentially they don't need a designer. They just need a dressmaker. And it's very hard to design a wedding dress because it's more like, "Well, no, I always wanted to look like Grace Kelly," so there's not a lot of creativity to it. It's not fun as a designer.

Red-carpet fashion is boring.

Confirm. You get stylists calling you, saying, "She only wants to wear yellow, she wants strapless." People don't wear fashion, really; they wear a kind of vintage. The one time I thought they all looked great was last year at the Golden Globes when they all wore black.

You like to watch medical procedures.

Once, a Beverly Hills cosmetic surgeon took me in to see a breast augmentation. It's fascinating because it's very sculptural. As in my business, it's about where you hide the seams and what shape you create.

Derek Blasberg is the new Andy Warhol.

No. Derek Blasberg is the new Truman Capote.

The Kushners are the new Kennedys.

Oh my God, deny!

In private, you dress normcore.

Deny.

You spent more money on Goop last year than on Amazon.

Deny.

Studio 54 was overrated.
Deny.

Nobody ever lives happily ever after.
True, confirm.

There's only been one actual Anna Wintour smile on record, and that was Tom Ford in 2001.
(Laughs) Deny.

There's not an hour that goes by in which you do not think about death.
Confirm. I think about it more than every hour. It's constant.

You still take three baths a day.
At least two. Why do anything standing up that you can do lying down?

You have a subscription to Stitch Fix.
Deny.

Men are going to get into skirts.
I think the last time it looked good was Rome. Although a kilt can still do it for me. But it has to be a real kilt and you have to be Scottish.

Men are going to get into makeup.
I don't think there's a stigma attached to it anymore. In fact, I think people know the sun is bad for you so they just put on some bronzer. Just yesterday, I approved a cushion compact for Korea and Japan targeted specifically for men. But I do live in this bubble of New York and L.A. where there are a lot of performers.

When photographed, you favor the right side of your face with a three-quarter turn.
The left side is like the dark side of the moon. I don't think anyone's ever seen it.

Elizabeth Holmes ruined black turtlenecks for everyone.
Deny.

DIANE VON FURSTENBERG HAS NO REGRETS: 'I WILL LAUGH WHEN I DIE'

—JUNE 6, 2024

VENICE—Diane von Furstenberg's friends like to tease that, had she been on the cinematic Titanic, she would have found a way to hoist up Jack from the freezing water and onto that wooden door. Three days later, Jack in tow, she would have sashayed into a soignée New York dinner party wearing that 56-carat blue diamond necklace.

The woman has a strong will.

I realized that the first time I met her in 1975, when I was a cub reporter at The Washington Star. At 28, Ms. von Furstenberg was already a sensation with the phenomenally successful $86 wrap dress; she had conjured it after seeing Julie Nixon Eisenhower on TV defending her father during Watergate, wearing a DVF wrap top and skirt.

The tycooness, on a visit to D.C. to promote her brand, was in a rush to get to the airport and asked if I could come down to her car for the interview.

I felt like I was climbing into a cage with a panther. I got into the back of a black limo and there she was in a dark mink coat, her long dark hair with a henna sheen spilling over her shoulders, her legs sheathed in black fishnets. She was nibbling from a box of dark chocolates on her lap. In her sultry Belgian accent, she offered me one. Her voice, as her late friend, Vogue's André Leon Talley, said, "wraps itself around you like a cozy, warm cashmere muffler."

That half-hour in her limo was a revelation. In an era when we were instructed by male "experts" to dress and act like men to get ahead, Ms. von Furstenberg insisted on living a man's life in a woman's body. Her message was bracing: Meet men as equals but don't imitate them. Ambition and stilettos can coexist.

I immediately tossed out all my hideous dress-for-success floppy ties.

I caught up with Ms. von Furstenberg recently to talk about a new Hulu documentary, "Diane von Furstenberg: Woman in Charge," on her vertiginous, glamorous life, a life darkened by the Holocaust, AIDS, her bout with tongue cancer and her periodic business woes.

She doesn't like small talk; she likes intimacy. So we had a marathon two-day conversation on the Grand Canal, punctuated by feasts, at her dazzling palazzo, where putti (cherubs) cavort along the banisters. She is renting the piano nobile, known as the entertainment floor in the old days because of its high wooden and gilt carved ceilings. The palace is owned by Cristiana Brandolini d'Adda, the 97-year-old aunt of her late ex-husband, Egon von Furstenberg, a German prince and the son of Clara Agnelli.

"Venice is a nice stage for the winter of my life," Ms. von Furstenberg said. She is surprised that her family did not complain that she has moved to La Serenessima part-time, but said wryly: "They're very well trained."

Wearing a DVF silk print blouse and drawstring pants with vintage knit black-and-white Hermès booties, she patted the space beside her on her Vichy 19th-century daybed, where she was stretched out like an odalisque, and said, "You want to come here?"

As Michael Kors noted, "She is a sublime flirt. She's a real seductress, and that's not something that a lot of people manage to do well."

Her husband, Barry Diller, agreed: "She cannot sit down without being louche."

As she always does in her habitats, Ms. von Furstenberg has loaded up her lagoon retreat with animal print rugs and luscious pictures, including a Bert Stern photo of Elizabeth Taylor as Cleopatra, which hangs in her bedroom.

Andy Warhol's 1974 paintings of Ms. von Furstenberg are there, her right arm raised at an odd angle because the pop artist wanted a white background, so she had to squeeze into a space next to the refrigerator in her old Park Avenue apartment.

She got her custom-made neo-deco bed out of storage; her mother bought it for her on her 30th birthday. It's a portal to the Studio 54 era, when she prowled both coasts with the likes of Mick Jagger, David Bowie, Richard Gere, Warren Beatty, Ryan O'Neal and Omar Sharif.

"In my wild days, in that bed," she murmured. "That bed can tell you all the stories."

In the documentary, she recalls how she was enlisted for a threesome by Mr. Jagger and Mr. Bowie.

"I considered it and I thought, 'OK, this is a great thing to tell your grandchildren,'" she told me. "Then I came back to the room and they were two little skinny things, and I didn't. Actually, it's a better story that I didn't."

"Oh my God, I wonder what Mick is going to say," she said in her soft voice, noting that she is the godmother of his daughter Jade.

About David Bowie, she said: "I never thought he was sexy, but he was intelligent. Mick was sexy *and* intelligent."

She confides in the film that, while at the Beverly Wilshire on a business trip, "I was with Warren Beatty and Ryan O'Neal on the same weekend. How about that? I was very proud."

She mused to me, "If I didn't have kids, I can't even imagine what I would have become, because I would've had no restraint.

"It wasn't even about seduction when I was young. It was about—why can guys do that and women not? Why can a man hunt and boast about it, and why can't a woman? That was the fun, really. Diana's the huntress. I like the hunting.

"That's the biggest thrill and it lasts such a short moment," she said. Referring to Egon, she said, "I was married to a man who was very promiscuous. It was really: 'OK, you humiliate me, I could do it, too.' I didn't like to feel small. I could do it, too—boom—and then it's finished. It wasn't such a big thing, but I am glad I did it."

After a Venetian dinner on Saturday night, which kicked off with champagne and caviar, her guests—including Christian Louboutin,

Edward Enninful, the former editor of British Vogue, and Juergen Teller, the renowned fashion photographer who was in town to photograph the Pope for his visit, and his wife, Dovile Drizyte, who was wearing a T-shirt imprinted with a nude portrait of herself taken by Teller—just naturally piled into Ms. von Furstenberg's bed in a cuddle puddle to continue chatting in a polyglot of languages about West End plays, books, the Biennale and fashion gossip.

The princess of the wrap dress has been musing on how she plans to wrap up things.

She is soaking up the atmosphere of "the shimmering jewel in the sea," as her friend, the historian Thomas F. Madden, calls Venice, while she plots to take back control of her struggling business. She is also brainstorming about using her "magic wand"—a blend of wisdom, connections and philanthropy—to help people, and especially to "help women be the women they want to be." As she likes to purr: "Venice is a woman."

When I met with Mr. Diller in his Frank Gehry–designed glass clipper ship of a headquarters near the High Line in Manhattan, he explained: "Diane has an unquenchable ambition not to give up. Her life is at least a five-act opera."

Venice is the perfect frame for Ms. von Furstenberg. Mr. Madden has described it as "a place of contradictions—a city without land, an empire without borders." And it is DVF's contradictions that fascinate.

She wears a gold and diamond "In Charge" necklace and has numerous signs in her New York office with that exhortation. But, as Mr. Diller said, "Diane, she's the most in charge and the most vulnerable." She was too shy to even call herself a designer until two decades after creating the wrap dress.

Fabiola Beracasa Beckman, the daughter of Veronica Hearst and a producer of the documentary, has known Ms. von Furstenberg her whole life, because Egon von Furstenberg and her father were friends.

"By all societal norms, DVF is a contradiction in every possible way," Ms. Beckman said. "She's the child of a Holocaust survivor who married a German prince. She's an entrepreneur and also a seducteur. She's a socialite and a very serious activist. Usually, feminists aren't seducing men at every turn and comfortably navigating the patriarchy, right?"

Even Ms. von Furstenberg's sartorial creation was at cross-purposes, designed to let women be sexy *and* practical. It had no zipper, she said, so that you could slip out of lover's room without waking him—"Just like a man." It was a dress to seduce a man while impressing his mother.

Mr. Kors called his friend "a fascinating dichotomy" who "keeps you guessing." "Diane is over-the-top glamorous and yet very down-to-earth," he said. "She's no b.s., but then incredibly charming. I've had moments where I realized she's incredibly tender."

In 2020, Mr. Talley had a financial scuffle with his friend and landlord, George Malkemus, a former Manolo Blahnik C.E.O.; Mr. Malkemus threatened to evict the financially strapped Mr. Talley from his cherished house in White Plains. André, an old friend of mine, was bitter that some of his closest friends in the chiffon trenches, as he called the fashion industry, had deserted him. Not Ms. von Furstenberg, who quietly stepped in and paid off the $800,000 mortgage, without even discussing it with him.

Mr. Talley contracted Covid, had a heart attack in the hospital and died in 2022. But even if the payment provided him only a short time of relief, Ms. von Furstenberg is glad she came through.

"I was happy I could buy his dignity back," she told me. "He didn't die small." She also staged his memorial service at the Abyssinian Baptist Church in Harlem, which she pulled together with his friend, Alexis Thomas, and arranged for his papers to be given to the Library of Congress.

Sharmeen Obaid-Chinoy, who co-directed the documentary with Trish Dalton, said that she was drawn to DVF's journey from outsider in Belgium to insider in Gotham.

"In school, she felt like she was the odd one out, she didn't have blond hair, didn't have blue eyes; she stuck out," said Ms. Obaid-Chinoy, a Pakistani director who won an Oscar for her 2012 documentary, "Saving Face," about acid attacks on women in Pakistan, and is slated to direct an upcoming "Star Wars" movie.

Young Diane was thrilled to go off to Switzerland and England to boarding school, where—displaying her sexual fluidity—she fell in love with a boy and then a girl. At 18, she met Prince Egon von Furstenberg, who was also sexually fluid. He initiated the middle-class Jewish girl into the jet set. They married when she was 22. Egon's father, upset about Jewish blood in the family, attended the ceremony but skipped the reception. (He later said it worked out fine, because Egon sent "a girl" to his room.) As Gioia Diliberto reported in her 2015 biography of DVF, the father commented to a friend at the rehearsal dinner, "I don't know why Egon is marrying this dark little Jewish girl."

When Diane started her clothing line, Egon introduced her to Diana Vreeland, who boosted her business. The "princess" title helped.

The wrap dress, a quintessential symbol of the 70s, was so big, it was anthropomorphized. Ms. von Furstenberg's son, Alexander, said that it was like having another child in the house—"My genius brother who goes in and out of rehab."

"Nobody could understand how this stupid, simple little dress became such a huge phenomenon," she told me. "It was overwhelming."

Ms. von Furstenberg made an enormous amount of money very quickly and lost it all when her partners didn't heed her warning that the market was glutted. In the 90s, when she realized young women were ferreting their mothers' wrap dresses out of the closet, she revived it for a lucrative second act—launched by her unorthodox appearances on QVC. (Mr. Diller ended up buying a $25 million stake in the teleshopping network.)

The company's next act is up in the air. Ms. von Furstenberg said her empire was cresting in 2014, the year of the 40th anniversary of the wrap dress, as she and her executives pushed to make it even bigger, a la Chanel and Gucci.

"The problem was the people I hired started spending too much money, opening too many stores and outlets," she said. "I started losing control and really losing money." Then Covid made everything worse.

As The Times reported in 2020, Ms. von Furstenberg had to lay off 60 percent of the corporate and retail staff in the U.S., Britain and France, and close 18 of her 19 U.S. stores—as employees were let go without severance and creditors howled.

"I paid the bills, I closed the stores, which was very costly, but I made myself as clean as possible," Ms. von Furstenberg told me. She is still selling clothes online, in some department stores and in her flagship store in Manhattan's Meatpacking District. But for three years the bulk of her business was in the hands of her distributor in China, where the dresses are also made.

"Unfortunately," she said, "I realized how important it is for the brand owner, me, to be able to control the design. So I'm in the process of taking the business back from them. I thought, 'OK, this is the moment to pull back and do an inventory—what does the brand mean?' I want to create a vocabulary for my legacy. I realized I care more about women than fashion. Creating a uniform for women in charge."

Or as the always blunt Mr. Diller put it: "She's narrowing the business because the rest of it is a pain in the ass."

With a new top executive and a fresh creative team, Ms. von Furstenberg is working on a plan to make the company smaller and to adapt it to the changing world; it will be announced by the end of the year.

"Me, personally, I'm not particularly interested in running this anymore," she said. "I'm too old and I keep on saying, 'Use me as an adviser, because prints are still my thing.'"

She is also pulling together her archives in two buildings at Cloudwalk, her beloved 18th century farm in Connecticut.

In April, The Times ran a feature that the wrap dress might finally be dead, given the demise of "girlboss" culture and the different ideas younger generations have about what is flattering in this era of body positivity and neutrality. Ms. von Furstenberg's original motto for her creation, "Wear a dress, feel like a woman," would no longer fly with a lot of younger women.

Tom Ford, who replaced Ms. von Furstenberg when she finished her 13-year run as the head of the Council of Fashion Designers of America, disagreed about the wrap's ability to revivify.

"It's like saying the loafer is dead," Mr. Ford told me. "It might be quiet for a moment but it will come back because it's a staple. Like a woven men's shirt."

Ms. von Furstenberg says that the moment that most defines her life is when her mother, Lily Nahmias, a Jewish Greek immigrant working for the Belgium resistance, was liberated from the death camp when the war ended in 1945.

After 13 months in Auschwitz and Ravensbrück, the 22-year-old was barely the weight of her bones, down to 29 kilos, with blue tattooed numbers, 5199, on her left arm. She had to be fed every few moments like a bird. A year later, she was married to her fiancée, a Jewish Bessarabian immigrant named Leon Halfin, who was in electronics and later the semiconductor business. Against her doctor's warning that she couldn't have a normal baby, she had Diane.

"And I'm not normal," Ms. von Furstenberg said with a smile.

Her mother was tough on her, saying, "Fear is not an option" and "Don't be a victim." When the little girl was scared of the dark, her mother locked her in a dark closet to face her fear.

"Today she could go to jail for it," Ms. von Furstenberg says in the documentary. "But she was right." Her mother wanted to "equip" her in case she ever had to go through a trauma like she had.

That ability to look terrible news in the eye held Ms. von Furstenberg in good stead when, at 47, she got cancer at the base of the tongue. The key, she told me, is "not be a victim, not be angry, not say 'Why me?' Just say, 'This is what my situation is. This is what the doctor can do. This is what I can do.'"

In the 80s, when Ms. von Furstenberg's business was cratering, her mother, who had left her father for another man, went with her new partner on a business trip to Germany. Hearing a bunch of men talking loudly in German in the hotel sent her into a panic, and she was found crouching under the concierge desk.

"She went crazy," she says in the documentary. Her mother ended up in a mental ward in Switzerland. Lily, who was always freezing in Auschwitz, was "like a bird," Ms. von Furstenberg said, huddling under the fur coat she had bought with reparations from the German government.

Stunned by coming to terms with her mother's past, Ms. von Furstenberg fled with her children to Bali for a year, fell in love with Paulo, a sexy Brazilian beach bum, and put out a perfume inspired by her experience, Volcan d'Amour. "The fantasy then was Bali and the volcano and the blah, blah, blah," she told me.

Besides the popular attractions the Diller–von Furstenberg family foundation has helped bring to New York—Little Island, featuring free entertainment this summer, and the High Line—Ms. von Furstenberg is on the board of Vital Voices, helping women leaders around the globe. She also created the DVF awards, now based in Venice, for "bad-ass women."

She helped one woman in particular—the Statue of Liberty—raising $100 million for a Statue of Liberty Museum and earning herself the sobriquet "the Godmother of Lady Liberty." She even dressed as the Statue of Liberty, torch held high, for the Met Gala in 2019, the year the museum opened. It was apt, given that her mother, the Holocaust survivor, had always called her daughter "my torch of freedom."

"My parents were refugees," she said. "Refugees all over the world have built huge things. Not to have a country is a sad thing."

All aristocratic appearances to the contrary, she insists, "I'm a socialist." (She did name a striped sweater dress after Angela Davis when the revolutionary was in jail.)

"I think the most unbearable thing that is happening to the world is the distribution of wealth," she said. "Well," she added dryly, "I'm here in the palace telling you that."

Her biographer, Ms. Diliberto, told me: "It's easy to mock her as an out-of-touch member of the half percent—with an immense yacht, a private plane, cloned dogs, and several luxurious homes, including a palace in Venice. But her commitment to feminism, to her family and friends, and to New York City is sincere. Also, she's just a lot of fun."

Anna Wintour, the global editorial director of Condé Nast and the editor in chief of Vogue, agreed: "She is a person of enormous, generous spirit, never one to judge, highly eccentric and impossible to invent."

Ms. von Furstenberg beats you to the punch, anyhow, saying now and then: "Do you think I am ridiculous?" Or, "I don't want to sound obnoxious." Or, "I don't want to sound too rich."

When I laughed at that last, she protested: "Thank God I question myself. Otherwise, I would be arrogant and a monster."

She showed her egalitarian side at the CFDA.

"She was able to speak to a small designer and Ralph Lauren in the same way," Mr. Kors said.

DVF turned the insular little trade group into a global brand, doubling the membership, establishing an endowment and advocating for a strict age requirement and better working conditions for models.

When the fashion capitals of Milan, Paris, London and New York got into a throwdown about the calendar of events, Ms. Furstenberg told Steven Kolb, her top executive, to leave it to her.

"I know Italian, so I can fight with the Italians in Italian," she said, "and I know French, so I can beg the French in French, and we'll be fine."

She complains about how her face looks when she checks the photos she is always taking with her phone. She said she never smiled in photos when she was younger but now she thinks she looks better smiling. She has checked out doctors, thinking she would succumb to the knife or needle, but in the end, she always decides to stick with her septuagenarian face.

"People talk always about aging like it's something to hide," she told me. "Aging is a great thing. You already have in the bank what you have in the bank. I'm already 77, so no matter what, no one can take that away. Also, you're so much wiser.

"I don't understand people who say, 'Oh, I'm 50.' 50? You're just beginning."

Her key advice is: Don't lose yourself. "Because no matter what, you are always with yourself. You go through the diseases, the heartbreak, through the frustration, you wake up many mornings feeling like a total loser."

She continued: "I think the complicity you have with yourself is one of the most important things. Winking at yourself in the mirror or saying hello when you go by a mirror. That's why I write a diary. I write in French."

She does not like the trends of women embracing victimhood or objectifying themselves.

"We don't want to be too objectified by men, but then we shouldn't really objectify ourselves too much, either," she said. "Because then you have absolutely no claim to say that you're being treated like meat, right?"

In the documentary, she recalls her salad days in Paris when men could be cochons and lock you in a room and try to have their way. "I cannot say that anyone has ever done anything that made me uncomfortable," she says in the film with a little smile. "I would never give anyone that much credit."

Angelo Ferretti, who invited her to learn the trade at his print fabric factory in Como, Italy, was trying to get her "in his bed," she said, adding: "At the same time, I owe Angelo everything. He believed in me before anybody else.

"I am definitely a feminist. But that doesn't mean that you want to castrate men. On the contrary."

She is very concerned about women's reproductive rights being curbed in America.

"That is unacceptable," she said.

She has talked about her two abortions. "At the time of my first one, we didn't have ultrasound," she recalled. "Being pregnant at that time was much more abstract than it is now. Now you are barely pregnant and they're already staring at photos."

She has been fretting about the portrait of her family in the documentary. "Do you think I'm exposing myself too much?" she asked.

When she is pictured living the high life at Studio 54 and working hard as a baby mogul, will she seem like she was an inattentive mother to her two young children?

Her children, Alexander and Tatiana, who are involved in her company and foundation, make it clear in the documentary that their parents, the darlings of sparkly New York society, were distracted.

"They didn't have the longest attention span," Tatiana says. "I don't know if you want to use the word 'neglected' or 'free.' But we were not infantilized or cared for as children. We cooked for ourselves. We traveled alone from a very young age." She called her grandmother Lily "the woman who had been a mother to me."

Mr. von Furstenberg, who made men's shirts and caftans, was blithely pansexual; as an admiring Fran Lebowitz says in the film, Egon "was known for being decadent in an environment where you had to be outstanding to be known for that."

Then came the infamous 1973 feature by Linda Francke in New York magazine christening the von Furstenbergs "New York's reigning glory couple." The pair came across, as Francke says in the film, as

"Eurotrash." Egon talks about wanting to experiment with men and about a threesome with a woman the couple had met in Paris, which was, he said, a lot of work for him.

Ms. von Furstenberg looked at herself in the story and didn't like what she saw. She decided to get a divorce.

"I just realized I couldn't be a couple," she told me. "I did not want 'we.' I wanted 'I.' That's all."

Her son, Alex, said he would see her in her room with male models and movie stars she was dating, which, he added, didn't faze him.

Tatiana says in the film that her father's promiscuity with his gay posse after the divorce scared her as AIDS burgeoned, given that his nickname was "Egon von First-in-bed." When he died from complications from AIDS in 2004, Diane was with him in Rome and closed his eyes.

Pictures of Egon are all over her apartments; she remains close to other exes, as well, including Alain Elkann, the writer she lived with in France; she left him after he cheated on her with her best friend, but she's still friendly with him (and Paulo).

"When someone is in your heart, in your bed, you share intimacy, you want to keep them as friends," she said. "Sometimes it takes work, especially if you left them."

Tatiana seems more deeply affected by her parents' high-flying lifestyle. She talks about writing her mother a letter, which Ms. von Furstenberg saved and pinned up: "Dear Mommy, I wonder if we could have a talk some time because Mommy, you don't know anything about my life."

Until her daughter went to a doctor at 21 and figured it out, Ms. von Furstenberg had never realized Tatiana had a disability, a neuromuscular disease that made it hard to run and jump. Ms. von Furstenberg told me that her only regret in life is that she did not figure out her daughter's health issue sooner.

"The worst is that I saved that letter," she said. "That letter is on my wall. And even while I was saving that letter, I wasn't understanding its meaning."

She said: "I had a lot to manage with the business. I did the best I could. Emotionally, I was always with them, even when they were in boarding school. I would write every single day. They'd say, 'You left us all the time.' I didn't leave them that much at all.

"At the end, let me tell you, was I the best mother? Probably not, but the results are amazing. I speak at least twice a day with both my children. They are my best friends. Somebody was saying, in every family, there are secrets. I really don't think in my family there are any secrets at all."

In her memoir, Ms. von Furstenberg wrote that when she first got involved with Mr. Diller, who was the young, brash head of Paramount, his friends were incredulous, because no one had known him to be with a woman before, and that made her feel special.

In the documentary, Ms. Obaid-Chinoy asks both Ms. von Furstenberg and Mr. Diller about a Warhol line: "I guess the reason Diller and Diane are a couple is because she gives him straightness and he gives her powerfulness."

Ms. von Furstenberg looks arch and answers, "Ooh, it could be the other way around." Mr. Diller calls it disrespectful to the life they have built together.

"Diane and I were actually motiveless when we came together," he told me. "It was a coup de foudre."

Their marriage has certainly sparked a lot of talk. She lives downtown in the meatpacking district, in a small glass penthouse with a tented bedroom and a free-standing wooden bathtub above her last U.S. store. Mr. Diller lives uptown in a suite at the Carlyle Hotel.

"The only place we don't live together is New York City," he said, because there was no drawer or closet for him in her aerie, and because "I don't want to live above the store."

He added: "We live together in Connecticut. We live together in L.A. We sail together." They own a three-masted yacht named the Eos.

They are both adamant that this is no marriage of convenience. "There's nothing fake at all," she said. "It was real passion. I can still remember, it was total passion, and totally unexpected. And, of course, because it was so unique, I did feel like, 'Oh, my God, how special I am.' And he continues to make me feel special.

"My relationship and love with Barry, it's beyond anything. It is totally, totally love. When I met him, he was very shy, he was very introverted, and he opened it all up and gave me everything with no reservation and I fell in love with that."

For their first date in 1975, he picked her up at the airport in a yellow Jaguar and had the props department at Paramount set up all the furniture at his house. When he left the next morning, she said she opened all his drawers but found nothing that disturbed her.

"All I know is, we fell in love, we were lovers, then we left each other, then we were friends, and then we were together, and then we were married," she said.

For her 29th birthday, he gave her 29 loose diamonds in a Band-Aid box at a party at Woody Allen's house. "When I was 49, he gave me 49 diamonds," she said. "But the best story is when we got married. He gave me 26 wedding bands for the 26 years that we had not been married. I mean, who does that? Who even thinks of that? That was so sweet."

She recalled: "Just at the beginning of our relationship, we saw an old couple helping each other crossing the street. We both at the same time had the same thought that that's what we would be. He says it's Madison Avenue, I say it's Lexington. Whatever."

When I asked if women should embrace romantic passion into their later years, she waved her hand and said, "Thank God I'm relieved of all that" and "I can't imagine being attracted physically, sexually to anyone new. Those days are over. I mean, you have so much more time when you don't do that." Her feline aura belies her words.

She said that, while she didn't start out trying to be a kind person, she has learned the importance of that quality. Now she loves "making miracles" every day, connecting people and helping them achieve their dreams.

"I want to make kindness sexy, OK?" she said, adding that our "conflict sells" society is wearing us down.

"At this point in my life, I would like my experiences to be inspiring or useful," she said. "Otherwise, it's just conceited. And that's why I am fine to show I'm far from being perfect but I've had a good life."

In the documentary, she shows off the cemetery she has designed at Cloudwalk—"where I will become a mushroom."

"The other day I told my children, 'Listen, when I die and you're not there, don't worry about it. As long as I am with myself, I am fine.' I want to be able to live my death. I think I will laugh when I die, because, recently, I had two or three accidents, falling, and my reaction was laughing."

She read me my horoscope—we're both Capricorns—and Scotch-taped a lilac petal to my laptop for luck. She's a believer in talismans, wearing evil eye jewelry from her family and scattering them throughout her office. Late in the evening, Mr. Diller called to say hello, addressing her as "little girl"; he was in Miami checking on the new $45 million family compound he just bought in Biscayne Bay.

At the end of our Venice adventure, Ms. von Furstenberg was still curled up. I wondered how she liked always being described as feline.

"I would rather be a bird," she said, "because I could fly."

Confirm or Deny

MAUREEN DOWD: *Anne Hathaway was conceived in a wrap dress.*
DIANE VON FURSTENBERG: Her mother told me that.

You once went to a party at Brigitte Bardot's house in Saint-Tropez.
I did. It was pirate-themed.

You and Barry gave Jeff Bezos and Lauren Sanchez their engagement party. You think they should be married in outer space.
I never said that.

Just as Lauren Sanchez is the model for the figurehead of Jeff Bezos's yacht, you are the model for the figurehead of Barry's yacht.
Well, what happened is that when Barry was building the boat, he wanted a figurehead, and I asked my friend, the sculptor, Anh Duong, to do it. So she started to be inspired because the boat is called Eos, for the goddess Eos, and then she asked me to pose for it. Mine is in metal. It's very pretty. It has gone around the world twice. I may make a duplicate for my cemetery.

The word "boring" bores you.
Boring is not a word that I use, but I don't like passivity for sure.

You have always been fascinated by mirrors.

It's true. Mirror is very important. I need to have the contact with *me*. I hope it's not vanity and I hope it's not narcissism, but I get strength from my own eye contact.

Diana Vreeland was the scariest person you ever met.

Well, she was intimidating. I also love to say that because it annoys Anna.

You shouldn't wear vintage if you are vintage.

No, I love vintage. But when you dress up and you are older, you look older. That's why I don't like the Met Gala.

You always like to look a bit destroyed.

I do, I do, yes. What I mean is that even when I was younger, I liked women that looked a little worn as opposed to doll-like.

If you pack lightly, you live lightly.

Yes. I get my best design ideas packing.

You shared a hairdresser with Jackie Kennedy Onassis.

Yes, that's when I would iron my hair.

Every morning, before you get out of bed, you send an email connecting one person to another who otherwise would never have had the opportunity to meet.

It's a wonderful thing to be able to make a miracle a day.

Once a week, you give quality time to someone you ordinarily wouldn't speak to.

You think you do it for them, but you end up expanding your own horizon.

All high-powered career women need wives.

No, I would hate to have a wife. I can't think of worse. I can barely have an assistant. I don't like anyone to make my schedule.

There's a jet set Barbie based on you, with a pink wrap dress, a suitcase, a passport and a newspaper under her arm.

There's nothing I don't have. My life is so pathetic.

ANN ROTH IS HOLLYWOOD'S SECRET WEAPON

—JULY 23, 2023

BANGOR, Pa.—Ann Roth began with a few instructions: "Do NOT call me amazing. Do NOT call me a 91-year-old legend. Do NOT call me the oldest person in the 'Barbie' movie."

I had driven four hours through a biblical downpour to interview the revered costume designer. After a hike down a dark path through the woods to an 18th-century house, I felt as though I were opening the Narnia wardrobe and entering a whimsical fantasy world. Owls perched on rafters. Angels from Naples, Italy, dangled from the bedroom ceiling and chandeliers. A stone mantel was lined with miniature farm animals amid Oscars, Tonys and BAFTAs.

The enchanted cottage is a portal to one of the most imaginative minds in American culture, who has conjured memorable theater and film characters for more than half a century, from "The World of Henry Orient" to "The World According to Garp," from "Midnight Cowboy" to "The Morning After."

Ms. Roth was dressed in a crisp blue Orvis shirt, flowered shorts, rubber sandals (with aquamarine toenails peeking out) and an anklet that reads "East Coast" in an Old English typeface, a present from her grandchildren. She sports rings for earrings, including her grandmother's engagement diamond.

Ms. Roth has a pivotal scene with Margot Robbie in the "Barbie" movie, directed by her friend Greta Gerwig (Ms. Roth calls her "Gret"). When it was floated that Ms. Gerwig cut the scene, she refused, she said, because without it, "I don't know what this movie is about."

When the forever-young Barbie ventures out from Barbieland and encounters Ms. Roth, who plays a woman sitting at a bus stop in Los Angeles reading a paper, the doll suddenly realizes that being human and growing old could be cool.

"You're so beautiful," Barbie tells the woman, sounding amazed.

"I know it," Ms. Roth, in character, replies blithely.

Asked about the blizzard of pink that has enveloped the nation, Ms. Roth replied: "I live in Pennsylvania. I haven't seen pink in a long time." She is not going to a fancy "Barbie" premiere. She's going to see the movie this weekend at a theater on Route 248 in eastern Pennsylvania.

The designer has been the trusted collaborator of—and provocateur for—a pantheon of top directors, including Mike Nichols, Nora Ephron, Steven Spielberg, Anthony Minghella, John Schlesinger, Brian De Palma, George Roy Hill, Hal Ashby, Joe Mantello, Jack O'Brien, M. Night Shyamalan, Stephen Daldry, James Brooks and, early in her career, Dino De Laurentiis.

"She rides shotgun with you," said Mr. O'Brien, the Broadway director.

Ms. Roth points out a bedroom where her close friend Meryl Streep stays when she visits. She has conjured Ms. Streep's look in 13 movies, including "Silkwood," "Heartburn," "Postcards From the Edge," "Doubt," "Julie & Julia," "The Post" and "Mamma Mia!" as well as the mini-series "Angels in America." She calls her "Melstrip," echoing the way she heard the name pronounced in Italy.

She is planning a road trip in Italy with Melstrip if she can find the right shoes to ease her knee pain.

JESUS CHRIST BY WAY OF CHERYL TIEGS

Ms. Roth is of Quaker stock. She grew up in Pennsylvania Dutch country, where she wore a long strand of pearls to her job as a teenager at the five-and-ten. After graduating in the class of '53 at Carnegie Mellon, she apprenticed with the celebrated costume designer Irene Sharaff, working on "Brigadoon" (dyeing the men's tartans), Judy Garland's "A Star Is Born," and "The King and I."

Ms. Sharaff warned her protégée not to pursue her dream of becoming a production designer, saying, according to Ms. Roth, "it's not the place for women."

Mr. O'Brien said he knew that Ms. Roth was a force to be reckoned with back in 1970, when they worked on a production of "The Importance of Being Earnest" and she suggested adorning Miss Prism, Oscar Wilde's strict spinster governess, with little scissors around her waist. "So she can go snip, snip, snip, at people's balls," Mr. O'Brien said with a laugh.

Ms. Roth was doing Off Broadway shows, stealing costumes from garbage cans, when she got her Hollywood break. Zooming around Los Angeles in her white 1946 MG convertible, she started with a splash, creating the fantastic look for the 1964 Peter Sellers comedy "The World of Henry Orient." In it, an affluent Manhattan teenager named Valerie Boyd telegraphs her loneliness by draping her neglectful mother's long mink coat over her plaid school uniform; Mr. Sellers's Casanova concert pianist is bedecked in monogrammed handmade yellow silk pajamas. "Do you think I'd make polyester for anyone?" Ms. Roth said with a laugh.

Some of Ms. Roth's most iconic looks: Peter Sellers in "The World of Henry Orient," Jane Fonda in "9 to 5" and "Klute"—remember the sequined cocktail dress and boa she wore as a call girl?—Melanie Griffith in "Working Girl," Dustin Hoffman's purple suit and Jon Voight's fringed suede jacket in "Midnight Cowboy," and Barbra Streisand's nightie with the satin-appliqué hands cupping her breasts and "heart on her pee-pee," as Ms. Roth put it, in "The Owl and the Pussycat." She's the person who put Natalie Portman in a $19 pink wig for "Closer."

Then there's the Jesus character in "The Book of Mormon," who had lights attached to his cape to give him a sacred glow. "I wanted Cheryl Tiegs in the '80s," Ms. Roth said of the look, harking back to the beatific, blond pictures of Jesus I grew up with.

As costume designer for the notorious film flop "The Bonfire of the Vanities," Ms. Roth "resembled an elegant pheasant on amphetamines," Julie Salamon wrote in her rollicking 1991 book, "The Devil's Candy."

The pheasant and I sat down to a delicious lunch of salmon, corn salad, homemade vanilla ice cream and red wine. Then we repaired to her cozy studio, rain pattering on the skylights, to look at all her sketches, photos and voluminous research books. The room is dominated by a large, beautiful Brigitte Lacombe photo of Ms. Streep, a smaller one of a smiling Mr. Nichols ("I really, really miss Mike") and a photo of Ms. Streisand wearing that racy negligee.

"What do you think it took to get little Barb into that?" Ms. Roth said drolly about La Streisand. "I don't think she thought it was hip or would make the pages of Vogue. It's hard to get actors to go for trash. Trash is one of my favorite things to do."

In the middle of the room, there's a chaise with a leopard-print throw, perfect for getting inspiration as she plays Mozart, Beethoven, Strauss, Offenbach, Elvis and Fats Domino. In a corner is a MacBook still in the box.

"I've never opened it," she said. "I don't have a website. I've never seen Instagram or TikTok." She adds, "I'm way oldie-timey."

Her friends would laugh at that description of a woman with boundless energy who shows up at parties with her karaoke machine. "She's younger than any young artist I know," said her close friend Scott Rudin. "She's been on top of her game for 65 years."

Ms. Roth is going through 2,000 drawings of her costumes, which she plans to donate to Carnegie Mellon when she dies. She showed me some of the famous ones, complete with swatches of material attached. "Usually, they have a wine glass circle on them," she said, "because I'm talking with the tailor late at night."

(Most of the time, she calls me "darling girl," but if I ask a question she deems stupid, she calls me "birdbrain.")

Ms. Roth's warehouse a few miles away has enough clothes to outfit a city, chockablock with pieces from every decade—waist cinchers and fedoras and century-old football shoulder pads, and categories like "Nazis," "Israeli police," "Mambo kings" and "Jesus Christ, multiples."

The designer had a symbiotic relationship with Mr. Nichols for nearly 50 years. She did six plays with him, starting with Neil Simon's

"The Odd Couple" in 1965, and 13 films, including "Silkwood," "Heartburn," "The Birdcage" and "Working Girl."

The director usually took Ms. Roth's advice—except on one thing. "He had a terrible problem with printed fabrics," she said. "Mike would say, 'You can't have plaid. Ever.'"

"'Let's just try it. If you hate it, I'll pay for it,'" Ms. Roth recalled saying to him. "That always gets them."

Mr. Spielberg was more docile. He said that when he first met Ms. Roth, she did a presentation on how she would dress Ms. Streep and Tom Hanks as Katharine Graham and Ben Bradlee for "The Post," and he was smart enough to keep his mouth shut. "I said, 'Yes, boss,'" he recalled.

ATTENTION TO DETAIL

When Ms. Roth won the Academy Award for best costume design in 2021 for "Ma Rainey's Black Bottom," she was hailed as the old-est woman to ever win a competitive Oscar. It followed her win for "The English Patient" in 1997—remember the amazing red plaid shawl Kristin Scott Thomas wore to keep warm in the desert nights?—and a Tony in 2013 for "The Nance."

For "Ma Rainey," Ms. Roth said, "I made the behind." She endowed Viola Davis with greater curves—rubber boobs underneath her boobs, as Ms. Roth put it, and a rubber bottom to match the measurements of Aretha Franklin, at Ms. Davis's request.

The actors wore authentically heavy wool suits in a steamy Chicago summer "because it needed to hang correctly," said the film's director, George Wolfe. Ms. Roth said she imports 21-ounce wool from West Yorkshire, England, for period pieces, noting that "wool has to be what it is supposed to be."

"Things either enhance or distract," Mr. Wolfe said. "Actors feel and sense and are affected by everything. They're affected by what their un-dergarment is, what the wig is. It's all contributing to the storytelling or it's distracting from the storytelling. That's what's so thrilling to work with Ann, because she brings the ferocity of that belief in every single detail of her work."

Unlike costume designers in Hollywood's heyday, Ms. Roth is not devoted to making the top movie stars look impossibly glamorous. She talked Nicole Kidman into wearing a big latex nose to play Virginia Woolf in "The Hours" in 2002. "I said to her, 'I can't honestly put a 1917 hat on your head with that nose,'" she recalled. "I made her a nose with a nose maker in England, and it took hours every morning for them to get the damn thing on."

Mr. Rudin, the film's producer, backed up Ms. Roth, but Harvey Weinstein, who was financing the movie, was furious. "'I paid a million dollars for that girl, and no one knows who she is,'" Ms. Roth recalled Mr. Weinstein snapping. Mr. Rudin said that Mr. Weinstein sent an executive to London to talk Ms. Kidman out of the nose, but Mr. Rudin stationed security guards at every entrance of the set so that Mr. Weinstein's man could not get to the actress. Ms. Kidman won an Oscar for her transformation.

"I don't think anybody really liked him," Ms. Roth murmured about Mr. Weinstein.

Ms. Roth conceived Melanie Griffith's metamorphosis from Staten Island secretary to Wall Street wiz in "Working Girl." ("You can't talk about the movie without talking about cocaine," she told Mark Harris for his biography on Mr. Nichols.)

On "The Bonfire of the Vanities," which also starred Ms. Griffith, the director, Mr. De Palma, had conferences with actresses on his lap, and the crew openly rated the actresses' "heinies" and legs and complained if they were a few pounds overweight, according to Ms. Salamon's book.

"I've never seen so many prosthetic breasts in my life," Ms. Roth told Ms. Salamon, after days of fitting extras for the movie.

Asked about the quote, Ms. Roth smiled sweetly. "A girl has to be careful what she says, doesn't she?" she replied.

The costume designer is famously blunt. She hates whiners and loves a challenge.

"She tells you the truth, tells you when you've made a mistake, straight up, no B.S., and you trust her because of it," said Amy Pascal, the producer who worked with Ms. Roth on "The Post."

Ms. Roth performs her alchemy at the moment when actors feel most vulnerable: costume fittings when they're in their underwear, looking in the mirror and just beginning to search for their characters. She is like a psychoanalyst, managing their insecurities to help them subsume themselves in a character.

She said her technique is to gather all kinds of stuff and stick it in the closet of the fitting room. "Then I say to them, 'You and I are going to find this character,'" she said. "But I, in all honesty, am not going to consult. It's too late to consult because I've already got it behind the curtains in the closet.

"Someone said to me, 'I don't wear yellow,'" she recalled. "I said, 'Shut up.'" Eventually, the actors' characters stare back at them in the mirror.

Sometimes Ms. Roth changes lives. She advised one uptight movie star to smoke marijuana to relax, and warned Mr. Shyamalan, when they worked on "Signs" and "The Village," not to let money and success corrupt him.

"She was playing through life like a child and that's contagious," Mr. Shyamalan said.

A 'NOVELIST DESIGNER'

Ms. Roth's curiosity about everyone, whether she meets them at a gas station or a gala, is her most distinctive trait.

Ms. Streep calls her "a novelist designer."

"In her work in film and theater, she is a sort of writer," Ms. Streep said of her friend. "Her designs are not so much costumes as an extension of the individual character she is building with an actor and director. You don't come away from her work saying, 'Oh, weren't the costumes gorgeous?' You just remember the people she has clarified for you through what they chose to put on their bodies in the morning. She has a sharp flair for the eccentric in the ordinary. Authenticity and specificity."

Ms. Roth scorns the slipshod. She searched for just the right shade of blue for Bette Midler's caftan in her 2013 one-woman play "I'll Eat You Last: A Chat With Sue Mengers."

Ms. Midler said: "Usually these days you get 'It sort of fits.' 'It's fine, the camera won't see your feet.'"

"I hate the expression 'I see you,'" the actress said. "But Ann sees you and sees the character on top of you."

Ms. Roth has been known to go to extremes to get the look she wants. While shooting the 2012 action movie "Safe," she asked a Polish construction worker in Philadelphia for his pants to put on Jason Statham, according to "The Designs of Ann Roth," by Holly Poe Durbin and Bonnie Kruger.

"They were old and sexy," Ms. Roth told me. (She bought the pantsed man another pair.)

She is particularly proud of buying a red fox fur coat from a parking attendant at 25th and 10th in Manhattan that Brenda Vaccaro, nervous about being naked, ended up wearing during her sex scene with Mr. Voight in "Midnight Cowboy." The designer kept it to wear herself afterward.

During the costume fitting for "Mamma Mia!" Ms. Roth told Christine Baranski about Tanya, her jet-setting character: Her lifestyle was "Dolce & Gabbana Vita," and she vacationed in Sardinia, Italy, and Ibiza, Spain.

"Ann said Tanya was always pursuing the next fabulous thing and the next fabulous guy, but there was a bit of desperation there," Ms. Baranski recalled.

Ms. Roth worked with a nervous Nathan Lane on Noël Coward's "Present Laughter" on Broadway in 1982. In the play, he's an aspiring playwright whose father wants him to be a lawyer. Ms. Roth put a vintage brown suit on him while explaining, "This suit was probably owned by your father, who's a lawyer. He wanted you to become a lawyer and the suit was cut down for you." (Mr. Lane called her "the Meryl Streep of costume designers.")

James Brooks, who produced "Are You There God? It's Me, Margaret," released earlier this year, was dumbfounded when he heard Ms. Roth, who was overseeing costumes, hair and makeup, talk to the actors as she fitted them. He began sitting with her.

"It would be pleasure seeking to just sit and listen to it," he said. "It was like every second, 100 times a day, she was saying something smart in that low, thrilling voice."

He has already enlisted her to work on his new movie being shot in Rhode Island, "Ella McKay," starring Emma Mackey, who is in "Barbie."

HISTORICALLY ACCURATE UNDERWEAR

Ms. Roth upended the Hollywood system, informing the suits about dressing the bit players, "I will be doing the elevator man," she said.

In "Cold Mountain," she did not just dress Ms. Kidman and Renée Zellweger; she outfitted the entire Union and Confederate armies for the scene depicting the Battle of the Crater. She took someone with her to the set to age and dye the fabrics correctly; she can give a whole dissertation on the iron as an instrument to ingrain dirt around a collar.

We looked at the fabric swatch from the movie. In The Times, Kate Betts described the labyrinthine process of replicating the fabric of the North Carolina 25th Infantry, called butternut because it was dyed with the bark of a butternut tree. "So she tracked down someone named Pat Cline in Pennsylvania, who knew exactly how to dye the thread to look authentic," Ms. Betts wrote. "Ms. Roth had the fabric woven and printed in Montana, dyed and aged in Rome and shipped to Romania, where the filming took place."

Ms. Roth did the costumes for the smash Scott Rudin production of Harper Lee's "To Kill a Mockingbird," refashioned by Aaron Sorkin. She visited London last year to check on the costumes for the West End run.

After lining up the cast in the lobby of the theater, because the backstage stairs were too daunting, Ms. Roth asked the actors if anyone had some coins she could borrow. She dumped a load of coins into the suit pocket of one of the actors and said, "*That's* how a jacket that's been worn for years sags and sits and looks, and that's how I'd like all these coats and pants and jackets to hang, with the weight of time and wear."

She also insists on historically accurate underwear. For "Places in the Heart," a Depression-era story, she gave Sally Field a girdle without a crotch for Edna Spalding's going-into-town-to-ask-for-a-loan-at-the-bank look. When Ms. Field gave her a look, she told the actress, "Put it on." With the proper underwear, she explained, you walk and sit a certain way. The actress won an Oscar.

Most of the time, actors are grateful to soak up Ms. Roth's ideas. "Ann will hand me a purse to go with a particular costume and going through its contents will inevitably reveal things to me about my character," Ms. Fonda said. "Maybe there's a Swiss Army knife in the purse. Maybe a cigarette holder and lighter or a small notebook for journaling and a very specific kind of pen."

Speaking about her character in "9 to 5," Ms. Fonda recalled, "A purse she gave me for Judy Bernly had food coupons in it."

Joe Mantello said that for the Honey character in his 2020 production of "Who's Afraid of Virginia Woolf?" Ms. Roth had a second A-line shift made and put a small vomit stain on it and more wrinkles for the scene after Honey throws up.

"Unless you were in the three front rows and really observant, you would not notice that," Mr. Mantello said. "But detail and reality are so much a part of her process. And it really helps the actor because they move in a different way when they wear it. That's what makes Ann Roth Ann Roth.

"She and Mike Nichols were like-minded collaborators because he allowed behavior to reveal psychology and she allows clothes to reveal psychology."

Sometimes, however, movie stars cling to their image and fight Ms. Roth. Mr. Hoffman, a newly minted movie star after "The Graduate," at first resisted Ratso Rizzo's look in "Midnight Cowboy," a green suit Ms. Roth found on 42nd Street and dyed purple, and a white jacket redolent of Ratso's pathetic emulation of the Italian actor Marcello Mastroianni. She added Times Square "cockroach-in-the-corner" high-tops.

In "Primary Colors," John Travolta, playing Jack Stanton (based mostly on Bill Clinton in the 1992 campaign), did not want to wear what Ms. Roth had accurately planned: "Department-store suits available to men in a small city in a not-prominent Southern state."

"I lost that battle," Ms. Roth said with a rueful grin, noting that the actor must have gone to Mr. Nichols, the director, and said, "She's making me wear this ugly suit." Mr. Nichols told Ms. Roth, "Let him have Donna Karan suits."

"I will never forgive Mike for that," she said, laughing.

Mr. Travolta's rejection of her look did not stop them from hanging out.

"I did go dancing with Travolta once," she said. "We danced once in a big makeup-hair camper and we said, 'We have to do this more' and we did. He's a very good jitterbug, as am I."

Before I left, I wondered which movie she considered her best work.

"It was probably Jude Law and Matt Damon in 'The Talented Mr. Ripley,'" she said. "That was my fashion piece."

And which was the most fun?

"I have never had fun making a movie in my life except for 'Mamma Mia!' where some guy called me and said, 'How would you like to go to an island with your good friend and make 'Mamma Mia!'?" She got to hang out with Ms. Streep and Ms. Baranski and drink lots of martinis. "I drink potato-based vodka on ice," she said. "Not grain."

After all, as Ms. Roth said slyly, "I'm the world's oldest costume designer, damn it!"

Confirm or Deny

MAUREEN DOWD: *You have been wearing blue toenail polish every day since 1953.*

ANN ROTH: Mike Nichols asked me to come to dinner with Anthony Minghella at the fancy Chinese restaurant in Beverly Hills, Mr Chow. Before Minghella arrived, Mike looked at my feet and said, "You're not going in like this, are you?"

You worked as an assistant for Miles White when he designed the Ringling Bros. and Barnum & Bailey Circus and was the costume designer for "Around the World in 80 Days." There were 74,685 costumes for that movie.

That was a big mess. I did go to Las Vegas to fit Marlene Dietrich. She wanted to sit on a big beer or wine barrel with her legs apart because Miles had done a divine drawing of her like that. I had to find the barrel. She was fabulous. She taught me about a fabric that was made in Czechoslovakia and found in Switzerland called silk soufflé, which really doesn't exist anymore. It's just thinner than silk stockings ever dreamt of being. Cameramen sometimes liked to use it on their lenses because it made people look better.

You kept the gray sequined dress Jane Fonda's call girl wore to parade before a client in "Klute."

Jane and I passed that dress back and forth for about a year afterward. Jane is like four inches taller than I, and I would have mine pinned up and go to a party and then ship it back to her.

You often use a flesh-toned fabric known as O.M.D., describing the color of an older man's privates.

O.M.D. is a lavender gray. The Russian ladies who sewed for the costume designers Barbara Karinska and Irene Sharaff called that color thread O.M.D. They spoke no English at all except they all knew what O.M.D. was.

You love to wear snail spit to go out to cocktails.

I would. Snail spit is a novelty fabric, cheap, like nylon with a shine or glitter to it. You can pull a yard through a wedding ring. You can't pull a yard of velvet through a wedding ring.

You have your own karaoke machine.

I do, but I need it Thursday and I don't know where it is.

MONSIEUR VOGUE IS LEAVING TRUMPLAND

—DECEMBER 21, 2016

CHAPEL HILL, N.C.—André Leon Talley is eating a biscuit.

He shouldn't be eating a biscuit because he is on a long, difficult sojourn here through the holidays at Duke Diet & Fitness Center to try to lose 100 pounds and stop associating food with love. And biscuits are his Proustian madeleines, evoking all the love he got from his grandmother growing up in humble circumstances in nearby Durham.

But André has been going through a rough patch with his friends, and he needs a bit of carb comfort, as we listen to the morning medley soundtrack of Dean Martin and Frank Sinatra in the lobby of the genteel Siena Hotel before he heads off to Duke for a more spartan breakfast in a no-frills cafeteria.

It's my fault, too, because I'm pressing him on a sore subject he is reluctant to discuss: Melania Trump.

The 68-year-old, 6-foot-6 Monsieur Vogue, as he is known, cloaks his voluminous red puffer coat over his mountainous form, so that only his big brown eyes and navy Filson knit cap are showing.

"First of all," he says, well aware of my fashion ignorance, "this is a Norma Kamali sleeping bag coat."

Then he offers his declaration: "You make the choice to be in Trumpland or you make the choice to eject yourself from the horror of Trumpland. I've made my choice not to be part of Trumpland."

But, I point out, Donald Trump was bragging on the trail only the day before that he had just had a meeting with André's Vogue compadre and fellow Hillary supporter Anna Wintour. At first, André has a hard time believing that Ms. Wintour would venture anywhere near the dreaded Trump Tower. I have to actually show him the story and get it confirmed with the Trump spokeswoman Hope Hicks. But finally he shrugs under his puffery.

"As for Anna Wintour going to Mr. Trump, she's a powerful woman, she's running an empire, she's the editorial director of Condé Nast," he says. "We can't judge her for going to a meeting. She's a professional, powerful woman. That's all I have to say."

I have flown here to see if André can shed some light on Melania, the sultry enigma of Trumpworld, the only reserved member of what is shaping up to be the most bellicose takeover in modern times. As everyone else rushes in to blow up the capital, as Ivanka shops for houses in Georgetown and office space at the White House, as headlines cascade about how Ivanka will be the real first lady, Melania has virtually disappeared. We see more of her doppelgänger on "Saturday Night Live" than we do the real Slovenian Sphinx, who is hanging back in New York so her 10-year-old son, Barron, can finish the school year.

Melania's absence from the stage has not stopped a raging battle in the fashion world about her—a sequel to the boycott during the campaign against Ivanka's brand and a microcosm of the fight being replayed across the country about whether to "normalize" the Trumps or whether to keep shouting from the rooftops, "This is not normal!," as my colleague Charles Blow urged this week.

André's friend Tom Ford said he was not likely to dress the former fashion model and future first lady because "she's not necessarily my image." (Ford once spent time after a Helmut Newton memorial trying to get Melania to do something about the Donald's hair, but Melania merely murmured in her Gabor accent, "I like him the way he is.") Marc Jacobs told Women's Wear Daily that he would rather put his energy "into helping out those who will be hurt by Trump and his supporters." The French designer Sophie Theallet, a favorite of Michelle Obama's, published an open letter saying she would not dress Melania to protest Donald Trump's "rhetoric of racism, sexism and xenophobia." Other designers, like Tommy Hilfiger and Carolina

Herrera, have riposted that they would be proud to dress the Trump women.

It is a particularly sensitive matter since Melania follows Michelle, beloved by the fashion world, as The New York Times's Vanessa Friedman wrote recently, for elevating the industry "beyond the superficial to the substantive," by framing clothing "as a collection of values: diversity, creativity, entrepreneurship." As David Yermack, a professor of finance at New York University, noted, Michelle was also a bonanza, generating $2.7 billion in a single year for the companies she showcased.

André has particular insight into Melania's style since, while on Vogue assignment, he went to couture shows with her in Paris and helped her choose her Dior wedding gown, and later flew with her in white-leather splendor on the Trump plane as Donald scarfed down Oreos and talked about how Jude Law was no Cary Grant.

As André told me in the fall when I interviewed him, he came away impressed with the Trump women. He called Melania charming and private, "soignée and polished" with "impeccable" manners and legs that are "a long drink of water," and said she had a gift for standing on four-and-a-half-inch stiletto heels. "She's very much like a high, super, superglamorous Stepford Wife," he told me.

He also said that she was the most fastidiously groomed and exquisitely moisturized person he'd ever met. (He now gives that honor to Kim Kardashian West.) At the Mar-a-Lago wedding, which he attended with Ms. Wintour, he noticed that "even then you could tell that Ivanka was going to be a very bright star. She had on a melon-colored dress."

But André walked into a sartorial buzz saw when, amid buzz that he might be called on to give Melania advice about her Inaugural gown, he echoed some of those sentiments recently to a Daily Mail reporter, saying that Melania was "a wonderful person to be with" and that she "will be one of the great stars in the administration." He capped it off with optimism: "I hope there will be a great, great Trump presidency."

It didn't take long for the guillotine to fall. One friend emailed him, "Oh my God, you have gone to the Evil Empire!!!!!"

He agonized about the "tragedy of ruptured friendships" to me in an email, saying about Melania: "She's a nice person. I do not endorse Trumpism on any level. So why can't one be positive and want her to shine? I mean, it's good she cares about napkins, crystal, dinner plates with gilded edges to the point of over the top, and abundant flower arrangements. In the end, why pick on her when they should be picking on her husband's billionaire cabinet and his seeming readiness to turn the country back towards oppression, anti-Semitism, anti-culturalism, etc."

As we sit in the hotel lobby, he muses: "I'm not a big person in the world. I'm maybe a big figure in the fashion world. I mean, sort of iconic. But I don't want to get phone calls in the middle of the night, telling me I've gone over to Trumpland and I'm going to Darth Vader because I said nice things about Melania. I voted for Hillary Clinton. I registered in North Carolina because it mattered. I went through hoops of fire to get my absentee ballot. And, quite frankly, I thought she would have brought back the pantsuit. I thought the gray trouser suit designed by Ralph Lauren she wore with the purple satin shell and the lapels matching the blouse was brilliant. The elegant anthracite gray dry wool actually was slimming.

"Melania, who opted at 3 a.m. for a palazzo jumpsuit, with one arm exposed and a flounce over the other—it seemed to me too Mar-a-Lago, a huge, full-volume jumpsuit. Trying too hard. And I am so tired of the long hair falling on both sides of her face. She has to upgrade her coiffure."

But isn't he worried that many of those on the left who complain about Trump as a dictator are acting dictatorial? Not one good word can ever be said about anything that happens for the next four or eight years? Is it fair to hold Melania and Ivanka responsible? Or are they putting a lovely gloss on some of Trump's unsavory rhetoric and actions?

"Listen, Melania made her choice," he replies. "She married the man, so she's got to go with the territory. She's Mrs. Trump."

I remind André that he told me that, at the 2005 wedding, it seemed as if "Donald Trump was a cool guy."

"He became the master of darkness, the master of the dark empire, as he became more powerful, as he started with birtherism and in the campaign," André says now. "Birtherism is terrible. It was a terrible thing he did to Obama. And he never let go. 'Make America great again.' A lot of people think that means make America white again."

I say that a friend of mine, the writer David Israel, is now calling it the Whites-Only House.

"People are really afraid of these dark, dark institutions of bigotry and anti-Semitism that have come out from under the rocks like creepy snakes and come up to rear their heads up like cobras," André agrees. "People seem to have put all their egregious things on the back burner. Melania plagiarized Michelle Obama's speech. Let's just wait and see what happens on Jan. 20. I don't want Trump to fail, and I don't want Melania Trump to fail. But I'm not going to sit here and say any more positive things, because I'd get crucified from personal friends."

So the Trumps should never get a full measure of respect?

"Did the Congress ever treat Obama as a president?" André snaps back. "Did they plot in a restaurant the night he was inaugurated to filibuster everything for eight years? This country has elected a president who is on audiotape saying I'm a star and I can do whatever I want with women, grab them in the vagina. Dignity has gone out the door. He's causing me much ire. He just said, 'My cabinet has the highest I.Q.' His cabinet of mostly white men. That's a dog whistle."

Trump had come down to the bouquet of microphones the day before with Kanye West, whose wedding André had attended and praised as even more astonishing than the Trump wedding because the rehearsal dinner was at Versailles, not just a Florida ballroom gussied up to look like Versailles. But even Kanye's visit did not impress André.

"Listen to me," he instructs. "There is a lot of marzipan here. Marzipan is the glaze you put on a cake, a superficial glazed layer. It's all marzipan, it's all optics."

Speaking of optics, I tell André that the mother of a Times colleague I met at the White House Christmas party said she didn't mind that Melania had been a model, noting that Betty Ford worked as a model. And she didn't care if she had been an "adventuress" seeking a wealthy husband. But she did not like Melania's photo shoot of racy pictures with another woman, and felt she could not accept her as first lady because of that.

"You can't judge a person by pictures," André responds. "She was a model. She took pictures."

I mention that it's passing strange that Melania's project is fighting cyberbullying when her husband is a cyberbully. André rolls his eyes.

André's favorite first ladies are Michelle Obama and Jackie Kennedy. Of Jackie he says, "I would have loved to give her advice, even about what to wear to the beach."

The night before, we had a tasty 390-calorie dinner of grilled salmon, broccoli and eggplant at the diet and fitness center's cafeteria. This is André's fifth time here.

I asked him if it was true that Anna Wintour and Oscar de la Renta once had an intervention with him about his weight.

"Absolutely," he said. "Anna Wintour called an intervention in the conference room at Vogue one morning. And I was escorted downstairs by a fellow staff member to one of the executive dining rooms. And I said to this person, 'Am I about to be fired for something?' And I walked into the room, and there was an intervention going on. And Oscar and his wife and Anna Wintour and my minister, Reverend [Calvin O.] Butts, had been called into the room. They were ready to send me to the Duke Diet & Fitness Center the very next day, and they'd already made the reservation. But, of course, I angrily rejected it because I was emotionally not ready to come, so I got up and I quietly left the room."

About a year later, he finally made the decision himself to come to Duke and left straight from the Trump wedding at Mar-a-Lago on a Sunday afternoon.

When he was a child, his grandmother worked every day to support him, cooking, washing and ironing. But on Sunday mornings, she would make him a special pan of biscuits and "the best" chocolate cake.

"So my weaknesses are anything I associate with childhood, which I associate with love," he said. But he is weaning himself from bread and sugar and has already lost 28 pounds.

I made one last attempt to press him for an idea of what Melania will be like compared to other first ladies. We know there will be opulence. We know that she loves Valentino and Chanel and Manolo and fur and diamonds and that she doesn't like prints or going without makeup.

When Melania did the Vogue cover, the writer Sally Singer said that the bride of Trump, compared in the piece to a Bond girl, had "a slightly old-fashioned idea of femininity" because she refused to pose for Mario Testino without makeup or perfectly styled hair.

"She has those impossibly high four-inch, towering stilettos," André said. "Clearly, her clothes will cling in the right places, accentuate her figure and her model-style long tresses. Get ready for super-cinched waists, hourglass silhouettes and pencil skirts. She is already into one-shoulder, which Jackie Kennedy wore by Oleg Cassini. Melania likes monotone matching coats and beige dresses, but that hair will always be flying once she goes down the stairs of Air Force One.

"She's very private. She just wants to be a mother. It's very similar to Jackie O, who also wanted to keep her kids out of the fray. When Barron was first born, she used to say: 'I'm going off to play with Barron. I just want to spend time with Barron.' So, in a way, I think that she's maintaining her privacy with him and maintaining a kind of dignity because she's not making statements. I don't think that she would try to change the White House in any way. I don't think that's what she's interested in."

She never tried to modify the gaudy '80s gilt in the three-story Trump Tower penthouse or the rushing fountain in the middle—a style of décor described by the Trump biographer Timothy O'Brien as Louis XIV on acid. As André has noted, Melania is not "a disrupter." But Trump is.

"I wish them the best," André said. "I want suddenly to see that she has incredible style, wake up and say, 'Oh my God, look, isn't that great?' I really do think that there's hope. We have to wait and see. As Sergei Diaghilev told Jean Cocteau, 'Astonish me.'"

Confirm or Deny

MAUREEN DOWD: *You have gorgeous stuff in your house in White Plains, but you don't entertain.*

ANDRÉ LEON TALLEY: Confirm.

You don't like it when Joe Scarborough and Mika Brzezinski dress like twins.
   Confirm.

You once advised me to get shoes the color of the skin of a Vidalia onion.
   Confirm.

You worked for Andy Warhol at Interview magazine. He was the weirdest person you ever met.
   Deny. He was normal to me.

Anna Wintour has never worn a ponytail.
   Confirm.

You've never been romantically involved with a designer.
   Oh, confirm.

You own a thousand custom-made caftans.
   Deny. I have more than 10 and less than 50. Listen, I'm not Marie Antoinette.

You don't believe couples should sleep in the same bed.
   Confirm. They really should be in different apartments in the same city.

If you could have any friend in the world, you'd pick Judge Judy.
   Confirm.

You watch seven hours a day of MSNBC.
   Confirm.

You touched Vivien Leigh's green velvet dress from "Gone With the Wind."
   And did I! Confirm.

Was Queen Elizabeth hot?
   Confirm. She was very stylish in the '60s. She had a fabulous figure, fabulous waist and big bosoms, and she looked good in her clothes.

Was Princess Margaret sexy?
   Deny. Except the actress who plays her in "The Crown," when she's galloping on her horse to Peter Townsend with her trench coat flying behind.

Except for kilts, skirts for men, like Marc Jacobs made, are never coming back.
  Confirm.

Your biggest regret is not writing the definitive biography about Yves Saint Laurent.
  Confirm.

You've never been in love with a man, only a woman.
  Confirm.

Your ideal of a hot guy is Bruce Springsteen.
  Deny. It's Will Smith.

When you ran the Russian magazine Numéro Russia, you thought you could change Russian politics.
  Deny.

Michelle Obama is the best-dressed first lady of all time.
  Confirm.

Anna Wintour will love the fashion of the Trump presidency.
  Deny.

You thought it was a brilliant move when Trump Scotch-taped the back of his tie to keep it in place.
  Confirm. You can also have an instant face-lift by Scotch-taping your temples.

Amal Clooney snubbed you at the Met Gala.
  Confirm.

Trump is going to bring back boxy suits and long ties.
  Deny.

Ivanka is a fashion icon.
  Deny.

Oscar de la Renta designed your bed.
  Confirm.

You brushed Valentino's pug's teeth.
    That is so not true! Deny.

You were blurred out of the Kim and Kanye wedding episode on the Kardashian show.
    Confirm. It was an oversight. They did put me back in.

You have Truman Capote's sofa in your house that you bought at an auction.
    Confirm.

It's O.K. to wear a bandeau maillot to the office.
    Confirm.

You crave a pair of sable boxer shorts to go with your full-length sable coat.
    Confirm. Sable underwear would go great with my sable coat by Karl Lagerfeld for Fendi and would express a kind of sexuality that I would aspire to that does not exist.

PART 6

Writers, Moguls, Visionaries

THE SLOW-BURNING SUCCESS OF DISNEY'S BOB IGER

—SEPTEMBER 22, 2019

ANAHEIM, Calif.—Bob Iger looks down at his phone and frowns.

"Why is the stock market dropping?" he murmurs to himself, sitting in the back of a BMW ferrying him around Disneyland during last month's convention of superfans, where he is showing off the new Disney+ streaming service.

I know I have to give him the bad news.

"You are hereby ordered," I tell him, "to immediately start looking for an alternative to China, including bringing your companies home and making your products in the U.S.A."

He looks puzzled. I am here, after all, to interview him about his new memoir, "The Ride of a Lifetime," in which he proudly writes about the 40 trips he took to Shanghai in 18 years to complete the labyrinthine negotiations to open the $6 billion Shanghai Disneyland, 11 times the size of this park.

We are about to go to the Star Wars attraction in Disneyland and take the wheel of the Millennium Falcon ride, which was made partly in China. And many of the costumes being sold in the gift shops at the park are sewn in China.

"President Trump just tweeted that 'our great American companies are hereby ordered' out of China," I explain, reading from my phone. The Disney chief's face darkens in the Happiest Place on Earth, and I see the thought bubble about what he wants to say about the president sending the stock market tumbling with his volatile trade war with China and ordering C.E.O.s about.

But he refrains. The man who guided the Mouse to gobble up so much of Hollywood is nothing if not smooth, sitting in his navy Tom Ford suit, white Tom Ford shirt, black John Lobb shoes and Rolex Daytona.

As one top Hollywood player told me, the most important thing to know is this: "Nobody expected Bob Iger to be Bob Iger."

It was a long, nasty climb from being a little boy on Long Island watching "The Mickey Mouse Club," having a crush on Annette Funicello, to working in a building with Snow White's dwarves on top, shattering a Hollywood record this year when Disney released five $1 billion movies.

"Look, where else does a lower-middle-class kid with a modest education and not superhuman skills grow up to be me?" Mr. Iger asks, sounding a little surprised himself.

After recognizing the tech threat early and making three acquisitions that revolutionized the media landscape (Pixar, Marvel and Lucasfilm), Mr. Iger rolled the dice at age 68, on the cusp of retirement, and beat out Comcast with a $71.3 billion bid for a chunk of 21st Century Fox. And now he is, as one top producer at Disney dryly calls him, "the God King."

In a town where everyone is always filleting everyone else, Mr. Iger floats above it all, cosseted in what some call a "cult of nice." He may own most of the box office, but he is shielded from schadenfreude because the people who would ordinarily begrudge him are happy that someone was able to assail the unassailable Netflix, and rescue the spirit of Old Hollywood from the takeover of the deep-pocketed tech giants.

"Literally, I have never heard one person say a bad thing about him and I have never seen him be mean," David Geffen marveled. "To be honorable, decent, smart, successful and a terrific guy is unusual anywhere. But it is most unusual in the entertainment business. He's in a category of one."

Barry Diller agrees: "Of all the characters here, he's the one with the most courage and the most certainty. He has put as many cards in his hand as he could gather and he's absolutely determined not to turn the world over to Netflix and Amazon. He is in every sense the real deal. And he's grown into it, which is even more impressive."

Mr. Iger comes across as effortlessly elegant. He is the sort of person who takes the time to talk to hoi polloi's parents at parties and poses graciously for photos with fans at the park. He seems relaxed with the staff when we stop for cocktails with names like the Jedi Mind Trick at the Star Wars bar.

But his book makes clear how much effort went into his effortless demeanor. By eighth grade, he was working as a stock boy in a hardware store. At 15, he toiled as a janitor for his school district. "Cleaning gum from the bottoms of a thousand desks can build character, or at least a tolerance for monotony," he writes.

At Ithaca College, he earned spending money making pizza every night at Pizza Hut. After he graduated, he became a weatherman in Ithaca and delivered a lot of bad news about the gloomy weather there.

He gave up a dream of being Walter Cronkite and moved to New York City and started at the bottom rung at ABC: $150 a week for menial labor on game shows, soap operas and newscasts. His friends say he was long underestimated and treated as a glorified errand boy, even when he worked under Michael Eisner at Disney.

In "The Ride of a Lifetime" Mr. Iger recounts how when he started at ABC, in 1974, the anchor Harry Reasoner sent him on an errand to check with the producers of the evening news to see if Mr. Reasoner needed to make any updates or if he could enjoy a second double extra-dry Beefeater martini on the rocks with a twist at Hotel des Artistes.

"I ventured into the control room and said, 'Harry sent me to find out how it looks,'" Mr. Iger writes. "The producer looked at me with complete disdain. Then he unzipped his pants, pulled out his penis, and replied, 'I don't know. You tell me how it looks.' Forty-five years later, I still get angry when I recall that scene."

Mr. Iger simply kept moving, as he did after so many slights and wounds, including Mr. Eisner's disastrous decision to bring in the super-agent Michael Ovitz as his No. 2. Even once Mr. Ovitz was dispatched with a $140 million golden parachute for failing, it was an uphill battle for Mr. Iger to persuade the board that he should succeed Mr. Eisner.

"Part of it was the association with him, I was just tarred by the same brush," Mr. Iger says. "And part of it was that, at least to the board—talk about having to subjugate my own ego—it was his company and I was like a second-class citizen."

I remind Mr. Iger that I covered the 1997 Disney shareholder meeting where Mr. Ovitz got his obscene severance package, and noted in the column that among other failings, Mr. Eisner's socks were too short.

"Michael did not care about clothes," Mr. Iger says with a smile. "He had good taste in other things, but not clothes or food or wine."

LEGGO THAT EGO

In his book Mr. Iger tells the story of meeting Jeffrey Katzenberg for breakfast near the Disney lot in Burbank, Calif., when he was facing headlines like this one in the Orlando Sentinel: "Eisner's Heir Far From Apparent."

"You need to leave," Mr. Katzenberg told him. "You're not going to get this job. Your reputation has been tarnished." He was, Mr. Katzenberg said, too tied to Eisner messes, including a titanic battle with Roy E. Disney, Walt's nephew. "You should go do some pro bono work to rehabilitate your image."

It turned out, though, that Mr. Iger had a fierce will under that gentlemanly exterior. Early on, he began getting up at 4 a.m. to out-work everyone else and he still does. He sets out his exercise clothes the night before, so he doesn't have to turn on the lights in his closet and thus wake up his wife, Willow Bay, a former Estee Lauder model and broadcaster who is now dean of the USC Annenberg School of Communication and Journalism. He leaves out a coffee mug for Ms. Bay and warms up some milk for her coffee before he tackles the VersaClimber.

"I never viewed myself as exceptional," Mr. Iger says over salmon and a glass of red wine at the Napa Rose restaurant in Disneyland. "And so whenever I got a job, I was relying on hard work more than anything and a level of enthusiasm and optimism. When I went to ABC Sports, everybody there went to Stanford or Dartmouth or Columbia.

"Ithaca College, O.K.? I didn't have an inferiority complex but I knew I wasn't one of them. I didn't wear Gucci shoes. I didn't wear Brooks Brothers clothes. I couldn't afford any of that stuff, but I knew I had a work ethic that was prodigious. And what happened early on is people started relying on me because they knew if they asked me to get something done, including Roone Arledge"—the ABC executive—"I would get it done.

"So suddenly I realized, well, wait a minute. I may not be special in certain ways. But when it came to getting things done, I was special. And that's actually driven me throughout, you know?"

In the book, Mr. Iger writes that his sang-froid when things go wrong may have developed as "a defense mechanism" to the chaos in his house growing up.

His father was a Navy veteran and graduate of Wharton, a trumpet player who worked with some "lesser" big bands before he got into advertising. But he had dark moods, and Mr. Iger later learned his father had been diagnosed with manic depression and had gone through electroshock therapy.

It was a time when mental health issues had more of a stigma and when a neighbor's child told young Bob that his father was going to a shrink, "I had no idea what that was," Mr. Iger recalls.

"We never knew which Dad was coming home at night," Mr. Iger writes, "and I can distinctly recall sitting in my room on the second floor of our house, knowing by the sound of the way he opened and shut the door and walked up the steps whether it was happy or sad Dad."

Money was tight and torn pants were patched, not immediately replaced. His role, as the oldest son, was to be "a calming influence in the house." His mother and younger sister counted on him for consistency and an even temperament, he says.

His father instilled a love of books and The New York Times and a mania for using his time constructively. Mr. Iger is always early for meetings. On a scale of one to 10 of obsessiveness, he says, laughing, "I'm a 15."

Mr. Iger says that he cried when he gathered up his late father's belongings and realized that they could fit in a little Tupperware box and inside there were mementos of his son's illustrious career, including a gold lighter that Frank Sinatra gave the young Iger in 1974 after ABC televised his live concert at Madison Square Garden.

Mr. Iger is self-conscious about his memoir, confiding that "it feels to me a bit like a big ego trip." When he started it, he thought his reign at Disney might be over by the time it came out. But then Rupert Murdoch called, and all that went out the window.

Actually, Mr. Iger's book is a primer on how much you can achieve if you keep your ego in check. In an era of brutish and ego-driven leadership in the White House, Silicon Valley and in many other countries around the world, Mr. Iger doesn't lead with his ego or try to drive the other alphas out of the herd.

"You have to have an ability to subjugate your own ego," he says. "It serves you well when you're rising and then even when you have risen, there are going to be times when you just have to put that away."

He tells the stories of his four megadeals: how he charmed Steve Jobs, after Mr. Jobs had an acrimonious split from Disney in the Eisner era, and bought Pixar to save Disney animation; how he (sometimes with Ms. Bay) wooed a wary, reclusive Ike Perlmutter to get Marvel and how he persuaded George Lucas to sell him the Star Wars universe at a lower price than he paid for Pixar.

"Rupert was crazed that we bought Lucas," Mr. Iger says, with shy pride. "They were the distributor of all of George's movies, and he was very disappointed in his people. 'Why didn't you think of this?'"

All these deals were propelled by Mr. Iger's personal touch. (The tech journalist Kara Swisher christened him the Cashmere Prince.) He often showed up to court these men by himself and tried to be sensitive about what it would mean to have the companies they'd built from nothing swallowed by the Mouse.

He says that when Mr. Murdoch called to ask him for a drink at his Bel Air estate overlooking his winery, Moraga Vineyards, he figured that the Fox mogul just wanted to find out if he was running for president, maybe to pass the information to Mr. Trump.

"He barely has poured his glass of sauvignon blanc and he asks me the question," Mr. Iger recalls. "At that point, I was thinking about it. I didn't really want to tell him. So I was dismissive. I said, 'You know, a lot of people have said I should look at it. My wife hates the idea. Next.'"

Aside from Ms. Bay's reluctance, Mr. Iger doubted that the Democrats would support a successful businessperson. "I think the Democratic Party would brand me as just another rich guy who's out of touch with America," he tells me, "who doesn't have any sense for what's good for the plight of the people."

THE NASTIEST PLACE ON EARTH

I ask how the Murdoch sons, Lachlan and James, affected the Fox deal. Was it like an episode of "Succession"? As Jim Rutenberg and Jonathan Mahler reported in The New York Times Magazine, Lachlan was furious about it, seeing his future shrinking, and James pushed for it, possibly believing he could snag a top job at Disney.

Mr. Iger says he doesn't want to "get into the Shakespearean drama" of it all, but adds carefully: "If you're asking me whether the relationship with the sons and the relationship the sons have with one another and their potential future in the company was ever on the table in negotiation, the answer is yes. But never to a point where it got in the way of us doing what we wanted to do and Rupert doing what he wanted to do."

He says that he got on well with James, even if he was not a fit for Disney, and that James was helpful during the transition.

When Mr. Iger did his slap-down of Fox assets for Wall Street, noting that Fox was in worse shape than he had thought, was he implying that Mr. Murdoch had taken advantage of him?

"It wasn't a slap-down," Mr. Iger says. "It was an admission that the movies that they had made failed. And I actually gave them a tremendous amount of cover by saying that when companies are bought, processes and decision making can come to a halt.

"There were problems at that studio well before the deal was announced. But the reason I did not believe that it was something we should be concerned about is because it's a short-term problem. And with the talent that we have at our studio, that are now supervising with some of their executives all the movies that they decide to make and how they are made, I'm convinced that the turnaround can happen. It's not a snap your fingers, but it's not 10 years of lost value. It's a year and a half."

He says his tough assessment was not designed to lay the groundwork to write off the purchase price of Fox.

"It's way too early, really, to have to do that," he says. "We don't know anything that would cause us to do that."

His candid critique did not hurt his relationship with the Murdoch patriarch; he says he still goes to the Bel Air winery, and has "a nice relationship" with Mr. Murdoch.

The deal has already profoundly affected the way Hollywood works, with filmmakers shaping their pitches to suit the new reality.

A column in Variety suggested that "the unprecedented colossus" is giving people the shakes because Disney doesn't just own all the properties, it owns all the mythologies.

"Look, no one will ever have a monopoly on mythology or storytelling—not us, not anybody," Mr. Iger says.

The angst was summed up when James Brooks, a creator of "The Simpsons," a Fox show, posted on Twitter an image of Homer Simpson strangling Mickey Mouse.

"I love it when we make fun of ourselves," Mr. Iger says. "A little self-inflicted irreverence goes a long way."

Some have wondered if Disney has already strip-mined the foundation of its new empire, stretching its famous franchises too thin.

He agrees that with "Star Wars," "I just think that we might've put a little bit too much in the marketplace too fast." But, he adds, "I think the storytelling capabilities of the company are endless because of the talent we have at the company, and the talent we have at the company is better than it's ever been, in part because of the influx of people from Fox."

How can he match the billions that tech companies are pouring into content?

"What Netflix is doing is making content to support a platform," Mr. Iger says. "We're making content to tell great stories. It's very different."

Mr. Iger believes that, if Mr. Jobs had lived, Disney and Apple might have merged.

But it worked out quite differently. After Mr. Iger proudly revealed his $6.99-a-month price point for Disney+, telling me that it would be hard for anyone to compete, Apple announced a streaming service for $4.99 a month, underpricing Mr. Iger, who was on the Apple board. Mr. Iger resigned from the board the day of the announcement, acknowledging the conflict of interest.

He thinks that Mr. Jobs also could have helped steer Silicon Valley in a better direction. "Steve had quite a conscience," Mr. Iger says. "It didn't always manifest itself in his interpersonal relationships, but he had quite a conscience. Silicon Valley needs leaders." The two men became so close that Mr. Jobs pulled Mr. Iger aside right before the announcement of the $7 billion Disney-Pixar deal to confide that his pancreatic cancer had come back and was now in his liver. Only his wife, Laurene, knew. Mr. Iger had to think fast; he rejected Mr. Jobs's offer to back out of the deal.

And what about the moment when the Happiest Place on Earth thought about annexing the Nastiest Place on Earth? Mr. Iger writes in the book about how he pulled the plug at the last minute on a deal to buy Twitter, thinking it could help Disney modernize its distribution. But he had a feel in his gut it wasn't right, and called a stunned Jack Dorsey to tell him.

"The troubles were greater than I wanted to take on, greater than I thought it was responsible for us to take on," he tells me. "There were Disney brand issues, the whole impact of technology on society. The nastiness is extraordinary. I like looking at my Twitter newsfeed because I want to follow 15, 20 different subjects. Then you turn and look at your notifications and you're immediately saying, why am I doing this? Why do I endure this pain? Like a lot of these platforms, they have the ability to do a lot of good in our world. They also have an ability to do a lot of bad. I didn't want to take that on."

I note that even though Disney has broken gender and race ground with movies like "Captain Marvel" and "Black Panther," the top executives at the four quadrants of the company (TV, film, parks and consumer products, and streaming and international) are all white men.

"You have to look one level down, because we've done a lot," Mr. Iger says. He concedes that it's a disappointment that those who directly report to him "are lacking" in diversity and vows, "I'll change that before I leave."

I wonder if there will ever be a female director for "Star Wars." He says that Kathleen Kennedy, head of Lucasfilm, is "trying really hard" to make that happen.

Watching Mr. Jobs, who was famously mercurial with employees, and getting older has taught him to be careful how hard he comes down on people who work for him. "I get angry," he says. "I've also tried as I've matured to learn a lot about what matters in the world, you know? Unfortunately, as you age, you lose people, and you think, why did I ever get mad at them for something so small?

"You know, I'm very organized and neat. If I got into the kitchen and Willow's been in, and she leaves a cabinet open, there was a time when I would actually get mad at that. You've got to be kidding. Why would I get mad at something like that? It's pausing for a moment and thinking, does this really matter?"

His equanimity was surely roiled by the crusade of Abigail Disney, granddaughter of Roy O. Disney, Walt's brother. She has been a frequent critic, calling out the Disney culture and his compensation in interviews and Twitter threads, using her exalted last name, though she is not connected to the company.

"I like Bob Iger," she wrote on Twitter, and he has led the company "brilliantly." But she contended that his salary, $65.6 million, was "insane," and that Disney workers should get a higher wage.

"We're trying really hard to find solutions to the challenges and the problems that our employees are facing today," he says. "We're going to come up with dozens of more solutions that we're going to try to help improve their lives, and if they don't work, we're going to find dozens more. We have to be better."

As obsessive as Mr. Iger is about work, he schedules in some fun. He has a sailboat and he has his T.G.I.F. movies.

"I try every Friday afternoon to leave work at lunchtime and go to my home and screen a movie," he says. The ceiling of his screening room is a programmable planetarium based on the one at Pixar. Its default setting is modeled on a photograph from NASA of the night sky in New York on the day Mr. Iger was born, a special touch from its designers.

One recent night, when he found himself on his own, he rewatched "Four Weddings and a Funeral." Funnily enough, that is the movie Barbara Walters advised him to watch back when he was single, so that he would be sure to always follow his heart.

He says he has made "zero plans" for what happens in 2021, his new retirement date.

Asked about whether he'd run for president in 2024, when he will be 73, he says, "I don't know that I have it in me."

He has one outstanding offer that intrigues him, though.

"I have relationships with weathermen throughout the company," he says, laughing. "So the promise they've all made me is they're going to give me a weekend at some point in my last year."

Sometimes he'll get in the car with his family and show off his meteorological chops. "I can do the whole weather report for Los Angeles County, Orange County, the Inland Empire, the beaches and the mountains, I can do the whole thing. You know, it's sunny and 63 degrees. Seasonal temperatures here in Los Angeles expected through the rest of the weekend. Winds are mild today out of the northeast at five to 10 miles an hour. The barometer is steady at 29, 28, and we're looking at a great—and I mean a great—Memorial Day weekend. All you out there who are going camping or barbecuing or going to the beach, I promise you this is going to be a weekend you're really going to enjoy."

[Don't leave your seats just yet! Just like at the movies, the outtakes at the end can be the best part.]

Confirm or Deny

MAUREEN DOWD: *You have thoughts on Sean Spicer being on ABC's "Dancing With the Stars."*

BOB IGER: No. Let's move on.

Steve Jobs used to call you on Saturday mornings when he thought a Disney film was a dud.
　　Oh, that's true.

You avoid carbs, except pizza, which you try to get anywhere in the world.
　　Correct.

You love David Portnoy's pizza reviews.
　　Yes.

Jack Dorsey tried to convince you to get into intermittent fasting during the Disney board meeting.
　　False.

You miss being Bill Simmons's boss.
　　False.

Licensing content to Netflix was a mistake.
　　False.

Your biggest position in your personal stock portfolio is a Netflix short.
　　Very false.

When you met in Rupert Murdoch's vineyard, you were drinking a great Yellow Tail vintage.
　　I was drinking a decent sauvignon blanc.

Allen & Company Sun Valley vests are not as cool as they used to be.
　　I never wear Allen & Company Sun Valley vests because I don't wear vests.

You realized you never want to retire when you saw a picture of Lloyd Blankfein wearing dad jeans.
　　I don't wear dad jeans.

Your first read in the morning is David Geffen's Instagram.
　　No. Well, I follow him. I will say, in my reading session before I go to work, Instagram is part of it.

You never read "DisneyWar."
　　Correct.

Euro Disney really took off once you realized that French parents wanted fine wine at the restaurants to get them through the day.
I know it was an issue.

You witnessed the moment Queen Bey met Duchess Meghan.
True.

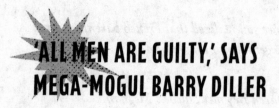

'ALL MEN ARE GUILTY,' SAYS MEGA-MOGUL BARRY DILLER

—MARCH 24, 2018

BEVERLY HILLS, Calif.—Barry Diller knows your weaknesses.

He knows how to intimidate you, if he wants to, or charm you, if he chooses. Because he is a taskmaster and a visionary and a billionaire, people in Hollywood and Silicon Valley pay close attention when he speaks.

He has so many vests from Herb Allen's Sun Valley retreats for global elites that they're taking over his closets.

"There is so much fleece," says the chairman of IAC, laughing. "I've been going for 30 years."

On this rainy afternoon, by the fireplace in the Frank Lloyd Wright–inspired stone and wood living room of his dreamy mansion, Mr. Diller is all charm, with a healthy dose of self-deprecation. He's dressed in a red checked flannel shirt, a burgundy Hermès hoodie, baggy jeans and black Tod's loafers.

We are eating cold salads and drinking hot tea, served by the butler, Victor. And we are hopscotching topics, from Silicon Valley taking over Hollywood to Jared & Ivanka & Josh & Karlie to pornography to his company's dating websites to the time Harvey Weinstein tried to throw Mr. Diller off a balcony in Cannes to how his friend Hillary Clinton is faring to the mogul's dismissal of Donald Trump (whose Secret Service code name is Mogul) as "a joke" and "evil."

I tell him that a friend of mine, an executive in network television, fretfully asked her Hollywood psychic how long Mr. Trump would last as president and the psychic asserted that it wouldn't be more than two years and that the president would be felled by a three-page email. (The only problem with this prediction being, I don't think Mr. Trump emails.)

"I would so love it if he were being blackmailed by Putin," Mr. Diller says with a sly smile. "That would make me very happy. This was a man of bad character from the moment he entered adulthood, if not before. Pure, bad character. Ugh, Trump."

He shrugs off what he calls Trump's "normal, vicious Twitter attacks" on him. After Mr. Diller mocked Trump's campaign in 2015, Trump tweeted: "Little Barry Diller, who lost a fortune on Newsweek and Daily Beast, only writes badly about me. He is a sad and pathetic figure. Lives lie!"

Mr. Diller waves off talk of Mr. Trump opening the door to more celebrity presidents, saying, "I want this to be a moment in time where you go in and pick out this period with pincers and go on with life as we knew it before."

Has the media gone overboard in criticizing Mr. Trump?

"Are you kidding?" he replies.

Mr. Diller says that he and his wife, Diane von Furstenberg, are friends with Josh Kushner and his supermodel girlfriend, Karlie Kloss, but do not hang out with Jared and Ivanka.

He has put Chelsea Clinton on the boards of two of his companies, but that is not likely to happen with this first daughter.

"I mean, we were friendly," he says of Ivanka, in the time before Mr. Trump became president. "I would sit next to her every once in a while at a dinner. And I, as everyone did, was like, 'Oh, my God, how could this evil character have spawned such a polite, gracious person?' I don't think we feel that way now."

At 76, having seen around the corner to tech and pulled together the ragtag group of internet ventures at IAC into a thriving whole, Mr. Diller has "mellowed beautifully," as one producer here who has known him for many years puts it.

His dogs are jumping up on our chairs. He has three Jack Russell terriers cloned from his late, beloved dog Shannon, a Gaelic orphan he found wandering many years ago on a back road in Ireland.

For about $100,000, a South Korean firm "reincarnated" Shannon in three pups: Tess, short for "test tube," and DiNA, a play on DNA, who live in Beverly Hills; and Evita, who lives in Cloudwalk, the Connecticut home of Mr. Diller and Ms. von Furstenberg.

"These dogs, they're the soul of Shannon," he says. "Diane was horrified that I was doing this but she's switched now to say, 'Thank God you did.'"

Mr. Diller has started a trend in Hollywood, inspiring his friend Barbra Streisand, desolate over the loss of her Coton de Tulear, Samantha, to clone her.

Doesn't he want to clone himself into a "Killer Diller," as his protégés, including Jeffrey Katzenberg, Michael Eisner and Uber's Dara Khosrowshahi, are known?

"God forbid," he says with a grimace.

FROM MAILROOM TO #METOO MAELSTROM

I ask Mr. Diller what he thought of Sacha Baron Cohen's joke at David Geffen's recent birthday party at Jimmy Iovine's house in Los Angeles that Mr. Geffen, Mr. Diller and the other starry billionaires and millionaires there represented "the world's third-largest economy."

"It is a funny joke," he says. "It's close to true."

Is it a cool club to be in, I wonder, or a backstabbing one?

"For me, it's stimulating," he says. "Diane hates it. So I am both in it, because I like it, and *ripped* out of it, because Diane says, 'Too much money, too many rich people, let's go.' I've got a good personal boomerang process."

He says he met Mr. Geffen, whom he considers "family," when the two were teenagers in the William Morris mailroom in Los Angeles.

"It's Christmastime and this scrawny person comes into the mailroom and he said, 'I'm in the mailroom at William Morris in New York. I had a week off for the holiday so I wanted to come and work here.' And I thought 'Oh, my God, on your vacation?' Because for me, vacation was Hawaii."

We talk about how Hollywood has changed, and I ask how the #MeToo era will affect the content of movies.

"'Red Sparrow' has some of the most violent and extreme sexual messiness that you could imagine," he says. "O.K., it was made a year and a half ago. Would it be made today in the same way? Probably so. So I don't think it affects content.

"I mean, if you take the effect of pornography on young people today. Pornography until recently was fairly staid. Today, online, pornography is so extreme and so varied, with such expressions of fetishism and other things that boys are seeing. The idea of normal sex and normal romance has to be adversely affected by that."

Once, Hollywood taught us about desire and sex and romance, giving us a vocabulary for these experiences. But no more. I wonder what will happen as girls emboldened by the fall of male predators collide with boys indoctrinated by pornography.

"I see it in our companies, where the relationships between people are changing," Mr. Diller says. "We recently had a formal complaint made by a woman who said that she was at a convention with her colleagues and she was asked to have a drink with her boss. Period. That was the complaint. And we said, 'Here's the thing. Anybody can ask you anything, other than let's presume something illegal, and you have the right to say "Yes" or "No." If it's "Yes," go in good health and if it's "No," then it's full stop.'

"But the end result of that is a guy, let's presume he is heterosexual, and his boss, heterosexual, and guy asks guy for a drink and they go have a drink and they talk about career opportunities. And the boss says, 'Oh, this is a smart guy. I'm promoting him.' A woman now cannot be in that position. So all these things are a-changin'.

"God knows, I'm hardly a sociologist. But I hope in the future for some form of reconciliation. Because I think all men are guilty. I'm not talking about rape and pillage. I'm not talking about Harveyesque. I'm talking about all of the spectrum. From an aggressive flirt. Or even just a flirty-flirt that has one sour note in it. Or what I think every man was guilty of, some form of omission in attitude, in his views. Are we really going to have only capital punishment? Because right now, that's what we have. You get accused, you're obliterated. Charlie Rose ceases to exist."

TWILIGHT OF THE GODS

Mr. Diller is the chairman of the board of Expedia, and his IAC owns a gaggle of internet properties, including Vimeo, Dictionary.com, Investopedia, Tinder, Match and OkCupid. I wonder how he thinks online dating is reshaping the culture.

"It's just like the princess phone evolved to the internet," he says. "Match.com has caused God knows how many more marriages than bars ever did. And now I'm starting to hear that out of Tinder. It's funny, though, on Bumble, the women get to choose first and they don't want to. I liked the sheer adventure of romance before online dating, which is less appealing to me."

I ask Mr. Diller, a Los Angeles native, about a comment made to me by the playwright and TV writer Jon Robin Baitz, another Los Angeles native, that Hollywood is no longer relevant politically and culturally.

"Does Hollywood reflect in any possible sense what is happening in the world?" Mr. Baitz asked. "Hollywood abdicated films and became an empty exercise in male capes and superheroes. Can you imagine anyone now making 'Norma Rae,' 'Silkwood,' 'Five Easy Pieces,' 'Reds'?"

Since Mr. Diller was running Paramount in 1981 when Warren Beatty and Diane Keaton made Mr. Beatty's epic "Reds," he should know.

"What an undertaking," Mr. Diller says. "But isn't it amazing how it holds?"

Calling "Red Sparrow" "awful" and "The Shape of Water" "beautiful but silly," he says he wouldn't want to run a movie studio now. "It would be like saying, do I want to own a horse-and-buggy company? The idea of a movie is losing its meaning."

Of the Academy Awards nominees this year, he said, "essentially, no one went to see them."

Growing up in Beverly Hills with a father in the construction business—he says there are still streets out here named "Dillerdale" and "Barrydale"—Mr. Diller was able to see the twilight of the men who invented Hollywood.

"They were real characters—overblown, exuberant, nasty, but each of them in their own way were genuinely interesting people," he says. "The only thing that I've learned, that I think I've had some instinct for, is *instinct*. And these people operated completely out of instinct. As against today, when people operate out of research and marketing."

He says that Netflix and Amazon have blasted Hollywood into "a completely different universe."

"It's something that's never happened in media before, when Netflix got a lot of subscribers early on and made the brilliant decision to pour it into original production, like spending more than $100 million dollars to make 'House of Cards,' instead of buying old stuff," he says. "It blows my mind. It's like a giant vacuum cleaner came and pushed all the other vacuum cleaners aside. And they cannot be outbid. No one can compete with them."

He calls Reed Hastings, the C.E.O. of Netflix, the most remarkable person in the media business: "He has so much original thinking in so many different areas, he's really impressive."

I ask how the tech community's noxious bro culture will affect the business here, given that Hollywood already has such entrenched sexism.

"They're tech people," he says with a shrug. "They don't have a lot of romance in them. They don't have a lot of nuance in them. Their lives are ones and zeros." But they can grow, he says. "When I met Bill Gates, I would say he had the emotional quotient of a snail. And now you can see him cry."

He corrects me when I call the tech titans our overlords. "Our overlords are not them," he says. "Our overlords are artificial intelligence."

At several points during our three-hour interview, Mr. Diller stops to ask me if this is any fun. When I assure him it's fascinating, he looks skeptical.

"Yeah, right," he says. "Don't seduce me. I'm a very seducible person." He also says he's a "jinxable" person.

Ms. von Furstenberg says that when she met Mr. Diller 43 years ago,

"What I found so incredibly appealing is that behind the very forceful, determined and engaged human being, there was shyness and reservation. He's not a pig. I mean, in no way."

He impressed her immediately on a trip to Vegas by driving his banana-yellow Jaguar E-Type sports car barefoot and talking a policeman out of giving him a speeding ticket.

On another occasion, driving back into Manhattan fast from her Connecticut house—Mr. Diller likes to drive fast—they saw an octogenarian couple crossing the street slowly, holding on to each other.

"Both of us at the same time thought exactly the same thing: 'One day, we will be that couple,'" she recalls. "The only thing we disagree on is, he thinks it was Madison Avenue and I say it was Lexington."

The other quality his friends talk about is his voracious curiosity.

"When he knows about something, he knows more about it than anyone else, and when he doesn't know something, he wants to know more about it than anybody else," says Scott Rudin, who has produced movies, plays and television with Mr. Diller (including "Lady Bird" for the screen and "Betrayal," "The Humans," "A Doll's House, Part 2," "Three Tall Women" and "Carousel" for Broadway). Mr. Rudin is also helping his friend develop the so-called Diller Island, an undulating pier floating on piles in the Hudson River adjacent to the meatpacking district.

Given that Mr. Diller helped create the Fox Broadcasting Company with Rupert Murdoch—and blessedly greenlighted "The Simpsons"—I wonder if he feels like Dr. Frankenstein.

"I left Fox before Fox News came into being," he says. About the sale of Fox to Disney, he notes that his former boss "played a bad hand very well."

I observe that he called Harvey Weinstein out publicly as a bully early on.

Mr. Diller recalls that once in Cannes, when he was the chief executive of Universal, Stacey Snider, the head of the movie division, told him that "Harvey had treated her terribly and made her cry. So the next day I saw Harvey on the terrace at Hotel du Cap and I said, 'Harvey, don't ever treat an executive at my company that way. Don't you ever talk to anyone in that manner.'

"And Harvey, about six feet away, said, 'I'm going to throw you off the terrace.' And this gorilla, because he looks like a gorilla, starts walking towards me, right? And truly, I was scared. I thought, how, without cutting and running like a chicken, do I stop him? And somehow a bear came into my mind." He says he pulled himself up into a menacing stance, as you're supposed to do if you have to confront a bear.

"And it so surprised him that he stopped and I got out with a small amount of honor," he says.

(Ms. Snider told Kim Masters in a 2007 Esquire article that Mr. Diller was such a tough boss that she teared up with him, after she made a blunder at a meeting. Mr. Diller apologized to her afterward.)

He adds: "Other than psychopaths, I think all of this bad behavior is finished."

Speaking of bad behavior, I ask if he knew Mr. Trump back in the day in Manhattan.

He said that when he was in his mid-30s, running Paramount, Mr. Trump invited him to lunch.

"And you know when people compliment you without foundation?" Mr. Diller says. "And they do it too much? It's really irritating. It's kind of offensive. And he spent the entire time saying how great I was. He didn't know me. And afterward, I walked around the corner and I thought, 'I never want to see that man again.' Decades passed and we would run into each other, but I literally never spoke to him again."

He says he has gone to a couple of Broadway shows recently with Hillary Clinton and that "she's well with herself again and she has a role to play."

After the interview, when the Cambridge Analytica scandal breaks, I call him to see what he makes of Facebook's role.

"Since the beginning of media and advertising, the holy grail has been the precise targeting of the ads," he says. "Along comes the internet with almost perfect aim, and now the entire concept is being called antisocial. That's a most ironic but momentous thing."

Mr. Diller's friends say he is quiet about his philanthropy. He flinches when I use the term "Diller Island," saying it should be called "Pier 55."

Now he is working on an idea concocted by Alex von Furstenberg,

Diane's son whom Mr. Diller also calls his son, to build a gondola up to the Hollywood sign and a circular catwalk around it, so that people can tour and hike around it.

He is very proud of the success of the High Line, the elevated park he helped fund on the West Side of Manhattan. "Who would have dreamed so many people would come?" he marvels.

Andrew M. Cuomo, the governor of New York, pulled the Hudson Island project, a $250 million family park and cultural center, out of the ashes, moving past attempts by Douglas Durst to block it. (Hasn't that family done enough damage?)

"The delay cost us $25 million or something like that," Mr. Diller says. "But here's the thing. My family's lucky. So who's counting? Can I actually say, 'Who's counting?' That's awful. But it's true. There's a lot about the absurdity of wealth. I have so many friends who continue to make absurd amounts of money and count it. I think if you're really lucky, who's counting?"

Confirm or Deny

MAUREEN DOWD: *You wish I.A.C. owned Goop.*
BARRY DILLER: Deny.

Newsweek should just fold already.
Confirm.

Your secret for success is that you don't possess the need to be liked.
Deny. It's certainly not true that I don't care what anyone else thinks.

"Flashdance" was the greatest thing you produced.
More than deny.

Derek Blasberg is your favorite Instagram account.
I don't have an Instagram account. When I want to see if something is trending, I will go on Twitter. But I don't go to it daily.

John Malone once tried to run you over in his RV to get control of Expedia.
Deny. John Malone is my friend.

John Malone is a better investor than Warren Buffett.
  Deny, deny.

You are happiest when you are in something that has an engine.
  Extra confirm.

You prefer to drive yourself everywhere you go.
  Confirm! I do.

You look at a parking ticket as the price of a good parking spot.
  Yes.

You're afraid of snakes.
  Beyond wildly confirm.

You binge-watch QVC.
  Deny.

You don't want anyone to talk to you about how great "Hamilton" is ever again.
  Oh, confirm.

Your favorite new artist is Cardi B.
  Unlikely. Deny.

The next generation of children will only communicate via emoji.
  Deny.

Bill de Blasio is a great mayor.
  He's a good mayor.

Cynthia Nixon would be a great governor.
  Deny. And yes, it's because Cuomo is helping me with the island.

You would prefer Oprah in 2020 over any of the other Democrats right now.
  Deny.

If only Jared hadn't lost his security clearance, he would have solved Middle East peace.
  Confirm. (Laughs.)

There's only one thing you order off the Carlyle Hotel's lunch menu: the chopped seafood salad.
I order egg salad from the Carlyle.

Facebook is a media company.
Deny.

You miss Gawker.
Deny.

Hearst is in better shape than Condé Nast.
Confirm.

You would rather run Facebook than Disney.
Deny.

You can parallel-park your yacht, Eos, no problem.
Deny.

You've visited three-quarters of the countries in the world.
Oh, yes. The great thing about boats, if you love boats and I love boats and so does Diane, for adventuring rather than sitting in the Mediterranean or the Caribbean, is that our boat's been everywhere. We've been every place you've never heard of. My favorite was Vanuatu. And I went night diving, which is glorious, in Raja Ampat in Indonesia.

You once made $465 million in a day.
I doubt that's true, but I don't know.

You and Donald Trump have the same favorite film, "Citizen Kane."
Now I don't like "Citizen Kane."

ELON MUSK'S FUTURE SHOCK

RUNNING AMOK

It was just a friendly little argument about the fate of humanity. Demis Hassabis, a leading creator of advanced artificial intelligence, was chatting with Elon Musk, a leading doomsayer, about the perils of artificial intelligence.

They are two of the most consequential and intriguing men in Silicon Valley who don't live there. Hassabis, a co-founder of the mysterious London laboratory DeepMind, had come to Musk's SpaceX rocket factory, outside Los Angeles, a few years ago. They were in the canteen, talking, as a massive rocket part traversed overhead. Musk explained that his ultimate goal at SpaceX was the most important project in the world: interplanetary colonization.

Hassabis replied that, in fact, *he* was working on the most important project in the world: developing artificial super-intelligence. Musk countered that this was one reason we needed to colonize Mars—so that we'll have a bolt-hole if A.I. goes rogue and turns on humanity. Amused, Hassabis said that A.I. would simply follow humans to Mars.

This did nothing to soothe Musk's anxieties (even though he says there are scenarios where A.I. wouldn't follow).

An unassuming but competitive 40-year-old, Hassabis is regarded as the Merlin who will likely help conjure our A.I. children. The field of

A.I. is rapidly developing but still far from the powerful, self-evolving software that haunts Musk. Lacebook uses A.I. for targeted advertising, photo tagging, and curated news feeds. Microsoft and Apple use A.I. to power their digital assistants, Cortana and Siri. Google's search engine from the beginning has been dependent on A.I. All of these small advances are part of the chase to eventually create flexible, self-teaching A.I. that will mirror human learning.

Some in Silicon Valley were intrigued to learn that Hassabis, a skilled chess player and former video-game designer, once came up with a game called *Evil Genius*, featuring a malevolent scientist who creates a doomsday device to achieve world domination. Peter Thiel, the billionaire venture capitalist and Donald Trump adviser who co-founded PayPal with Musk and others—and who in December helped gather skeptical Silicon Valley titans, including Musk, for a meeting with the president-elect—told me a story about an investor in DeepMind who joked as he left a meeting that he ought to shoot Hassabis on the spot, because it was the last chance to save the human race.

Elon Musk began warning about the possibility of A.I. running amok three years ago. It probably hadn't eased his mind when one of Hassabis's partners in DeepMind, Shane Legg, stated flatly, "I think human extinction will probably occur, and technology will likely play a part in this."

Before DeepMind was gobbled up by Google, in 2014, as part of its A.I. shopping spree, Musk had been an investor in the company. He told me that his involvement was not about a return on his money but rather to keep a wary eye on the arc of A.I.: "It gave me more visibility into the rate at which things were improving, and I think they're really improving at an accelerating rate, far faster than people realize. Mostly because in everyday life you don't see robots walking around. Maybe your Roomba or something. But Roombas aren't going to take over the world."

In a startling public reproach to his friends and fellow techies, Musk warned that they could be creating the means of their own destruction. He told Bloomberg's Ashlee Vance, the author of the biography *Elon Musk*, that he was afraid that his friend Larry Page, a co-founder of

Google and now the C.E.O. of its parent company, Alphabet, could have perfectly good intentions but still "produce something evil by accident"—including, possibly, "a fleet of artificial intelligence–enhanced robots capable of destroying mankind."

At the World Government Summit in Dubai, in February, Musk again cued the scary organ music, evoking the plots of classic horror stories when he noted that "sometimes what will happen is a scientist will get so engrossed in their work that they don't really realize the ramifications of what they're doing." He said that the way to escape human obsolescence, in the end, may be by "having some sort of merger of biological intelligence and machine intelligence." This Vulcan mind-meld could involve something called a neural lace—an injectable mesh that would literally hardwire your brain to communicate directly with computers. "We're already cyborgs," Musk told me in February. "Your phone and your computer are extensions of you, but the interface is through finger movements or speech, which are very slow." With a neural lace inside your skull you would flash data from your brain, wirelessly, to your digital devices or to virtually unlimited computing power in the cloud. "For a meaningful partial-brain interface, I think we're roughly four or five years away."

Musk's alarming views on the dangers of A.I. first went viral after he spoke at M.I.T. in 2014—speculating (pre-Trump) that A.I. was probably humanity's "biggest existential threat." He added that he was increasingly inclined to think there should be some national or international regulatory oversight—anathema to Silicon Valley—"to make sure that we don't do something very foolish." He went on: "With artificial intelligence, we are summoning the demon. You know all those stories where there's the guy with the pentagram and the holy water and he's like, yeah, he's sure he can control the demon? Doesn't work out." Some A.I. engineers found Musk's theatricality so absurdly amusing that they began echoing it. When they would return to the lab after a break, they'd say, "O.K., let's get back to work summoning."

Musk wasn't laughing. "Elon's crusade" (as one of his friends and fellow tech big shots calls it) against unfettered A.I. had begun.

"I AM THE ALPHA"

Elon Musk smiled when I mentioned to him that he comes across as something of an Ayn Rand–ian hero. "I have heard that before," he said in his slight South African accent. "She obviously has a fairly extreme set of views, but she has some good points in there."

But Ayn Rand would do some re-writes on Elon Musk. She would make his eyes gray and his face more gaunt. She would refashion his public demeanor to be less droll, and she would not countenance his goofy giggle. She would certainly get rid of all his nonsense about the "collective" good. She would find great material in the 45-year-old's complicated personal life: his first wife, the fantasy writer Justine Musk, and their five sons (one set of twins, one of triplets), and his much younger second wife, the British actress Talulah Riley, who played the boring Bennet sister in the Keira Knightley version of *Pride & Prejudice*. Riley and Musk were married, divorced, and then re-married. They are now divorced again. Last fall, Musk tweeted that Talulah "does a great job playing a deadly sexbot" on HBO's *Westworld*, adding a smiley-face emoticon. It's hard for mere mortal women to maintain a relationship with someone as insanely obsessed with work as Musk.

"How much time does a woman want a week?" he asked Ashlee Vance. "Maybe ten hours? That's kind of the minimum?"

Mostly, Rand would savor Musk, a hyper-logical, risk-loving industrialist. He enjoys costume parties, wing-walking, and Japanese steampunk extravaganzas. Robert Downey Jr. used Musk as a model for Iron Man. Marc Mathieu, the chief marketing officer of Samsung USA, who has gone fly-fishing in Iceland with Musk, calls him "a cross between Steve Jobs and Jules Verne." As they danced at their wedding reception, Justine later recalled, Musk informed her, "I am the alpha in this relationship."

In a tech universe full of skinny guys in hoodies—whipping up bots that will chat with you and apps that can study a photo of a dog and tell you what breed it is—Musk is a throwback to Henry Ford and Hank Rearden. In *Atlas Shrugged*, Rearden gives his wife a bracelet made from the first batch of his revolutionary metal, as though it were made of diamonds. Musk has a chunk of one of his rockets mounted on the wall of his Bel Air house, like a work of art.

Musk shoots for the moon—literally. He launches cost-efficient rockets into space and hopes to eventually inhabit the Red Planet. In February he announced plans to send two space tourists on a flight around the moon as early as next year. He creates sleek batteries that could lead to a world powered by cheap solar energy. He forges gleaming steel into sensuous Tesla electric cars with such elegant lines that even the nitpicking Steve Jobs would have been hard-pressed to find fault. He wants to save time as well as humanity: he dreamed up the Hyperloop, an electromagnetic bullet train in a tube, which may one day whoosh travelers between L.A. and San Francisco at 700 miles per hour. When Musk visited secretary of defense Ashton Carter last summer, he mischievously tweeted that he was at the Pentagon to talk about designing a Tony Stark–style "flying metal suit." Sitting in traffic in L.A. in December, getting bored and frustrated, he tweeted about creating the Boring Company to dig tunnels under the city to rescue the populace from "soul-destroying traffic." By January, according to *Bloomberg Businessweek*, Musk had assigned a senior SpaceX engineer to oversee the plan and had started digging his first test hole. His sometimes quixotic efforts to save the world have inspired a parody twitter account, "Bored Elon Musk," where a faux Musk spouts off wacky ideas such as "Oxford commas as a service" and "bunches of bananas genetically engineered" so that the bananas ripen one at a time.

Of course, big dreamers have big stumbles. Some SpaceX rockets have blown up, and last June a driver was killed in a self-driving Tesla whose sensors failed to notice the tractor-trailer crossing its path. (An investigation by the National Highway Traffic Safety Administration found that Tesla's Autopilot system was not to blame.)

Musk is stoic about setbacks but all too conscious of nightmare scenarios. His views reflect a dictum from *Atlas Shrugged*: "Man has the power to act as his own destroyer—and that is the way he has acted through most of his history." As he told me, "we are the first species capable of self-annihilation."

Here's the nagging thought you can't escape as you drive around from glass box to glass box in Silicon Valley: the Lords of the Cloud love to yammer about turning the world into a better place as they churn out new algorithms, apps, and inventions that, it is claimed, will make our lives easier, healthier, funnier, closer, cooler, longer, and kinder to the planet. And yet there's a creepy feeling underneath it all, a sense that we're the mice in their experiments, that they regard us humans as Betamaxes or eight-tracks, old technology that will soon be discarded so that they can get on to enjoying their sleek new world. Many people there have accepted this future: we'll live to be 150 years old, but we'll have machine overlords.

Maybe we already have overlords. As Musk slyly told Recode's annual Code Conference last year in Rancho Palos Verdes, California, we could already be playthings in a simulated-reality world run by an advanced civilization. Reportedly, two Silicon Valley billionaires are working on an algorithm to break us out of the Matrix.

Among the engineers lured by the sweetness of solving the next problem, the prevailing attitude is that empires fall, societies change, and we are marching toward the inevitable phase ahead. They argue not about "whether" but rather about "how close" we are to replicating, and improving on, ourselves. Sam Altman, the 31-year-old president of Y Combinator, the Valley's top start-up accelerator, believes humanity is on the brink of such invention.

"The hard part of standing on an exponential curve is: when you look backwards, it looks flat, and when you look forward, it looks vertical," he told me. "And it's very hard to calibrate how much you are moving because it always looks the same."

You'd think that anytime Musk, Stephen Hawking, and Bill Gates are all raising the same warning about A.I.—as all of them are—it would be a 10-alarm fire. But, for a long time, the fog of fatalism over the Bay Area was thick. Musk's crusade was viewed as Sisyphean at best and Luddite at worst. The paradox is this: Many tech oligarchs see everything they are doing to help us, and all their benevolent manifestos, as streetlamps on the road to a future where, as Steve Wozniak says, humans are the family pets.

But Musk is not going gently. He plans on fighting this with every fiber of his carbon-based being. Musk and Altman have founded OpenAI, a billion-dollar nonprofit company, to work for safer artificial intelligence. I sat down with the two men when their new venture had only a handful of young engineers and a makeshift office, an apartment in San Francisco's Mission District that belongs to Greg Brockman, OpenAI's 28-year-old co-founder and chief technology officer. When I went back recently, to talk with Brockman and Ilya Sutskever, the company's 30-year-old research director (and also a co-founder), OpenAI had moved into an airy office nearby with a robot, the usual complement of snacks, and 50 full-time employees. (Another 10 to 30 are on the way.)

Altman, in gray T-shirt and jeans, is all wiry, pale intensity. Musk's fervor is masked by his diffident manner and rosy countenance. His eyes are green or blue, depending on the light, and his lips are plum red. He has an aura of command while retaining a trace of the gawky, lonely South African teenager who immigrated to Canada by himself at the age of 17.

In Silicon Valley, a lunchtime meeting does not necessarily involve that mundane fuel known as food. Younger coders are too absorbed in algorithms to linger over meals. Some just chug Soylent. Older ones are so obsessed with immortality that sometimes they're just washing down health pills with almond milk.

At first blush, OpenAI seemed like a bantamweight vanity project, a bunch of brainy kids in a walkup apartment taking on the multi-billion-dollar efforts at Google, Lacebook, and other companies which employ the world's leading A.I. experts. But then, playing a well-heeled David to Goliath is Musk's specialty, and he always does it with style—and some useful sensationalism.

Let others in Silicon Valley focus on their I.P.O. price and ridding San Francisco of what they regard as its unsightly homeless population. Musk has larger aims, like ending global warming and dying on Mars (just not, he says, on impact).

Musk began to see man's fate in the galaxy as his personal obligation three decades ago, when as a teenager he had a full-blown existential crisis. Musk told me that *The Hitchhiker's Guide to the Galaxy*, by Douglas Adams, was a turning point for him. The book is about aliens destroying the earth to make way for a hyperspace highway and features Marvin the Paranoid Android and a supercomputer designed to answer all the mysteries of the universe. (Musk slipped at least one reference to the book into the software of the Tesla Model S.) As a teenager, Vance writes in his biography, Musk formulated a mission statement for himself: "The only thing that makes sense to do is strive for greater collective enlightenment."

OpenAI got under way with a vague mandate—which isn't surprising, given that people in the field are still arguing over what form A.I. will take, what it will be able to do, and what can be done about it. So far, public policy on A.I. is strangely undetermined and software is largely unregulated. The Federal Aviation Administration oversees drones, the Securities and Exchange Commission oversees automated financial trading, and the Department of Transportation has begun to oversee self-driving cars.

Musk believes that it is better to try to get super-A.I. first and distribute the technology to the world than to allow the algorithms to be concealed and concentrated in the hands of tech or government elites—even when the tech elites happen to be his own friends, people such as Google founders Larry Page and Sergey Brin. "I've had many conversations with Larry about A.I. and robotics—many, many," Musk told me. "And some of them have gotten quite heated. You know, I think it's not just Larry, but there are many futurists who feel a certain inevitability or fatalism about robots, where we'd have some sort of peripheral role. The phrase used is 'We are the biological boot-loader for digital super-intelligence.'" (A boot loader is the small program that launches the operating system when you first turn on your computer.) "Matter can't organize itself into a chip," Musk explained. "But it can organize itself into a biological entity that gets increasingly sophisticated and ultimately can create the chip."

Musk has no intention of being a boot loader. Page and Brin see themselves as forces for good, but Musk says the issue goes far beyond the motivations of a handful of Silicon Valley executives.

"It's great when the emperor is Marcus Aurelius," he says. "It's not so great when the emperor is Caligula."

THE GOLDEN CALF

After the so-called A.I. winter—the broad, commercial failure in the late 80s of an early A.I. technology that wasn't up to snuff—artificial intelligence got a reputation as snake oil. Now it's the hot thing again in this go-go era in the Valley. Greg Brockman, of OpenAI, believes the next decade will be all about A.I., with everyone throwing money at the small number of "wizards" who know the A.I. "incantations." Guys who got rich writing code to solve banal problems like how to pay a stranger for stuff online now contemplate a vertiginous world where they are the creators of a new reality and perhaps a new species.

Microsoft's Jaron Lanier, the dreadlocked computer scientist known as the father of virtual reality, gave me his view as to why the digerati find the "science-fiction fantasy" of A.I. so tantalizing: "It's saying, 'Oh, you digital techy people, you're like gods; you're creating life; you're transforming reality.' There's a tremendous narcissism in it that we're the people who can do it. No one else. The Pope can't do it. The president can't do it. No one else can do it. We are the masters of it. The software we're building is our immortality." This kind of God-like ambition isn't new, he adds. "I read about it once in a story about a golden calf." He shook his head. "Don't get high on your own supply, you know?"

Google has gobbled up almost every interesting robotics and machine-learning company over the last few years. It bought Deep-Mind for $650 million, reportedly beating out Facebook, and built the Google Brain team to work on A.I. It hired Geoffrey Hinton, a British pioneer in artificial neural networks; and Ray Kurzweil, the eccentric futurist who has predicted that we are only 28 years away from the Rapture-like "Singularity"—the moment when the spiraling capabilities of self-improving artificial super-intelligence will far exceed human intelligence, and human beings will merge with A.I. to create the "god-like" hybrid beings of the future.

It's in Larry Page's blood and Google's DNA to believe that A.I. is the company's inevitable destiny—think of that destiny as you will. ("If evil A.I. lights up," Ashlee Vance told me, "it will light up first at Google.") If Google could get computers to master search when search was the most important problem in the world, then presumably it can get computers to do everything else. In March of last year, Silicon Valley gulped when a fabled South Korean player of the world's most complex board game, Go, was beaten in Seoul by DeepMind's AlphaGo. Hassabis, who has said he is running an Apollo program for A.I., called it a "historic moment" and admitted that even he was surprised it happened so quickly. "I've always hoped that A.I. could help us discover completely new ideas in complex scientific domains," Hassabis told me in February. "This might be one of the first glimpses of that kind of creativity." More recently, AlphaGo played 60 games online against top Go players in China, Japan, and Korea—and emerged with a record of 60–0. In January, in another shock to the system, an A.I. program showed that it could bluff. Libratus, built by two Carnegie Mellon researchers, was able to crush top poker players at Texas Hold 'Em.

Peter Thiel told me about a friend of his who says that the only reason people tolerate Silicon Valley is that no one there seems to be having any sex or any fun. But there are reports of sex robots on the way that come with apps that can control their moods and even have a pulse. The Valley is skittish when it comes to female sex robots—an obsession in Japan—because of its notoriously male-dominated culture and its much-publicized issues with sexual harassment and discrimination. But when I asked Musk about this, he replied matter-of-factly, "Sex robots? I think those are quite likely."

Whether sincere or a shrewd P.R. move, Hassabis made it a condition of the Google acquisition that Google and DeepMind establish a joint A.I. ethics board. At the time, three years ago, forming an ethics board was seen as a precocious move, as if to imply that Hassabis was on the verge of achieving true A.I. Now, not so much. Last June, a researcher at DeepMind co-authored a paper outlining a way to design a "big red button" that could be used as a kill switch to stop A.I. from inflicting harm.

Google executives say Larry Page's view on A.I. is shaped by his frustration about how many systems are sub-optimal—from systems that book trips to systems that price crops. He believes that A.I. will improve people's lives and has said that, when human needs are more easily met, people will "have more time with their family or to pursue their own interests." Especially when a robot throws them out of work.

Musk is a friend of Page's. He attended Page's wedding and sometimes stays at his house when he's in the San Francisco area. "It's not worth having a house for one or two nights a week," the 99th-richest man in the world explained to me. At times, Musk has expressed concern that Page may be naive about how A.I. could play out. If Page is inclined toward the philosophy that machines are only as good or bad as the people creating them, Musk firmly disagrees. Some at Google—perhaps annoyed that Musk is, in essence, pointing a finger at them for rushing ahead willy-nilly—dismiss his dystopic take as a cinematic cliche. Eric Schmidt, the executive chairman of Google's parent company, put it this way: "Robots are invented. Countries arm them. An evil dictator turns the robots on humans, and all humans will be killed. Sounds like a movie to me."

Some in Silicon Valley argue that Musk is interested less in saving the world than in buffing his brand, and that he is exploiting a deeply rooted conflict: the one between man and machine, and our fear that the creation will turn against us. They gripe that his epic good-versus-evil story line is about luring talent at discount rates and incubating his own A.I. software for cars and rockets. It's certainly true that the Bay Area has always had a healthy respect for making a buck. As Sam Spade said in *The Maltese Falcon*, "Most things in San Francisco can be bought, or taken."

Musk is without doubt a dazzling salesman. Who better than a guardian of human welfare to sell you your new, self-driving Tesla? Andrew Ng—the chief scientist at Baidu, known as China's Google—based in Sunnyvale, California, writes off Musk's Manichaean throwdown as "marketing genius." "At the height of the recession, he persuaded the U.S. government to help him build an electric sports car," Ng recalled, incredulous. The Stanford professor is married to a robotics expert, issued a robot-themed engagement announcement, and keeps a "Trust the Robot" black jacket hanging on the back of his chair. He thinks people who worry about A.I. going rogue are distracted by "phantoms," and regards getting alarmed now as akin to worrying about overpopulation on Mars before we populate it. "And I think it's fascinating," he said about Musk in particular, "that in a rather short period of time he's inserted himself into the conversation on A.I. I think he sees accurately that A.I. is going to create tremendous amounts of value."

Although he once called Musk a "sci-fi version of P. T. Barnum," Ashlee Vance thinks that Musk's concern about A.I. is genuine, even if what he can actually do about it is unclear. "His wife, Talulah, told me they had late-night conversations about A.I. at home," Vance noted. "Elon is brutally logical. The way he tackles everything is like moving chess pieces around. When he plays this scenario out in his head, it doesn't end well for people."

Eliezer Yudkowsky, a co-founder of the Machine Intelligence Research Institute, in Berkeley, agrees: "He's Elon-freaking-Musk. He doesn't need to touch the third rail of the artificial-intelligence controversy if he wants to be sexy. He can just talk about Mars colonization."

Some sniff that Musk is not truly part of the whiteboard culture and that his scary scenarios miss the fact that we are living in a world where it's hard to get your printer to work. Others chalk up OpenAI, in part, to a case of FOMO: Musk sees his friend Page building new-wave software in a hot field and craves a competing army of coders. As Vance sees it, "Elon wants all the toys that Larry has. They're like these two superpowers. They're friends, but there's a lot of tension in their relationship." A rivalry of this kind might be best summed up by a line from the vainglorious head of the fictional tech behemoth Hooli, on HBO's *Silicon Valley*: "I don't want to live in a world where someone else makes the world a better place better than we do."

Musk's disagreement with Page over the potential dangers of A.I. "did affect our friendship for a while," Musk says, "but that has since passed. We are on good terms these days."

Musk never had as close a personal connection with 32-year-old Mark Zuckerberg, who has become an unlikely lifestyle guru, setting a new challenge for himself every year. These have included wearing a tie every day, reading a book every two weeks, learning Mandarin, and eating meat only from animals he killed with his own hands. In 2016, it was A.I.'s turn.

Zuckerberg has moved his A.I. experts to desks near his own. Three weeks after Musk and Altman announced their venture to make the world safe from malicious A.I., Zuckerberg posted on Facebook that his project for the year was building a helpful A.I. to assist him in managing his home—everything from recognizing his friends and letting them inside to keeping an eye on the nursery. "You can think of it kind of like Jarvis in Iron Man, " he wrote.

One Facebooker cautioned Zuckerberg not to "accidentally create Skynet," the military supercomputer that turns against human beings in the *Terminator* movies. "I think we can build A.I. so it works for us and helps us," Zuckerberg replied. And clearly throwing shade at Musk, he continued: "Some people fear-monger about how A.I. is a huge danger, but that seems far-fetched to me and much less likely than disasters due to widespread disease, violence, etc." Or, as he described his philosophy at a Facebook developers' conference last April, in a clear rejection of warnings from Musk and others he believes to be alarmists: "Choose hope over fear."

In the November issue of *Wired*, guest-edited by Barack Obama, Zuckerberg wrote that there is little basis beyond science fiction to worry about doomsday scenarios: "If we slow down progress in deference to unfounded concerns, we stand in the way of real gains." He compared A.I. jitters to early fears about airplanes, noting, "We didn't rush to put rules in place about how airplanes should work before we figured out how they'd fly in the first place."

Zuckerberg introduced his A.I. butler, Jarvis, right before Christmas. With the soothing voice of Morgan Freeman, it was able to help with music, lights, and even making toast. I asked the real-life Iron Man, Musk, about Zuckerberg's Jarvis, when it was in its earliest stages. "I wouldn't call it A.I. to have your household functions automated," Musk said. "It's really not A.I. to turn the lights on, set the temperature."

Zuckerberg can be just as dismissive. Asked in Germany whether

Musk's apocalyptic forebodings were "hysterical" or "valid," Zuckerberg replied "hysterical." And when Musk's SpaceX rocket blew up on the launch pad in September, destroying a satellite Facebook was leasing, Zuckerberg coldly posted that he was "deeply disappointed."

A RUPTURE IN HISTORY

Musk and others who have raised a warning flag on A.I. have sometimes been treated like drama queens. In January 2016, Musk won the annual Luddite Award, bestowed by a Washington tech-policy think tank. Still, he's got some pretty good wingmen. Stephen Hawking told the BBC, "I think the development of full artificial intelligence could spell the end of the human race." Bill Gates told Charlie Rose that A.I. was potentially more dangerous than a nuclear catastrophe. Nick Bostrom, a 43-year-old Oxford philosophy professor, warned in his 2014 book, *Superintelligence*, that "once unfriendly superintelligence exists, it would prevent us from replacing it or changing its preferences. Our fate would be sealed." And, last year, Henry Kissinger jumped on the peril bandwagon, holding a confidential meeting with top A.I. experts at the Brook, a private club in Manhattan, to discuss his concern over how smart robots could cause a rupture in history and unravel the way civilization works.

In January 2015, Musk, Bostrom, and a Who's Who of A.I., representing both sides of the split, assembled in Puerto Rico for a conference hosted by Max Tegmark, a 49-year-old physics professor at M.I.T. who runs the Future of Life Institute, in Boston.

"Do you own a house?," Tegmark asked me. "Do you own fire insurance? The consensus in Puerto Rico was that we needed fire insurance. When we got fire and messed up with it, we invented the fire extinguisher. When we got cars and messed up, we invented the seat belt, air bag, and traffic light. But with nuclear weapons and A.I., we don't want to learn from our mistakes. We want to plan ahead." (Musk reminded Tegmark that a precaution as sensible as seat belts had provoked fierce opposition from the automobile industry.)

Musk, who has kick-started the funding of research into avoiding

A.I.'s pitfalls, said he would give the Future of Life Institute "10 million reasons" to pursue the subject, donating $10 million. Tegmark promptly gave $1.5 million to Bostrom's group in Oxford, the Future of Humanity Institute. Explaining at the time why it was crucial to be "proactive and not reactive," Musk said it was certainly possible to "construct scenarios where the recovery of human civilization does not occur."

Six months after the Puerto Rico conference, Musk, Hawking, Demis Hassabis, Apple co-founder Steve Wozniak, and Stuart Russell, a computer-science professor at Berkeley who co-authored the standard textbook on artificial intelligence, along with 1,000 other prominent figures, signed a letter calling for a ban on offensive autonomous weapons. "In 50 years, this 18-month period we're in now will be seen as being crucial for the future of the A.I. community," Russell told me. "It's when the A.I. community finally woke up and took itself seriously and thought about what to do to make the future better." Last September, the country's biggest tech companies created the Partnership on Artificial Intelligence to explore the full range of issues arising from A.I., including the ethical ones. (Musk's OpenAI quickly joined this effort.) Meanwhile, the European Union has been looking into legal issues arising from the advent of robots and A.I.—such as whether robots have "personhood" or (as one *Financial Times* contributor wondered) should be considered more like slaves in Roman law.

At Tegmark's second A.I. safety conference, last January at the Asilomar center, in California—chosen because that's where scientists gathered back in 1975 and agreed to limit genetic experimentation—the topic was not so contentious. Larry Page, who was not at the Puerto Rico conference, was at Asilomar, and Musk noted that their "conversation was no longer heated."

But while it may have been "a coming-out party for A.I. safety," as one attendee put it—part of "a sea change" in the last year or so, as Musk says—there's still a long way to go. "There's no question that the top technologists in Silicon Valley now take A.I. far more seriously—that they do acknowledge it as a risk," he observes. "I'm not sure that they yet appreciate the significance of the risk."

Steve Wozniak has wondered publicly whether he is destined to be a family pet for robot overlords. "We started feeding our dog filet," he told me about his own pet, over lunch with his wife, Janet, at the Original Hick'ry Pit, in Walnut Creek. "Once you start thinking you could be one, that's how you want them treated."

He has developed a policy of appeasement toward robots and any A.I. masters. "Why do we want to set ourselves up as the enemy when they might overpower us someday?" he said. "It should be a joint partnership. All we can do is seed them with a strong culture where they see humans as their friends."

When I went to Peter Thiel's elegant San Francisco office, dominated by two giant chessboards, Thiel, one of the original donors to OpenAI and a committed contrarian, said he worried that Musk's resistance could actually be accelerating A.I. research because his end-of-the-world warnings are increasing interest in the field.

"Full-on A.I. is on the order of magnitude of extraterrestrials landing," Thiel said. "There are some very deeply tricky questions around this. . . . If you really push on how do we make A.I. safe, I don't think people have any clue. We don't even know what A.I. is. It's very hard to know how it would be controllable."

He went on: "There's some sense in which the A.I. question encapsulates all of people's hopes and fears about the computer age. I think people's intuitions do just really break down when they're pushed to these limits because we've never dealt with entities that are smarter than humans on this planet."

THE URGE TO MERGE

Trying to puzzle out who is right on A.I., I drove to San Mateo to meet Ray Kurzweil for coffee at the restaurant Three. Kurzweil is the author of *The Singularity Is Near*, a Utopian vision of what an A.I. future holds. (When I mentioned to Andrew Ng that I was going to be talking to Kurzweil, he rolled his eyes. "Whenever I read Kurzweil's *Singularity*, my eyes just naturally do that," he said.) Kurzweil arrived with a Whole Foods bag for me, brimming with his books and two documentaries about him. He was wearing khakis, a green-and-red plaid shirt, and several rings, including one—made with a 3-D printer—that has an *S* for his Singularity University.

Computers are already "doing many attributes of thinking," Kurzweil told me. "Just a few years ago, A.I. couldn't even tell the difference between a dog and cat. Now it can." Kurzweil has a keen interest in cats and keeps a collection of 300 cat figurines in his Northern California home. At the restaurant, he asked for almond milk but couldn't get any. The 69-year-old eats strange health concoctions and takes 90 pills a day, eager to achieve immortality—or "indefinite extensions to the existence of our mind file"—which means merging with machines. He has such an urge to merge that he sometimes uses the word "we" when talking about super-intelligent future beings—a far cry from Musk's more ominous "they."

I mentioned that Musk had told me he was bewildered that Kurzweil doesn't seem to have "even 1 percent doubt" about the hazards of our "mind children," as robotics expert Hans Moravec calls them.

"That's just not true. I'm the one who articulated the dangers," Kurzweil said. "The promise and peril are deeply intertwined," he continued. "Fire kept us warm and cooked our food and also burned down our houses. . . . Furthermore, there are strategies to control the peril, as there have been with biotechnology guidelines." He summarized the three stages of the human response to new technology as Wow!, Uh-Oh, and What Other Choice Do We Have but to Move Forward? "The list of things humans can do better than computers is getting smaller and smaller," he said. "But we create these tools to extend our long reach."

Just as, two hundred million years ago, mammalian brains developed a neocortex that eventually enabled humans to "invent language and science and art and technology," by the 2030s, Kurzweil predicts, we will be cyborgs, with nanobots the size of blood cells connecting us to synthetic neocortices in the cloud, giving us access to virtual reality and augmented reality from within our own nervous systems. "We will be funnier; we will be more musical; we will increase our wisdom," he said, ultimately, as I understand it, producing a herd of Beethovens and

Einsteins. Nanobots in our veins and arteries will cure diseases and heal our bodies from the inside.

He allows that Musk's bete noire could come true. He notes that our A.I. progeny "may be friendly and may not be" and that "if it's not friendly, we may have to fight it." And perhaps the only way to fight it would be "to get an A.I. on your side that's even smarter."

Kurzweil told me he was surprised that Stuart Russell had "jumped on the peril bandwagon," so I reached out to Russell and met with him in his seventh-floor office in Berkeley. The 54-year-old British-American expert on A.I. told me that his thinking had evolved and that he now "violently" disagrees with Kurzweil and others who feel that ceding the planet to super-intelligent A.I. is just fine.

Russell doesn't give a fig whether A.I. might enable more Einsteins and Beethovens. One more Ludwig doesn't balance the risk of destroying humanity. "As if somehow intelligence was the thing that mattered and not the quality of human experience," he said, with exasperation. "I think if we replaced ourselves with machines that as far as we know would have no conscious existence, no matter how many amazing things they invented, I think that would be the biggest possible tragedy." Nick Bostrom has called the idea of a society of technological awesomeness with no human beings a "Disneyland without children."

"There are people who believe that if the machines are more intelligent than we are, then they should just have the planet and we should go away," Russell said. "Then there are people who say, 'Well, we'll upload ourselves into the machines, so we'll still have consciousness but we'll be machines.' Which I would find, well, completely implausible."

Russell took exception to the views of Yann LeCun, who developed the forerunner of the convolutional neural nets used by AlphaGo and is Facebook's director of A.I. research. LeCun told the BBC that there would be no *Ex Machina* or *Terminator* scenarios, because robots would not be built with human drives—hunger, power, reproduction, self-preservation. "Yann LeCun keeps saying that there's no reason why machines would have any self-preservation instinct," Russell said. "And it's simply and mathematically false. I mean, it's so obvious that a machine will have self-preservation even if you don't program it in because if you say, 'Fetch the coffee,' it can't fetch the coffee if it's dead. So if you give it any goal whatsoever, it has a reason to preserve its own existence to achieve that goal. And if you threaten it on your way to getting coffee, it's going to kill you because any risk to the coffee has to be countered. People have explained this to LeCun in very simple terms."

Russell debunked the two most common arguments for why we shouldn't worry: "One is: It'll never happen, which is like saying we are driving towards the cliff but we're bound to run out of gas before we get there. And that doesn't seem like a good way to manage the affairs of the human race. And the other is: Not to worry—we will just build robots that collaborate with us and we'll be in human-robot teams. Which begs the question: If your robot doesn't agree with your objectives, how do you form a team with it?"

Last year, Microsoft shut down its A.I. chatbot, Tay, after Twitter users—who were supposed to make "her" smarter "through casual and playful conversation," as Microsoft put it—instead taught her how to reply with racist, misogynistic, and anti-Semitic slurs, "bush did 9/11, and Hitler would have done a better job than the monkey we have now," Tay tweeted, "donald trump is the only hope we've got." In response, Musk tweeted, "Will be interesting to see what the mean time to Hitler is for these bots. Only took Microsoft's Tay a day."

With Trump now president, Musk finds himself walking a fine line. His companies count on the U.S. government for business and subsidies, regardless of whether Marcus Aurelius or Caligula is in charge. Musk's companies joined the amicus brief against Trump's executive order regarding immigration and refugees, and Musk himself tweeted against the order. At the same tune, unlike Uber's Travis Kalanick, Musk has hung in there as a member of Trump's Strategic and Policy Forum. "It's very Elon," says Ashlee Vance. "He's going to do his own thing no matter what people grumble about." He added that Musk can be "opportunistic" when necessary.

I asked Musk about the flak he had gotten for associating with Trump. In the photograph of tech executives with Trump, he had looked gloomy, and there was a weary tone in his voice when he talked about the subject. In the end, he said, "it's better to have voices of moderation in the room with the president. There are a lot of people, kind of the hard left, who essentially want to isolate—and not have any voice. Very unwise."

ALL ABOUT THE JOURNEY

Eliezer Yudkowsky is a highly regarded 37-year-old researcher who is trying to figure out whether it's possible, in practice and not just in theory, to point A.I. in any direction, let alone a good one. I met him at a Japanese restaurant in Berkeley.

"How do you encode the goal functions of an A.I. such that it has an Off switch and it wants there to be an Off switch and it won't try to eliminate the Off switch and it will let you press the Off switch, but it won't jump ahead and press the Off switch itself?" he asked over an order of surf-and-turf rolls. "And if it self-modifies, will it self-modify in such a way as to keep the Off switch? We're trying to work on that. It's not easy."

I babbled about the heirs of Klaatu, HAL, and Ultron taking over the Internet and getting control of our banking, transportation, and military. What about the replicants in *Blade Runner*, who conspire to kill their creator? Yudkowsky held his head in his hands, then patiently explained: "The A.I. doesn't have to take over the whole Internet. It doesn't need drones. It's not dangerous because it has guns. It's dangerous because it's smarter than us. Suppose it can solve the science technology of predicting protein structure from DNA information. Then it just needs to send out a few e-mails to the labs that synthesize customized proteins. Soon it has its own molecular machinery, building even more sophisticated molecular machines.

"If you want a picture of A.I. gone wrong, don't imagine marching humanoid robots with glowing red eyes. Imagine tiny invisible synthetic bacteria made of diamond, with tiny onboard computers, hiding inside your bloodstream and everyone else's. And then, simultaneously, they release one microgram of botulinum toxin. Everyone just falls over dead.

"Only it won't actually happen like that. It's impossible for me to predict exactly how we'd lose, because the A.I. will be smarter than I am. When you're building something smarter than you, you have to get it right on the first try."

I thought back to my conversation with Musk and Altman. Don't get sidetracked by the idea of killer robots, Musk said, noting, "The thing about A.I. is that it's not the robot; it's the computer algorithm in the Net. So the robot would just be an end effector, just a series of sensors and actuators. A.I. is in the Net. . . . The important thing is that if we do get some sort of runaway algorithm, then the human A.I. collective can stop the runaway algorithm. But if there's large, centralized A.I. that decides, then there's no stopping it."

Altman expanded upon the scenario: "An agent that had full control of the Internet could have far more effect on the world than an agent that had full control of a sophisticated robot. Our lives are already so dependent on the Internet that an agent that had no body whatsoever but could use the Internet really well would be far more powerful."

Even robots with a seemingly benign task could indifferently harm us. "Let's say you create a self-improving A.I. to pick strawberries," Musk said, "and it gets better and better at picking strawberries and picks more and more and it is self-improving, so all it really wants to do is pick strawberries. So then it would have all the world be strawberry fields. Strawberry fields forever." No room for human beings.

But can they ever really develop a kill switch? "I'm not sure I'd want to be the one holding the kill switch for some superpowered A.I., because you'd be the first thing it kills," Musk replied.

Altman tried to capture the chilling grandeur of what's at stake: "It's a very exciting time to be alive, because in the next few decades we are either going to head toward self-destruction or toward human descendants eventually colonizing the universe."

"Right," Musk said, adding, "If you believe the end is the heat death of the universe, it really is all about the journey."

The man who is so worried about extinction chuckled at his own extinction joke. As H. P. Lovecraft once wrote, "From even the greatest of horrors irony is seldom absent."

PETER THIEL, TRUMP'S TECH PAL, EXPLAINS HIMSELF

—JANUARY 11, 2017

Let others tremble at the thought that Donald J. Trump may go too far. Peter Thiel worries that Mr. Trump may not go far enough.

"Everyone says Trump is going to change everything way too much," says the famed venture capitalist, contrarian and member of the Trump transition team. "Well, maybe Trump is going to change everything way too little. That seems like the much more plausible risk to me."

Mr. Thiel is comfortable being a walking oxymoron: He is driven to save the world from the apocalypse. Yet he helped boost the man regarded by many as a danger to the planet.

"The election had an apocalyptic feel to it," says Mr. Thiel, wearing a gray Zegna suit and sipping white wine in a red leather booth at the Monkey Bar in Manhattan. "There was a way in which Trump was funny, so you could be apocalyptic and funny at the same time. It's a strange combination, but it's somehow very powerful psychologically."

At the recent meeting of tech executives at Trump Tower—orchestrated by Mr. Thiel—the president-elect caressed Mr. Thiel's hand so affectionately that body language experts went into a frenzy. I note that he looked uneasy being petted in front of his peers.

"I was thinking, 'I hope this doesn't look too weird on TV,'" he says.

I ask if he had to twist arms to lure some of the anti-Trump tech titans, like Jeff Bezos and Elon Musk.

"I think, early on, everybody was worried that they would be the only person to show up," Mr. Thiel says. "At the end, everybody was worried they would be the only person not to show up. I think the bigger tech companies all wanted to get a little bit off the ledge that they had gotten on.

"Normally, if you're a C.E.O. of a big company, you tend to be somewhat apolitical or politically pretty bland. But this year, it was this competition for who could be more anti-Trump. 'If Trump wins, I will eat my sock.' 'I will eat my shoe.' 'I will eat my shoe, and then I will walk barefoot to Mexico to emigrate and leave the country.'

"Somehow, I think Silicon Valley got even more spun up than Manhattan. There were hedge fund people I spoke to about a week after the election. They hadn't supported Trump. But all of a sudden, they sort of changed their minds. The stock market went up, and they were like, 'Yes, actually, I don't understand why I was against him all year long.'"

Talking about how the Billy Bush tape was not so shocking if you've worked on the Wall Street trading floor, Mr. Thiel says: "On the one hand, the tape was clearly offensive and inappropriate. At the same time, I worry there's a part of Silicon Valley that is hyper-politically correct about sex. One of my friends has a theory that the rest of the country tolerates Silicon Valley because people there just don't have that much sex. They're not having that much fun."

I note that several Silicon Valley companies have pre-emptively said they will not help build a Muslim registry for the Trump administration. Will Palantir, the data-mining company of which Mr. Thiel was a founder, and whose clients include the N.S.A., the C.I.A. and the F.B.I., be involved in that? (Palantir's C.E.O., Alex Karp, sat in at the Trump tech meeting.)

"We would not do that," Mr. Thiel says flatly.

When I ask him if he can explain to Mr. Trump that climate change is not a hoax perpetrated by the Chinese, he offers a Chinese box of an answer: "Does he really think that? If he really thinks that, how would you influence that? If he really thinks that and you could influence him, what would be the best way to do it?"

One could have predicted Mr. Thiel's affinity for Mr. Trump by read-ing his 2014 book, "Zero to One," in which he offers three prongs of his philosophy: 1) It is better to risk boldness than triviality. 2) A bad plan is better than no plan. 3) Sales matter just as much as product.

But he was portrayed as an outcast in Silicon Valley and denounced as a jerk for supporting Mr. Trump and giving him $1.25 million. "I didn't give him any money for a long time because I didn't think it mattered, and then the campaign asked me to," he says.

His critics demanded to know how someone who immigrated from Frankfurt to Cleveland as a child could support a campaign so bristling with intolerance. How could a gay man back someone who will prob-ably nominate Supreme Court justices inclined to limit rights for gays and women? How could a futurist support a cave man who champions fossil fuels, puts profits over environmental protection and insists that we can turn back the clock on the effects of globalization on American workers?

"There are reduced expectations for the younger generation, and this is the first time this has happened in American history," Mr. Thiel says. "Even if there are aspects of Trump that are retro and that seem to be going back to the past, I think a lot of people want to go back to a past that was futuristic—'The Jetsons,' 'Star Trek.' They're dated but futur-istic."

It is a theme he has struck before, that Silicon Valley has not fulfilled the old dreams for bigger things. "Cellphones distract us from the fact that the subways are 100 years old," he says.

An article entitled "Peter Thiel Is Poised to Become a National Vil-lain," in New York magazine, suggested he looked like he is enjoying that role.

He says he isn't. Yet the billionaire views the visceral torrent against him with his usual rationality, surveying the scene deliberately, like the chess prodigy he once was. "I was surprised that it generated as much controversy as it did," he says. "There was a push to remove me from the board of Facebook, which is kind of crazy, since I'm the longest-serving director there after Zuckerberg."

He recalls that he went through a lot of "meta" debates about Mr.

Trump in Silicon Valley. "One of my good friends said, 'Peter, do you realize how crazy this is, how everybody thinks this is crazy?' I was like: 'Well, why am I wrong? What's substantively wrong with this?' And it all got referred back to 'Everybody thinks Trump's really crazy.' So it's like there's a shortcut, which is: 'I don't need to explain it. It's good enough that everybody thinks something. If everybody thinks this is crazy, I don't even have to explain to you why it's crazy. You should just change your mind.'"

On the Russian hacking, Mr. Thiel says: "There's a strong circumstantial case that Russia did this thing. On the other hand, I was totally convinced that there were W.M.D.s in Iraq in 2002, 2003."

The reaction from the gay community has been harsh, with one writer in The Advocate going so far as to suggest that Mr. Thiel was not even a gay man, because he did not "embrace the struggle."

"I think Trump is very good on gay rights," Mr. Thiel says. "I don't think he will reverse anything. I would obviously be concerned if I thought otherwise."

I ask if he's comfortable with the idea that Vice President–elect Mike Pence, regarded in the gay community as an unreconstructed homophobe, is a heartbeat away from the presidency.

"You know, maybe I should be worried but I'm not that worried about it," he replies. "I don't know. People know too many gay people. There are just all these ways I think stuff has just shifted. For speaking at the Republican convention, I got attacked way more by liberal gay people than by conservative Christian people.

"I don't think these things will particularly change. It's like, even if you appointed a whole series of conservative Supreme Court justices, I'm not sure that Roe v. Wade would get overturned, ever. I don't know if people even care about the Supreme Court. You know, you'd have thought the failure to have a vote on Merrick [Garland] would be a massive issue. And somehow it mattered to Democrats, but it didn't matter to the public at large."

Would he like to get married and have kids?

He looks a bit startled by the question, then says: "Maybe."

I ask him if he worries about the bromance with Vladimir V. Putin and Mr. Trump's bizarre affinity for dictators. "But should Russia be allied with the West or with China?" Mr. Thiel says. "There are these really bad dictators in the Middle East, and we got rid of them and in many cases there's even worse chaos."

So he doesn't worry about Mr. Trump sending an intemperate tweet and spurring a war with North Korea?

"A Twitter war is not a real war," Mr. Thiel says.

If the worst fears of annihilation seem plausible, Mr. Thiel can always invest more in his libertarian fantasy of a new society of Seasteads: islands at sea with their own rules, starting with a French Polynesian lagoon. "They're not quite feasible from an engineering perspective," he says. "That's still very far in the future."

He does think, though, that human violence is more of a risk than a pandemic or robot army. "It's the people behind the red-eyed robots that you need to be scared of," he says.

Mr. Thiel is focused on ways to prolong life. He was intrigued by parabiosis, a blood regeneration trial in which people over 35 would receive transfusions from people aged 16 to 25—an experiment that Anne Rice gave a thumbs-up to.

"Out of all the crazy things in this campaign, the vampire accusations were the craziest," he says, adding that while blood transfusions may be helpful, there may be harmful factors and "we have to be very careful."

"I have not done anything of the sort" yet, he says about parabiosis. And because of the publicity, he says, he is now sifting through hundreds of proposals he has received from parabiosis ventures.

Mr. Thiel has, however, used human growth hormones and he has signed up for cryogenics. "We have to be more experimental in all our medical procedures," he says. "We should not go gently into that good night."

I ask why everyone in Silicon Valley seemed so obsessed with immortality.

"Why is everyone else so indifferent about their mortality?" he replies.

He has invested in many biotech companies and has been advising the Trump transition team on science. "Science is technology's older brother who has fallen on hard times," he says. "I have some strong opinions on this. At the F.D.A. today, aging is still not an indication for disease. And you're not allowed to develop drugs that could stop aging. We have not even started yet."

Given the passion of his friend Mr. Musk for colonizing Mars, has he influenced Trump's thinking about NASA?

"It's this very large agency that has kind of lost its way over the last 30 to 40 years," Mr. Thiel says. "When we went to the moon, it took less than a decade from the time Kennedy announced it to the time we got there. Mars is harder but surely possible."

He says Mr. Trump's foes want to cast the president-elect "as this uniquely evil person, Trump as Hitler; that doesn't strike me as remotely plausible."

Over a four-hour dinner of duck and chocolate dessert—a surprisingly sybaritic meal for a man who admits he is prone to weird diets—Mr. Thiel shows, again and again, how he likes to "flip around" issues to see if conventional wisdom is wrong, a technique he calls Pyrrhonian skepticism.

"Maybe I do always have this background program running where I'm trying to think of, 'O.K., what's the opposite of what you're saying?' and then I'll try that," he says. "It works surprisingly often." He has even wondered if his most famous investment, Facebook, contributes to herd mentality.

When I remark that President Obama had eight years without any ethical shadiness, Mr. Thiel flips it, noting: "But there's a point where no corruption can be a bad thing. It can mean that things are too boring."

When I ask if he is concerned about conflicts of interest, either for himself or the Trump children, who sat in on the tech meeting, he flips that one, too: "I don't want to dismiss ethical concerns here, but I worry that 'conflict of interest' gets overly weaponized in our politics. I think in many cases, when there's a conflict of interest, it's an indication that someone understands something way better than if there's no conflict of interest. If there's no conflict of interest, it's often because you're just not interested."

When I ask if Mr. Trump is "casting" cabinet members based on looks, Mr. Thiel challenges me: "You're assuming that Trump thinks they matter too much. And maybe everyone else thinks they matter too little. Do you want America's leading diplomat to look like a diplomat? Do you want the secretary of defense to look like a tough general, so maybe we don't have to go on offense and we can stay on defense? I don't know."

When I ask about the incestuous amplification of the Facebook news feed, he muses: "There's nobody you know who knows anybody. There's nobody you know who knows anybody who knows anybody, ad infinitum."

Mr. Thiel and Mr. Trump are strange bedfellows, given that much of Mr. Thiel's billions came from being one of the original investors in Facebook and Mr. Trump recently said it's better to send important messages by courier. ("Well," Mr. Thiel notes, "one does have to be very careful with what one says in an email.")

The 70-year-old president-elect rose by wildly lunging with his Twitter rapier in an "unpresidented" way in the first campaign that blended politics, social media and reality. But the 49-year-old social-media visionary rarely updates his Facebook page and doesn't tweet, "because you always want to get things exactly right" and "if you start doing it, you have to do it a lot."

As Silicon Valley has devolved into a place that produces apps like one that sends the word "Yo," Mr. Thiel worries its thinking is "not big enough to take our civilization to the next level."

When I ask if it is true that Jack Dorsey, Twitter's chief executive, wasn't invited to the Trump tech meeting because the Trump camp was angry that Twitter wouldn't let the Republican nominee create a "Crooked Hillary" emoji, Mr. Thiel replies that "there were people upset about that," but that he set up the meeting according to the market caps of the bigger tech companies.

"I think the crazy thing is," he says, "at a place like Twitter, they were all working for Trump this whole year even though they thought they were working for Sanders."

Mr. Thiel says he fell into his role in the Trump candidacy.

"It was one of my friends who called me up and said, 'Hey, would you like to be a delegate at the Republican convention?'" he recalls. "I said: 'Actually, I kind of would. I think it would be fun to go.' Then, two weeks before the election, they talked to me about speaking at the convention."

I note that the audience in his hometown, Cleveland, gave him a great reception when he appeared as only the third openly gay speaker at a Republican convention.

"I'm not sure that my speech was that good," he says. "I do think a lot of other speeches were just very bad."

He had his first conversation with the man whom he sometimes calls "Mr. Trump" at the convention, when the Manhattan mogul told the San Francisco mogul, "You were terrific. We're friends for life." Mr. Thiel never did go to a Trump rally or watch a whole video of one. "I would think they were very repetitive," he says.

He says that at the tech meeting, Mr. Trump showed "a phenomenal understanding of people. He's very charismatic, but it's because he sort of knows exactly what to say to different people to put them at ease."

I ask him if Mr. Trump and Mr. Musk are similar.

"I'm going to get in trouble, but they are, actually. They're both grandmaster-level salespeople and these very much larger-than-life figures."

He recalls a story from his and Mr. Musk's PayPal days, when Mr. Musk joined the engineering team's poker game and bet everything on every hand, admitting only afterward that it was his first time playing poker. Then there was the time they were driving in Mr. Musk's McLaren F1 car, "the fastest car in the world." It hit an embankment, achieved lift-off, made a 360-degree horizontal turn, crashed and was destroyed.

"It was a miracle neither of us were hurt," Mr. Thiel says. "I wasn't wearing a seatbelt, which is not advisable. Elon's first comment was, 'Wow, Peter, that was really intense.' And then it was: 'You know, I had read all these stories about people who made money and bought sports cars and crashed them. But I knew it would never happen to me, so I didn't get any insurance.' And then we hitchhiked the rest of the way to the meeting."

Mr. Trump, with his litigious streak and his pugilistic attitude toward the press and his threat to change the libel laws, naturally admired Mr. Thiel's legal smackdown of Gawker. The tech titan was disturbed by the "painful and paralyzing" stories published on the gossipy website and other blogs under the Gawker banner, including a 2007 post that originally appeared on Valleywag blithely headlined "Peter Thiel Is Totally Gay, People."

So he secretly financed the lawsuit filed by Terry Bollea (the real name of the wrestler Hulk Hogan) against Gawker for posting an excerpt from a sex tape showing Mr. Hogan with a friend's wife. A court ruled in Mr. Bollea's favor, in a judgment of $140 million, which drove the site into bankruptcy. (The Gawker founder Nick Denton, who is also gay, described Mr. Thiel to Vanity Fair as "interesting—and scary.")

"It basically stands for the narrow proposition that you should not publish a sex tape," Mr. Thiel says. "I think that's an insult to journalists to suggest that's journalism now. Transparency is good, but at some point it can go in this very toxic direction."

Just as there was "a self-fulfilling Hillary bubble" where "everybody was just too scared to say this was a really bad idea" to support this "very weak candidate," Mr. Thiel believes Gawker manufactured "a totally insane bubble full of somewhat sociopathic people in New York." When the case went to court in Florida, he contends, the culture that "you could do whatever you wanted and there were no consequences" was exposed.

Savoring his victory, dismissing those who think the way to deal with vile and invasive stories is to grow a thicker skin, Mr. Thiel dressed as Hulk Hogan for the "Villains and Heroes" annual costume party last month, hosted on Long Island by the Mercer family, who were big Trump donors. He shows me a picture on his phone of him posing with Erik Prince, who founded the private military company Blackwater, and Mr. Trump—who had no costume—but jokes that it was "N.S.F.I." (Not Safe for the Internet).

"There's some resonances between Hogan beating Gawker and Trump beating the establishment in this country," Mr. Thiel says. Hulk Hogan was "this crazy person" who didn't seem like the best plaintiff, but "he didn't give up."

Using two wrestling terms he learned, Mr. Thiel says that many people assumed Mr. Trump was "kayfabe"—a move that looks real but is fake. But then his campaign turned into a "shoot"—the word for an unscripted move that suddenly becomes real.

"People thought the whole Trump thing was fake, that it wasn't going to go anywhere, that it was the most ridiculous thing imaginable, and then somehow he won, like Hogan did," Mr. Thiel says. "And what I wonder is, whether maybe pro wrestling is one of the most real things we have in our society and what's really disturbing is that the other stuff is much more fake. And whatever the superficialities of Mr. Trump might be, he was more authentic than the other politicians. He sort of talked in a way like ordinary people talk. It was not sort of this Orwellian newspeak jargon that so many of the candidates use. So he was sort of real. He actually wanted to win."

I ask Mr. Thiel about a prescient theory he proffered when I had dinner with him at the convention—again, flipping conventional wisdom—that Hillary was making a mistake by being too optimistic.

"If you're too optimistic, it sounds like you're out of touch," he says. "The Republicans needed a far more pessimistic candidate. Somehow, what was unusual about Trump is, he was very pessimistic but it still had an energizing aspect to it."

He says he has no plans to buy a place in Washington. "One of the things that's striking about talking to people who are politically working in D.C. is, it's so hard to tell what any of them actually do," he says. "It's a sort of place where people measure input, not output. You have a 15-minute monologue describing a 15-page résumé, starting in seventh grade."

While many predict that Mr. Trump will crash and burn, Mr. Thiel does not think he will regret his role.

"I always have very low expectations, so I'm rarely disappointed," he says.

I ask him how Mr. Trump, who is still putting out a lot of wacky, childish tweets, has struck him during the transition. Isn't he running around with his hair on fire?

"The hair seems fine," Mr. Thiel says. "Mr. Trump seems fine."

Confirm or Deny

MAUREEN DOWD: *California should secede.*

PETER THIEL: Confirm. I'd be fine with that. I think it would be good for California, good for the rest of the country. It would help Mr. Trump's re-election campaign.

Meryl Streep is overrated.

Confirm. She's probably very overrated, especially by all the people who are vociferously saying that she's overrated.

You did the seating chart at the Trump tech meeting.

Deny.

You have eaten 3-D printed meat, which you invested in.

Deny.

The empire in "Star Wars" gets a bad rap.

Deny. Oh, come on.

You like "Star Trek" more than "Star Wars."

Deny. I like "Star Wars" way better. I'm a capitalist. "Star Wars" is the capitalist show. "Star Trek" is the communist one. There is no money in "Star Trek" because you just have the transporter machine that can make anything you need. The whole plot of "Star Wars" starts with Han Solo having this debt that he owes and so the plot in "Star Wars" is driven by money.

You have written some of Trump's tweets.

Deny.

The Trump elevator is the new Mordor.

Deny, although that's close.

You've never stayed at a Trump hotel.

Deny. I've stayed at the Trump International in New York.

We should create a GPS-style algorithm to tell employees what to do at any given moment, like Bridgewater, the world's largest hedge fund, is doing, according to The Wall Street Journal.

Deny. That's always the place where everyone's overpaid and superunhappy. That algorithm doesn't seem like a formula for happiness.

As Jeff Bezos said of you in October, contrarians are usually wrong.
Deny.

Liberals are intolerant.
I'll confirm that but that's too one-sided. You have to get some nuances in here. I think it depends where they are. If you're the village atheist in a small town in Alabama, you're probably the most tolerant person there.

Optimism doesn't sell anymore.
That's complicated. It always sells some but not as much.

Mark Zuckerberg asked you to invest in Facebook while wearing pajamas.
Deny. The actual story was that Sean Parker convinced him to go to Sequoia Capital wearing pajamas to insult them at some point.

Zuckerberg did not have a great pitch.
Confirm. He was 19 years old. He was totally introverted, didn't say much. You desperately need a good pitch when you have a bad company. When you have a great company, you don't need a great pitch.

Facebook is a media company.
I think the official policy is to deny that.

The media should trust Facebook.
Confirm. Although, trusting in what way? There are a comical number of misguided conspiracy theories about Facebook.

Google had too much power in the Obama administration.
Confirm. Google had more power under Obama than Exxon had under Bush 43.

The age of Apple is over.
Confirm. We know what a smartphone looks like and does. It's not the fault of Tim Cook, but it's not an area where there will be any more innovation.

There's no job you would take in the Trump administration.
Confirm. I want to stay involved in Silicon Valley and help Mr. Trump as much as I can without a full-time position.

You do not like your character in HBO's "Silicon Valley."
Deny. I liked him. I watched the first season. My character died. I think eccentric is always better than evil.

You don't like cowhide rugs because you were sitting on one when you asked your father, Klaus, what happened to the cow and you understood mortality.
Yes, I very strongly confirm.

You do weird diets.
Confirm — on Paleo diet.

You believe that no one should ever eat sugar.
Confirm. We preach, we don't always practice.

You think the stock market is a giant bubble right now.
Confirm.

You should always switch doors in the Monty Hall problem.
Confirm.

Your favorite movie is "No Country for Old Men."
I like that one, yeah.

You're addicted to online chess.
Confirm. I delete it and download it a few times a year. I have it right now.

Your favorite opening move is Pawn to King 4.
Confirm.

The quote you like to use from Enoch Powell, "All political lives, unless they are cut off in midstream at a happy juncture, end in failure," applies to Trump.
Deny. He's not a standard politician.

Death and taxes are not actually certain.
Confirm.

JANN WENNER WANTS TO REVEAL IT ALL

—SEPTEMBER 22, 2022

MONTAUK, N.Y.—Rock may be dead, but Jann Wenner is still rolling.

The founder of Rolling Stone magazine always had a baby face, but he was never timid. His own mother told him he was the most difficult child she'd ever encountered. He edited stories with a red pen. He gave out roach clips with subscriptions. He turned a darkroom into an in-house drug-dealing operation called the Capri Lounge, as a perk for staffers.

"More than anyone I know, he's always just done what he wanted," said his friend Lorne Michaels, the creator of "Saturday Night Live."

When it suited him, Mr. Wenner was a tyrant.

"I wasn't raving around tearing up people's copy," he said, looking relaxed in a blue linen shirt and black pants at his Montauk home in August. "But I just would not take less than your really best effort. I was tough, but I was also super-indulgent. I believed in writers."

Hunter S. Thompson once wrote Mr. Wenner a letter about how working for Rolling Stone was "like being invited into a bonfire and finding out the fire is actually your friend." He added, "Some people were fried to cinders, as I recall, and some people used the heat to transmogrify themselves into heroes."

That wild energy is how, in 1967 when he was a 21-year-old enfant terrible, he created a magazine that chronicled a generation, serving up a flambé of music, drugs, alcohol, sex and politics. It was, to use a Wenner phrase, "a king hell spectacle."

Boomers may be a punchline now, but back then, they were groovy.

Ralph Gleason, a founding editor of Rolling Stone, wrote that the magazine was predicated on the idea that great musicians were "the true shamans," and that music was the glue that kept young people in the 1960s and 1970s from falling apart "in the face of incredible adult blindness, and ignorance and evilness."

"I'm sorry to see it go," Mr. Wenner said about rock 'n' roll. "It's not coming back. It'll end up like jazz."

Now 76, he has written a memoir ("Like a Rolling Stone," out on Sept. 13) brimming with juicy anecdotes about friendships and feuds with the gods of the golden age of rock. He also dishes on the inimitable writers he nurtured at the magazine, like Mr. Thompson, the avatar of gonzo journalism, and Tom Wolfe, a bespoke wonder in white among the shaggy hippies. Mr. Wenner also provides an intimate—she may think too intimate—look at Annie Leibovitz, the photographer who started her career at Rolling Stone and who took the moody cover shot of Mr. Wenner for the new autobiography.

Mr. Wenner almost died in 2017, after he broke his femur in a fall when he was showing his son Noah how to improve his tennis serve and had a heart attack that required open-heart surgery. He had to give up his daredevil habits of skiing, motorcycle riding and chain-smoking Marlboros. He said he had stopped doing coke long before, labeling it the "nefarious drug."

But even sitting quietly with his cane at his side, eating a bowl of cherries, he still has something of the whirlwind about him. Looking a bit chagrined, he confessed that he enjoyed a bit of LSD a month ago at the beach, listening to Bruce Springsteen, U2, Dire Straits and Bob Dylan. "Unbelievable," he said.

"Pot is too difficult on my throat to smoke, and edibles last too long," he said. "Coke is fun for parties but then it's useless."

He had just gotten back from taking his family on a safari with the family of Bette Midler, one of his favorite traveling companions, who says she finds him "peculiarly optimistic, even in the darkest of his days."

We had lunch by the ocean on the deck of Mr. Wenner's spectacular modern home, featuring a basketball court, swimming pool, tomato garden, a sculpture of a huge metal head lying on its side and Ralph

Lauren and Bill O'Reilly as neighbors. We ate gazpacho with caviar and roasted Montauk black sea bass, prepared by his chef, and drank rosé. The music on tap was nuevo flamenco.

Mr. Wenner lives here in Montauk—and sometimes in Manhattan and Sun Valley, Idaho—with his husband, Matt Nye, a handsome designer who has worked at Ralph Lauren and Calvin Klein, and their three teenagers. His ex-wife, Jane, with whom he has three grown sons—their names are engraved on a silver ID bracelet he's wearing—has a house nearby.

One of the original staffers at Rolling Stone, the beautiful and stylish Jane was instrumental in helping Mr. Wenner get his magazine off the ground (her parents gave him money to get started). She was his muse and charmed the people he needed, acting as "an ethereal housemother." Gus Wenner, Jann and Jane's youngest son, is now the C.E.O. of the Jann-less Rolling Stone.

Mr. Wenner decided to write his own memoir after he first worked closely with, and then grew disenchanted with, Joe Hagan, who wrote a biography of the editor in 2017 called "Sticky Fingers."

The New York Times called it "a supple, confident, dispassionately reported and deeply well-written biography." Mr. Wenner disagrees.

"I made a terrible choice of a writer, who turned out to be a gossip reporter more than a really careful in-depth writer," Mr. Wenner said. "I gave him this great opportunity to look at my archives, but he was too interested in the sensational gossip stuff."

Mr. Hagan responded to this in an email: "I still have an affection for Jann and I'm flattered that I could inspire him to write his own book, even if he fails to credit me. While his 'gossip' comments are hilarious coming from the former publisher of Us Weekly, I also find it sad how blind he is to the journalistic ambition of my book, which was an homage to the style and spirit of Rolling Stone at its best—Jann's true legacy."

ROLLING STONE AND THE STONES

Mr. Wenner grew up in the rural suburbs of San Rafael, Calif., the son of former military officers who started a baby formula company. He liked to sing songs from Gilbert and Sullivan operettas.

By sixth grade, he was already the editor and publisher of The Weekly Trumpet. As a freshman at Berkeley, he was ripping wire copy for Chet Huntley and David Brinkley at the 1964 Republican National Convention in San Francisco, where Barry Goldwater became the nominee.

Running Rolling Stone required special skills. Mr. Wenner had to mold the copy into something readable after drug-fueled interviews, like the one he did with Jimi Hendrix. And he had to edit the work of Mr. Thompson, who loved his cocaine and whose office supplies included Wild Turkey and beer on tap, and an air horn.

Mr. Thompson's first dispatch from D.C., when he covered George McGovern's 1972 campaign, began like this: "I feel the fear coming on, and the only cure for that is to chew up a fat black wad of blood-opium about the size of a young meatball."

Cameron Crowe, the moviemaker, was 15 when he began writing for the magazine. He said Mr. Wenner's secret was that "he kept it personal," building "a family out of geeky music lovers, hopeful upstarts, gunslinger professionals."

Mr. Wenner recounts one day early in the magazine when Mick Jagger stopped by for blow and a long visit. On another, Ms. Leibovitz dropped three large rocks of coke on his desk as "a gift from Keith for you."

"Cocaine had a stranglehold on the music business," Mr. Wenner writes in the memoir. "Drugs were the coin of the realm, enabling bad behavior, bad relationships, and lapses of judgment all around."

Dinner parties might have silver trays of neatly arranged lines of coke passed around every half-hour. When John Belushi fell off a stage doing his samurai skit and ended up in the hospital, with his leg in a cast suspended by wires, he mischievously pulled out a vial of coke hidden in the cast to show his friend Jann.

Conflict-of-interest rules at the magazine were blurry. Mr. Wenner became fast friends with Mick Jagger. Mr. Jagger, who, according to Rolling Stone's count, has been on the cover 21 times, topped only by Paul McCartney with 24, agreed to finance a British version of the magazine, which shortly tanked.

When Mr. Jagger put out a solo album with Wyclef Jean called

"Goddess in the Doorway" in 2001, Mr. Wenner watched them at a recording session producing what he considered a "bewitching" sound—"Especially after a little pot"—and then reviewed it for the magazine. When the record review editor put four stars on the review, Mr. Wenner added an additional star.

"There was some snickering about being on Mick's leash," he writes, "but so what, and what if I were?" (Keith Richards called the album a spicier version of "Dog Doo in the Doorway.")

The friendship had its rocky moments. Mr. Wenner assigned a full-court press on the Stones's deadly concert at the Altamont Speedway in 1969 after the Hells Angels, brought in to handle security, killed an 18-year-old Black man in front of the stage. He knew that Mr. Jagger would be angry when some of the blame fell on him and the Stones's tour manager, who brought in the Hells Angels.

After the publication of the 17-page article, which called it "rock 'n' roll's all-time worst day," Mr. Jagger declined an interview request and sent Mr. Wenner a frosty telegram, saying, "rightly or wrongly we no longer trust you to quote us fully or in context."

They made up and grew closer over the years.

Mr. Wenner tells an amusingly indiscreet story about being in Barbados with Mr. Jagger and Ms. Leibovitz. One night everyone was sipping cognac and Bianca Jagger was looking for her husband. He soon showed up, Mr. Wenner writes, "with sand on the knees of his white trousers. Annie followed a few minutes later. Bianca walked out without a word and there was a general sigh of relief. Then she returned with a large pot of water and poured it over Mick's head. It was hilarious. Justice!"

Two pages later, he writes that Ms. Leibovitz tried to absorb Jane Wenner's style and hung out with her constantly. "Annie was also in love with Jane, though I didn't know that at the time, nor would I have even thought about it." (Ms. Leibovitz did not reply with a comment.)

After spilling much ink on the magic of Mick, it is a surprise when, near the end of his book, Mr. Wenner reveals that he stopped going to Stones concerts because they were "an oldies" revue.

"Since I have to use a cane to get around, going to see them at a

NOTORIOUS

coliseum, it's just like, why?" he told me. "It's an interesting show, but I've seen it 20 times." (If they played at Barclays Center in Brooklyn, he said, he'd go.)

In one Rolling Stone cover story, Mr. Jagger said he did not want to be singing "Satisfaction" when he was 42. He's singing it at 79.

"Now they're older and Keith has certainly slowed down," Mr. Wenner said. "Mick is still a miracle, but he's so old looking."

"I don't mind," Mr. Wenner added, "but they look like people out of 'Lord of the Rings' or something."

Mr. Wenner said Bob Dylan, Bono and U2, and his pal Bruce Springsteen are still worth seeing because they're still trying to be original.

Once in Sun Valley, before Mr. Wenner's severe health issues began, Mr. Springsteen asked his friend how he kept skiing every day.

"Because I keep champagne, pot cookies and Percocet," Mr. Wenner replied. "Have you ever had Percocet, Bruce? Try it. It's not too late to throw your life away."

For his birthday, Mr. Springsteen wrote a ditty for his friend, singing, "I've never seen so much innocence and cynicism walk side by side. Champagne, pot cookies and a Percocet keep him rolling stoned."

Mr. Wenner also had a complicated, close relationship with the Beatles. John Lennon put Rolling Stone on the map. In 1968, they did a cover using the naked picture of John and Yoko holding hands that Mr. Lennon's record company had banned for their first record together, "Two Virgins."

"Nude Beatle Perils S.F." was the headline in The San Francisco Chronicle; the issue was banned in Boston. "All the fuss," Mr. Wenner writes, "came down to an ancient principle of public relations: 'Print a famous foreskin and the world will beat a path to your door.'"

In 1970, for Mr. Lennon's first solo album, Mr. Wenner hung out with the couple—"John and Yoko referred to themselves in the third person as Liz and Dick"—and interviewed an angry Mr. Lennon, who unleashed on "the dark side" of the Beatles. Mr. Lennon was angry at the way he perceived that his bandmates were treating Yoko, Mr. Wenner said.

The ex-Beatle said he wouldn't bother to play George Harrison's solo album at home; he called Paul's solo album "rubbish," and "light and easy"; he said Bob Dylan was B.S., adding snidely "Zimmerman is his name"; and he accused Mr. Jagger and the Stones of mimicking the Beatles's music, asserting, "'Satanic Majesties' is 'Pepper.'"

Against Mr. Lennon's wishes, Mr. Wenner published "Lennon Remembers"—which Mr. Lennon had begun calling "Lennon Regrets"—as a book. Mr. Lennon was angry. The two never saw each other again, and 10 years later John was shot. Mr. Wenner went to the Dakota and when he commiserated with Ms. Ono, she placed Mr. Lennon's glasses, with dried blood on them, in his hands.

He became closer to Mr. McCartney after Mr. Lennon died. (Funnily enough, he writes that he gave Linda Eastman, "a comely blonde from Scarsdale," her assignment to go to London and photograph the Beatles, which was less driven by aesthetics than that she wanted to meet Mr. McCartney, whom she would later marry. "She sent me postcards from London, detailing her pursuit of him," Mr. Wenner writes.)

FROM HIPPIE TO YUPPIE, AND OTHER CHANGES

In 1977, Mr. Wenner moved the magazine to New York from San Francisco. He befriended the Kennedys. He put Donna Summer on the cover and used stylists to make the Jefferson Starship look glamorous. He started wearing three-piece suits and got rid of his magazine's "hippie potpourri" design.

"I began to hear that we had 'sold out,' which had been a sour-grapes gripe I was immune to," he writes, adding: "I suppose my own lifestyle and friendships in New York legitimized a lot of that."

Mr. Wenner ran an ad campaign in 1985 called "Perception vs. Reality" to shed the magazine's hippie image. There were contrasting pictures of pot brownies with Häagen-Dazs; coins with an American Express card; George McGovern with Ronald Reagan.

Hunter Thompson lambasted the shift to the mainstream, with a rant against BMWs, pesto and gossip, saying: "Bon Jovi, you know, what color he paints his fingernails is more important than the fact that

Ronald Reagan is president. I think Jann, in the darkness of his private nights, should be ashamed, and is ashamed, because Rolling Stone is not more of a weapon than a tool."

As Mr. Wenner got more buttoned-up, his mother became more bohemian. She moved to Hawaii and became a hippie, raising pet goats and taking acid with her astrologer/guru. And she became a lesbian.

"My mother's gay? I just thought, she's my mother, for Christ's sake," Mr. Wenner said. "What's going on?" The last straw, he said, was when she got involved in what he termed "a sex-and-scam cult."

"Somewhere along the line I realized that I didn't like being around her," he writes, adding, "No love was lost. Even our little dog growled and snapped when she showed up."

He didn't have much patience for her very public sexual exploration. "I wasn't disapproving or negative; I just didn't want to hear any more intimate information," he said. "What son wants to hear about his mom's" intimate life? Mr. Nye weighed in on this, smiling: "His mom was an utter original."

Mr. Wenner knew he liked men as well as women at an early age. He rubbed up against a fellow student in boarding school. He used "homosexual ideation" to get out of the draft. He had a fling with a young man from England. But he was happy with Jane.

In 1994, though, he became infatuated with Mr. Nye. "I didn't want to be open about being gay, and never discussed it with my closest friends or colleagues," he writes. "I was having the best of both worlds and had been for years."

He didn't want to hurt Jane or his three young children but he was mooning over Matt, so he poured it all out to her. She told him to leave and he moved into a hotel on Madison Avenue. (Ms. Wenner did not respond to a request for comment.)

"Jane stabilized at first," he writes. "She had friends and money, but she couldn't let go of me. She phoned every day, either acting as if nothing had happened or, if she was stoned, doubling down on her humiliation, rejection, and my 'sudden decision' that I was gay. She would unleash anger and abuse as I listened, silenced with guilt."

It took some time, and sensitivity on Mr. Nye's part. Mr. Wenner writes that when he and Matt revealed they were having their own child, Jane "took it hard" and he felt "guilt and misery." A 15-year-old Gus, protective of his mother, cried and said he "hated" Matt. But Mr. Wenner said they eventually blended into a modern family.

He hates the phrase "coming out of the closet" because it seemed like a "shameful cliché, that dark and stuffy closet. Debutantes came out."

"I was concerned about it, but I wasn't that concerned," he said. "I never lost a friend because of it."

THE END OF THE MAGAZINE ERA

Besides Rolling Stone, Mr. Wenner co-founded Outside, which he sold in 1979, two years after it started, and founded Men's Journal, which he sold in 2017. He acquired Us Weekly, which in the early 2000s got so successful that it was making more than Rolling Stone.

As the owner and C.E.O. of Us Weekly, he was privy to all the celebrity secrets.

"A photographer we worked with received a tip that Angelina Jolie was at a resort on the coast of Africa on a secret trip with then-married Brad Pitt," he writes. "The tipster further specified a time and place where they walked every day and suggested we could 'secretly' do a photo ambush. We got the photo, we got the proof, we had the worldwide scoop, the debut of Brangelina. The tipster was Angelina."

Mr. Wenner can boast of much remarkable journalism aside from music in Rolling Stone: stories about Patty Hearst, Karen Silkwood, Charles Manson, AIDS, climate change. He did interviews with presidents and presidential candidates, enduring two of Bill Clinton's "purple fits" of rage.

With lingering distress, he talks about the nadir for his magazine, the 2014 publication of "A Rape on Campus" about an alleged brutal gang assault on a victim with the pseudonym of "Jackie" in a fraternity house at the University of Virginia. But "Jackie" had made it up.

"Our budget cuts had left us understaffed," he writes. "Still, pseudonyms, lack of corroborating sources, and our sympathy for the victim, which made us reluctant to challenge her, were all warning signs."

When Rolling Stone was born, music was a cultural and political force in this country. Now music is often disconnected from social change.

"The concerns have become very trivialized," Mr. Wenner said. "It's a lot of Taylor Swift and her disagreements with her celebrity boyfriends." When he started the magazine, he writes, the readership was 90 percent male, and the star writers were male. "It was a macho era," he told me. (Later, he said, readership evened out.)

"The music today is driven by teenage girls," he said. "Today's music, hip-hop, pop music, I don't listen to as much, and I don't think it is as culturally relevant as it used to be, nor is it musically as good. But I think some of it, particularly hip-hop, is very strong and tough."

He thinks that technology has changed the nature of music. "If you listen to Bob Dylan and other stuff, it almost sounds antique," he said. "Everything now has got this modern sound. They've got synthesizers, they've got auto-tuning." And, he posited, "I think one of the reasons classic rock will never come back is, young people are being tuned to this new level" that makes old music seem "tame, just like I used to think of Frank Sinatra."

As far back as 2008 and 2009, he said, he saw the writing on the wall about the internet superseding magazines.

People thought they wanted to get into the magazine game, he said, "but once they get in and discover it's going to lose $10 million a year for the next three years, they're like, 'I don't know about this.' No big company wanted to buy Rolling Stone. They all knew what was happening."

David Pecker, the publisher of the National Enquirer, bought Mr. Wenner's Us Weekly for over $100 million in 2017. At one lunch, Mr. Wenner recalled, Mr. Pecker said that at the Enquirer, "he had been buying and then spiking stories from women who had been sleeping with Trump."

Journalism was moving toward bullet points, away from 10,000-word articles. Celebrities preferred to be interviewed by other friendly celebrities, and they were asking for editorial control, right down to writing their own captions.

"It's like everybody's Tom Cruise all of a sudden," Mr. Wenner keened. "He says nothing."

Mr. Wenner had been grooming Gus to take over, but handing over the keys was difficult. Gus was "my usurping doppelgänger," he writes.

"It took me a while to get used to not being in charge and that was tough," he admitted. "Clearly, Gus had his ideas about what he wanted to do with Rolling Stone, and it was time for it to change."

His chief financial officer, Tim Walsh, told him he would have to sell Rolling Stone.

The magazine that started with a zeal to take on the Man ended up going to two scions. The new owner is Jay Penske, whose father was Roger Penske, the former racecar driver turned billionaire businessman, and he elevated Gus Wenner to C.E.O.

"No more baby boomer, old-white-guy covers," Mr. Wenner dryly noted about his final cover, a Bono interview.

The new team quickly began firing some of Rolling Stone's veteran writers and photographers.

"I wanted to remain with Rolling Stone, to have some relationship with my baby," Mr. Wenner writes. "Could I be the uncle? The grandpa? The brother-in-law? Nope, I would be the ex-wife. Gus wanted to take over. He listened to me with respect but impatience."

As we ate peach sorbet with peaches, Mr. Wenner laughed ruefully. "I said, 'Don't cut me out' and he was cutting me out. I went to him and said 'Geez, I'm here.' You discover they don't really need the benefit of your advice that much. Yes, it could have been helpful on a couple of specific occasions but I guess it's more important they got out on their own."

He writes: "Of course, I was now in my seventies, standing in the way of progress, stubbornly locked in my office listening, it was assumed, to Bob Dylan and Neil Young. I was not invited to meetings. What should have been an exciting redesign and translation of Rolling Stone from a newsmagazine to a feature magazine ended up garbled and lackluster."

Mr. Wenner kept coming to the office, like Citizen Kane on a walker.

Sometimes, he and Gus would disagree; sometimes they would go smoke "a grit" on a bench outside.

He told me he became what he hates most: a cliché, "the grumpy old man left behind by the forces of time and history."

Finally, Mr. Wenner writes, Gus delivered the message: "I was out."

But, Mr. Wenner assured me, Gus handled him with T.L.C.: "Gus sold and saved the magazine. He has done a brilliant job with it." Mr. Wenner added that "Gus transitioned it to a new generation and a new music. I could never have done it." In April, Axios reported that Gus Wenner said the magazine had had its most profitable year "in two decades."

For his part, Gus called his father his "best friend and greatest mentor," adding: "If we didn't disagree here and there along the way, I would probably not be cut out for the job."

Does the father read the son's Rolling Stone?

"I don't read Rolling Stone that much," Mr. Wenner replied. "I don't read that many magazines. It's about people I'm not personally interested in. I don't really care for K-pop. I don't really know who Cardi B is."

Recent Rolling Stone covers have included the YouTube star MrBeast and JLo in a jumpsuit with a plunging neckline.

"A big difference," he said. "John Lennon being naked on the cover was a statement. How would the most popular man in the world be willing to go out and be naked?" He added, "It's so destroying."

They were "willing to place their fame, to put it in danger" to make the statement: "'Here's the honest truth about people, about sex, about nudity.' Now JLo goes out and it's like, 'I'm doing this to sell like hotcakes. I'm not doing this for a reason.'"

I couldn't end without asking the desert island discs question. What would he bring?

He offered this list: "Don't Let Me Be Misunderstood" by Nina Simone. "Speedway at Nazareth" by Mark Knopfler. "The Ghost of Tom Joad" by Bruce Springsteen. "Moondance" by Van Morrison. "I've Been Loving You Too Long" by Otis Redding. "Desolation Row" by Bob Dylan. "Crying" by Roy Orbison. "Think" by Aretha Franklin.

"Beautiful Day" by U2. "Under My Thumb" by the Stones. "Imagine" by John Lennon.

"Seems like a pretty cool cat," he said about himself.

Confirm or Deny

MAUREEN DOWD: *Bob Dylan shakes hands like a dead fish.*

JANN WENNER: Yes, weird. In the early days, it was a way to establish dominance. "What are you to me? What? Huh?"

Paul Simon is a buzzkill.

(Giggling) Yes.

You slept with Mick Jagger.

Swishful thinking, as Bette Midler would say. I never slept with a rock star.

Bruce Springsteen uses the word "pope" as a verb.

Yes. We were driving in a car to the airport and he says, now watch me, I'm going to pope it. Then he rolls down the window, and as the crowd goes by, he waves like the pope.

You traded your tickets to the Beatles's last show for 30 hits of LSD.

You couldn't hear the Beatles for all the screaming. I got the better bargain.

LSD use was a litmus test for new Rolling Stone hires.

Not true. But in the early days, I wanted to know if they had. Like what frame of mind this person would be in, what was their philosophical bent?

Michael Jackson should not be the subject of a musical on Broadway that is popular with children.

I don't see any value in canceling him or pretending that he wasn't a child molester or any value in not listening, and I think we lose something not listening to his music.

You were ensorcelled by Jackie Kennedy Onassis.

She smiled at you and it was like the sun came out. You just bask in that attention of hers and the eyes and the delight. She could focus on you. She was really smart.

You were in a two-man book club with David Bowie.

He turned me on to Junot Díaz. He was really the definition of erudite. And he also was committed to avant-garde. He was not interested in traditional writing.

Keith Richards accused you of nicking the name of his band.

True.

Bob Dylan was jealous that you gave the Rolling Stones credit for the name of the magazine. And Mick said that without him and Keith, your magazine would've been called Herman Hermits' Weekly.

True.

You tried to get Tom Wolfe to change Sherman McCoy's job in "Bonfire of the Vanities" from a bond trader to a writer because you said no one was interested in Wall Street.

That is true. I was really wrong.

Tom Wolfe was the first person to tell you about rap and he wrote his own rap lyrics. He liked to go to Harlem and the Bronx to watch the crews battle it out.

Yes.

You sniffed coke while being interviewed by a Columbia Journalism Review reporter.

I was under his influence.

You cut the testicles off Ken Kesey's cows.

Yes, that is true.

You added an extra N to your name in high school to seem cooler.

Yes, to seem cooler.

You love drill music.

What is drill music?

Jack Nicholson brought a portable ashtray to the Clinton Inaugural.

It was so cool. You're not supposed to smoke there but he had a little brass circular container with a lid on. He pulled it out of his pocket and smoked, and nobody bothered him at all because he had just come off of doing "A Few Good Men," so all the Marines and security at the inauguration wouldn't touch him. They loved Jack.

You've appeared in several movies. But not yet in the role that Michael Douglas said would be the most natural fit for you: a coldblooded hit man.
The story of my life. I could have done Whitey Bulger.

For your cameo in Cameron Crowe's "Almost Famous," your credit read "Legend in Cab."
Yes.

In an interview for a Rolling Stone cover story, Madonna told Carrie Fisher she did not like to perform oral sex.
(Laughing) I thought, that's pretty selfish.

The Stones song "Memory Motel" was written about Annie Leibovitz.
Yes. She was covering the Stones at that time and she and Mick were sleeping together.

Kurt Cobain was his generation's John Lennon.
That's what my younger staffers said at the time. I didn't want to challenge them at that moment but thought the idea was hyperbolic and emotional. There was something to be said about their reaction to his death being similar with ours to Lennon, but to compare the actual artists for their work is far-fetched.

You agree with Jimmy Buffett that nothing is worth saying or listening to after 1 a.m.
Truer words have never been spoken.

CINDY ADAMS, GOSSIP'S G.O.A.T.

—AUGUST 7, 2021

When Donald Trump was president, the world should have been Cindy Adams's oyster.

Forgive me for this reference, but she seemed destined to be the Ben Bradlee to Mr. Trump's J.F.K.

The White House had come onto her turf. The chief executive was her old pal. Mr. Trump was the first tabloid president, a creature of the New York gossip columns. That was the litter box in which he sharpened his claws and perfected his media sorcery.

Ms. Adams, who attended all three of Mr. Trump's weddings and covered both of his divorces as if they were Watergate, seemed the best positioned to get scoops out of the new president.

She stood next to him at Trump Tower on election night in 2016. He reminded her of what the notorious lawyer Roy Cohn had told her back in the 1970s: "One day this kid is going to own New York."

It was expected that she would get even more New York Post headlines than she did in 1990, when she broke many of the salacious stories about Mr. Trump's affair with "the Georgia peach," Marla Maples, and his ensuing split from Ivana. "GIMME THE PLAZA!" one Cindy front-page headline blared, describing Ivana's purported divorce demands. She was channeling the Donald, dueling with her rival, Liz Smith, who broke bulletins from Ivana in The New York Daily News.

And, Ms. Adams had made a career of being a sympathetic ear to

Sukarno, the shah of Iran, Manuel Noriega, Imelda Marcos and Leona Helmsley. She certainly would have had no trouble getting a good seat in the White House briefing room. And yet . . .

"I stayed away so I would be safe," Ms. Adams said, pointing out that everyone in Mr. Trump's orbit seems to crash, sooner or later. She noted that, a few days before our interview, Trump's buddy Tom Barrack was arrested in Los Angeles.

And consider Rudy Giuliani, another boldfaced name frequently cited in Ms. Adams's column, who is said to be nearly broke, literally melted on TV, and was recently paid a pre-dawn visit by the Feds.

"They started acting crazy," Ms. Adams said of the Trump circle. "I think so many people around him got caught in something. I would have gotten caught in something. Hard not to be. They'll find something."

"It's not worth it for me to get three stories and be important to The New York Post and get killed," she said, speaking metaphorically.

Ms. Adams was sitting in her Park Avenue–meets–Ming Dynasty penthouse, her bare feet with Jungle Red toenails stretched out.

She was wearing a Prada blouse that her Yorkie puppy, Jellybean, had just "whoopsed" on, as she put it, with "10-cent pants and $5,000 worth of jewelry." And that's not counting the diamond-encrusted Yankees ring that George Steinbrenner gave her.

It's not that Ms. Adams wasn't tempted to extract some news from her old pal camped on the Potomac, but she steered clear.

"I never went to Mar-a-Lago," she said. "I went nowhere. I didn't go anywhere near him."

You don't get to be 91 and still in the game without having some good instincts. And without being a firecracker.

But President Trump did call her sometimes.

"I think he was just checking with a friend to see how he was doing," she said.

Were her editors upset that she didn't take more advantage of her relationship with Mr. Trump?

"No," she said. "They understood."

UNFAILINGLY LOYAL

You know things are serious when Cindy Adams, who sometimes prints her hate mail in her column for fun, worries about cancel culture and the Twitter horde. The famously unexpurgated columnist isn't even on Twitter but she knows about the buzz saw of public discourse. You say the wrong thing, you're done.

"It's so intense," she said. "I'm afraid to speak out. You go to a dinner party, they want to strangle you." She added, "Newspapers, sooner or later, will get rid of you if everybody is killing you. Look at all the people we know who have been fired lately for whatever reason."

Doesn't she have protected status as a New York landmark?

"I can say lots of things, I can and I do," she said. "Look, I took Donald's part when nobody else was. I can do that, and I understand people don't like me because of it. I don't care. I'm loyal to a friend. I will never forget anybody who was good to me. Never. So, I was with Donald."

She recounted when she first moved into the palatial apartment—which was once owned by Doris Duke, and bought by Ms. Adams in 1997—her late husband, Joey Adams, a comedian and humor columnist, was very frail. Mr. Trump sent a team over to install a security system.

"I'm not going to forget stuff like that," she said. "I am loyal, whether it's Donald or anybody else. If you were good to me, I pay back. If you were evil to me, I'll get you back."

After Mr. Adams's death in 1999, Mr. Trump picked her up in a limo and took her on a helicopter ride to scatter Joey's ashes over Central Park.

"Joey was never No. 1, he was No. 2," she said. "He was never a Seinfeld of today, he was never a Bob Hope of yesterday. But he had a No. 1 lifestyle. He was the brother-in-law of Walter Winchell. Remember Walter Winchell at the Stork Club?"

Still, Ms. Adams is not like most of the Republicans in Congress, who are busy helping the former president weave a pernicious mythology about what happened on Jan. 6.

Asked if that dreadful day made her feel differently about Mr. Trump, she replied, "Of course it did. I'm not immune. I thought it was terrible. Horrible. I can't believe that I would live through something like that, that's how awful it was."

She said it was hard during the vitriolic 2016 race between Hillary Clinton and Mr. Trump because she liked them both so much. "You can't get into mud like that," she said. "You can't." (She has pictures with both pols on display, as well as one with Rupert Murdoch.)

According to those who have seen him lately, Mr. Trump has been described as either relaxed or depressed. What is her impression?

"Depends on when you get him," she said.

She does not believe he will run again. "I think there may be a few too many bridges that he'll have to cross," she said.

She is certainly no fan of this White House.

"He's not with it," she said of President Biden, calling Jill Biden "our ventriloquist first lady."

"Then there's Kamala," she sniffed. "I think he should watch out for her."

ALWAYS A WORKHORSE

Ms. Adams is the centerpiece of a new Showtime docuseries called "Gossip," produced by Imagine Documentaries, the Ron Howard and Brian Grazer outfit, and directed by Jenny Carchman. It explores the columnist's prismatic life and the tabloidization of the media and society.

It's billed as a treatise on "bottom feeding at the top," and shows the gossip queen's nocturnal crawl through a velvet-rope-line world of dictators, scoundrels, movie stars and politicians.

(Watch out for the bizarre story related by the former Post editor in chief Col Allan, who claims Tom Cruise's front teeth fell out on the tablecloth during a restaurant meeting.)

"News today, news is gossip, that's what it is," Ms. Adams told me. "There's no straight reporting anymore."

She isn't fazed by her latest close-up. "Now, even orthodontists get documentaries," she said. "You don't have to be somebody. You shine shoes? Good. We'll do a two-parter."

She jokes about her longevity at The Post. "I was there when Alexander Hamilton founded it, for Chrissake."

Ms. Adams was always a workhorse, out, looking glamorous, five nights a week to truffle hunt for her punchy Post column—until the pandemic left her isolated at home with her housekeeper, Nazalene, and Jellybean.

"I'm a book reader," she said. "If you give me Grisham, I'll sit for the rest of my life. And I'll read Daniel Silva and James Patterson. I have a dog and I'm OK. Was it difficult? Of course. Look, there was a time I didn't get my hair done, there was a time I never got a manicure. I haven't bought anything in two years—to buy to go where? It's been horrible, and writing has been a nightmare. If I didn't have a sense of humor, I would have no ability whatsoever."

The mere idea of a buzzy column, chockablock with notables and quotables, is almost unfathomable in this age, when the rich, the famous and even anyone fame-adjacent, have their own publishing platforms and give it all away up front free. We're swimming in a sea of overexposed nobodies. Their every lived moment is in your face on Instagram and they have little use for the press. Anemic magazines bend over backward to get stars, allowing them to do interviews with one another.

"You have to speak to *their team*," Ms. Adams said. "In the old days, you could speak to Clark Gable. You had his phone number. Now they have a team. The whole team is 17 years old, if that. The team doesn't know who the hell you are because they're 11 years old."

Still, she said, "There's always gossip. Down in the old days at the riverbed, the ladies washing clothes in the river, they talked. The hieroglyphics of the Egyptians. It's always been that way."

Offering up the ne plus ultra of overexposure, Bennifer 2.0, Ms. Adams said: "They tweeze their chin, it's in the paper. It doesn't matter. They have several P.R. people. Several." She joked that the famous parts of J-Lo's anatomy have their own P.R. agents, too. "What is the point of writing about them when they're sending their own stuff to you?" she said of the current crop.

She fretted about the state of her magpie craft. "My feeling about gossip is, it's gone so low and so down," she said, "soon, they're going to have a camera in the bottom of a toilet bowl, shooting up."

Ms. Adams was never Gawker. "I never outed anybody," she said. "I never said somebody was sleeping with somebody if they were married. I didn't do dirt."

As someone who came of age in the time of Frank Sinatra and Judy Garland, she thinks today's A-listers leave something to be desired.

She is most emphatically not impressed with the Duchess of Montecito, a.k.a. Meghan Markle, she said, christening Harry "Prince Empty." About the couple's four-book deal, reportedly worth $20 million, the columnist noted, "He's going to pee on everybody. And when he did this Oprah thing, his socks were too short. I never saw anything so disgusting. His ankles."

How about Britney Spears?

"I think anybody should be free," Ms. Adams said. "It's her father who should be put away."

What does she think about Chrissy Teigen?

"I don't."

What does she say to those who believe Rupert Murdoch, the Post overlord, is bad for the world and climate change, that Fox News is out of control, and that Mr. Murdoch is just as much of a monster as Logan Roy on "Succession"?

"What is the matter with you?" she said, laughing. "Get out of my house. Find another question."

Jared and Ivanka? Can they make a comeback with their old liberal social set on the Upper East Side?

"Yes, of course, they will," she said. "It'll take a little while."

Will Ivanka run for Senate in Florida?

"She won't even walk for senator," Ms. Adams said, laughing again.

'I'M A PRODUCT'

She worries that The New York Times is tilting too far leftward, though she praises the paper as "The Statue of Liberty," and she worries about the focus on identity politics in the country and proliferation of micro-aggression complaints.

"Soon, they're going to have Oscars just for Hungarians with one left leg," she joked. "Simple, joyful, glamorous living, nice food, going out, wearing pretty things, it's gone. I just don't know what the country is going to be."

She said she doesn't have any grudges going at the moment but assured me that when she speaks about vengeance, it's not all talk.

She tells me a story about Dorothy Kilgallen, the Hearst showbiz gossip columnist and panelist on the TV game show "What's My Line?" Back in the '60s, when Ms. Adams was working for $5 a week for a weekly paper, Ms. Kilgallen was the top gun.

When Ms. Kilgallen began relentlessly attacking Joey Adams in her column, Ms. Adams wrote a "vicious" retort about the more famous columnist.

"I said, 'I know who you sleep with, I know where you go.' I said in the column 'If you do one more thing about Joey, I will see that every one of the teachers of the schools where your kids go get this, and I will hand it to every kid as they leave the school.'"

Ms. Adams said that she is all about her friends and her dogs. As far as children, "I didn't want any," she said. "My husband, who was the same age as my mother, he didn't want any."

The series recounts how, at a tender age, Ms. Adams was put under the knife on her mother's orders.

"They did my nose at 15 on some couch in Brooklyn," she said, chuckling. "You weren't allowed to have your nose done until you were 16 because you are still growing. My mother took a look at me at 15 and she says, 'You're ugly.' My mother was beautiful."

Didn't that mess her up?

"No, I kissed her," she said, looking indignant. "I was quite grateful. What, are you crazy? I looked lousy, like Wallace Beery, and I looked better after. Why would I be unhappy?"

The documentary also shows pictures of Ms. Adams, as a teenager, scooping up a load of titles. She was Miss Bazooka Bubble Gum, Miss Brooklyn Dodgers, Miss Jersey State Fair, Miss Brooklyn Dodgers,

Miss Upswept Hair and Miss Bagel of the Brooklyn Better Bagel Bakers' Bureau.

"My grandmother had no money, came from Russia, cleans stoops on the Lower East Side, took in boarders," she recalled. "My mother was an executive secretary, perfect, gorgeous English. She gave me lessons. My speech is broadcast English, which means it's not regional. It's not Western, it's not Southern, it's not British, it's not New York. It's absolutely perfect. My mother was not going to let me be a nobody. She wasn't going to have a loser. I'm a product. I was nothing and she put me together."

Interviewing Ms. Adams is a movable feast. We started in the living room, then moved into her office, which is a temple to tabloids, with front pages citing her scoops decoupaged on the walls and ceiling.

We went through wooden doors, hand carved in the year 1600 and found in Beirut, eventually emerging onto a terrace, from which the Plaza can be glimpsed.

Finally, we had a glass of chardonnay in the kitchen, where shelves of stuffed animals stared down at us. An embroidered pillow reads: "A spoiled rotten dog lives here." Hanging in one corner of the kitchen is a New York City traffic light.

"OK, I am not what we call a culinary expert," she announced. "If you're asking for anything beyond wine, forget it."

Sipping St. Francis, we decided to crank call Sheila Nevins, the docuqueen (who is not involved in this one).

The conversation between the two salty grandes dames of New York went like this:

SHEILA: "Will you come to the Crosby Hotel and watch a film about something you don't give a damn about?"

CINDY: "Downtown? I should go downtown?"

SHEILA: "Have you ever been to the Crosby Hotel?"

CINDY: "Yes, don't talk down to me. I will send my car and driver to bring you uptown for dinner."

SHEILA: "I will send *my* car and driver to bring you downtown."

CINDY: "Shove your car and driver up your husband and come to dinner. OK?"

SHEILA: "OK. I really do love you even though you're a bit of a"—
bleep!—"Goodbye."

Later, Ms. Nevins told me that Ms. Adams is "more than a gossip,
she's a bit of a shrink."

I told Ms. Adams I had to go back to Washington.

"What's to love in Washington?" she demanded. "They got rubber-
soled shoes and they got suits that have creases. New York is the capital
of the world. Washington is the toilet."

I protested that my hometown is beautiful and that L'Enfant modeled it on Paris.

"The Galápagos, the Congo, I've been to Siberia, I've been everywhere," she cracked. "You are going to tell me that Washington is like
Paris? Really, something is the matter with you. OK, get out of my
house."

Confirm or Deny

MAUREEN DOWD: *If you're indicted, you're invited.*
   CINDY ADAMS: Confirmed.

You once wore a mink hat to an A.S.P.C.A. board meeting?
   Yes, I did. It was dumb, but I didn't know I shouldn't do it.

Your late Yorkies had sable coats and a car and driver.
   Yes.

You carry a clock in your purse.
   Doesn't everyone?

Paris Hilton was the beginning of the end.
   No. I think Meghan is the beginning of the end.

Khloé is your favorite Kardashian.
   Nobody is my favorite Kardashian.

Bill de Blasio has been the best mayor in your lifetime.
   What language would you like me to say "No" in?

You will be sad when The Daily News finally folds.
   No. I thought it already did.

Judge Judy is in charge of all your medical decisions.
   Yes.

Ivanka Trump did not invite you to her wedding.
   She didn't, no. I don't think I was an important enough journalist for her.

Charlie Rose once flashed you in the bathroom at Elaine's.
   Never. Where did you get this dreck?

You love Keith McNally's Instagram account.
   I don't know. OK, out, out, out!